Christianity and the Holocaust
of Hungarian Jewry

Other Books by the Author

The Struggle of Man—Religious and Social—as a Central Motive in the Writings of Shmuel Yosef Agnon

Shai Olamot—Mekorot Le'Agnon (Rabbinical Sources for the Writing of Agnon)

Dinim Uminhagim (Laws and Customs)

The Great Divide: A Jewish Answer to Christian Missionary Activity (with M. E. Katz)

Christianity and the Holocaust of Hungarian Jewry

Moshe Y. Herczl

Translated by Joel Lerner

NEW YORK UNIVERSITY PRESS
New York and London

NEW YORK UNIVERSITY PRESS
New York and London

Library of Congress Cataloging-in-Publication Data
Herczl, Moshe Y., 1924-1990.
Christianity and the holocaust of Hungarian Jewry / Moshe Y.
Herczl : translated by Joel Lerner.
p. cm.
Translation from Hebrew.
Includes bibliographical references and index.
ISBN 0-8147-3503-7
1. Jews—Hungary—History. 2. Antisemitism—Hungary—History.
3. Christianity and antisemitism. 4. Holocaust, Jewish (1939-1945)—
Hungary. 5. Hungary—Ethnic relations. I. Title.
DS135.H9H46 1993
305.892'40439—dc20   92-47500
CIP

New York University Press books are printed on acid-free paper,
and their binding materials are chosen for strength and durability.

Manufactured in the United States of America

10 9 8 7 6 5 4 3 2 1

To the memory of Shimon Herczl, his children—Fradi, Ceri, Malka, Bluma, Jocheved Miriam, and Avraham Menachem—and Chaim and Gitel Rosenberg, all of whom were murdered in 1944.

To the memory of Sarah Rivka Herczl, who died in 1938.

And to the memory of the six million.

Contents

3. 1944

Preface and Acknowledgments

After the Holocaust, my late husband felt that it was his duty as a survivor to research and recount that aspect of the catastrophe which befell his family and his people and which is described in this book.

Unfortunately, he did not live to see his work published, but he left a complete Hebrew manuscript. It was his testament and it has been my responsibility to bring it to publication.

While every effort has been made to ensure that the book is free of errors, I am ultimately responsible for any mistakes that may have inadvertently been made. I have aimed for standardization of Hungarian names and terms and have consciously omitted the use of Hungarian accents throughout the book.

This book would not have been possible without the efforts of our daughter Tova, who edited the Hebrew manuscript and the English translation. In addition, I want to thank several other individuals who helped my husband or me in various ways: Louis Gluck, Herman Goldberger, Ivan Harris, Clara Irom, Eliot Osrin, Martha Vorhand and Zvi Yekutiel.

Special mention must be made of the Kaplan-Kushlick Foundation, whose generosity enabled the publication of this book.

I am grateful to all of the above for their invaluable assistance in publishing Moshe's contribution to Holocaust research.

Jerusalem   RACHEL HERCZL

I

The Preparatory Years

Introduction

The tragedy of Hungarian Jewry reached its climax between May 15 and July 7, 1944. During this period nearly half a million Jews were expelled from Hungary to the death camps. The removal of the Jews from Hungary—except for those of the capital, Budapest—was absolute, and was executed rapidly and efficiently. This dramatic event, unusual even against the background of the Holocaust, did not take place in a vacuum. Its roots grew out of a relationship that had persisted over generations between an expelled people and the population from which they were removed.

March 19, 1944—the day Germany invaded Hungary—is an important milestone in the fateful events that struck the Jews of Hungary in the summer of 1944. Nevertheless, the background to this day, and to these events, is crucial. As noted by the historian Jacob Katz,

> If our intention is to compare the run of events during the Holocaust period in the different countries involved, with regard to the behavior of the surrounding populace, we must broaden the scope of our examination to include the relations between the Jews and their environment in the generations preceding the Holocaust. A country such as Holland, where Jews could move among the general population with heads held high, bears no resemblance to Hungary, where Jewish heads were lowered before the catastrophe struck.[1]

I will discuss here the history of Hungarian Jewry from the arrival of Jews in Hungary at the end of the seventeenth century up until the late 1930s. The Jewish community experienced many significant changes during its time in Hungary. Its numbers grew, and it sought to integrate itself by actively contributing to the economic, scientific, cultural, and artistic development of Hungary.

Hungarian Jews' relations with their neighbors have a long history. In the middle of the nineteenth century, the Jews fought with dedication against the Hapsburg regime in the Hungarian War of Liberation. In the 1880s, the community bore the brunt of a blood libel that stirred up

3

antisemitism throughout the state. After World War I, bloody pogroms were waged against the Jews, and the early 1920s saw the introduction of discriminatory anti-Jewish legislation. And, while the civil status of the Jews was rendered equal to that of other citizens in the 1860s, they were compelled to fight for three additional decades to attain full recognition for Judaism.

In the fight against the official recognition of Judaism, both the church and the priesthood played central roles, on occasion even leading antisemitic forces.[2] The Catholic church even set up a special political party, the Catholic People's party, to wage the parliamentary war against recognition. Various Christian parties evolved out of the Catholic People's party and continued their antisemitic efforts for years, until the early 1940s.

The church and the priesthood actively emphasized the differences between the Christian and Jewish populations of Hungary. They stressed time and again the "foreignness" of the Jews, their intrinsic "difference" from the rest of the populace, and promoted the idea that Jews had no place in Christian Hungarian society.

As a result of this history of antisemitism, the Jewish community in Hungary rang in the year 1938, which marked the beginning of the period of anti-Jewish legislation, with its head bowed.[3]

Background

On August 29, 1526, a Turkish army led by Sultan Suleiman II, "The Magnificent," defeated the Hungarian army in a battle near the town of Mohacs in southern Hungary. To this day the Hungarians call the battle and its consequences "the Mohacs disaster," and for good reason. Most of the Hungarian army was destroyed, the king of Hungary was killed, and the kingdom of Hungary was exposed to a Turkish invasion. The Turks advanced without hesitation toward Buda, the capital, and successfully conquered much of Hungary's territory. The Turkish occupation lasted about 150 years, during which time Hungary served to a large extent as a battlefield between two rival powers, the Ottoman and Hapsburg empires, that waged war with each other for hegemony over central Europe. From time to time local Hungarian princes joined this struggle, fighting each other under the auspices of the rival empires.

The Hapsburgs triumphed in the end, taking Buda in 1686, and the Turks withdrew from Hungary. The retreating Turkish army was joined by most of the Jews living at the time in Hungary. The conquest and ensuing wars laid Hungary to waste and decimated its population.[4] In order to restore the land, the Hapsburgs transferred large groups of the people under their control to Hungary. Among these were Jews.

The Jews came mainly from the northwest, from Moravia, and from the northeast, from Poland. This migration, which began toward the close of the seventeenth century, laid the basis for the Hungarian Jewish community in the modern period.

This Jewish migration continued after the organized migration of various national minorities had come to an end, and the Jewish increase was larger than that of the Hungarian population in general. Thus, the number of Jews in Hungary grew steadily until World War I. In 1720, about twelve thousand Jews lived in Hungary; in 1787, about ninety-three thousand;[5] by 1880, less than a century later, their number had reached 625,000. On the eve of World War I, in 1910, Hungarian Jews totaled 911,227.[6] The proportion of Jews, when compared to the entire population, grew as well: in 1815, Jews made up 1.8 percent of the population, whereas in 1880 this figure had reached 4.4 percent and in 1910 5 percent.[7]

Upon their arrival in Hungary, most Jews settled in the villages adjacent to the border they had just crossed on their way to Hungary. During the ensuing decades, many moved to cities, mainly to the capital, Budapest. The Jewish population of the capital grew accordingly: in 1815, 1,734 Jews lived in Budapest, but within thirty-five years this number had grown tenfold, reaching about seventeen thousand by 1850, while in 1910 over two hundred thousand Jews lived there. This figure was equivalent to about 23 percent of the population of the capital, and the Jews of Budapest made up almost 22 percent of the entire Jewish population of Hungary.[8]

The internal migration of Hungarian Jewry resulted in basic changes in the social and spiritual structure of the Jewish community.[9] In the words of the historian Katzburg,

> In Pest, and the largest of the country towns, there was evolving from the beginning of the nineteenth century a Jewish bourgeoisie, out of which there grew, during the development of a capitalistic economy, an aristocracy of wealthy Jews. . . . This stratum of financial giants, large bourgeoisie, and well-off middle class, was not characteristic of the entire Jewish community, though contemporaries tended to identify it with the Jewish community, by means of superficial generalization.[10]

From statistical data relating to the first decade of the twentieth century, it seems that the two main sectors from which most of the Jews make their living are trading and credit. Out of the 225,000 engaged in these sectors, some 110,000 are Jews, more than half of whom are self-employed—i.e., shop-keepers and small-scale traders.

In the various branches of craftsmanship there are some 85,000 Jews, half of whom are self-employed and half employed by others. Two oc-cupations in this sector in which the Jews are employed in especially large numbers: bars (12,000 Jews as against 29,000 non-Jews) and tailoring (5,000 Jews as against 25,000 non-Jews).

In agriculture the Jews appear in considerable numbers as owners and as lessors of large and middle-sized estates, especially from the last third of the nineteenth century onward....

Jews stand out in the free professions in four fields: law, medicine, journalism and art. Out of 11,000 lawyers...some 5,000 are Jewish.... Out of 2,100 doctors engaged in private practice some 1,300 are Jews. They stand out also among government doctors (40 percent) and doctors employed in clinics and hospitals (over a third in each of the two classes). Out of 1,214 newspaper editors, 516 are Jews. Out of artists (painters, sculptors, actors, musicians, etc.) some 20 percent are Jews.[11]

The Jews would never have reached such heights had they not been granted equal rights. The process was a continuous one, full of struggles between Jews and the liberal circles that had supported equal rights for Jews, on the one hand, and their opponents, on the other. In 1848–49, Hungary fought a war of liberation against the yoke of Austria and the Hapsburg dynasty. The Jews participated in the war of liberation, both as fighters and as suppliers of the army, which had quickly been orga-nized. The Hungarian writer, Mor Jokai, wrote,

> When the minorities of various races and of various nationalities, who had enjoyed full freedom in our homeland and whom Hungary had released from their fate as vassals, making them masters of their lands—when these minorities launched an armed attack against Hungary, in this very struggle the Hebrew race sacrificed its own blood, its own self, and its very soul upon the altar of the defense of legal freedom. In this way the Hebrew race acted, unique in that only the Jews were not granted equal civil rights among the millions in our homeland.[12]

The Hungarian revolutionary leader, Lajos Kossuth, stated, "Twenty thousand Jews fought bravely in our army." Some scholars feel that this number is exaggerated, but nevertheless it is clear that Jews did take part in the war, and even reached the rank of officers: no less than eight Jewish officers served at the rank of major, together with more than fifty Jewish doctors. The revolutionary commanding officer, Gorgey, said of the Jew-ish soldiers: "In their discipline, their personal courage, their devotion, and in every positive military characteristic, they performed honorably together with the other soldiers."[13]

As an expression of the Hungarian revolutionary government's appreciation of the Jews' patriotic stand, the government proposed granting the Jews equal rights. The law was adopted while the fighting was still going on, on July 28, 1849, a short time before the collapse of the revolution. In broad terms, the law stated that "anyone professing the religion of Moses born within the borders of the state of Hungary or who has settled in Hungary in a legal fashion—partakes of all those political and civil rights enjoyed by anyone professing any other faith."[14]

With the collapse of the revolution, the Austrians imposed on Hungary an absolutist regime. Up until 1867 they did away with parliamentary activity and ruled Hungary directly during most of this period. Thus the decision to grant the Jews equal rights remained meaningless from a practical standpoint—especially since the Austrians were enraged at the active role the Jews had played in the revolution. As they put it, "a decisive majority of Hungarian Jews furthered the revolution by criminal activity; without their participation the revolution would not have been able to reach those dimensions it in fact achieved."[15]

In 1867 the Austrians and the Hapsburg monarchy reached a "compromise" with the Hungarians. The Austrians recognized the independence of Hungary, its Parliament, and its government. At the same time, the Hungarians agreed that foreign, military, and financial affairs would be administered together by both states.

The renewal of parliamentary activity put the question of Jewish emancipation back on the public and parliamentary agenda. The government presented a bill that was intended to solve the problem. The bill was worded as follows:

[1] The Jewish inhabitants of the country are hereby declared to have rights equal to those of the Christian inhabitants, as far as political and civil rights are concerned.
[2] Every law, custom or order that contradicts this declaration is hereby declared null and void.

The law was adopted by Parliament without reservation, unanimously, and in the Upper House, too, it was adopted that year by a large majority.[16] It should be noted, however, that granting civil rights to Jews as individuals did not include granting the Jewish religion full recognition. Even after the adoption of the Law of Emancipation, the legal status of the Jewish faith was inferior to that of the Christian churches.

The adoption of the Equal Rights for Jews Bill was followed by an antisemitic awakening, organized antisemitic activity, and even the appearance of an antisemitic party in Parliament in the late 1870s. On April 8, 1875, parliamentary delegate Gyozo Istoczy made an antisemitic speech, proudly claiming that he was the first to deliver an antisemitic speech in any parliamentary forum in Europe. He asserted that his influence was felt in other countries as well, and viewed himself as the leader of European antisemites. He was later joined by five members of Parliament, and these six delegates formed the nucleus of the Antisemitic party, which arose a short time later. In the 1884 elections the Antisemitic party won seventeen parliamentary seats out of a total of 457 seats. On the eve of these elections, the Antisemites were assisted by priests.[17]

The party's success can be ascribed to a considerable extent to the excitement that permeated Hungary in the wake of the blood libel of Tisza Eszlar (discussed below), and to the priesthood, which supported the party's election campaign. The Antisemitic party was active outside Parliament, too, with considerable success.[18]

As a result of internal personal rivalries, the Antisemitic party lost strength, and in the 1887 elections it returned only eleven delegates to Parliament. Nevertheless, before it vanished from the public eye, it succeeded in placing Jew-hatred on the public agenda, as well as setting the precedent of creating a political party based on the antisemitic concept. In a bill the Antisemitic party presented to Parliament in 1884, it stated, "Antisemitism merely means Christian peoples adopting a stance of self-defense against Jewish semitism."[19] The idea of antisemitism being an act of self-defense was eagerly snapped up by various circles in Hungary, and haunted the Jews for many years to come.

The Blood Libel of Tisza Eszlar

The Blood Libel of Tisza Eszlar shocked Hungarian Jewry in 1882. The event had its effect on the non-Jewish population of Hungary as well, contributing to antisemitism and exerting an influence upon the relations of Jews with their neighbors that lasted for years.[20]

Tisza Eszlar was a tiny village in northeastern Hungary. At the time of the blood libel, some twenty-five Jewish families lived there, in the midst of the twenty-seven hundred Christian residents of the village. On April 1, 1882, a fourteen-year-old Christian girl named Eszter Solymosi disappeared. Additional information would seem to indicate that she committed suicide by jumping into the river. The day she vanished was "Shabbat Ha-Gadol," the Saturday before Passover, and on that day the village was host to three candidates for the twofold position of the Jewish community's cantor and ritual slaughterer.

The presence in the village of strange Jews when the young girl disappeared ignited the imaginations of the simple folk of the village, and the proximity of the date to the Jewish Passover festival raised the suspicion that the Christian girl had been murdered to satisfy the ritual needs of the Jews.

The importance of the happening did not warrant its becoming anything more than a provincial event. The court of the provincial capital of Nyiregyhaza was authorized to deal with the matter, and, indeed, for a month and a half the event remained unknown outside the province. It was the local Catholic priest, Jozsef Adamovics, who worked stubbornly to turn the national and international spotlight on this village event. For this he had at his disposal the services of the clerical organ *Magyar Allam* and of a few antisemitic members of Parliament. He was not satisfied with the accusation of Jewish ritual murder in a court in the provincial capital and strove to have the veracity of the blood libel accepted legally throughout the nation and the world.

A short time after the event in Tisza Eszlar, the deputy notary public of the Nyiregyhaza court, Jozsef Bary, was appointed to the post of judicial investigator. Bary said of himself, "I was brought up in the spirit of a strong Calvinist faith, and in the environment in which I grew up Christian love, respect for others, faith and respect for freedom of religion were the central values affecting our lives."[21]

Bary also describes the Jews in the area in which he lived:

They were seeking a new homeland for themselves. Who are these people? They are the same rubbish that was filtered out of the Moscovite sieve and escaped to Galicia. There they were filtered out once again. The good ones remained, and the scrap material continued to wander.... They arrived here without anyone asking them: from where and for what purpose? What have they brought with them? In what way will they earn their living, what are their intentions, and what is their profession?

They continued to arrive, bundles on their backs, deceitful scales in their hands, and a poisoned drink in their barrels. They came here with their fierce hatred of Christianity.... They came with their mercantile inventiveness which they have developed over hundreds of years. They have even brought their views with them, views that teach them that it is permitted to deceive others and that harming others is not considered evil.... They kept coming, more and more. They came by tens, by hundreds, and by thousands.[22]

Bary believed the blood libel. This belief accompanied him in his role as judicial investigator, and he overlooked nothing in his attempt to prove his belief correct. He played an important part in turning this local event into an international sensation.

Bary's first suspicions fell on "the strangers," the three cantors/slaughterers who were spending that Saturday in Tisza Eszlar. He arrested them quickly, and, after brutal torturing, the accused admitted their guilt.

Bary sought out an eyewitness to the murder of the girl, and selected the weak, fourteen-year-old son of the local slaughterer. The boy was taken from his family and, after a period of detention, moved into the roomy home of the official in charge of the provincial headquarters, who became his guardian. Members of his family and other Jews were not permitted to meet with him; Bary provided him with two Catholic tutors.[23] His hosts and mentors gave him antisemitic newspapers, and the Catholic priest visited him on occasion to tell him of other blood libels.[24]

This brainwashing lasted for months and produced results far beyond those considered desirable. The boy described at the trial how he witnessed the murder of the girl through the synagogue keyhole. At the trial the boy showed such disgust and hatred for his father, for the others accused, and for Jews and Judaism that even the president of the court— who believed the blood libel had occurred—was forced to ignore the boy's testimony, for it was clear to him that it could not be considered acceptable in court. In this fashion the evidence given by the state's main witness was disqualified, and the accused were acquitted for lack of proof.

For a month and a half the topic remained a provincial one; but, on May 20, 1882, the local Catholic priest, Adamovics, published an article in the clerical paper *Magyar Allam,* under the heading "The Mysterious Event of a Girl's Disappearance." A portion of the article read,

This river of ours, this Tisza of ours, pure, unsullied and miserable? No one doubts that you are blameless of the innocent blood spilled in vain. No one assumes that you have sinned. On the contrary, everyone here knows with absolute certainty who the guilty parties are. A girl of fourteen, going shopping in the village, vanished in the vicinity of the Jewish synagogue. That is a fact! Who is guilty? It cannot be that you suspect this to be a case of a despicable, fanatic Jewish assassination. Are the Jews guilty of this mysterious event taking place just before their Passover festival? Is it their fault that by chance a few strange slaughterers appeared in Tisza Eszlar and spent the night in the synagogue? . . . For they are decent citizens, expressing their thanks for their emancipation by sacrificing Christian blood to their god. And the Jewish population is already at work:

they have already begun their noble campaign to have this matter put to rest in a speedy and desirable fashion.[25]

The priest was not satisfied with the publication of his article. He appealed in writing to the representative of his district in Parliament, Geza Onody, to raise the subject in the legislature, and Onody did indeed act at the instigation of the priest. On May 23, 1882, Onody spoke of the Tisza Eszlar events:[26]

> According to the Talmud, the Jews need the blood of Christians for ritual purposes on certain festive occasions. On April 1, the fourteen-year-old girl went to the shop to buy paint. Witnesses saw her pass by the synagogue, and it was there that all trace of her vanished.... The slaughterer enticed her to enter the synagogue, bound her hands behind her back, gagged her mouth and, according to rumor, they murdered her in order to use her blood in baking matzoth.... There are also witnesses who overheard her calls for help.[27]

On the following day the opposition newspaper, *Fuggetlenseg,* prominently published Onody's speech in its entirety. At a later stage, the editor of the paper, in his book *Masters of the Land,* described what had convinced him to publish Onody's speech, though its author was not considered an influential politician:

> He came to my office and described the details of the event to me in an interesting fashion. He told me in great detail everything he knew. He showed me the letter written by the priest Adamovics, a letter that had encouraged him to intervene.... In light of this I had no doubt the event was a serious one. I summed up the data and published them in my newspaper in an extremely objective manner.[28]

From that point on, the *Fuggetlenseg* became the flagbearer of antisemitic incitement as far as the blood libel was concerned.

Bary testified to the role played by the Catholic priest in escalating the affair out of all proportion: "At the instigation and encouragement of the Catholic priest Jozsef Adamovics, Onody began to roll the snowball of Tisza Eszlar into an international sensation... and even brought about the evolution of a widespread antisemitic movement in Hungary."[29]

To attract parliamentary interest, the priest Adamovics appealed in a letter to Istoczy, the leader of the Antisemitic party in Parliament,[30] who quoted from the letter in a speech he delivered in Parliament: "It is clear that the story of the sickening Jewish assassination is not merely an invention.... If the newspapers follow this topic attentively, this may influence the judges investigating the affair to ensure that the guilty are punished most severely, as they deserve, so that their punishment will serve to deter others as well."[31]

In his speech, Istoczy analyzed the possibility that the murder had not been linked with ritual needs, but rather was committed for its own sake, only to ultimately reject this notion: "Consider the fact that the slaughterer committed the murder, the man whose function in the Jewish community is to slaughter according to ritual requirements, and consider the fact that the murder was committed in the synagogue, and consider the fact that it was committed just a few days before the Passover festival."[32]

Istoczy was agile in exploiting the event to further his own political aims. "The Tisza Eszlar event served the interests of Istoczy in that it served to further his stubborn, bitter, and consistent antisemitic campaign."[33]

And so it may clearly be seen that the match that ignited the barrel of gunpowder of the blood libel was lit by the village Catholic priest. He acted in three intertwined directions: he wrote an article that was published in the clerical paper; he appealed to his district representative in Parliament, Onody; and he wrote to the leader of the Antisemitic party in Parliament, Istoczy.

The prime minister and the minister of justice both replied to Istoczy's inquiry. They spoke calmly and moderately and promised a proper investigation.[34] But these calm responses were not successful in moderating the hostile atmosphere that had been generated, and the very treatment of this serious allegation leveled against the Jews nourished this antisemitic atmosphere. In other words, turning the local event into a national topic suited the antisemitic propaganda prevalent at the time.[35]

The trial began on June 19, 1883. For its duration, the clerical newspaper *Magyar Allam* was consistent in its antisemitism. In the trial's first stage, the fourteen-year-old son of the slaughterer was called to the witness stand. The semiofficial government newspaper *Pester Lloyd*, appearing in German, noted on June 22, "It seems more and more evident to any unbiased reader that the court in Nyiregyhaza is dealing at present with an allegation based on the hallucinations of a fourteen-year-old child."[36] *Magyar Allam* reacted to this in an editorial on June 26: "We well understand the reasons for the Jewish press's attitude and approach to this subject. But we are entirely unable to comprehend the reason for the stand taken by the semiofficial paper in adamantly and emotionally defending the slaughterers."[37]

The accused, too, were called to the witness stand, where they refuted the confessions they had made under duress and torture when first interrogated. The testimony given by the accused in court did not match the expectations of those circles favoring the blood libel, who now saw their prey slipping through their fingers. *Magyar Allam* served as the mouthpiece of these circles:

> The Jews have gone too far. They have freed themselves of all their embarrassment and give their testimony as if they are reading it from a written document. In their new testimony they are denying their previous statements, which were included in the investigation report. They are full of contradictions. There is no limit to what they are doing: the witness stand is flooded with false testimony.[38]

The newspaper *Nemzet,* the government organ, reported the progress of the trial without expressing support for those who accepted the blood libel. *Magyar Allam* responded on July 11: "In its defense of the slaughterers the newspaper *Nemzet* has surpassed even the Jewish press. It has been exploiting every admission, every comment made by the defense attorneys and has been presenting the case in a manner best serving the interests of the accused."[39]

In addition to the state prosecution, a private prosecutor representing the mother of the missing girl appeared at the trial. In his summing up he said,

> I stand here and ask the honorable court to do justice in the case of this crime, which has caused the mourning mother so much sorrow. The Jewish purse, which has been recruited in support of the slaughterer's knife, is here challenging Christianity and the culture of love of all creation. The slaughterer's knife is here in confrontation with the Cross.... Just as our magnificent ancestors succeeded in overcoming the Ottoman lion, so we, too, their miserable offspring, shall succeed in overcoming the Jewish hyena.[40]

In other words, the event was regarded in some circles as nothing but an expression of the conflict between Christianity and Judaism.

The verdict was handed down on August 2, 1883. The court drew no conclusions concerning the fate of the girl, and the accused were acquitted. The verdict, however, did not determine unambiguously that the blood libel was baseless. And so, the various antisemitic circles that accepted the blood libel were left some room to maneuver. Istoczy expressed the feelings of these circles precisely in his speech in Parliament on November 21, 1883: "Did they acquit the accused? This proves nothing concerning their innocence. The only thing to be learned from the acquittal is that once again Jewish money did its job.... Everyone is convinced in the depths of his heart that the poor girl from Tisza Eszlar came to a sorry end there in the synagogue of her village."[41]

The trial and the publicity it received aroused strong and widespread antisemitic feelings. Consequently, the transition from antisemitic rhetoric to antisemitic action was immediate. Pogroms had already broken out in some twenty different locations in the early stages of the obsession with the blood libel, with the encouragement of local intelligentsia, teachers, and priests.[42] The hesitant verdict aroused a new wave of rioting that broke out during the months of August and September 1883:

> This rioting was more severe than the rioting of 1882, both in size and in seriousness: this time there was rioting in about fifty places, which—in contrast to the 1882 riots, which were aimed mainly against property— included cases of physical violence and even several cases of murder. Furthermore, cemeteries were damaged.[43]

The cardinal archbishop, Janos Simor, head of the Catholic church in Hungary, had his offices in the town of Esztergom. Jews of the town turned to him in the hope that he would express a negative opinion of the blood libel. His reply: "Would that the Almighty fulfill your request and that of all those of your faith, and you would enjoy—in our land— respect, tranquil lives, and happiness as a result of your engaging in justice, in law, and in love of all creatures."[44] The cardinal's reply does not contain any negative reference to the blood libel; on the other hand, it may include a swipe at the Jews in that he advised them to engage "in justice, in law, and in love of all creatures."

At the instigation of ten or fifteen priests of the Reformed church, two landowners with estates, and various public figures, a convention took place in the town of Tapolca, in the province of Zala, in western Hungary, on July 31, 1883, a few days before the handing down of the verdict. Some two hundred people took part in the convention and adopted a resolution containing three paragraphs, which was to be presented to Parliament:

> [1] The Emancipation Law of 1867 should be abrogated, because "the Jews set themselves off from Christianity, especially by means of their observance of the laws of Kashruth and ritual purity, which debase Christians and insult them."
> [2] So long as the Emancipation Law is not abrogated, the separatist Jewish education should be forbidden.
> [3] Members of the Jewish race must be forbidden to acquire real estate in Hungary.[45]

The petition, bearing the signatures of 2,174 citizens of Zala, was presented to Parliament.[46] Work on the petition had involved antisemitic factors in various parties.[47]

Ten and a half years after the adoption of the Law of Emancipation, the Reformed priests rushed to propose its abrogation. The hostile atmosphere prevailing throughout Hungary in the wake of the blood libel trial certainly helped their message to be absorbed.

During the public debates on the question of the blood libel, the priest Imre Tatay from the town of Szekesfehervar sought to prove the guilt of the Jews. He related that when he was a child, Jews attempted to kidnap him in order to commit a crime aimed at providing them with their needs in their religious rituals. Only by a miracle was he saved.[48]

After the trial was over, the priest of the Evangelical Church of Nyiregyhaza, Janos Bartholomeides, became aware of rumors to the effect that he had doubted the guilt of the accused in the blood libel trial after the verdict had been handed down. The priest hurriedly published a denial of the report. In his letter to the editors of the newspapers he wrote, "I shall believe in the innocence of the slaughterers only if it is proved that the girl vanished in a way unlike that which was described in their indictment."[49]

The Reformed church priest serving in Tisza Eszlar at the time of the trial, Janos Lapossy, collected the official court records of the trial and deposited them for safekeeping in the church building, available for viewing by anyone interested. In addition, the church also had volumes of the local newspaper containing "The Tisza Eszlar Diary" from the time of the trial. On June 25, 1885, about two years after the verdict was handed down, the priest jotted down on the first page of one of these volumes,

> Since I know that in the future my views of the events of the trial, in which the Jews were accused of ritual murder, will be important, and since I was in a situation where I was directly familiar with the conditions under which the event took place, with the characters involved, and with the development of events—therefore, now, after a considerable period of time and when I am free of the excitement which the trial aroused, and so long as I am in full possession of my physical and mental qualities—I hereby declare that I fully believe that Eszter Solymosi was murdered by the Jews in the synagogue in Eszlar on April 1, 1882. Furthermore, I also believe the murder was committed for the purpose of a religious ritual, and not for any other purpose.[50]

Indeed, many Christians in Hungary accepted the suspicions against the Jews as if they were proven facts. Bary enjoyed telling how the population punished the prime minister for taking a liberal stand in this affair:

> When the verdict was made public, elections were being held for the position of chief guardian [a mainly honorary position, empty of any real meaning] in the Transtisza province of the Reformed church. The candidates for the position were Prime Minister Kalman Tisza and Janos Valyi. Under other circumstances the members of the Reformed church would have been proudly happy to be given the chance to elect the prime minister to this honored post. But under the conditions then prevailing, the vast majority of Reformed church members in the province of Transtisza could not agree with the government's attempts at covering up in the Tisza Eszlar trial. The surprising result of these elections was that, as compared with the 258 votes the prime minister received, his rival was elected—with 299 votes.[51]

The antisemitic newspaper *Fuggetlenseg* reported the event: "The Calvinistic masses celebrated the election of the new chief guardian with a torchlight procession voicing antisemitic slogans. Why does the prime minister not settle for his guardianship over the slaughterers?"[52]

The private prosecutor representing the mother of the missing girl, who took advantage of the trial to describe Judaism as challenging Christianity and the "slaughterer's knife" as "confronting the Cross," has been previously discussed. His was not the only opinion of this sort. In a book the editor of *Fuggetlenseg* wrote after the trial, he considered the usefulness of the trial:

> Even if the blood of the poor widow's daughter, though screaming to Heaven, was unsuccessful in saving further victims from the yoke of fanaticism; even if the struggle on this subject—known as "the Jewish Question"—had no result other than the fact that from every church pulpit announcements were made of the victory, the triumph, the success of the Christian spirit and of the proof that the whip of Jesus had struck our contemporary parasites; even if this trial had no results other than the fact that this struggle has erected a barrier in the path of the view attempting to replace Jesus' exalted doctrines, teaching us of the love of our fellowmen, by the poisonous, rotten doctrines of "the chosen people," aimed at furthering the separate existence of this race with its queer customs and rituals that keep it separate from the society it exploits as if members of this society were its bondsmen; even in such a case this legal battle has provided an extremely important service for all mankind.[53]

The image of the village girl was exploited well by antisemitic circles, which depicted her as a martyr, complete with halo, whose life was ended by murderers, enemies of Christianity. Her image even played a respectable role in the antisemitic propaganda of later decades. In 1943, sixty years after the trial and a year before the expulsion of Hungarian Jewry to Auschwitz, there appeared a book on the blood libel of Tisza Eszlar. In the introduction to the book, a poem is dedicated to the girl who vanished, a poem that speaks for itself:

> The judge has had his say
> and the trembling wearers of the kaftans
> are free to go their way.
> They did not murder Eszter Solymosi,
> they are not criminals,
> they are not murderers,
> and they did not bake matzoh
> with human blood.
>
> The judge has had his say
> and the "persecuted" Jews
> breathed freely,
> but the "tale" still lives.
> "The superstition" is spreading
> through the poor Hungarian people.
>
> The spurt of blood has become a stream,
> the stream—a mighty river,
> a river roaring and rushing
> down to a sea of blood,
> an eternal sea, a chasmic one,
> a depth with no bed.
> Blood like the blood of Jesus,
> son of God, redeemer of the world,
> the blood of the debased martyr:
> the blood of Eszter Solymosi.[54]

The Catholic People's Party

In the early 1890s there appeared on the stage of Hungarian public life a political party organized by the Catholic establishment. The party appeared in the wake of government legislative action on the question of personal and religious status in Hungary.

The Law of Emancipation of 1867 granted the Jews equal rights as individuals, but did not deal with the status of the Jewish religion, which remained inferior even after the adoption of the Emancipation Law. At the time, the Hungarian constitution granted different statuses to different religions. The great Christian religions were defined as "accepted religions" (*Bevett Vallas*), whereas the Jewish religion was defined as a "recognized religion" (*Elismert Vallas*). The accepted religions enjoyed official status, internal administrative autonomy, and government assistance in various fields. Their leaders were members of the Upper House of the legislature. These religions were equal to one another in their legal and religious status, and a member of one accepted religion was permitted to convert to another accepted religion, though not to a religion that did not enjoy "accepted" status. The "recognized religions" were also recognized by the state, but their autonomy was more limited than that of the accepted religions. Their leaders did not represent them in the Upper House and, as already noted, the mutual conversion right did not apply to their members. The Jews were in fact the only large religious community whose religion was not an "accepted" one. From a legal-constitutional point of view, the Jewish religion was discriminated against, though individual members of the Jewish religion enjoyed full civil and political rights in accordance with the Law of Emancipation. The government was interested in correcting the situation, and so it prepared legislation of a liberal kind concerning "the freedom of religion and the equality of the religious communities." The government's proposed legislation was comprehensive, and included far-reaching changes in the relationship of religion and state. Questions concerning personal status had up until now been under the jurisdiction of the churches, and now the government proposed adopting civil marriages and divorces. The churches viewed this planned governmental legislation as an intrusion and as an attack on topics specifically Christian, and thus opposed it vehemently. The churches even rejected the idea of rendering the status of the Jewish religion equal to that of the Christian faiths, and recruited all their resources for the struggle against the government's legislative proposal.[55]

The bill was presented to Parliament in 1869. The Catholics expressed their opposition, and it was removed from the agenda. In 1881 the bill succeeded in reaching the parliamentary law committee, but it was not adopted. In 1882—the year of the blood libel—the government felt the time was not right for debating the bill. In 1883 the debate was renewed. The law was adopted in Parliament by a large majority, but was rejected by the Upper House, where the strength and influence of the church representatives were maximal. The process was repeated, with similar consequences, in 1884, and so the bill was shelved for a number of years.[56]

On November 21, 1892, the prime minister announced that the bill concerning the status of the Jewish religion and religious freedom was soon to be presented to Parliament. The heads of the Catholic church reacted swiftly. On December 15, 1892, a conference of Catholic bishops—both Roman Catholic and Greek Catholic—from all over the country convened in Budapest. Cardinal Archbishop Kolos Vaszary chaired the conference, which prepared a memorandum that was presented to the Hungarian government, to the pope and to the emperor, Franz Jozef. The memorandum said, in part:

> The difference between Christianity and the Jewish religion is so great and so profound, that it is not at all possible to word a bill which speaks of "converting from Judaism to Christianity or vice versa." The Christian religion is not limited to a single nationality, and by virtue of its universal character all the nations of the world are able to believe in it without their nationality being damaged.... The Jewish religion is a national religion and was only a preparation for Christianity... and the Christian nations are not able to unite with it in its religion, for religion and nationality are intertwined in Mosaism extremely closely, just like body and soul. For just this reason, while a Hungarian can be Catholic or Protestant without inhibiting his nationality in any way, no one can follow the way of Mosaism without sacrificing his nationality.[57]

The bishops were not satisfied with sending memoranda; they published a "Shepherds' Epistle" in which the heads of the church warned the public of the danger threatening the Catholic religion from the proposed reforms. The priests who read the Shepherds' Epistle from the pulpits of their churches added their own embellishments. The incitement against the Jews was stressed, especially by the Catholic press.[58]

The government, for its part, did not give up on its intention to have the law adopted, whereas the priesthood amassed all its resources to thwart the government's plan. The struggle was fierce and lengthy. Several governments fell because of this question. The Upper House rejected the bill time and again. The speaker for the opposition in the Upper House, Nandor Zichy, expressed well his view and that of his colleagues from the Catholic aristocracy: "The interests of the Magyar state and of Magyar society are not served by strengthening the power of non-Christian religions." Judaism was the only non-Christian religion in Hungary, and so the intent of the speaker was clear. It was only toward the end of 1895 that the government succeeded in its undertaking. The law was adopted, and the Jewish religion in Hungary thus won full formal recognition.[59]

In the elections of 1892 Istoczy's Antisemitic party was soundly defeated, no more than six of its representatives being elected to Parliament:[60]

The Catholics realized that they would lose a parliamentary struggle as long as no party enjoying public support backed them up, and so they began to found their own political party. The party, founded at the beginning of 1895 under the name Katolikus Neppart [the Catholic People's party], set itself the goal of protecting the Christian nature of Hungary and the status of the Catholic church, and of opposing every law opposing the Christian spirit.... The party's clerical and conservative nature and its appearing in the middle of the struggle for religious legislation gave the party from the very onset an antisemitic character.... The new party became the political flagbearer of antisemitism, after the weakening of Istoczy's Antisemitic party.[61]

The Catholic People's party relied on the religious emotions of the populace to gather strength. It went so far in this that the minister of culture spoke out in the Upper House against its electioneering tactics:

> I must strongly protest against the persuasive tactics adopted by the People's party. How can they permit themselves to drag the intimate religious feelings of the people into the political arena? The use of religious reasoning for political purposes is extremely dangerous, and it can only embitter the struggle between the members of the various religions.[62]

The culture minister's warning did not deter the Catholic People's party from its campaign. Its continuing use of religious belief to achieve its political aims led the government, some five years after the founding of the party, to insert into the Protecting the Purity of Elections Act a special paragraph that was called the Church Pulpit Paragraph:

> The results of the elections will be null and void, if during the three months preceding the elections the candidate for election will have appeared in a place intended for religious ritual or at a meeting convened for the purpose of a religious ritual and made any declaration which might influence the outcome of the elections.... This shall apply if the candidate shall have made the use, or the denial of said use, of religious articles conditional upon the vote, as well as if he shall have voiced a threat concerning the punishments a voter can expect in the next life.[63]

The Catholic People's party made efficient use of the various church institutions throughout the state. In cities, in towns, and in villages, existing churches made up the nucleus about which party circles organized. With the active assistance of church employees, groups were founded to serve the needs of the various population groups. By 1908 the party was already active in about thirteen hundred settlements. All of this activity was directed by a central national body based on the hierarchy of the Catholic church. Its leadership at its various levels was made up of church leaders and religious and lay activists. A newspaper article that appeared in mid-1908 and signed by "a Catholic priest" declares, "This hierarchic organization promises us a united leadership, rapid action, and a decisive approach.... There is a huge army which is organizing here, ready to respond immediately to the slightest hint on the part of the leadership, to come to immediate attention and to make its voice heard on each and every question."[64]

The Catholic People's party declared war on liberalism. It claimed that the Jews—and especially the Jewish press—played a significant role in the evolution of liberalism: "The Jewish press created heretic liberalism, which in its turn created socialism. Public opinion must be delivered from the influence of the Jewish press, and we must return to our Christian fundament."[65]

The Catholic People's party strove to be a popular party, and was interested in attracting the workers, both urban industrial workers and landless agricultural laborers. The Christian Socialist organization began to function in 1902–1903 as a counterbalance to the socialist movement and with the aim "of saving Hungary from revolutionary socialism." One of the prominent spiritual leaders of the new movement was the priest Ottokar Prohaszka,[66] and others became known as leaders of the antisemitic reaction after World War I.

Among the steps taken by the Catholic People's party in the economic-social sphere, one must note the founding of the consumers' unions, companies for purchasing and for marketing, and credit companies. The economic institutions sprang up at the instigation of local branches of the party, starting from the second half of the 1890s. In 1904, some two hundred associations were linked to the national center. From a Parliament member who belonged to the Catholic People's party, we learn that the purpose of organizing the consumers' unions was to protect the small-scale farmers from "the rule of wealth" and to protect themselves from the "collectors of exorbitant interest ... and acts of deceit in trade."[67]

Bishop Prohaszka interpreted the hints included in these expressions:

> The Jewish cancer has eaten at the Christian Hungarian nation until it wore it down and presented it as a naked skeleton. It has turned most of the Hungarian people into beggars. Judaism is a blight everywhere ... it lowers the moral level and transforms corruption into an accepted way of life. No one has ever stolen and robbed as much as the modern, liberal Jewish economic regime.
>
> The fact is that the most typical representatives of modern capitalism are the Jews. Their religious outlook requires them to amass property, and to accomplish their goal they have to resort to all kinds of tricks, cunning,

and misrepresentation—limitless and shameless. The Jew has become the
master, the Hungarian—the beggar.... No one can aid Hungary, nothing
can save her, other than a popular uprising against the oppressive usury.
"Consumer Societies" are the concrete expression of such an uprising.[68]

A writer quoting Prohazska added his own explanations and evalu-
ations: "He has encouraged the priesthood on a regular basis to support
the idea of cooperative societies, for he saw in such a concept the only
way of escaping the claws of Jewish blackmail and the usury they have
been collecting."[69]

While the consumers' societies were being set up in the country, a
boycott was imposed on Jewish shopkeepers. This was swiftly followed
by a drop in Jewish income, and some Jews had to seek a livelihood
elsewhere.[70] The priesthood, which had succeeded over a period of fifteen
years in delaying the adoption of the law granting the Jews full equality,
could not in the long run withstand parliamentary ambition, but when
the law was adopted, the priesthood transferred its struggle outside Parliament, into the economic and social sphere, where there was considerable room for political maneuvering.

As for the matter under consideration, the very existence of the Catholic People's party is extremely important. From the time of its inception
up until World War I, it was a flagbearer of antisemitism in Hungary.
It will be shown below, that during the period between the two world
wars various antisemitic groups—including leaders of the Catholic priesthood—as well as antisemitic Christian parties identified strongly with
the Catholic People's party and with its antisemitic positions. In this
identification these groups hoped to bestow upon their antisemitic positions a dimension of historical depth, the roots of which were anchored
in the nineteenth century.[71] The Catholic People's party is thus to be
viewed as a mother party to the antisemitic movements that sprang up
out of its roots, and as a party of long-range influence over the antisemitic
setup controlling Hungary in the 1930s and 1940s.

At the turn of the century, Hungary was facing the urgent problem
of millions of landless agricultural workers. Two main groups enjoyed
the profits gleaned from the widespread farmland territories: the landed
aristocracy, and the priesthood—especially the Catholic priesthood,
which also owned large estates. Naturally, the landowners feared any
liberal government that might arouse public attention—especially the
attention of the agricultural workers—concerning the distribution of land
and its significance. Thus, presenting liberalism as the product of a Jewish
Weltanschauung was well suited to the needs of aristocratic and priestly

circles, especially since liberalism had appeared in Hungary at the same time as the granting of rights to the Jews.

Despite these activities, World War I found the Jews of Hungary enjoying full civil and religious equality. The regime was indeed liberal and viewed the equality of its citizens as an immutable fact of life.

The Revolutions and the White Terror

World War I had disastrous results for Hungary. When the war came to an end, the Austro-Hungarian monarchy broke up. Historical Hungary was partitioned and most of its area and population distributed among its neighbors. What was left of Hungary came to less than a third of its earlier territory, some ninety-three thousand square kilometers. Of some 21 million original inhabitants, only about 7.5 million remained within its new borders. On June 14, 1920, in the Trianon Palace at Versailles, Hungary signed the agreement determining its new borders.[72] The birth pangs of this new period rocked Hungary and its population fiercely, and the Jews in Hungary were among those to suffer most from these developments.

Besides the devastating blow to the national pride of the Hungarians resulting from their loss of the war and of the larger portion of their homeland, there were additional reasons for the atmosphere of frustration prevalent in the country. The long war demanded many sacrifices in both life and materiel. It diminished the national reserves as well as private property. Officers and soldiers returned from the front with but little chance of being absorbed into the civilian economy. Tens of thousands of Hungarian refugees arrived from the territories that had been transferred to other sovereignties. These were largely government clerks, teachers, doctors, and other members of the middle class. Territories that had formerly provided foodstuffs and raw materials for industry were now cut off from Hungary. For many years the economy did not recover, grow, or begin producing for peaceful purposes. This new situation confronted the Jews with problems.

Until World War I the population of Hungary was variegated nationally: about half was not Hungarian. The Hungarians viewed the merging of the various nationalities as one of their most significant national aims, and within this framework, some of the Hungarians viewed Jewish attempts at assimilation favorably.[73] At the end of the war, however, the population of Hungary remained almost homogeneous, and aside from a group of German speakers, the approximately half-million Jews were the only large minority in Hungary. The idea of a merger of peoples had vanished, to be replaced by anger at the minorities that had previously resided in Hungary but were allegedly hostile to her. The Jews were a convenient target for the Hungarian frustrations developing against the minorities.

Enmity toward the Jews was quickly rationalized. It was claimed that the Jews in Hungary blocked the way toward self-improvement of the lower classes, as well as of the Hungarian refugees who had arrived from the countries of the confrontation, for in the fields where they sought their livelihood there were many Jews. More than anything else, however, the Hungarians were furious at the Jews with regard to the short-lived Communist regime that ruled Hungary in the summer of 1919 and that was headed by a Communist of Jewish extraction.

On October 31, 1918, after more than four years of warfare, the Hungarian government resigned, to be replaced by a new government headed by the leader of the liberals, Count Mihaly Karolyi. The historian Macartney explains,

> Karolyi...was able to convince a confused and desperate people that if Hungary, with him as her leader, proclaimed her independence of the Hapsburgs, all her ills could be cured by the one operation. The war would end: the oppressive and reactionary...regime associated with the Compromise would be swept away; even the nationalities, no longer fearing oppression and denationalization, would return to the fold.[74]

Karolyi even hoped that the triumphant powers would regard favorably a democratic Hungary that no longer had relations with the Hapsburgs or with Germany.

Except for the cutting off of Hungarian relations with the Hapsburg dynasty and the dissolving of the Austro-Hungarian monarchy, none of Karolyi's plans were realized. The various nationalities—Czechs, Serbs, and Rumanians—not only refused to return to "the fold," as Karolyi had hoped, but even took control of large sections of Hungary, including territories stretching beyond the regions that were inhabited by their compatriots. Even the victorious powers did not improve their hostile attitude toward Hungary, and despite Karolyi's efforts at liberalization, refused to regard her positively.

At home, too, things did not progress as Karolyi had expected. Vicious propaganda from Communist Russia caused unrest among the people of Hungary. Karolyi was unsuccessful in keeping his promises, and he did not hold elections. He lacked the decisiveness necessary to carry out an agrarian reform. And as if their internal problems were not enough, Karolyi had to face difficulties caused by external factors as well. A chain of occurrences resulted in a French demand to evacuate extensive territories in East Hungary, and as a result the Karolyi government fell.

At this stage a Communist of Jewish extraction named Bela Kun appeared in the Hungarian political arena. Kun had been a member of the Social-Democratic party in his youth. He had served in the Hungarian army and had been taken captive on the Russian front, where he joined the Communist party.

Kun proposed a way to save Hungary from the French threat. He claimed that if a Communist government were installed in Hungary, the Bolshevik Russians would come to the aid of Hungary, thus preserving Hungarian territorial integrity. In fact, Kun succeeded Karolyi, and Hungary was proclaimed a Soviet republic. Though Kun came to power with the agreement of many—including non-Communist groups—disappointment with his regime came swiftly. The Russian Red Army did not come to the assistance of Hungary, and the army under Kun's control operated with no noticeable success.

Furthermore, Kun's activities in the public and economic fields caused him to lose his popularity very rapidly. His regime applied brutal and extreme measures against both the rural and urban populations. He succeeded in arousing against him the fury of broad sectors of the public, and even his own Social-Democratic party abandoned him.

At the end of July Kun organized a military campaign against the Romanians, but the Hungarians were defeated. Kun fled to Vienna on August 1, 1919, thus bringing the short-lived Communist regime in Hungary to its end.[75]

This regime left behind unpleasant memories. Of the twenty-nine members of the Communist government, eighteen had been Jewish, and so Hungary—after the fall of the Communist regime—readily identified communism with Jewry. This identification gradually became a turn of phrase widely used by the media, by public figures, and even by the general public.

True, eighteen of the twenty-nine members of the Communist government were indeed of Jewish origin. Yet there was clearly no connection between their Communist activity and their Jewish religion. But the intelligentsia, itself the source of socialist thinking, included large numbers of Jews. The Jews who stood out in the revolutionary movements had no links with the Jewish community, and some even went so far as to convert. For its part, the Jewish community identified in the main with the previous regime, and had no expectations of advancement when it fell and was replaced by a regime dedicated to aiding those social strata with which the Jews, by and large, had but little to do. Despite these mutual reservations—of the Jewish Communist leaders regarding their religion, and of most of the Jews concerning communism—the gentile population of Hungary formed a generalization whereby Jews and communism were inextricably entangled with one another.[76]

It should be noted that not only had the Communist regime not discriminated in favor of the Jews, but in fact its negative effects upon the Jews were more severe than upon the population in general. Of the 342 victims of the Communist revolution, forty-four were Jewish, two and a half times their relative weight in the general population.[77]

During the days of the Kun regime, an anti-Communist group began to organize in southeast Hungary, in a region not under Communist control. On May 5, 1919, an antirevolutionary government was installed in the town of Arad, and at the end of May the group moved to the town of Szeged, where it joined with the local "anti-Communist Committee." In Szeged the group began to organize "a national army" under the command of ex-Admiral Miklos Horthy.[78]

On November 16, 1919, Horthy entered Budapest at the head of his army, and on November 24, a temporary national government was installed, led by Karoly Huszar.[79]

The regime set up by the counterrevolution ruled Hungary until its conquest by the Russians in 1944–1945. The declared goal of the white counterrevolution was the purifying of Hungary from communism and Communists. Since at the time, as we have noted, the Jews and communism were identified with one another, the ire of the counterrevolution, of the national government, and of the national army at its disposal was primarily aimed at Hungarian Jewry.

When the national army left Szeged and found its way to Budapest blocked, it circumvented the capital and entered the western parts of Hungary. The national army began brutal purifying operations. The precise number of victims of "the White Terror" will never be known, but it would seem that there were some three thousand fatalities, most of whom were Jews.

Most of the murders were carried out in August–September 1919. The wave of murders resumed in April–May 1920,[80] but sporadic acts of murder went on until 1924–1925.[81]

These acts were carried out with the knowledge and, sometimes, the encouragement of the government. As one historian put it, even if the perpetrators of a murder were arrested, "they got off with light punishment.... When the same courts dealt with ... offenses by the right, the 'extenuating circumstance of patriotic motives' was always taken into consideration. Sentences . . . were not carried out."[82]

One of the leading commanding officers of the national army was Pal Pronay, who himself commanded the officers' unit that made up the vanguard of the national army in its war against Jews/Communists. In his memoirs, published in 1943, he described with nostalgia and with apparent pleasure the brutal acts he and his men had carried out:[83] "The headquarters of 'the national army' was located in Siofok, where the most brutal murders were committed. A few hundred of his men were murdered by units under the command of Pal Pronay."[84]

Another unit, under the command of Baron Antal Lehar, also attempted to operate in the spirit of Pronay's officers' unit, and during the night between September 9 and 10 they organized a pogrom in Tapolca, moved on to Diszel armed with hand grenades and machine guns, and murdered all the Jews there. In another town, Celldomok, the soldiers broke into a synagogue while services were being held and incited the population to murder the Jews.[85]

The Rumanians retreated from Hungary in the middle of November. On November 15, 1919, the day after the Rumanian evacuation of Kecskemet, one of the officers of the national army, Ivan Hejjas, appeared in town with his unit. With the assistance of local leaders, including the Apostolic Bishop Istvan Revesz and three teachers of theology at the church school, he prepared a list of those to be murdered. That night, sixty people[86] were murdered in the nearby forest, after being tortured. When Horthy and his army entered Budapest on November 16, 1919, the pogroms spread to the capital as well.[87]

The counterrevolutionary national army fought for a number of causes; these causes won the favor and the support of the most respectable Christian body in Hungary, which was also the most influential in the Hungarian Catholic church—the Synod of Catholic Bishops. This body met once every half-year under the leadership of the head of the Catholic church in Hungary, the cardinal archbishop. The protocols summarizing these sessions are an important instrument in understanding the spiritual leadership of the Catholic church during that period.[88]

The Synod of Bishops convened on August 22, 1919, a short time after the collapse of the Communist regime. The bishops considered at length the regime that had collapsed, and laid down plans of action for the future:

The terrible rampaging of Bolshevism has shocked the public conscience and aroused recognition of Christian self-value. Christian organization is progressing at a rapid rate, for only on the basis of Christian morality can we hope to stabilize the regime and strengthen the national idea anew. The Christian political organization has caused the Jews to panic.[89]

The Synod of Bishops entrusted Bishop Prohaszka with the preparation of a Shepherds' Epistle to reflect the spirit of its discussions:

> Violent groups took control of us and fought with all their might to realize their imaginary ideas.... It was not Hell that opened up its mouth to swallow us down, nor was it Hell that set her red demons upon us. It was the curse of fanaticism, lack of conscience, and brutality that struck at us.
>
> Now, with your own eyes you have seen the world that drifted away from its Christian foundation. You have been able to appreciate that our society has ceased being a human society, and has degenerated into a den of dangerous animals.... Those who ridiculed the Gospel beat down liberty under the feet of tyrants.... They have turned Mankind into a bloodthirsty beast!
>
> It was Hell on Earth, and not God's earth. Such a world as this is not worthy of being a refuge for human beings, and with horror we turn our backs on it. But it is not sufficient to express our horror. Let us all rise up as a single person, let the entire nation rise up in defense of Christianity! Let us defend our faith, our morality, our righteousness, and our honesty.
>
> Dear believers, it was possible to see that it was not the ambition to improve the lot of the proletariat that was on the agenda; neither was it the desire to lift up the downtrodden from the dung heap. These tyrants had completely different interests. Their main resource was hatred for Christianity.
>
> All the corruption, sin, and curses penetrating our Christian society do not originate in Christianity—on the contrary: they originate in a denial of Christianity. Let us oppose evil and stand up strongly for our principles, so that in the next elections we vote only for candidates standing firm on the basis of their Christian faith, supporting religious schools, desirous of applying the principles of Christianity in all areas of their lives.... Let us lead ourselves and not trust those who are capable only of destruction, yet are unable to build. Behold, we are all human beings, brothers, children of God in Jesus.... Let us follow practical Christianity as a basis for un- derstanding and respecting the law.

Prohaszka concludes his epistle with a quotation from the New Tes- tament: "And may the God of Peace swiftly trample Satan under your feet, and may the pleasantness of our Lord, Jesus Christ, the Messiah, be upon you" (Paul to the Romans 16: 20).[90]

The epistle was distributed in September 1919 in 2,450 copies.[91] While the word "Jew" was not mentioned in the epistle, in light of the note in the protocol about causing "the Jews to panic," there is no doubt who was referred to, especially since the Christian public to whom it was distributed was aware of the opinions of Bishop Prohaszka, the compiler of the epistle.

On July 29, 1919, less than a month before the convening of the Synod of Bishops, Prohaszka published an article in which he wrote:

> The Jews eat and consume us, and we must defend ourselves against this flea epidemic.[92] True enough, there are decent Jews as well, but Jewry in general is a foreign power conquering, oppressing Christians and taking control of us.... We are dealing here with the rampaging of a tricky, corrupt, disbelieving, and immoral race which is waging against us a campaign resembling the military campaign of rats, and is working against us by flooding us like invading fleas. The question before us is how to defend ourselves: are we to defend ourselves against them, or hand our country over to their control?[93]

It should be noted that at the time the Synod of Bishops' Shepherds' Epistle was being published, the antisemitic rampaging had reached a climax, and the epistle only strengthened the hate for the Jews. With this as background, several secret or semisecret organizations rose in support of government actions. In 1919 twenty-two patriotic organizations were founded, 101 more in 1920, forty in 1921, and forty-nine in 1922. These data do not include the secret organizations.[94]

What all these organizations had in common was their desire to strengthen the counterrevolution. They were antisemitic, and maintained relations—overt or covert—with various government officials who played a double role, often being leaders of these organizations while holding their positions as government officials.

Outwardly, these organizations strove to restore to Hungary her honor and her pristine greatness from before the war, by nullifying the Trianon Agreement that shrunk the borders of Hungary. Their internal aim was to purify Hungary from the harmful influence of Jews and Judaism, Communists and communism.

A section of a "voice" put out by one of these organizations, Etelkozi Szovetseg[95]—in short, Eksz—expressed in summary these ambitions: "War against destructive Jewry and freemasons, war against bolshevism and internationalism. War for the integrity of the state."[96]

Among the leaders of this organization—just as among their colleagues—there were representatives of the priesthood. In addition to Bishop Prohaszka, who quickly identified with every antisemitic movement, I shall mention only a few: Istvan Zadravecz, a Franciscan priest who later became a military chaplain; the priest Janos Gyarmathy, who was the confessor of the wife of Admiral Horthy and was also a member of the committee that received Pronay, the commander of the "officers' unit," as a member of Eksz and swore him in when he joined the group; and the Franciscan priest Boris Arkangyal.[97]

The latter was not satisfied with the activity of the counterrevolution's national army, and in his meeting with Horthy "he criticized severely those who delayed the National Christian development... and requested the Regent to drive out of public life those who prevent the fitting progress of the National Christian trend. He also demanded the curbing of the rampage of the Jewish press."[98]

His appeal to the leader had its desired effect. At the session of the Synod of Catholic Bishops the priest's request was brought before them "to grant support to the units under his command." The Synod of Bishops decided that "his movement, with its patriotic trend, was worthy of support and the Synod of Bishops recommends that he be supported. Donations are to be sent to the military chaplain, Istvan Zadravecz."[99]

Paralleling its civil institutions, the Eksz maintained a military arm known as Kettoskereszt Verszovetseg (Blood Alliance of the Double Cross). This choice of name conveyed a dual message: a mention of the double cross in Hungary's official seal and emphasis on the Christian nature of the organization.

From a numerical point of view, these two organizations were not large, numbering together less than ten thousand members. Yet their influence upon small organizations and individuals was great.[100]

The main aim of the various organizations was very much the same. Yet each organization decided for itself where it would put the emphasis while addressing a certain sector of the populace. A network of such organizations succeeded in meeting various requirements.

Macartney sums up these developments as follows: "When the counter revolution came, there was plenty for 'patriotic associations' to do. There were the embers of Karolyi's and Kun's revolutions to be stamped out, Communists to be tracked down and Jews disciplined... contact to be established with counterrevolutionaries in other countries... and help given them."[101]

At this time one organization stood out especially:

> The political and military body behind the White Terror was the Union of Awakening Hungarians, which was the most important organization of the extreme right in Hungary. Antisemitism constituted the most important component of its ideology and practical activity. The Awakening Hungarians obtained their ideas from various sources. Some elements were derived from nineteenth-century Hungarian antisemitism, others were

new, and bore the imprint of contemporary developments.... Another motif... was the base morals of the Jews, which corrupted Christian society. ... The ideology of the Awakening Magyars also gave prominence to the "Christian" nature of the struggle against the Jews.... As the same memorandum stated: "It is the unalterable will of the Ebredo Magyarok Egyesulete [the Union of the Awakening Hungarians] to reestablish the reign of pure Christian morals and national feeling throughout the country and to exterminate those destructive doctrines spread by the Jews which already contaminated the Christian population of Hungary to a degree that our nation appears in a perfectly false light in the eyes of the foreign nations."[102]

The Awakening Hungarians adopted a Christian line in their propaganda. They stressed the differences between Jews and Christians, spoke at length of Christian superiority to Judaism, and blamed the Jews for the defeat of Hungary in the war and for the tribulations that followed that war. Priests and church public leaders were among the activists of the organization.

At a convention held in Budapest at the end of November 1919, one of the central speakers was the priest Dr. Gyula Zakany. He said that the Communist regime in Hungary had merely been an unsuccessful attempt on the part of Jewry to take control of Hungary. He added that it was the fault of the Jews that Hungary's territorial integrity was still in danger. He called for repealing the recognition of the Jewish religion.

The priest Zakany was the one who worded the resolutions voted on by the participants in the conference:

[1] The violent and destructive activity of Jewry in the field of food supplies and various consumer products drives the nation into a state of chaos. Taking this fact into consideration, these products must be placed under military supervision.

[2] We propose the registration of food and heating materials stored in vast quantities in the basements and storehouses of the Jews. They are to be distributed to the robbed and tortured Christian populace suffering from the cold. This distribution will be undertaken by the executive committee of the Awakening Hungarians.

[3] The Jews are the restless component of cosmopolitanism, which leads to the destruction of nationality, they are a constant threat to the peace of the world.... as a result of features stemming from their very destructive and immoral racial heritage. The Jews are successful in taking control of such occupations as allow them to spread their filth. This phenomenon must be prevented. The Jews must be scattered among the various nations in accordance with the relative weight to be attributed to their occupations in the various fields.[103]

The Awakening Hungarians invited the public to a mass rally in Budapest. A flier distributed in the streets of the capital under the headline "Christians! Hungarians!" read,

> The dams of destruction have burst once again. The international Jewish mob strives for the complete destruction of dismembered Hungary. . . . They will try again to establish in our poor homeland their Jewish Empire upon the graves of hordes of laborers.
>
> Our base and disgraced enemies lie in wait for easy prey, but they are going to be very disappointed. We stand ready to meet their treacherous attack, and the rally will be devoted to the idea of standing up in a life-and-death struggle.

The first speaker at the rally was the priest Antal Buttykay, the head of a province in the order of the Franciscans.[104]

In actual fact, there was almost no difference between the "national army" and the Awakening Hungarians. These two bodies were executive arms of the national government and carried out their activities on its behalf. Many of the activists of one of these bodies also played roles in the other. Most of the leaders of the Awakening Hungarians were members of Parliament. Horthy, who owed his election to the position of regent (March 1, 1920) to the support of the army, in his turn supported the rule of terror and its leaders.[105]

Before Pronay's officer unit left Szeged on its murderous campaign on July 15, 1919, the unit dedicated a unit banner. The dedication was held according to Christian ceremonial rules, in the yard of the dormitory of the St. Gelert school, where a special altar was erected for this purpose.[106] The ceremony was led by the Franciscan priest Istvan Zadravecz. He was ordained a bishop in the summer of 1920, and then appointed to the post of military bishop.[107]

The banner continued to play an important role, and the Awakening Hungarians later held a ceremony to mark the rededication of the banner. In honor of the event they convened a countrywide convention in Budapest on December 19–20, 1925, to which the public at large was invited. The Central National Leadership of the Union of Awakening Hungarians put up signs announcing the event, and held special prayer services. The ceremonial prayer service in the Evangelical church was led by Bishop Dr. Sandor Raffay, and in the Reformed church by Bishop Dr. Laszlo Ravasz. These two bishops led their churches in Hungary. The Catholic church also held a special ceremonial prayer service.

Besides the prayer services, there was a mass rally in one of the large auditoriums of Budapest. The central speakers were men of the cloth.

Bishop Raffay spoke in the name of the Evangelical church, while two priests who were members of the Council of Awakening Hungarians in the capital spoke for the Catholic and Reformed churches.[108]

Even assuming that at the time of the dedication of the banner in the summer of 1919 the priest Zadravecz was not aware of Pronay's intentions, in December 1925, at the time of its rededication, the deeds of the unit that acted under the auspices of the banner were well known. Nevertheless, the Christian churches and their leaders played significant roles in this event and in saluting the ideas it represented. Thus the Christian population of Hungary could view the participation of its spiritual leaders in the ceremony as granting legitimacy, even a posteriori, to the murders perpetrated by Pronay's officers' unit.

This is the place to note the special charm of the banner and the willingness of the church to honor it. Fifteen years later, in December 1940, the banner was returned to its town of origin, Szeged. In the cathedral of the city a special ceremonial prayer service was held, during which the Catholic bishop of the province, Dr. Gyula Glattfelder, rededicated the banner. After the service, Pronay marched at the head of his officers to the place where the flag was originally dedicated, the dormitory of St. Gelert. There a memorial plaque was unveiled, commemorating the events of 1919 and honoring those who served under the banner.[109]

Mention has already been made of the session of the Synod of Bishops that gave rise to the Shepherds' Epistle written by Prohaszka. The main topic of that session was an evaluation of the evil influence of the Communist regime and a search for ways to neutralize that influence. The bishops decided upon two main ways to achieve these aims: support for the Christian Socialist party, and support for the Catholic press. The Synod of Bishops was consistent in this regard, extending support for the two up until 1944.

Antisemitism was one of the foundation stones of the Christian Socialist party, which the priesthood saw fit to support:

> Under present conditions, the Synod of Bishops views the political union of Christians as important, and for its part would support the Christian Socialist party.... Even Bishop Raffay has recently expressed his agreement to the Protestants joining the Christian Socialist party. The bishops are requested to make contact with the Party and praise it strongly.[110]

The Christian Socialist party discussed at the session of the Synod of Bishops was, in many senses, the offspring of the Catholic People's party founded in 1895 by the Catholic church.[111] However, contrary to the oppositional stand adopted by the mother party toward the liberal governments of Hungary until World War I, its political offspring of the period between the wars generally took part in the government and even supplied prime ministers. Even when party representatives did not actually participate in a government, the party played the part of a favorable opposition. The party was an organ of expression for the church in political life, and played executive roles on its behalf. And so, even if indirectly, the church was involved in the activities of the regime. The role played by the church in society, in government, and in economics transformed it into an integral part of the regime.[112]

The Christian Socialist party continued to exist up until World War II, and during the years it existed it underwent splits, unifications, and name changes. The denominator common to the party and its component parts over the years was twofold: first, uncompromising antisemitism, and second, the use of the term "Christian" in their names—to stress their negative approach to anything or anyone not Christian. The party was called the National Christian party, the United Christian League, the United National Christian League, the Economic National Christian party, the National Socialist Christian party, and so on.[113]

In order to extend its influence among the laborers and as a counterweight to the social-democratic movement, the Christian party organized its own professional society, once again following in the footsteps of its mother party, the Catholic People's party, which had set up a professional society at the onset of the twentieth century.

After a few months of preparation in which the church itself took part, the United Christian National League was formally founded in December 1919. Count Pal Teleki was elected president. He served two terms, in different periods, as prime minister. During his terms of office anti-Jewish legislation was enacted, and he was the chief architect of these laws. Karoly Wolf was elected party chairman; over the years, until his death in 1936, he proudly bore the banner of popular antisemitism. The party also elected cochairmen. These included the bearers of high-ranking positions in the various Christian churches: the Catholic bishop of Szombathely, Count Janos Mikes; the Catholic bishop of Szekesfehervar, Ottokar Prohaszka; the president of the Calvinist Alliance, Istvan Bernath; and the Evangelical Bishop Bela Kapi.[114]

The resolution taken by the bishops on August 22, 1919, regarding making contact with the Christian Socialist party, brought about a response on the part of the government, who viewed the resolution as an invitation for cooperation between the two bodies. The basis for cooperation between government and the Synod of Bishops was laid, cooperation that lasted twenty-five years.

In the spirit of this recommendation of cooperation, the governor of Trans-Danubia, Count Pallavicini, requested of the Cardinal Archbishop Csernoch on October 19, 1919, that he instruct the priesthood to participate actively in the distribution of the government program in such a way as to precipitate a favorable reaction by the public. The governor informed the archbishop that for this purpose the government was prepared to send top-notch experts to priestly gatherings, whose main job would be "to instruct the active, respected priesthood, and to teach them so that the priests become national Christian propagandists." The governor dispatched similar letters to all the Catholic bishops and to the leaders of the Protestant churches in his region.[115]

In his reply of December 6, the archbishop wrote that when he heard of the organization he expressed his desire

> that my priesthood take part in it actively.... The fact that the chairman of the Propaganda Committee in Estergom province is one of my priests causes me great pleasure [the seat of the archbishop of Hungary is in Estergom. Both the province itself and the provincial capital are known by that name]. Naturally, the fact that a few priests, both of the local priesthood and from other towns and villages, participate on the Executive Committee makes me very happy.

The bishop of Szombathely replied on November 4 that he agreed with the governor completely and that "the priests in my area will readily take part in Propaganda Committees, they will do whatever they are able, and I for my part shall encourage them in this activity of theirs."

The Reformed Bishop Elek Petri announced in his response of December 10 that he agreed "that the priests and church officials take part in the aforesaid work, for its aims are well suited to the aims of the Reformed church."[116] Other bishops replied in a similar vein as well.

The dates of this correspondence in the Trans-Danubia region are extremely important. While the heads of the churches were expressing their pleasure at the opportunity given them to participate in the activities of the regime, representatives of that regime were imposing terror upon the inhabitants of the region. This correspondence between priesthood and government leaders gave the representatives of the regime a feeling that their activity in situ suited the positions adopted by the prominent representatives of the various churches.

The cooperation between these bodies bore fruit in another field as well. A newspaper report from that period reads,

We have been informed that there has been strong and effective activity in the towns of Trans-Danubia for the Christian press. In the meantime it has been decided in forty towns and villages, that they will in the future not allow any destructive newspaper into their domains. They will muster all their strength to support exclusively only those newspapers which serve the national Christian line, and they will distribute only those. This decision should serve as an example for all Hungarian towns and villages.[117]

The Protestant churches held a mass rally in Budapest at the beginning of December 1919. The subject of the rally was "the spirit of Christian unity." At this rally, too, the familiar voices of antisemitic incitement could be heard. Dr. Andras Csillery, a former government minister, declared that "we bear witness to the war of liberation of Christianity against Jewish Talmudism."

Istvan Haller, a government minister, claimed at that rally that

the decision of the Christian populace to insist on its right to succeed in life in opposition to the Jewish oppression from which it has suffered until today—is not antisemitism. Just as an oak tree has a natural right to grow, to spread and to be stronger than the thorny bushes and shrubs growing at its base, so we have the right to grow and become powerful on our own soil. The path which shall best serve our ambition to guarantee our territorial and political integrity is that which follows Christian policy. The fact that the various minorities have shown hostility toward us was merely the result of the Jewish policy we adhered to. Let us adopt Christian policies—and they will return to us.

And so the conclusion reached at the Protestant church rally reads that "our terrible disaster was brought about by the destructive international policy which acted against our Christian and national spirit."

Though one of the speakers at the rally, Gyorgy Szekely, the chairman of the Protestant committee in the National Union party, announced that "tolerance and magnanimity toward those of other faiths and those of other nationalities are based on the fundamental outlook of the Protestant church in Hungary," his words clearly omitted the attitude of participants in the rally toward Jews.

Evangelical Bishop Sandor Raffay and the Reformed Bishop Elek Petri, the spiritual leaders of the two Protestant churches in Hungary, also spoke at the rally. Their speeches were not cited at length in the newspaper report, but the latter does note that the two bishops announced "their churches' enthusiastic support" of the ideas expressed at the rally.[118]

This Christian-national-social organization was not limited to the halls in which its rallies were held. The organizers appealed in various ways to the public at large, making use, among other tactics, of placards in city streets. During the election campaign of January 1920 the United National Christian League, which enjoyed—as already noted—the support of the Synod of Bishops, published a placard:

> We are perched on the edge of a whirlpool threatening us with the nightmare of destruction. That which was not taken from us by the war's parasites and blackmailers and remained in our possession after the world war which was imposed upon us—was taken from us by force by the band of robbers operating under the guise of a proletarian dictatorship.... Thousand-year-old Hungary lies insulted and mocked.
>
> Who caused all this?
>
> A small hostile minority group, foreign to the national and Christian concept, is the group that exploited its organizational force and imposed its desires upon us.... There is but one way to revival and rehabilitation: our own firm, strong organization. We must impose the Christian and national concept on all our public and social lives.
>
> Brethren!
>
> If you do not want the dark days to return, if you want to guarantee by institutionalized means that the racial, Christian Hungarian will be master of his own fate in his own homeland: let us organize! We are raising the flag, the flag of the United National Christian League! Our goals: to illuminate the eyes of our Hungarian brethren in day-by-day work, orally and in writing, constantly and without laxity, in order to give expression to the national concept of Christian Hungary. We demand that the establishment impose Christian morality upon public, social life and upon private life in both industry and trade.[119]

On the same occasion the Awakening Hungarians distributed a manifesto of similar content, containing the following passages:

> After decades of sophisticated preparation, the Jewish leaders succeeded in shunting onto Russian tracks the fate of our ravaged, weakened, and unaware people.
>
> Awaken, Hungarians! Stand upon your own feet, open up your eyes, and behold—you have no future, unless you administer the affairs of your people with your own hand. You must prevent damage to our rehabilitative process by destructive elements. Remove those persistent leeches from your fainting body!
>
> Awaken, Hungarians! Let us unite so as to be able to restore our ruined, mocked homeland, so as to be able to further the peace, the morality, and the culture of the world, and so as to be able to break down the destructive activities of the international Jewish race.
>
> We demand a Hungarian Christian press, a Christian spirit in public life, in public office, in the economy, and in trade. We demand that Christian progress be assured officially so that we will be able to prevent in advance the danger of future infection.

We shall fight stubbornly, untiringly, with strong means which will get ever stronger, until the last Semite has left our homeland, of which they have made a mockery. May God help us![120]

There is a great deal of resemblance among the three publications—the Shepherds' Epistle of the Synod of Bishops, the placard of the United National Christian League, and the manifesto of the Awakening Hungarians. These documents, published upon the establishment of the new regime after the unrest brought on by the war, set a precedent with regard to the level of antisemitic argument that was to be heard in Hungary over the following twenty-five years. The fact that one of these documents was the Shepherds' Epistle of the Synod of Catholic Bishops granted them a status worthy of emulation. And so, a stream of antisemitic publications flooded the Hungarian population. Most of these documents presented positive Christianity opposing negative Judaism, and enjoyed great popularity.

The following is a sample taken from a pamphlet published during the January 1920 election campaign:

> We must return courageously to the Cross, we must return to our thousand-year-old Hungary, to Christianity.... Judaism is a parasitic being and, just like a mushroom, it, too, flourishes and develops best in a place overwhelmed by rot: on the dung heap. Life according to the Christian faith and following in the footsteps of Jesus is the only effective cure for corruption and rot.[121]

Regarding the practical way to achieve liberation from the Jewish political yoke, the writer of the pamphlet goes on:

> Breaking Jewish political power depends only upon us. We shall engage in Christian politics, and in the fateful elections before us we shall not give our vote to the corrupt champions of industry, nor shall we suffer traitors among us. We shall entrust the running of the State to decent, dedicated people.... There is no possibility of maintaining legislation in the Christian spirit and Christian education in a region infected by Judaism. Thus, we must burn out the abominable Jewish nest, the roosting region of moral and cultural poison.[122]

The election rallies of the Christian Socialist party were exploited for antisemitic incitement. An election rally held in December 1919 sent a special delegation to the prime minister, demanding the removal of "Galician Jewry" from Hungary or, alternately, their immediate transfer to concentration camps.[123]

The United National Christian party received fifty-nine seats in the elections, and came in second after the Smallholders party, which won ninety-one seats.[124]

Despite other differences between these two parties, on the question of their attitude to the Jewish problem the differences between them were minor. Thus, Istvan Nagyatadi-Szabo, leader of the Smallholders party, declared at an election rally in Kecskemet on December 1, 1919, "Now is the time to correct all that was ruined by liberalism. Hungarian Christian society must be liberated from the blackmail of Judaism."[125]

The cooperation between the Christian party and the Awakening Hungarians did not cease with the elections. In a joint flier signed by the Union of Awakening Hungarians and the Leadership of Christian Socialist Professional Unions, these two groups called Christian workers to a joint protest rally:

> Christian workers! Awakening Hungarians!
> The social-democratic-communist camp is once again trying to lift up its head.... They feel the ground is slipping away beneath their feet, and so they reject no means in their attempt to retake control of the fortress of the Institute for the Assurance of Laborers, which was at one time a hothouse of the Red commissars and of the Jewish inciters.
> This time they are in error! The Institute for the Assurance of Laborers belongs to Christian workers.... Whoever is not with us—is against us, and we shall surely keep an eye on them. We have had enough of Communist deceivers.[126]

In fact, the damage done by the short-lived Communist regime was felt more by the Jewish public than by its neighbors: with the collapse of the Kun government, the non-Jewish public in Hungary was liberated from Communist rule. This was not so for the Jewish public: with the rise of the white counterrevolution to power, it found its scapegoat in the form of the Jewish public, and the red stain that adhered to the Jews in 1919–1920 accompanied them all the way to 1944.

The counterrevolutionary regime and its various agencies enjoyed the positive attitude taken by the priesthood and the constant support of the churches. Members of the priesthood were among the leaders of the Awakening Hungarians and other similar groups. With regard to making the lives of the Jews difficult, the basis for cooperation between the churches and the counterrevolutionary regime was laid as early as the stormy days of 1919–1920, and this continued to serve the aims of both sides during the entire period of counterrevolutionary rule.

The Catholic Press

The high-level Catholic priesthood was aware of the potential influence of a guided press, and was eager to assist the counterrevolutionary regime, then taking its first steps, whose plans and activities suited the desires of the church leaders. The bishops, at their very first session after the collapse of the Communist regime, in August 1919, devoted their attention to the question of establishing the appropriate means for the expression of their views:
Their attitude is reflected in the protocol of the session:

> the Synod of Bishops considers reviving the Catholic press and raising it to a high level to be a task of first-order importance.... The Synod of Bishops will see to it that all those dealing with the Catholic press operate together in mutual coordination. To this end the Synod of Bishops shall make contact with the Central Press Project.[127]

The Central Press Project was the means by which the Synod of Bishops' financial support was channeled to the various Catholic newspapers; at the same time, it served as a pipeline for the transmission of the stands adopted by the Synod of Bishops to the Catholic press. To subsidize the Catholic newspapers and, apparently, to bring the subject to the awareness of the public, the Synod of Bishops imposed upon the believers a special "culture tax," which was to be collected by the bishops.[128]
The Catholic press constantly occupied the Synod of Bishops, and from the protocols it seems that the press was discussed in most of the sessions held over a period of twenty-five years.
At the top of the list of newspapers supported by the Synod of Bishops was the morning daily *Nemzeti Ujsag* (National Newspaper), the semiofficial organ of the Catholic church.[129] On the front page of the newspaper there appeared the heading "Political Christian Daily Newspaper."
The following is a selection of extracts from editorials written during the period when the shaping of the regime was underway, and the attitude of the Catholic press to the regime and to the Jews was being formulated. The viewpoints that crystallized during this period continued to exert influence over the following twenty-five years.
On economic subjects the paper wrote,

> The general atmosphere prevalent in our country permits us to hope that the political struggle which has just begun in our country between the national Christian outlook, on the one hand, and the destructive, homeland-less Jewish strata, on the other, will end in the triumph of the National Christian outlook. It will, however, be erroneous to think that with the

end of the political struggle everything will be the way it should be. Not at all! Only after the completion of our victory in the political struggle will the real siege of the fortresses of Judaism begin: the economic fortresses of Judaism. With the assistance of public opinion, which has recently regained consciousness, it will not be difficult to take control of the political positions, but with regard to the fight against the Jews' greater economic power, we shall have to be ready for a bitter, drawn-out struggle, for the economic roots of Judaism have penetrated deeply into Hungarian soil.

Anyone deluding himself into thinking that we have an easy fight before us does not know Jewish capitalism and its willingness to fight.... It will be an error to regard with scorn this economic power.... We must take such strong action as to shock the very foundations of Jewish economic power.[130]

Another editorial attempts to list the reasons for the shortage of food-stuffs, fuel, and other raw materials in the winter of 1919–1920 and points fingers at those considered responsible:

Truth to tell, on Dohany, Rombach, and Dovl Streets [streets in the poor section of the Jewish ghetto in Budapest] the authorities are hunting down and capturing the Jews who escaped to us from Galicia. These sewer rats should not be blamed for worrying about their livelihoods. However, be-hind the backs of these small peddlers the really guilty people are hiding, those who enjoy exaggerated profits and make our lives difficult and in-tolerable.... These champions of the black market are identical with those vast financial institutions which during the World War began shamelessly to hoard goods.

We call for government intervention in the spirit of the National Chris-tian trend—the same trend that brought it to power. The time has come for the government to begin the great purge which will be received gladly and eagerly, both by the Christian middle class and by the public of Hun-garian Christian workers.... No damage will be done if the government warns the large goods-hoarders unambiguously that the age of open rob-bery is past, that the period of corrupt government which made it possible for Jewish price-raisers to transform Hungary into their own Eldorado has come to an end.[131]

Another editorial that appeared in the "Christian Daily Newspaper" criticizes the very presence of Jews in Hungary, lists the damage they cause, and suggests ways to correct the situation:

The Jew did not come to our land with a sword in his hand. He sneaked in secretly, like a destructive bacterium sneaks into a human body. He has come in vast numbers with a flask of poison in his hand.... He himself is the rot which consumes everything. Even if we defeat him, our victory will only be a despicable victory, whereas if he defeats us, we shall never rise again.

While we were starving and trembling with cold, the greed of our uninvited invaders, scions of the foreign race, consumed our food, burnt the fuels for our heating, robbed us of our money, and took control of the power centers of our country. We failed to persuade them to leave us. They reside here and even behave as if they intend to remain with us. Is it possible to expel their spirit, which controls the press and the financial network?[132]

We have to set up a concentration camp in Hajmasker in order to save ourselves from whatever damage we can still be saved from. To isolate them completely we have to construct a defensive wall around the concentration camp. But that is not enough! We will have to construct a defensive wall around Hungarian land, around Hungarian spiritual life, and around Hungarian power sources. We will have to be constantly awake in supervising these walls, so as to defend those values important for our race: Only by means of putting these additional steps into operation will there be real value to the isolation of the Jews in the concentration camp.[133]

Yet another editorial dealt with the interpretation and appreciation of a certain speech delivered by Bishop Prohaszka:

It will be most desirable and even important for the Hungarian Christian public opinion to devote suitable attention to the words uttered by the great, most admired bishop of Szekesfehervar, Ottokar Prohaszka.... Many are they who delude themselves into thinking that after the fall of Jewish imperialism, known as Bolshevism, they may rest on their laurel wreaths. Yet behold, the great apostle of the Hungarian Christian public has arisen to warn us loudly and publicly: "Our homeland is in danger!"

The clear voice of the great bishop warns us of the danger of terrible destruction threatening with a moral revolution everything that the two-thousand-year-old Christian culture and the thousand-year-old Hungarian culture have succeeded in introducing into the souls of the people and their moral understanding. The obstinate evil spirit, with its cruel logic, attacks Jesus of Nazareth again and again. That same evil spirit is unwilling to accept the fact that it was defeated on the hill of Golgotha. It is consistent in its dedication to its wild materialism, in its worship of capitalistic Satan.

Only that powerful democracy that rests on the union of all Hungarian Christians, only a merger of all those who believe in Jesus of Nazareth, will be able to save our souls and our future. The oriental phantom, this dark, threatening shadow which follows us around like a shadow following its body, will invoke upon your head a curse of fire and brimstone if you walk in the ways of God and if you lift up your eyes unto the

Cross and to Him who was crucified. Take care, be cautious, do not fall into the net of those whose eyes yearn for only a single star: the selfsame star the Chaldean astrologist called "the Great Star of Mammon."[134]

The tone adopted by the semiofficial organ of the Catholic church and the content of its editorial articles suited the outlook of the Awakening Hungarians. This organization published in flier form its "Ten Commandments" as a guide to "the Christian Hungarian populace" on how to save "the homeland ruined by the Jews." Mention is made of "immoral Judaism" and "Red Judaism," and various ways are proposed "to beat the Jews." The last five commandments do indeed open with the expression, "Beat the Jew," and each commandment contains practical suggestions for beating the Jews: do not speak with a Jew, do not listen to a Jew, do not buy from a Jew and do not sell him anything, do not invite a Jew to your home, do not let a "Red-international" Jew into your club, your company.... The ninth commandment states, "Beat the Jew by not buying his filthy newspapers and not reading them, nor his morality-corrupting books, which might poison your soul and that of your family. You must read only Christian newspapers." The first newspaper mentioned in the list of reading material recommended by the Awakening Hungarians is *Nemzeti Ujsag,* the semiofficial newspaper of the Catholic church.[135]

The antisemitic coalition—in which the counterrevolutionary government, the Christian Socialist party, and the organizations headed by the Awakening Hungarians participated—included the high-level Catholic priesthood as well. The priests wanted their voice to be heard among their believers. The Shepherds' Epistle written by Prohaszka was the opening shot in a lengthy antisemitic campaign. It was clear to the priests that a one-time appeal, no matter how strong, had its own disadvantages. For this reason they supported the Christian press, which functioned according to their spirit and their dictates. Most of the bishops did indeed realize the importance of mass communications,[136] and all the newspapers that were aided by the Central Press Project expressed well the views of the church and its partners in the antisemitic coalition.

The "Numerus Clausus" Law

In light of the antisemitism spreading through clerical and journalistic circles, as well as other sectors in Hungary, it is not surprising that in the fall of 1919, while preparing for the opening of the academic year, strident protests by Christian students took place against the participation of Jewish students in university studies. Teachers at the universities joined these protests, which rapidly became violent demonstrations that forced the authorities to close the universities.

The immediate result of the disruptive events at the universities was that the government prepared a bill limiting the number of Jews at institutions of advanced learning. The law was aimed at limiting the percentage of Jewish students to 6 percent, comparable to their relative representation in the entire population. The efficiency demonstrated by the government in preparing the bill suggests that perhaps the student rioting, rather than forcing the government to invoke the "numerus clausus" act, actually provided the government with an excuse to do so.

The teachers at the Peter Pazmany Catholic University of Budapest played a pioneering role in the war waged by the institutions for higher education against Jewish students. At a meeting of the Faculty of Humanities, opinions were voiced to the effect that "the participation in studies of those elements tending toward Communism and Internationalism should be prevented. The possibility that antireligious and antinational elements receive their spiritual repast between the walls of the university must be ruled out."

A faculty member, summing up in a memorandum the stand adopted by the faculty, wrote, "Even had I not mentioned this explicitly, it would still have been clear that one of the main aims, if not the sole aim, of the proposed 'numerus clausus' bill is to set up a dam blocking the unbridled stream of Jewish students into our institutions." Of all the teachers in the Faculty of Humanities, there was only one who claimed "that he does not see the urgency in imposing 'a numerus clausus' at this stage."[137]

Other university faculties (of law, medicine, and theology) adopted similar stands. The university council discussed the topic and its own stand, which was summed up by the dean of the Law Faculty:

> Since the proletarian dictatorship was explicitly anti-Christian and was administered by Jews, the young generation strives to have those who belong to the Jewish race refused entry into the university forever. The young generation should be given suitable guarantees to assure them that the required purge will indeed be carried out among the university youth.[138]

In other words, the teachers and students at the Catholic university went beyond the government proposal. The latter strove to limit the number of Jewish students, but not to prohibit their studies altogether, whereas the university faculty and students demanded that the gates to their institution be shut to Jewish youth.

The administration of the Technological University of Budapest also held discussions on the "numerus clausus." After the various faculties had decided on their stands, the university council resolved to request the minister of religion and education to impose a "numerus clausus." "The large number of Jews endangers the intelligentsia . . . one must ensure that Judaism is unable to behave in the future in the way it behaved in the past."[139]

A memorandum presented by the Faculty of Medicine to the minister of religion and education described, in a style considered exceptional in an academic institution, the character of the Jewish doctors who had graduated the faculty, and proposed drawing conclusions with regard to the acceptance of Jewish students in the future:

> The Jewish race is an element undesirable to the Faculty of Medicine and to the profession of Medicine, and so it is desirable to remove it and we are indeed determined to do so. . . . Our patriotic approach requires us to maintain the Faculty of Medicine at a suitable moral level in accordance with proper professional ethics. In light of this it would be considered a crime, treason, to educate in the Faculty Jewish intelligentsia ready for any destructive and treacherous activity.
>
> A person growing up until his eighteenth year among people who jack up prices, among black marketeers, purchasers of stolen goods, usurers, and pimps—among people whose sole desire, whose only thought, whose only ambition is to pursue Mammon, and who reject no way or means of achieving it. . . . The moral outlook and ethical concepts of a person growing up in such an atmosphere must be as base, disgraceful, and abominable as those in whose environment he grew up.
>
> For the sake of the truth: if we concede five percent of the places in our institutions of higher education in favor of this Jewry, it will be a gift they are not worthy of. It will be bestowed upon them by that same Hungarian nation whose land was cut up and remained fragmented, those responsible being the Jewish Bolsheviks.[140]

The memorandum prepared by the Faculty of Medicine, together with additional memoranda, led the government to present the bill. The minister of religion and education, Istvan Haller, presented it on July 22, 1920, and in his speech boasted that "no one has preceded us in such legislation."[141]

The first participant in the debate on the bill was the priest Gyula Zakany, who supported it.[142] Bishop Prohaszka also spoke out in favor of the bill, declaring that he viewed it as a self-defense measure:

We have reached a situation where Jewry has become a factor limiting our steps.... Christianity senses, on every side, that it is in retreat before the Jewish attack upon it. We are in the very process of liquidating Christianity in our land.... I would feel scorn for Hungarian culture, were it to ignore the fact that while the Jews trample it underfoot and turn its blood into water, it does not have the strength to raise its voice and to voice its protest and declare: "As long as I have any energy at all left, I shall devote it to opposing such a trend, and as long as I breathe, I shall participate in the formation of our own way of life."

Similarly, Dezso Szucs, lecturer in theology and representative of the Reform church, viewed the "numerus clausus" law as a self-defense measure. "In order to defend our national culture we have need of a bill, for the vast surplus of Jewish intelligentsia endangers the national nature of our culture."

Emil Kovacs, a priest of the Reformed church, found the government's proposal inadequate, and suggested that its principles be applied to high schools as well.[143]

In Haller's rebuttal there appeared numerous antisemitic remarks. He found support in excerpts from the speech made by Bishop Prohaszka and stressed the bishop's reasoning. The law was indeed adopted by a decisive majority—fifty-seven votes in favor, with only seven opposing it—and was published on the eve of the opening of the academic year 1920–1921. The adoption and application of the law did not satisfy the young, and the riots that broke out in the fall of 1920 brought about a postponement in the registration for the universities and in the opening of the academic year.[144]

The "numerus clausus" law achieved its aim, and the number of Jewish students in Hungarian institutions of advanced education plummeted steeply. In the academic year 1917–1918 the University of Budapest had 4,288 Jewish students out of a total of 10,643, or some 40.3 percent, whereas in the academic year of 1920–1921 the number of Jewish students there dropped to 459 out of a total of 5,800 students—only 7.9 percent.[145]

Jewish youths were compelled to move out of Hungarian territory in order to study at an academic institution. Thus, in the academic year of 1920–1921, some eleven hundred Jewish students from Hungary studied at the University of Prague. Jewish students wandered as far afield as Austria, Italy, and Germany.[146]

Jewish organizations in Western Europe were perturbed by the law. In addition to the damage it caused the Jews of Hungary, these organizations feared the law might be construed as a precedent to be applied by other governments. Central Jewish associations in England and France appealed to the League of Nations against the "numerus clausus" law, which violated the Trianon Agreement signed by Hungary in 1920. The League of Nations, in its turn, approached the Hungarian government on the subject, only to be met by delays and other evasive tactics. Nevertheless, in October of 1927, as a result of continuing international pressure, the Hungarian government announced its intention of introducing certain changes into the law.

This announcement immediately aroused fierce opposition in Hungary. In November the Awakening Hungarians held a protest rally. Both Count Pal Teleki and Gyula Gombos, who served as prime minister at various times between the 1920s and the 1940s, took part in the rally, which came out in support of the continued application of the law in its present form. It should be noted that even the Christian Economic party— which during this period generally supported the government—opposed the proposed changes in the law. Despite the opposition, the changes went into effect about two years later, in October 1929, but they were little more than cosmetic changes, for they had no real effect upon the Jewish population.[147]

The two ministers of education who engaged in the preparation and adoption of the law—Istvan Haller and Karoly Huszar—were members of the Christian Socialist party whose connections with the leading institutions of the various churches have been described above. These ministers of education based their explanations of the necessity of the legislation on the need "for defending Christians and Christianity." The priests that took part in the debate on the proposed law supported it without reservation, and even demanded the broadening of its application.

During the debate on the proposed law, the Jews and Jewry were again and again defined as a "race." It was still over a decade before the "doctrine of race" would be inscribed in the lawbooks of Nazi Germany. Not only did the priesthood not speak up against the use of the term "race" to define a group of citizens in order to discriminate against them legally—it even supported this approach.

The significance of the "numerus clausus" law was that the Jews were separated from the rest of the populace by means of formal discriminatory legislation. This precedent facilitated the broadening of the discrimination in the future and symbolized the end of the full equality of rights that the Jews had enjoyed for twenty-five years— from 1895 to 1920. In both of these years the church was active in causing the Jews discomfort.

The Consolidation of the Twenties and the Christian Antisemitism of the Thirties

The 1920s saw a measure of decline in the official negative approach of the government toward the Jews; yet the 1930s were accompanied by a renewed viciousness in the antisemitic approach of both government circles and broad popular sectors—up until 1938, the year marking the beginning of the passing of a series of anti-Jewish laws.

The chairman of the Christian party, Karoly Wolf,[148] was one of the most prominent spokesmen of the approach that declared the existence of a violent clash of interests between Jews and Christians, between Judaism and Christianity, and the necessity of the anti-Jewish struggle. A number of excerpts from his statements clarifying his approach on these subjects will be adduced below. During his period of public activity, his party enjoyed the financial and moral support of the Synod of Bishops.

On April 14, 1921, Count Istvan Bethlen was appointed prime minister. He was one of the founders of the Christian Socialist party at the beginning of 1919. During the period of Communist rule, Bethlen had been in Vienna, where he worked to undermine Bela Kun's regime. There, together with Karoly Wolf and others, he founded the United National Christian League, which he served in leading roles. Bethlen, like most Hungarians of his generation, opposed the Trianon Agreement, but as a sober statesman he preferred to work for its abrogation by peaceful means. He realized that it was vital for faith in Hungary to be restored, especially the faith of international economic circles. Thus he strove to achieve stability in his country, and for this purpose he had to put an end to the antisemitic terrorism and to cooperate with Jewish economic sectors—despite his own violent hatred of the Jews.[149]

At the same time, in light of the stand adopted by the right wing of his party, Bethlen did not enjoy a free hand in determining policy. The antisemitic atmosphere prevalent in broad sectors of the population prevented any possibility of a return to the liberal regime that had ruled Hungary before World War I.[150] For his part, Bethlen persevered in his attempts to stabilize the situation, including that of the Jews, as he himself testified: "Luckily, the anomalous approach which existed here after the war is gradually fading away, and the situation of the Jews is becoming normal once again."[151] His ten years in office are generally known as "the years of consolidation," but as a consequence of the world economic crisis of 1929–1930 he was compelled to resign in 1931 and was replaced as prime minister by Gyula Gombos.

Gombos was one of the men of Szeged and was a confidant of Horthy's. He had an extensive network of connections with many, variegated antisemitic circles, including Russian exiles supporting the czar, Ukrainians, Mussolini's movement at its inception, and right-wing circles in Germany, including Hitler's movement while it was still insignificant. The German Nazis even received financial support from Gombos while they were still taking their first steps, and Rathenau's assassins found temporary refuge in Gombos's villa. In September 1925 he organized an international antisemitic conference in Budapest.[152]

During the 1920s Gombos became one of the central figures in the activities of the Hungarian extreme right.[153] As he was one of the men of Szeged, Gombos believed that the new regime in Hungary should be based on Christian line ideas, and he and his government were interested in stressing the Christianity of Hungary.[154]

Unquestionably the loudest speaker for the line that demanded emphasizing the Christianity of Hungary and basing the Hungarian regime on a Christian foundation was Karoly Wolf. He had been a member of the Catholic People's party prior to World War I.[155] During the period of Communist rule in Hungary, Wolf remained in Vienna, and, like Gombos, he worked there to undermine the Bela Kun government. He was one of the leaders of the Anti-Communist Committee, which was even named after him: "Wolf's Secret Group." After the collapse of the Communist regime, the group came back to Hungary, where it reorganized under the name "the United National Christian League," with the position of chairman given to Wolf himself. This party founded the Urban Christian party in Budapest, which took control of the Budapest Municipal Council and ran it in accordance with its own principles.[156]

The Catholic church appreciated the contribution made by Wolf's party to the development of a Christian atmosphere in Hungary, and rewarded it accordingly. According to the resolution adopted by the Synod of Bishops, which met on August 22, 1919,[157] this body materially supported the Christian party and the professional organization it set up for some twenty-five years.

In October 1920 the Synod of Catholic Bishops discussed the request of the National Union of Christian-Socialist Professional Organizations for support amounting to the sum of two million crowns. The following resolution was adopted: "The Synod of Bishops warmly recommends that the land owners contribute generously." The cardinal archbishop, who chaired the synod session, took the lead in making contributions, announcing his donation of two hundred thousand crowns.[158]

In October 1925 a ranking priest, Prelate Sandor Ernszt, appeared before the Synod of Bishops and made the following request in the name of the National Christian party:

> The great landowners of Hungary once granted the then People's party their fixed annual financial support.... However, now the financial sources of the National Christian party have dried up to such an extent that the party is compelled to request the grant of a hundred thousand golden crowns' annual support. The party sees itself as the heir to the People's party and strives to be worthy of this support.... The party prefers to maintain its independent political activity, and would like to begin proper preparations for the elections expected in 1927.[159]

The resolution adopted by the Synod was as follows: "The Synod of Bishops is of the opinion that the party is worthy of support to the extent of the sum requested."[160]

The protocol of spring 1926 read, "The Christian Socialist party has sent a detailed report of its last year's activities.... The Synod of Bishops informs the 'Union' of its positive and encouraging attitude toward it."[161]

From the year 1932 the subject of support for the professional organization of the Socialist-Economic Christian party, in its various evolutionary stages, became a routine part of the sessions of the Synod of Bishops. The resolutions on support for the coming year and for the level of this support were generally adopted at the autumn sessions of the synod. On occasion the bishops added moral encouragement to their financial support by praising the activities of the Christian Socialist party. The following is an extract from one of the relevant protocols:

> The Catholic population can rely on the Socialist-Economic Christian party and does indeed do so.... One of the efficient ways of defending the public and parliamentary interests of the Catholic populace is by identifying with the aims of the party and by efficiently supporting them. We must view affectionately and positively the activity of the Christian party. We must encourage it to act courageously in Parliament. We must promise the Christian party that the Synod of Bishops puts its faith in it.... The Synod of Bishops requests that the Cardinal convey the view of the Synod of Bishops to the party leadership and inform it that the Synod favors its activity and shall continue to support it in the future as well.[162]

The recipients of this support appreciated the favor bestowed upon them by the bishops and reacted accordingly:

> The professional organization stresses that the Synod of Bishops' financial support is what has enabled its activities on behalf of the Socialist Movement of Christian Workers over the past two years of difficult struggle.

We are prepared to continue eagerly with this work in the future, yet without this financial support it will be impossible.[163]

At their October 1939 session the bishops resolved that "the Synod of Bishops declares its support for the 'Socialist Christians' and its heart-warming attitude toward them, just as it has always done, and it enjoins the various bishops to support the party."[164] The last resolution of support appearing in the collection of protocols dates from just before 1944, having been adopted at the session of the Synod of Bishops held in the autumn of 1943.[165]

These excerpts are mere samples of the vast amount of material on this topic; in addition to them, the matter of support for the Christian party and its professional organization appears about twenty times in the records of the discussions held by the Synod of Bishops. The bishops' support for the ideas the party represented and spread among the public is reflected in most of the protocols. It is well worth tracing the development of these ideas.

The unquestioned spokesman for the Christian party was, as we have already mentioned, its chairman, Karoly Wolf. At the annual general convention of the United National Christian League, Wolf demanded a final confrontation with the ghetto spirit and expressed his joy at the prime minister's promise that "the line guiding the administration is the Christian *Weltanschauung*." Wolf added, "A line of thought claiming that it has no desire to rule according to the Christian *Weltanschauung* will be unable to reach us again.... The surrender of influential circles to the ghetto spirit may once again bring about a national tragedy. We shall not repeat this."

The speaker went on to refer to Hitler's coming to power, and linked the events taking place in Nazi Germany with the Christian revival:

Declarations matching the ghetto spirit have described events in Germany as transient events.... Germany is engaged in her national renaissance. The negative atmosphere has failed throughout the world. The golden calf has collapsed, Vienna's Judeo-Marxism has rotted away, and is gradually declining.... The negative atmosphere is unable to rule, for our Lord Jesus has been reborn.

The chairman of that convention, too, referred to these topics, saying, "The fact is that the resurrection taking place at the present time in Germany is based on moral foundations. Hungary, too, should base its development upon paths within faith and Christianity."[166]

At a rally called by Wolf's party, the Urban Christian party of Budapest, held at the same time as the convention of the national party, the chairman warned, "In light of the fact that liberal politics are once again beginning to lift up their head, our party must demand even more strongly the practical realization of Christian policy." Wolf's statement, made at that rally, clarified the matter: "I shall demand that there be carried out a thorough examination of the identity of the employees of the banks and of the large concerns. We must discover just how many of these employees are indeed Hungarian citizens and even Christian."[167]

At a mass rally of his party in Budapest Wolf spoke of "practical politics" in Hungary:

> The only practical politics are those which provide the justified material and moral needs of Hungarian Christians. . . . I am unable to observe calmly the ambitions of a foreign race to take control of us. . . . We are not racist, but our policy is based on the only correct Christian way. If some resident of Galicia pops up and founds some company somewhere in a dank and shadowy basement, the entire government need not support him immediately with the economic power of our national bank, the Galician receiving immediate support under the guise of "protecting a business enterprise."[168]

Urban Christian party representatives on the Budapest Municipal Council invited their voters to hear of their activity in the municipality. At the rally it was Karoly Wolf who spoke:

> In economic matters we must guarantee the supremacy of Christian Hungarians over those foreigners who have fallen upon us from foreign lands and, during the liberal period, taken control of economic, industrial, and financial life. . . . The firms and factories must be compelled to dismiss these uninvited foreigners. I have no desire to see my Christian colleagues in an inferior situation.[169]

Thousands participated in the celebration organized by the Urban Christian party in Wolf's honor. The master of ceremonies mentioned Wolf's courage in "daring even to touch on that sect which until now has been 'untouchable,' just like a similar sect in India. This sect has attempted to ensure itself the right to run wild and wreak havoc throughout our land." Wolf added,

> The wickedness of these has brought down upon Hungary intolerably heavy blows. We have been ineffectual in not daring up until now to apply in practice the truths of Jesus the Nazarene. The concepts of liberalism, democracy, and equality have caused Christian Hungarians harm. . . . I am prepared to admit that minorities, too, have some culture, but a one-sided, racist culture and not an absolute, universal one like Christian culture. . . .

It is not possible to base New Hungary upon elements of treachery, insincerity, and the expectations of easy profits, and those on the opposite side of the barrier had best be warned that our patience is running out! We shall not be prepared to give in out of motives of false humaneness. We are at war with Judeo-Marxism![70]

At a rally held by yet another wing of his party, the Party Union of Hungarian Christian Women, Wolf spoke of the purity of Christian and Hungarian blood: "I am a Catholic, not only in church but also in public life. There is nothing more ludicrous than a Jew who has become a Catholic who comes to advise me about Catholicism and my own Hungarian nature. To a person of this kind I say: before coming to give me advice, make sure your own blood becomes Hungarian and Catholic."

Wolf also spoke of the German orientation of Hungarian foreign policy and, using Christian rationale, fully supported this orientation:

Liberal and democratic circles and freemasons claim that, in light of German antisemitic tendencies, we must not draw near to her. The approach of these circles is based on their heart's desire, whereas I—my Christian outlook is based on a practical approach...and I seek links with the German people, for that nation is invaluable to the human race. The practical application of my Christian outlook and my steadfast perseverance in my faith are a guarantee of this political view of mine.[71]

The United National Christian League organized a series of lectures, and Karoly Wolf delivered the opening speech:

Only a nation bearing within itself general cultural values can be sure it will never disappear. What are these general cultural values? They are Christian cultural values! I am often accused of conducting an antisemitic policy. This is simply untrue. I am not antisemitic, but I am devoted to furthering the Christian idea, which is the sole representative of comprehensive universal culture.

Christian culture is the only eternal culture, and is immeasurably superior to any other culture promoted by any racial group. I am not willing to give up even the smallest part of Christian culture; anyone willing to make such a concession is nothing but a sinner and a misleader.... We must apply our national Christian outlook in a practical manner in order to promote our own rebirth.[72]

As New Year's Day, 1936, drew nearer, the functionaries of Karoly Wolf's party wished him well. In his reply he said,

Foreigners are attempting to take control of our national values, and their cunning plots have enabled them to lay their hands upon our most sacred of values. They have contaminated our literature, and the ghetto spirit

predominates upon the stages of our theatre. Even in the economic realm
we are no longer our own masters.[173]

He took steps to broaden his own personal involvement and the arena
of his activities beyond Budapest's municipal limits. A delegation of over
a hundred people, members of the Urban Christian Party Club, traveled
to Szeged to take part in a series of rallies aimed "at strengthening
Christian Hungarian industry, trade, and press and at expressing their
support of them." Wolf declared at the rally,

> Only eternal moral values are capable of directing the lives of humanity.
> Though we hear in our day all kinds of fashionable slogans, these are
> designed merely to cover up for personal interests or for the interests of a
> foreign race. Marx, too, devised all kinds of slogans, but they in no way
> served the interests of the workers.... In this town Christianity must be
> imposed upon economic life, upon the university, and upon all walks of
> life. We shall not permit others to drive us out of industry and trade.[174]

Karoly Wolf died in 1936. A few years later, his party disintegrated,
but the Christian professional organization, founded by the founders of
the party, survived into World War II. For many years it was Karoly
Wolf who bore the standard of Christian antisemitism. As noted above,
he was generously rewarded in his lifetime by the Synod of Catholic
Bishops. After his death, too, the ranking official of the Catholic church
in Hungary paid him homage. At a lecture on "Cooperation between
Church and State" he delivered a few months after Wolf's demise, the
head of the Catholic church, Cardinal Archbishop Justinian Seredi, stated,

> We Catholics have to be united, in order to be able to offer our assistance
> to the needy.... Each and every Catholic must be prepared at all times to
> declare his principles and to bear responsibility for those principles, just
> as the late Karoly Wolf did—in Parliament, in the municipality, and in
> public life (the assembly paid its respects to the illustrious memory of Karoly
> Wolf by standing at attention for a number of minutes).... In our struggle,
> aimed at restricting our common foe, the state may consider the church
> to be frankly interested in the state's welfare, without living in expectation
> of any benefits to itself.[175]

The assembly that had paid its respects to Wolf and his opinions was
certainly able to identify the "common foe" Seredi was referring to.

We thus note the cooperation between the Christian party and the
Synod of Catholic Bishops, the division of labor between them serving
the interests of both sides: Wolf expressed opinions favored by the Synod
of Bishops, and they rewarded him accordingly. The instance described

below involves a bishop who was not in need of any outside assistance in expressing his views.

Janos Meszaros, the bishop in charge of the cardinal's Budapest offices,[176] summoned the Catholic priests of the capital to a meeting. He clarified for them the stand adopted by the Catholic church on various matters of public importance, and also instructed them what to do in connection with these matters:

> Despite our many occupations, we must not back off from dealing with urban politics. We have to participate in this activity, and we must exert our influence to ensure that the atmosphere prevailing in the Budapest municipality is truly Christian. Let us recall the day when unrestrained liberal dogma ruled the municipality. Freemasons, internationalists, non-Christian and Marxist bodies all collaborated there with one another.... Such a situation was the consequence of the lack of Catholic self-appreciation on the part of the residents of Budapest. Among members of the municipal council there were those who had become Catholic by conversion. These assisted the non-Christian, anti-church trend.... This was the situation which led to the moral decline, which expressed itself fully in the Communist Revolution.
>
> This is the background of the self-organization of the population of Budapest, of its turn to the right, and of its takeover of the municipality by means of the Urban Christian party.... The schools have recently been purged of their destructive elements. May the priesthood remain faithful to the existing regime! Then we shall be able to sit quietly and securely, knowing that the spiritual life of Christian Budapest will continue flowing through the appropriate channels!

The press report stresses that "the appearance of Meszaros before the priesthood took place with the prior knowledge and explicit agreement of the Cardinal Archbishop."[177] The similarity between the speeches by Wolf and the instructive words of the bishop can immediately be seen.

Wolf often made use of reasoning acceptable to his audience. He often appealed to their patriotic emotions and to their moral obligation as Christians. He described their enemies as "internationalists" and "anti-Christian." Linking the two topics—Christianity and nationality—with Christian Hungarians, while simultaneously linking anti-Christianity and internationalism with their opponents of "the foreign race," is a sign of Wolf's sophistication. His words were picked up by eager ears, especially after the events of 1919. The cooperation between the Synod of Bishops and Karoly Wolf lasted for years, and they continued their support of his organizations even after his death.

Popular Antisemitism of the Thirties

Hungarian Jewry experienced the 1930s in the shadow of renewed outbreaks of antisemitism in broad population sectors differing from one another in their cultural, social, and economic status. Their organizations aimed to remove the Jews from their midst and to boycott them professionally, commercially, and socially.

Most of the antisemitic organizations that sprang up during the 1930s had a common denominator: the explicit desire of the organizers to preserve the Christian character of their organization, and their attempt to protect their Christian members from their potential rivals, the Jews. The following examples may render more tangible the hostile atmosphere prevalent in Hungary at that time toward the Jews.

The National Alliance of Hungarian Doctors sent a memorandum to the prime minister in the name of 3,500 Christian physicians. In their memorandum they called his attention to the possibility that,

> as a result of the Christian policies now being implemented in Germany, various Jewish elements may be compelled to leave that country—including doctors—and these doctors may arrive in Hungary. This would mean that the number of doctors would rise to a considerable degree, and as a result of the addition of undesirable elements, the medical profession may deteriorate.... Thus the Christian doctors request the prime minister to prevent most energetically the entrance of Jewish doctors from Germany. Similarly, the prime minister is asked to guarantee the careful application of the "numerus clausus" law.[78]

Elections were held in Budapest for the bar association. The Christian lawyers were not satisfied with the results, and they organized a Christian Executive Committee, which appealed to their colleagues:

> The results of the elections do not reflect the general interests of the lawyers. ... The Christian Executive Committee finds that the Bar Association, in its present composition, is not able to represent effectively the National Christian idea. Therefore, those Bar Association members who were candidates of Christian lawyer organizations and were also elected by them hereby resolve that their representatives shall leave the Bar Association immediately.... An appropriate message has been sent to all Christian lawyers.[79]

Even a window cleaner, an employee of the electricity company in the town of Miskolc, published fliers in which he appealed to the Christian population:

Please open your eyes, the eyes which have been blinded by ghetto dust, and see how the Jews plan to strike at your faith, at your family, at your nation, and at your liberty. Now, after waiting for two thousand years, we are about to enjoin Jesus of Nazareth, who was crucified by the Jews, who has come to destroy all their Talmudic works. Now that we have reached that point, are you going to continue your dance about the golden calf?

My brothers! My Hungarian brethren! Please think! Wake up! Where is your thousand-year-old faith? Stay away from those whom even Jesus of Nazareth scorned; do not support them, and be worthy of bearing honorably the title "Christian."

The window cleaner's flier goes on to call upon the Christian populace to support Christian craftsmen exclusively: Christian laborers, traders, lawyers, and doctors.[180]

The Christian-nationalist organization Turul rose to the defense of Christian building contractors. The leaders of the organization had learned that the construction of the university chapel in the town of Debrecen had been entrusted to a Jewish contractor. The organization lodged an official protest with the minister of religion and education, "expressing its amazement at the fact that the construction had been entrusted to a foreign contractor, of the Jewish race. This fact makes a mockery of the Christian and racial concept the government represents. ... The Jewish contractor must be denied this project, which should be entrusted to a Christian of the Hungarian race."[181]

The newspaper reporting this refers also to the closing down of forty-five different journals under government decree. The newspaper expresses its satisfaction with the closing down itself, and its happiness at the government having liberated the Christian public from the harmful influence of these journals:

Christian society rejoices that after so many years the government is finally beginning to impose order, and it is good that this is being done forcefully. Some of these journals pursued a racist, Jewish policy of incitement with bold, Hebrew impudence.... With their closing we are already able to believe that the time has come for Christian action, and that the government will indeed protect Christian society, in its institutionalized fashion, from the destructive activity of the racist left.[182]

At the onset of the 1930s, the Christian student associations organized riots that led to the temporary closing of the universities. They even published a petition asserting their demands, which was intended for the government:

Christian friends! The struggle being waged by Christian youth for fourteen years for the supremacy of the Christian race obliges us to act in a common framework.... We demand the application of the "numerus clausus" law in such a way as to ensure the relative number of all Christian students in each and every faculty.... We demand careful scrutiny of the foreign, pushy, uninvited race.[183]

Students at the Technical University of Budapest resolved at their convention that "in the classrooms, in the laboratories, and in exercises they would compel the Jewish students to concentrate in a 'ghetto.' They would allow them to enter the university, but would ostracize them absolutely."[184]

The antisemitic activity that went on in the institutions for higher education in Budapest had its effect upon universities outside the capital. Rioting, ostracizing, and beating Jewish students spread quickly to the universities in the various provincial towns.[185] The Christian students at one university in such a town distributed a manifesto in which they stated that "the leaders of the Christian student body have informed the Jewish students that they had better refrain for the present from continuing to frequent the university ... the Dean of Students has indeed suggested that they absent themselves from the university for a few days."[186]

The student struggle won respectable patronage. The Union of Awakening Hungarians took them under its wing and ensured them of its support. The governing body of this union debated the events taking place at the universities and resolved, "The 'Union of Awakening Hungarians' congratulates the students for recent events and ensures the students that in the future, too, it will extend to them full moral and material support."[187]

Five student organizations signed the petition of the Christian students that was intended for the government. It should be noted that four of these were in some way connected with the church. The Catholic Student Alliance and Emericana student organization operated within the framework of a Catholic organization known as Actio Catholica.[188] The names of two additional organizations indicated their church connections: the St. Imre Colleges of Buda and of Pest.[189]

The Hungarian civil service had never gone out of its way to employ Jews, and for this it won the support of an illustrious religious personage. The head of the Reformed church in Hungary, Bishop Ravasz, complained of the procedures enabling a person belonging to a certain church to be employed by the civil service, even when a person belonging to another church was more suited to that position. The bishop expressed his wish that in the future, employees would be engaged according to their suitability alone, whether they were Catholic, Evangelical, or Reformed. Yet he added, "Of course, this demand of mine does not include people of the foreign race."[190]

Ravasz's opinion of the Jews found other modes of expression as well: about six months before his comment on "people of the foreign race" he delivered a lecture on "The Connection between the Jewish Question and Reformed Christianity." In this lecture he referred picturesquely to Jews praying alongside the Wailing Wall:

> How exciting it is to see the Jews gathering alongside some stone wall in Jerusalem and wailing there some prayer in a monotonous voice: "Build, O Lord, your house which is in ruins"! This is a lament over some ruins. How much more sublime than this Jewish approach is the exalted Cross of Golgotha, above and beyond their tragedy! The Cross bathes in colored lights, and the voice of Jesus, our High Priest, calls to us in his prayer: "Let us be united, just as I am united with You, my Father who are in Heaven."[191]

Ravasz's Catholic colleague, Bishop Glattfelder, expressed his opinion of the Jewish question in his own style. At a Catholic rally in 1936, attended by hundreds of thousands of believers, he spoke the following words:

> The red Bolshevik Satan seeks his prey everywhere. The edges of the firmament have become red throughout the world, and bloody tracks mark the path of the Antichrist. Hungarian Christian village! Do not put your faith in the mocking emissaries of the Red tyrants, for they hate your Christian belief, they envy you your home, your fields, your children, and even your wife. And you—village priest, teacher, magistrate, doctor, and landowner—please do not abandon those of your race in their hour of severe distress, in the hour of this terrible crisis, for you bear upon your shoulders heavy responsibility in this tragic struggle being waged between opposing worlds.[192]

Glattfelder's speech contains a plan for the future as well. The speech was delivered in the fourth year of Hitler's rule, at a time when the very last of the believers was already aware of the identity of the two camps standing on opposite sides of the barrier in what the bishop defined as "the tragic struggle being waged between opposing worlds." The bishop left no room for doubt in the minds of his audience as to just where, in his opinion, their place was in that struggle.

One finds a similar stand in a Catholic journal that published an article entitled "Jewish Control of Hungarian Economic Life," where the writer urges his readers to act so as to bring about a change in the situation:

Our very national survival and independence are endangered. The present situation is intolerable, it is unbearable, and we have no choice but to solve the problem.... The protests made by Christian society against Jewish economic control and the Christian vetoing of Jewish trespassing are not merely empty words.... The very fact that we have to act against the prevalent situation is decisive proof that we are discussing the question of the survival of the Hungarian nation.[193]

The writer complains that the role played by the Jews in Hungarian economic affairs was greater than the Hungarian economy required, and caused Christian Hungarians harm. In truth, the Christians had not engaged widely in commerce—for historical reasons embedded in the social understanding of the middle class. Until World War I engaging in commercial activity was considered dishonorable by various social strata, who preferred to work in the civil service, including the armed forces. When Hungary was dismembered the requirements of the civil service were greatly reduced, and many found themselves unemployed. Some considered engaging in commerce, but they found the field largely occupied by Jews. Their need to enter into the field led them to organize in order to make it easier for Christian groups to take part in and take control of commercial life. The churches supported this organization and encouraged it.

And so, at the onset of the 1920s, the Baross Szovetseg (Society) was born. The aim of the organization was "to increase as far as possible the number of independent Christian craftsmen and merchants in Hungary."[194] Baross Szovetseg set itself the goal of undercutting Jewish merchants and replacing them with Christian merchants in every commercial field, both within Hungary and between Hungary and other countries.

Some time after it was founded, in 1924, the organization appealed to the Synod of Catholic Bishops "and requested its support for the Christian merchants and craftsmen. The organization also asked the Synod of Bishops to assist in convincing the Christian populace of its economic significance, thus granting the organization moral support." The bishops agreed to the request, and decreed that "the Synod of Bishops views this movement positively."[195]

The encouragement by the Synod of Bishops fulfilled its aim, and respected public figures did indeed support the organization and its goals. Among its supporters there were priests, even high-ranking ones. The organization, for its part, expressed from time to time its appreciation for its leading supporters, and awarded them the Baross Chain. Among those who received the chain were the antisemitic leader, Karoly Wolf,[196] Cardinal Seredi, and Premier Kalman Daranyi.[197] At the ceremonial awarding of the Baross Golden Chain to the cardinal and the prime minister, the chairman of the organization said, "Voices of protest are coming at present from the orthodox liberals. They are protesting against the 'Baross' organization's energetic activity in exports and in supplying public institutions. These voices are merely the roaring of aggressive beasts of prey now afraid of losing their prey. . . . We are not a nomadic mob that replaces its homeland in accordance with its needs and exploits for its own benefit the prosperity and economic surfeit in one country or in another."

At the same ceremony the minister of commerce and industry delivered a speech in which he lauded "the vision of Bishop Ottokar Prohaszka regarding the role of Christianity in the future. Prohaszka's figure and vision hover constantly before the eyes of the government." The nature of Prohaszka's vision and figure was common knowledge. The speech delivered by Prime Minister Daranyi at that ceremony included a hint of what was to come: "I emphasize that the government will do whatever it can to further those very ideas represented by 'Baross.' Government activity will lead to a situation where in Hungary there will be as large a number as possible of Christian craftsmen and Christian merchants."[198]

A year later Daranyi and his government prepared and presented to the Hungarian legislature the first anti-Jewish bill.

Bishop Ravasz, head of the Reformed church, was present at that same ceremony, together with Cardinal Seredi. The presence of the leaders of the two great churches in Hungary[199] accorded additional weight to the speech made by the prime minister—the speech in which he laid down the guidelines for his government's future policy. The fact that the cardinal shared the Baross organization's antisemitic platform with the prime minister in the receipt of an award testifies to his support both of the organization and of the prime minister's speech.

The bishop of Csanad appeared at a national rally of the Baross organization and said,

> For the last hundred years the slogan of freedom has served to camouflage unrestricted looting in our country. . . . The looted masses must wake up, they must become aware of the unlimited possibilities made available by the use of the power of the general public. Vast economic opportunities may open up before the Christian masses, on condition that these masses cease their subservient behavior, which bears witness to their self-deprecation before people of a foreign race. . . . This is a clear Hungarian Christian program, crystal clear and unambiguous.[200]

In addition to the organizations and associations noted above, the Actio Catholica was active in Hungary from 1932 on. This organization was different from the other organizations mainly in that the Synod of Bishops founded it in accordance with the recommendation of the pope; that is, it was the direct creation of the Catholic church.[201] When it first appeared, the organization had a positive effect. Its role was defined by its leaders in Hungary as follows:

> The Actio Catholica will be the institution which knows everything, directs everything, represents the Catholics but does not cause harm and does no damage to bodies whose aims are honest and decent, and it will support whoever is worthy of support. The existing [Catholic] organizations will focus on the framework of the Actio Catholica while preserving the particular nature of each organization, its field of activity, and its aims.[202]

Actio Catholica viewed itself as a nonparty organization, headed by Cardinal Seredi. The organization's council was made up of the representatives of twenty Catholic bodies representing the entire Catholic population of Hungary, whereas the day-by-day leadership was in the hands of known Catholic public figures.[203]

From the very inception of the organization its leaders stressed the importance of cooperation between their organization and the state authorities. At the organization's founding convention, Cardinal Seredi spoke out on this topic:

> The more energetic and comprehensive the activities of the Catholic church, the more useful they will be to the state. . . . Behold, your eyes perceive— and this very convention proves—to what degree both the state and Actio Catholica strive to express by means of their representatives at this convention that very same internal harmony which prevails between them, for the benefit of their citizens and their believers.

Another speaker at the same convention, the priest Bela Bangha, claimed that the concept of Actio Catholica had existed ever since the inception of Catholicism, and as proof of this "he pointed out many historical examples of the close cooperation between the church and the secular authorities in the fields of culture, economics, society, and social work and—in the Middle Ages—even in the military field."[204]

This Catholic organization, however, fitted itself into the antisemitic atmosphere that prevailed in Hungary, and even contributed to its advancement.

An official publication of the National Leadership of Actio Catholica dealing with the subject of the liberal press wrote:

> Certain newspapers are proving great experts in covering up subjects the publication of which may prove to be of use to the Catholic populace. . . .

If it happens that the rabbi of the Dohany Street Synagogue [the central synagogue of the Jewish community of Budapest] voices in his patter some confused "philosophy," those newspapers devote entire pages to the "wonderful sermon by the Chief Rabbi of the poetic soul." Yet if the Cardinal of Hungary delivers the most brilliant of speeches, those papers ignore it completely.... For the existence of such a situation we have only ourselves to blame. Let us unite and remove the handle from the hatchet! Let no one give money to those of the foreign race. Let us read only Catholic newspapers and then the hatchet will remain without its handle.[205]

At a certain national Catholic convention the participants included government ministers, the Synod of Bishops headed by the cardinal, and many other notables from both government and church circles. One of the speakers at the convention was the deputy chairman of the Actio Catholica, Karoly Huszar, who served as prime minister during the period of the White Terror. He spoke about "Christianity and Social Justice." Among other things he said, "If we do not reorganize to defend our faith, the danger of annihilation will threaten Christianity. Thus we need to base our society upon Christian viewpoints. It is not enough to remove the Jews from economic positions of power. We are obligated to introduce a true Christian spirit and Christian morality as well into each field of our lives."[206]

A newspaper article dealt with the topic, "Is Antisemitism Opposed to Catholicism?" The writer of the article claimed that he was an active member of Actio Catholica, and by virtue of his role there he often visited the branch offices of the organization throughout Hungary. As he put it, the opinion expressed in his article reflected loyally the opinion of the organization and most of its members.

And thus he wrote:

Is the defense of the Hungarian race opposed to Christianity, and does Antisemitism contradict Catholicism? Not at all! Ever since the inception of Christianity, a struggle with no compromise has been waged unceasingly between the church and Judaism. Our Lord Jesus began this struggle on a practical level when he drove out at whip's end the moneychangers from the Temple.[207]

He also fought them verbally, with strong language:

"Satan is your progenitor, and you desire to execute his will. You do not believe me because I speak the truth" (John 8:42–45). Ever since the end of the persecution of the Christians—which took place at the instigation of the Jews—and since Constantine the Great became ruler of the Roman Empire, and the persecuted Christians were able to come out of the Catacombs, the popes and church councils, year after year, generation after generation, have engaged in legislating laws to limit the rights of the Jews and to issue decrees aimed at achieving this goal.[208]

The writer lists many of these laws and decrees, such as prohibiting Jews from employing Christians, prohibiting Jews from performing certain services for Christians, forbidding Jews to live together with Christians, obligating the Jews to wear a yellow patch and various garments to identify them, and so on. He concludes, "No one has ever canceled these papal edicts and church laws. And so they are all valid in our day as well."[209] It should be noted that this newspaper article appeared while the second anti-Jewish bill was being debated in Parliament, and the encouragement included in it for the legislators is all too evident.

At a summer university of the Catholic church, held in Esztergom in 1937, the national director of Actio Catholica, the priest Zsigmond Mihalovics, who was also a member of the Upper House, participated. He spoke of the nature of his organization and its significance, saying, "The Actio Catholica is the most important contemporary Christian movement, adjusting itself to the spirit of the times and working for Christianity in accordance with the needs of this spirit."[210]

Awareness of the usage of the contemporary vernacular, as will be demonstrated below, explains the concept of "the spirit of the times." In a newspaper article that appeared just before the holding of the summer university, there appeared the following:

> The liberal-democratic-Jewish regime which ruled Hungary until recently is the source of all the troubles in our land, but the wonderful, triumphant "spirit of the times" is the dynamic force of the National-Socialist idea. Only nationality, born and bred in the concept of Hungarianism and Christianity, can serve as a basis upon which to build our national Hungarian future.[211]

On another occasion, the priest Mihalovics spoke before the council of the Central Catholic Circle about "The Importance of Catholic Circles in Changing Times." In his speech Mihalovics lauded the leading role played by the Catholics in their struggle against the dangers that were threatening Catholics and Hungary:

> They blinded the eyes of the masses by describing the advantages of the liberal state. This picture, hovering in front of their eyes, was merely a mirage. After the numerous forces of the Jewish Freemasons took control of our economic lives, they were about to take control of our spiritual lives as well. The Catholics were the first to perceive—out of this heavy spiritual unconsciousness—this terrible danger. The time which has passed since

then has justified the stand taken by the Catholics as well as their ambitions.[212]

While the period of anti-Jewish legislation was underway, the bishops, at one of their conventions, dealt with all aspects of the desired attitude of the Catholic church toward this legislation. They were afraid of the legislation harming converts to Christianity and of the government's position on racial questions. The bishops resolved to make use of the services of the Actio Catholica to bring their views before the general public, and decided "that the standpoint of the church on this issue will be clarified at rallies of the Actio Catholica."[213] In light of the organization's antisemitic stand, it is no wonder that its members rendered the bishop's strict standpoint even stricter by their interpretation.

As already noted, Actio Catholica was founded at the instigation of the pope, and was not uniquely Hungarian. A similar organization existed in Germany, and not surprisingly it supported Hitler consistently. When Hitler announced that Germany was leaving the League of Nations, he received many congratulatory telegrams, including one from the Actio Catholica, which announced its unanimous support of him.[214]

In summary, the antisemitic outbursts of the 1930s placed the Jewish population in opposition to various sectors that strove to block their advancement. Such organizations as Actio Catholica, which grew up out of the church and out of Baross, which favored them, did not contribute to general calm. In the 1930s, the Jews of Hungary found themselves in a situation that tended to remind them of that of their ancestors in the Middle Ages: the possibility of their employment in various fields was limited, while their Christian coworkers labored to put an end to their livelihoods and to drive them out of society.

Cross Movements and the Arrow-Cross Party

The leaders of most of the antisemitic movements in Hungary went out of their way to point out the Christian nature of their movements, for they realized that in this way they would stir up interest in joining on the part of the general public. As early as the end of the nineteenth century the People's party stressed its Catholic nature, and the consumers' unions that were founded by it stressed their aim: to protect the Christian population from Jewish exploitation. Karoly Wolf's antisemitic party, too, in its various stages of development, was consistent in including the term "Christian" in its various names.

After World War I the cross itself found its way into use by the antisemitic parties, who added it to the expression "Christian" already in their names, in their logos, or in both. This Christian symbol became a visual aid in the antisemitic struggle.

We have already mentioned the Blood Alliance of the Double Cross,[215] which was the military wing of one of the murderous organizations active during the White Terror period. Thereafter there appeared additional cross movements. From 1929 the Cross Scythe, headed by Zoltan Boszormenyi, was active in Hungary. Its leader met with Hitler in 1931, and the movement was the first significant national-socialist organization in Hungary. In the framework of this movement paramilitary units were organized, called "Storm Troopers."

In March 1935 Boszormenyi published the "Ten Commandments," a guide for the members of his party in general and the Storm Troopers in particular. Their obligations were described as follows:

> A member of the Storm Troopers is the gardener causing the Hungarian race to blossom, he is the scythe bringing death and oblivion to the criminal Jews and their adjuncts.... He also sounds the knell of death in the ears of those who would undermine our country's internal security and in the ears of those who would oppress the Hungarians, of the violators of law and order, of the usurers—the Jewish-Red-Bolshevik propagandists.[216]

In the mid-1930s the Blue Cross movement was active in Hungary. This organization was founded in order to fight Bolshevism, but its activities were mainly loud, antisemitic demonstrations and violence against the Jews in the city streets, especially in Budapest.[217]

In the spring of 1938 a mass international Catholic convention was held in Budapest, the Eucharistic Convention.[218] To mark the event the Christian organization of merchants and craftsmen, Baross, recommended that for the duration of the convention the members of the organization put crosses in the windows of their stores and businesses. A Jewish weekly reacted:

> The organization has already given up the idea that at the end of the convention the signs with the crosses be removed from the windows. It is clear that this is the introduction of intolerance into commercial life, the intolerance we encounter in various aspects of our public lives. With regard to the Cross Enterprise of the Baross organization, we must note that we respect the cross greatly as a religious symbol, but we feel the use of a religious symbol for commercial propaganda does not add to its honor. ... In our view, the cross—copied from church towers to store windows— is not in a place which gives due honor to its status.[219]

The Christian Hungarian population did not share the opinion of the Jewish weekly. During that period many joined the most extremely antisemitic Hungarian cross movement, the Arrow-Cross party, to be discussed below.

At that time antisemitic movements bearing the cross in their names and their symbols were active in other European countries as well: the Cross of Fire in France, the Iron Cross in Rumania, the Thunder Cross in Latvia—in addition to the Ku Klux Klan's fiery cross in the United States.[220]

Rumors of these cross movements reached Hungary, and so members of the Hungarian cross movements viewed themselves as active partners in an all-European movement, based upon Christian foundations and coming to shape a renewed Europe in the spirit of Christianity. In the background of all these cross movements there stood the symbol of the central cross of the era—the swastika. A considerable portion of the media in Hungary described the swastika as a symbol of the forces defending European Christian culture, struggling bravely against the danger of Red expansion from the east and against the Bolshevik-Jewish *Weltanschauung*. It served as a source of inspiration for the various cross movements, including the Arrow-Cross party.

The leader of the Arrow-Cross party was Ferenc Szalasi. The party was founded in 1935 from the union of some six extreme antisemitic movements, organizations, and parties, including the remains of Boszormenyi's Cross-Scythe, which was left leaderless after he fled to Germany in early 1938.[221] Furthermore, a group of members of the National Christian party joined the Arrow-Cross party after the death of their leader, Karoly Wolf. The leader of this faction, Andras Csillery,[222] announced, "We must absorb the successful ideas prevalent beyond our borders that have registered appreciable achievements there. I refer here to the idea of Hitlerism."[223] Another body to join the Arrow-Cross party was the Blue Cross.[224]

For a number of years the party operated under various names, such as the Wish of the Nation party, the Hungarian Socialist party, the Hungarianism Movement, the National Socialist Movement, and so on. From March 1939 it was called the Arrow-Cross party.[225]

According to the Arrow-Cross party regulations,

> Hungarianism believes in God and believes in Jesus. . . . We are aware of the existence of constructive factors and destructive factors. Jewry is not a nation, but rather a race, and is unable to put out roots in the soil of the homeland—it is destructive. . . . There is no way to resolve our struggle

against the old-fashioned capitalistic system without first solving the Jewish question.

Of the Hungarian initiative in the final solution of the Jewish problem, the regulations say:

> It is a fact that the efforts we made in 1920–1939 to solve the Jewish problem left our country in danger of an economic collapse. During that period the efforts made by the Jew to take control of the entire world reached their climax. In Russia, Jewish totalitarianism made use of the Communists to suppress the national war of liberation of the Russian people. Similar efforts were made in other European countries as well. Under such conditions we were unable to solve the Jewish problem alone. But it is a fact that the activities carried out during that period by the Hungarian nation and the Hungarian race were an opening step toward the solution of the problem, a step which by virtue of being a pioneering step, was of historical significance.

Of the moral foundations of Hungarianism the regulations say:

> Our national awareness supports the carrying out of our tasks in a moral manner and by bestowing respect on each and every man. We have absorbed this awareness from the truths of Jesus of Nazareth. The Hungarian National-Socialistic State will act so as to realize the most important values of the Christian faith in the lives of the Hungarian nation—all by means of a sense of love for the church and the readiness to sacrifice oneself for national unity. True and deep faith in God and in Jesus of Nazareth leads to a pure love of the nation and of the homeland, and vice versa: a pure love of nation and homeland leads to a deep realization of God and of Jesus of Nazareth. Hungarian National-Socialism cannot be separated from the Jesus movements.
>
> The aggressive, practical application of world order based on Jewish morality is Communism, whereas the practical application of the moral world based on the doctrines of Christian Jesus is Hungarian National Socialism, which is expressed in "Hungarianism."[226]

With the assistance of the Germans, the party leader Szalasi deposed Horthy on October 15, 1944, and on the following day took power and imposed a reign of terror upon the capital. During the months of his rule many thousands of Jews were murdered. After the war he was executed as a war criminal. This chapter does not deal with the period of his rule, but touches on his views, as expressed in the regulations of his party and his own utterances. The support of the Arrow-Cross party offered by some of the priests must be studied carefully in light of Szalasi's utterances.

A U.S. army intelligence officer in charge of the initial interrogation of the Hungarian war criminals after their apprehension says of Szalasi, "In his way he was a religious man. He constantly requested that we send him a priest."[227]

While awaiting trial Szalasi was interviewed by a psychoanalyst, who described his conversation with Szalasi on the question of his religious views and the influence of these views upon his political path:

> "I am a Catholic. I imbibed, together with my mother's milk, the value of a belief in God and my belief in him.... Only the full confluence of Socialism, Nationalism, and the doctrines of Jesus Christ can guarantee a happy Hungarian future."
>
> "Is this mixture represented by Hungarianism?"
>
> "Yes."
>
> "Does it include all of Jesus' doctrines, such as loving one's neighbor?"
>
> "Yes."
>
> "In our last conversation you said that you believe in God. Are you also a religious man?"
>
> "Yes."
>
> "Can you sum up in a single sentence the goal of 'Hungarianism'?"
>
> "Hungarianism is a combination of the doctrines of Jesus the Nazarene, Socialism, and Nationalism."
>
> "Do you accept the Ten Commandments as a basis for your moral outlook?"
>
> "Certainly. In full."
>
> "Do you accept the Christian assumption that one must not wish his neighbor that which he himself detests?"
>
> "In the positive Christian sense, that is, You should do for your neighbor whatever is good for you, too."
>
> "Does this include the concept of 'loving one's neighbor as oneself'?"
>
> "Certainly."
>
> "Are you convinced that in your feelings and your deeds you have always served the spirit of Christian outlooks?"
>
> "Certainly."[228]

This conversation took place after the war. Almost ten years passed between the time the Arrow-Cross party platform was composed and Szalasi's conversation with the psychoanalyst. It would seem that his religious outlook remained stable during this period. The Jewish question dealt with in the party regulations did not come up in his conversation with the psychoanalyst, but was mentioned at his trial. The following is an excerpt from the dialogue between the president of the panel of judges and Szalasi.

Szalasi: The carrying out of the ideas of socialism and nationalism fits in with Jesus' doctrines.... Ever since I have existed in this world I have lived according to his doctrines.

President: What would Jesus have said of your racial doctrines?

Szalasi: Racial purification does not contradict Jesus' doctrines.

President: Jesus' doctrines were morally based upon the principle of loving one's neighbor.

Szalasi: Loving one's neighbor relates only to a person who behaves like a neighbor, and not to a person who is unwilling to assume the obligations of a neighbor.

President: In accordance with your racist outlook, you in one of your speeches once referred to a claim made by a member of your party who said that there exist many decent Jews. Your reply was: "If a housewife cleaning her house discovers a large number of fleas she doesn't classify them or distinguish between those which had already stung and sucked blood and those which had not yet managed to do so. She crushes them all. This is true of the Jews. There are decent Jews and there are indecent Jews. Just as each and every flea can be expected to sting and to suck blood, so each and every decent Jew is to be expected to commit an indecent act."

Szalasi: Solving the Jewish question was one component of the aims of "Hungarianism."[229]

At its inception the arrow-cross was known as the anchor-cross, and the use of the symbol was initially quite hesitant. For example, the growers of onions in the town of Mako were not satisfied with the price they received for their crop. The fact that some of the onion growers were Jewish led to antisemitic outbursts, including the inscription of antisemitic remarks on the walls of Jewish homes. On the walls of their homes there also appeared a new symbol: a cross with arrowheads added to its four extremities. A newspaper item relates,

On occasion we encounter swastikas, too, but in most cases we see anchor-crosses drawn on the walls of Jewish homes. Members in Mako relate that in the adjacent province there are two thousand members organized in the Cross Scythe movement, and it cannot be denied that a very large number favor them.... Their leader approached me with a declaration that their foundations are firmly based on a Christian outlook, and that their only ambition is to be able to struggle for Hungarian racial national interests.[230]

What was said in Mako reflected the policies of the leaders of the Arrow-Cross party. A poster inviting the public to a meeting with Szalasi in a town nearby Budapest appealed to "all Christian Hungarians whose emotions are dedicated to their nation and their race."[231] The tone binding the ideas of the Arrow-Cross party with its members' Christianity prevailed at party rallies. For instance, under the heading "Tens of Thousands Demonstrated in Favor of Arrow-Cross Ideas," a newspaper item reports that a party activist declared in his speech that "the strength of National Socialism is anchored in religious faith.... Our idea will triumph, it must triumph, for God's will is for it to triumph."[232]

In an article published in a paper defining itself as "an independent Christian-National political paper," a Catholic priest went into very great detail concerning his approach to "the new movement." The writer of the article appeals emotionally to his priestly colleagues, especially to those serving in the countryside:

A new era lies before us, which will be different from that of heretic liberalism, which laid upon the table the interests of a foreign race which attempted to drown us all and to block our revival.... This new movement can be strengthened only on the basis of the doctrines of Jesus of Nazareth, as made clear by the leader of the political left, who is loved by all: Laszlo Endre.[233] We must carefully continue to respect the historical churches.

Our Lord Jesus taught us the elements of love; we must even forgive our enemy. But when we are discussing an ambition to take control of the world by people of the race that, beginning with the crucifixion of our Lord Jesus of Nazareth, can be met wherever there are revolutions, wherever the peace and quiet of entire nations is violated, wherever there is a violation of basic ethics, we do not have to hide behind the idea of Christian love...let us not be led astray by the Jewish press. Let us not come out in support of the Jews, but rather protect our own Hungarian race. Let us grant guidance to the frustrated Arrow-Cross man and watch how the people of your own villages love you more! See how thankful the villagers are toward you! I have discussed this subject with many of our leading, experienced clerical colleagues, and the fact is that this approach of ours achieves good results.[234]

During one of the events of the Eucharistic Convention in the spring of 1938, priests and priests-in-training marched in a body under the banners of the church. As they passed the building housing the central committee of the Arrow-Cross party, known by a name made up of its address, "Andrassy Ut 60," the priests dipped their flags and saluted the building, its inhabitants, and the viewpoints they espoused.[235]

The support for the Arrow-Cross movement was not restricted to the lower-class clergy, as indicated by the unambiguous statement made by one of the bishops of the Catholic church, Jozsef Grosz of Szombathely. Here are extracts from his speeches as quoted in the media:

Our ambition is for the younger generation to be a generation of believers and not one of heretics. This generation will swear in the name of Jesus' Cross, will be guided by the star of Bethlehem and not by the Red Star of the Soviets.... I have no claims against Arrow-Cross, nor against national-socialism, as long as they do not fight against Jesus the Nazarene and his Gospels. I am not bothered if they greet each other with the salutation "Courage!" ["Courage" was the greeting used by Hungarian antisemitic groups. The greeting was said with a raised-arm salute, like "Heil Hitler."] Alongside the cross there is room for an arrow, and as long as the Arrow-Cross members go to church and pray to Jesus, we have no complaints against them, and we are not fighting them.[236]

The writer of the editorial, quoting the bishop's words, adds:

The fact that his Holiness, Bishop Jozsef Grosz, defended our movement, the Hungarian National-Socialist Movement, openly and unambiguously, fills us with great satisfaction. From the very start of our struggle we have stressed that we stand on the ethical basis of Christian faith.... Our ideal is not Red Spain, murdering priests and destroying churches, but rather General Franco, struggling for his religion and his homeland. As we are determined to struggle for our political ideas in the shadow of the Arrow-Cross, so the Cross shines, in its full glory, in our hearts and in the depth of our souls.[237]

Grosz's open support of the antisemitic Arrow-Cross party did not disturb his superiors in the Catholic church. On the contrary, the *Osservatore Romano,* the Vatican's official organ, reported that "Pope Pius XII has appointed four new Hungarian bishops." The name of one of these was Grosz, whose status was advanced from acting bishop to provincial bishop of Szombathely.[238] Grosz's promotion through the Catholic hierarchy continued. The pope appointed him bishop of Kalocsa in the spring of 1943, thus circumventing bishops with more seniority than he had. This new role of his was the second most important in the Catholic church hierarchy in Hungary, second only to that of the cardinal.[239]

A priest named Gabor Szijjarto invoked divine blessings upon the heads of the Arrow-Cross party. He wrote an open letter to his priestly colleagues, which was published as an editorial under the heading "May God bless you, men of Arrow-Cross." In the letter, he wrote:

Our lives now flow more rapidly, and you, men of Arrow-Cross, are the force operating the nation, and you shape its character. In humility, in deep admiration, and with a joyful heart, I bow my head before your sacred obstinacy. You have believed in your mission, you still believe in it, and you were indeed right. Without your prodding, the government would not have responded to the demands of the Arrow-Cross party. The government's proper legislative program [the anti-Jewish legislation] results from the pressure applied by your tensed muscles.

Men of Arrow-Cross! Continue your struggle with consistent enthusiasm, untiringly, and the results will not be late in coming. Your reward will be the eternal thankfulness of the Hungarian people!

May God bless you, men of Arrow-Cross![240]

The edition that published the letter also brought out the opinion of the head of the Hungarian Reformed church, Bishop Laszlo Ravasz, on Judaism:

The Jews were once a people representing prophetic morality. The world was nourished by their vision and their prophecies for thousands of years. This spirit has now become negative and heretic. There once was a people that created great things; but that very people itself now appears on occasion before the world in the shock of revolutionism and ruin.[241]

A Catholic priest named Zoltan Nyisztor held a meeting with Szalasi, and he wrote in his memoirs, "I spoke with him at length, wanting to learn just what was transpiring in his soul. I must state that before me stood a man of noble spirit and good intentions. He was a spotless personage in both his past and his present."[242]

At a certain stage Nyisztor proposed to Cardinal Seredi "that the Catholic movements cooperate with Szalasi's party, and the Catholic church support Szalasi, so as to raise his party to power by legitimate means."[243] While Nyisztor's proposal was not adopted, the very fact that a priest could make such a proposal to the cardinal speaks for itself.

Szalasi did indeed take power by illegitimate means, and about two weeks later, on October 29, 1944, met with Seredi. After the meeting Seredi jotted down in his diary that from his conversation with Szalasi he "learned that Szalasi was a believer, and one could not doubt his good intentions."[244]

Less than a week later, on November 4, 1944, Seredi ordered all the teachers in Catholic schools—who by virtue of their positions were civil servants—to swear an oath of allegiance to Szalasi. Other church leaders followed Seredi's precedent.[245]

While the events described in the last two paragraphs took place outside the temporal framework of this study, they have been adduced here in order to show that even while their party's programs were being carried out in practice, they enjoyed the cardinal's encouragement. While thousands of Jews were being murdered in Hungary, and the death marches were leaving Budapest one after the other for the Austrian border, Szalasi, the leader of Hungary by virtue of German bayonets, sat in the royal palace in Buda, and the head of the Catholic church came to shake his hand. The foundations for such a meeting had been laid years before. It is reasonable to assume that the cardinal, like his bishop, Grosz, who was cited above, held that "as long as the Arrow-Cross men visit the churches and pray to Jesus, we have no complaints against them." The regulations of the Arrow-Cross party and Szalasi's various utterances make it clear that he and his party did indeed "pray to Jesus."

An editorial in the official Arrow-Cross party newspaper appearing just before Easter 1938 provides more information about the party's ideological background, which made appropriate the meeting between its leader and the cardinal. The writer of the editorial adduces the antisemitic struggles of his party in describing Jesus' battles, together with many quotations from the New Testament. In this way he succeeded in giving the words of the New Testament renewed actuality and in deepening the reader's identification with this ancient struggle against Judaism, being carried on energetically in his day by the party. The headline of the article was phrased accordingly: "In the Footsteps of Jesus, the Redeemer":

> Hungarian National-Socialist Brethren!
> I have good tidings for you. They have crucified Jesus of Nazareth. He has died, they have buried him, but, three days later, he rose up to new life.... Who was Jesus? He was the incarnation of Justice, and so he has been the light of the world for the last 1938 years. Contrary to those who do not understand the significance of our period (Matthew 16:3), the spirit of truth has revealed to us (John 16:13) the spirit of the times of the twentieth century.
> We have gone to war to realize the spirit of the times. Of our own free choice, of our own goodwill and our love we have undertaken to continue to march in the thorn-strewn path of our Redeemer. We have entered the narrow gateway of life (Matthew 7:13).... We have suffered willingly the suspicions and humiliations handed down by that race which, according to Holy Scripture, "lives in sin," and none of whom speak the truth. They are all useless, treacherous spillers of innocent blood, corrupt and corrupting (Epistle to the Romans 3:9–18). They are all liars, cheats, traitors, heretics in Jesus, and sons of Satan (First Epistle to John 2:26; Second Epistle to John 1:7; the Gospel according to John 8:37–59). Those in whose hearts Jesus is lacking hate us, but this hate does not harm us, for they already hated Jesus before they began to hate us (John 15:18).
> Hungarian National-Socialist Brethren!

Who stand in our way? . . . Those who fight us are those who curse Jesus (Epistle of Jacob 2:6–7). Those who fight us are the hypocritical Pharisees (Luke 12:1), sons of the serpent (Matthew 3:7), who hold back the wages of the employed while the screams of those they oppress cut through to Heaven (Epistle of Jacob 5:4). . . . Those who oppose us are those who exploit the fear of God as a source of profit (First Epistle to Timothy 6:5), those who pretend to be merciful, but have no knowledge of mercy (Second Epistle to Timothy 6:5).

Hungarian National-Socialist Brethren!

We do not distort the commandments of God. We present our ideas in the name of justice to the entire population and to its conscience before the face of God. We are overjoyed, for we are hungry and thirsty, persecuted and suffering, for Hungarian justice. The persecutions, the tortures, the exiling, and the violence only add to our strength and our power (Second Epistle to the Corinthians 12:10).[246]

Thus, as the writer of the article put it, starting from the beginning of 1938, the Arrow-Cross movement became stronger and stronger. Its popularity spread extremely rapidly. Its growth was not gradual, the movement reaching its maximal size within a year and a half.[247] In April the party had to create additional offices in order to register new members, and according to certain estimates, in Budapest alone some sixty-five thousand members joined by the end of May.[248]

In May 1939 elections to Parliament were held. A little over a half-million voted for the old-time, well-based Smallholders party, while the Arrow-Cross party received no less than 750,000 votes.[249]

The success of the Arrow-Cross party provided various bodies, including high-ranking ones in the church and outside it, with a source of encouragement. These claimed that they had to support various antisemitic steps to offset the success of Arrow-Cross.[250]

Two central ideas guided the Arrow-Cross party: uncompromising antisemitism and Christian piety. Another factor in its doctrines—the denial of capitalism and appropriate social changes—was never clearly defined, remaining vague in the minds of the party supporters. But the outlook that the Jews were wealthy capitalists, from whom the wealth was to be returned to its rightful owners, was well understood. Antisemitism intertwined with Christianity, as demonstrated by the Arrow-Cross party, reached the hearts of the masses, and the latter flocked to the party.

Conclusion

About 250 years passed between the beginning of Jewish immigration into Hungary and the 1930s. During only twenty-five years (1895–1920) the Jews enjoyed full equality of rights, whereas at the end of this period (1919–1920) the bloody events of the White Terror took place. With the change in regime at the end of World War I, the attitude toward the Jews changed as well, and the civil equality awarded them before the war was taken from them after it was over.

Alongside the changing attitude of the regime toward the Jews, there was also another element whose attitude toward them remained constant. This was the church. Throughout the vicissitudes of government, it constantly supported the body that was hostile toward the Jews. Before World War I the church opposed the stands taken by liberal governments, whereas after it was over the church fully supported antisemitic governments. The church's antisemitism was a matter of principle, not of opportunism.

The blood libel trial of Tisza Eszlar and the stand adopted by the clergy in this connection, the antisemitic petition drawn up by Reformed priests, the Catholic church's obstinate and drawn-out fight against granting the Jewish religion full recognition—all these left their impression on the final decades of the nineteenth century. The church adjusted its antisemitism to the developments of the twentieth century: even before the dissolution of the Austro-Hungarian monarchy the church linked Christianity and Hungarianism, exploiting this link to support its antisemitic outlook. When the monarchy disintegrated, this stand grew stronger and served to cause Jews harm.

The changes in regime during 1919–1920 provided the clergy with new conditions, new partners, and new opportunities for activity and for the realization of its views. During the bloody events of 1919–1920 the clergy stood unanimously behind the persecutors, to whom they awarded their support and their prestige.

The rapid promotion enjoyed by those priests who spoke up in public in support of blatant antisemitic opinions—Zadravecz and Grosz—indicates the approach taken by the church in its antisemitic incitement, which was common in broad circles.

The expression "foreign race" was synonymous with "Jew," and was commonly used by Hungary's secular leaders and its clergymen. This expression describes "the foreign race" as different from the "sons of the homeland"—inferior to them. Jews were uninvited citizens who were undesired in Hungary and in various Hungarian walks of life. This concept was the basis for the antisemitic propaganda that grew stronger during the 1930s.

At that time the realization was forming that practical steps had to be taken to remove "the sons of the foreign race," and conditions were growing ripe to channel the emotions hostile to them by means of a formal framework. The circumstances were well suited for the beginning of anti-Jewish legislation.

2

Anti-Jewish Legislation

Introduction

The anti-Jewish legislative process began in the spring of 1938 and lasted for some six years, up until the German invasion of Hungary in the spring of 1944. Earlier, Hungarian Jewry had enjoyed some equal rights for some seventy years, ever since the adoption of the Law of Emancipation in 1867, and as early as 1895 the status of the Jewish religion was rendered equal to that of the great Christian faiths. Equality before the law was absolute except for the limits imposed upon Jewish students under the "Numerus Clausus" Act of 1920. It was thus natural for the Jewish public to view as a serious blow to its position the tabling of an anti-Jewish bill in Parliament and the public debate that ensued, with various public figures in Parliament and in the Upper House voicing strong antisemitic sentiments. This besmirching of Jewry and of Judaism was strongly reflected in Hungarian public opinion, as demonstrated, among other things, by the results of the parliamentary elections held in May 1939. The Hungarian electorate lavishly rewarded the extreme right-wing circles that supported the anti-Jewish legislation, while severely punishing those parliamentary factions that opposed it. Experienced public figures and politicians, sensitive to the mood of the Hungarian masses, did everything possible to meet their expectations. The speeches delivered by many members of both Parliament and the Upper House were saturated with antisemitic incitement and with derogatory references to Judaism and to Jews. The masses and the national leadership reinforced one another, creating an axis linking them with a common topic and a common aim: persecuting Jews and removing them from as many fields of endeavor as possible.

This axis was joined by the top-ranking leaders of the Christian churches of Hungary, who, by virtue of their posts and their status, enjoyed membership in the Upper House. The strength of their antisemitic sentiments, voiced during the consideration of the proposed bills, was no less than that expressed by leaders of both the government and the extreme right wing, as will be demonstrated below. The church joining this axis, representing the people and their leaders, added yet another

81

dimension to the anti-Jewish campaign, and created a triangle that was to play a significant role during the entire period of anti-Jewish legislation.

Since the parliamentary debate was characterized by repeated mention of the confrontation between Christians and non-Christians, and between Christianity and Judaism, the debate aroused the Christian public to a greater degree of awareness of the differences between them and their non-Christian neighbors, the Jews. Furthermore, since the denigration of the Jews and the antisemitic incitement had their origins in the highest of government circles, expressions of antisemitism that in the late 1920s and early 1930s might have been considered vulgar now won legitimacy, becoming commonplace and desirable even in the most respectable of drawing rooms. When the heads of the Christian churches added their voices to those besmirching Jews and Judaism, a dimension of religious devotion was added to this antisemitic trend—a dimension that enjoyed considerable influence in Christian Hungary.

The anti-Jewish legislative process that went on for years was in fact the reading of a lengthy indictment against Jews, against Judaism, and against the characteristics of each. The damage caused by the corrupt traits of the Jews to the economic, social, cultural, and spiritual life of Christian Hungarians was spelled out from several points of view. The expressions used to describe Jewish corruption became so commonplace that even in the summer of 1944, when the Jews were faced with the danger of expulsion from Hungary, and even after most of them had already been expelled and then murdered in the gas chambers, those expressions still served the church leaders.[1]

The First Anti-Jewish Act

The first official intimation of the government's intention to legislate an anti-Jewish act came directly from the Hungarian prime minister, Kalman Daranyi, in a speech he delivered in the town of Gyor, on March 5, 1938:

> There is a Jewish question in Hungary . . . and it forms one of the unsolved problems of the nation's public life. . . . The kernel of the problem . . . lies in the fact that Jews living in Hungary, partly by reason of a special disposition for commerce and also because of the indifference shown by Hungarian Christians, play quite a disproportionate role in certain branches of economic life. Moreover, the large concentration of Jews in the Hungarian capital has naturally influenced the cultural and economic life of Budapest, and that influence does not always square with the vital requirements of the Hungarian people. . . . A solution should be found whereby

Jewish influence in cultural and other domains of national life will be reduced. Such a solution will grant the Christian section of the community a just share in the industry, commerce, and finance of the country.[2]

On the following day, Balint Homan, the minister of religion and education, made a speech in the town of Szentes, where he spoke in a similar vein:

> The Jewish problem is one demanding discussion . . . and it involves two questions—one economic, the other ideological. Economically, a disproportionate influence and participation in economic fields is enjoyed by Jews because of their special capacity. . . . Similarly, cultural endeavors and the press are dominated by Jews, many of whom express views alien to the Hungarian mentality . . . they live a separate, peculiar life, with a separate, peculiar ideology; and they are considered as aliens by the Hungarians. Certain of them have participated in subversive movements and in propagating dangerous theories.[3]

It should be noted that the concept of limiting the activities of the Jews by means of appropriate legislation had been raised in government circles long before the prime minister's Gyor speech. Though the idea of anti-Jewish legislation had not yet been explicitly formulated, indications of such thinking had been voiced earlier. In a speech delivered by the prime minister in February 1937 at the annual convention of the Baross Szovetseg, an organization whose raison d'être was the advancement of Christian trade and industrial interests at the expense of those of the Jews, the premier had said, "I must stress that the government shall do its very best to cultivate the ideas represented by the Baross Society. The government shall strive to achieve a maximal increase in the number of Christian industrialists and traders in this land."[4]

In March 1937 the president of the Hungarian National Bank, Bela Imredi, had prepared a memorandum for Premier Daranyi in which he dealt with the Jewish problem and with proposals for its solution. He suggested adopting measures to reduce Jewish influence over the press and to increase the number of Christians in middle- and upper-class economic projects.[5] In January 1938 General Karoly Soos, a retired minister of war, presented the regent of Hungary, Horthy, with a similar program. He proposed to reduce Jewish influence in economic activity, mainly by granting benefits to Christians, and to remove Jewish influence from the press and from cultural life by means of suitable legislation. The regent referred Soos to Premier Daranyi.[6] The economics minister, M. Fabinyi, said in a speech he made in the town of Pecs on January 16, 1938, "The desire is growing among Hungarian Christians to occupy those posts in industry and commerce which they had for so many years been content to leave to others."[7] He made no attempt to explain who the others were.

A week before the prime minister's Gyor speech there appeared an article written by a Catholic priest, which included these remarks: "We must admit the fact that there exists a Jewish problem in this country. Each and every one of us is called upon to support only those shops owned by Christians. We must see to it that the banks, the shops, and the land belong to sons of the Hungarian race alone. We must achieve this by appropriate legislation."[8]

If the Gyor speech aroused grave unrest in the hearts of the Jewish population, as well as a genuine fear of things to come, to an equal extent it excited the imaginations of the antisemitic circles, which hoped that the anti-Jewish legislation would usher in a new period in Hungarian history. Some two weeks after the Gyor speech an exuberant party was thrown, with the participation of high-ranking notables from both Catholic church and government circles, in honor of Bishop Istvan Zadravetz's receipt of a prestigious medal of excellence from the regent of Hungary, Horthy.[9] The aftermath of the Gyor speech was very apparent at the party, where an atmosphere of expectation prevailed. The opportunities for predictable change, which now appeared over the horizon, excited the imaginations of the guests, who expressed their innermost thoughts in their speeches. Zadravetz himself expressed the general appreciation of the Gyor speech and of its ramifications:

> The Hungarian Catholic Church and millions of Hungarian Catholics desire to work together for the rehabilitation of our beloved homeland. Whenever our country is considered, we must take into account its thousand years of history, the soul of those thousand years, including its exalted morality and principles. All of these converge on a single word: Christianity. ...The topics, the problems, and the matters discussed these days in the Gyor speech are like tree trunks, thick branches, arranged in such a way that they can become a raging bonfire, a triumphant flame illuminating our glorious future. To set this bonfire, this flame, alight we must place coals beneath them. The coals exist! They are simply the fire of Jesus Christ! We need an eternal flame, a fire never to be extinguished, for our great and joyous homeland and for the next thousand years for our nation. "I have come to ignite a fire in the world—can I not desire this fire to burst out?" (Luke 12:49)[10]

The bill was tabled in Parliament on April 8, 1938, and was known as the "Bill for a More Effective Guarantee of a Balanced Social and Economic Life." The preamble to the bill strives to give it a dimension of historical depth and links it with the Clerical People's party, which had struggled at the close of the nineteenth century against granting recognition to the Jewish religion: "The Catholic People's party, which was founded in the year 1894, has already waged war upon the anomaly which existed in political life, having been created as a result of liberal political views. In the political bearing of the People's party and in its practical activity in the various walks of public life, its intention in attempting to solve the Jewish problem has been clearly discernable."[11]

The preamble also mentions that the bill was intended to benefit the Hungarian nation by removing the Jews from various economic sectors and by making it more difficult for them in a variety of cultural fields, especially journalism:

> Under present circumstances certain sections of the population find their way blocked to various economic positions, as a result of the Jewish control of these positions above and beyond their proportion in the population. The national public opinion considers this situation unjust, unreasonable, and unacceptable. This disturbance of the economic balance is stressed by the fact that the vast majority of this sector [the Jews] does not partake of our traditional national feelings.

Paragraph 2 of the proposed bill deals with the limits placed upon Jews engaging in journalism, designed to reduce their part in influencing Hungarian public opinion. In explanation of the paragraph, the preamble says,

> The practical execution of this idea may be achieved most effectively by legislation which will guarantee the unification of journalistic endeavor within an organized association enjoying decisive influence over the formulation and direction of public opinion. In this way it will be ensured that the press functions in a spirit both national and Christian, on the one hand, while on the other, it will be guaranteed its independence within the framework dictated to it by the public interest. By means of this independence the nation will be able to rest assured that the freedom of the press will be expressed in the most noble fashion without being exploited for undesirable ends.[12]

The bill was adopted by an overwhelming majority in Parliament and was brought before the Upper House for its approval. As already noted, the heads of the Christian churches were members of the Upper House by virtue of their positions.[13] The church representatives encountered difficulty in voting for the bill. For operational purposes the bill included a definition of the term "Jew," defining as Jews even those converts to Christianity who had converted after August 1, 1919, upon the collapse of the Bela Kun Communist regime. The church delegates would not accept this definition, claiming that it was completely unreasonable for members of their churches, their flocks, to be considered Jewish. This became a bone of contention that aroused considerable debate concerning the bill, but could not prevent its adoption. The church leaders fought boldly for the interests of the members of their congregations, repeatedly stressing that they were not opposing the bill itself insofar as it imposed limitations upon the Jews. Regarding the desirable approach, as they saw it, to the Jewish problem, their utterances generally matched those of government members and supporters. The church leaders draped their utterances in religious, historical, economic, and other ideologies, as befitted their status in the church.

The head of the Evangelic church, Bishop Sandor Raffay, said,

> I cast no doubt, not even for a single moment, upon the necessity of tabling this proposal. Neither do I doubt that Jewry could have prevented its tabling. It could have done so by means of a substantial change in its behavior, and by means of such a change it would not have compelled us to consider this proposal.

The bishop went on to propose amendments he considered significant. One of these was for the date of August 1, 1919—the decisive date, according to the proposed bill, for recognition of valid conversions to Christianity and for exemption from the requirements of the bill—to be postponed until the 31st of that month. He also spoke of the need for consideration of those who had converted, "thus attuning themselves to us and already becoming like us." After proposing additional minor changes in the wording of the various paragraphs of the bill, he concluded his speech with the following declaration: "I accept the proposed bill."[4]

The head of the Reformed church, Sandor Ravasz, took the opportunity to expound upon the Jewish problem, its origins, the nature of Jews and Judaism, possible solutions to the Jewish problem, and the proper conduct required of Jews:

> As a legislator I sense the importance of taking a stand on the matters under discussion.... The Jewish problem has been the bane of humanity for about two thousand years. It is an important matter still awaiting its solution, and until it is eventually solved it will be accompanied by much suffering, many struggles, and a great many difficulties.... I am convinced that the adoption of this bill will serve well not only the welfare, the tranquillity, and the security of the state, but also those who today protest vehemently against its adoption.... Since the bill is intended to put in order economic issues such as providing employment opportunities and a fairer

division of revenues, I should like to believe that this is merely the first step in a broader, general program of planned legislation.... In discussing this bill it is impossible to refrain from dealing with the origin of the Jewish problem. We must state that during the modern, liberal period, the period that came to an end on the eve of the Great War, it was customary to view the Jewish problem as a religious one. The time has come for Hungarian public opinion to liberate itself from the opinion that the Jewish problem is a religious one. Were the 430,000 Jews of Hungary to convert all at once to Christianity, so that not a single Jew was left in Hungary, would in such a case the Jewish problem be solved? Of course not. It would become more complex and more difficult.

Ravasz continued:

Judaism is not a religion. If such is the case, what is it? Judaism is a race, with strong racial characteristics which prevent its assimilation. Though the Jews mingle with people of other races, yet Judaism continues stubbornly to maintain those racial characteristics.[15] Consider a nation with a strong racial awareness, which has existed for thousands of years, a nation with a fierce sense of national uniqueness, people for whom the very concept of being chosen has become bone of their bone, flesh of their flesh. This concept of theirs has grown and developed, together with their concept of their national god who grows with them, parallel to their exaggerated expectations of life. After much suffering and difficult crises this nation has altered its national form, adopting the form of a "diaspora"... living among the nations and at their expense.

Honorable Upper House! Is it any wonder that a nation living under such historical conditions for two thousand years develops certain psychological characteristics?... The diaspora and world trade are interwoven, and it is impossible to learn which came first. Is it any wonder that such a society, whose composition cuts across nations and countries, has selected for itself as a means an object which may be stored in the narrowest of places, which in comparison with its size represents the greatest value, which reflects great strength, and which is capable of attaining great influence?—and this means is nothing but money! Does this not mean that this society has come to dominate international capital and has become the controller of world credit? The natural consequence is that wherever it arrived, even within nations which have conducted their lives properly for hundreds of years, this scattered populace has sought out the cracks in the accepted social systems, just as parasitic, crawling plants do the same, climbing up on the host plant, sinking their roots deeply into it in order to enable them to subsist at its expense, even in tempestuous, stormy, dangerous times. Thus there are many who are stunned by the destructive ambitions of this race. We should not be surprised! Destructiveness is the basic characteristic of this race,[16] for it seeks to live, and if we do not want its life to be destructive, as at present, we have to work for a change in the relations between Jewry and its host nation.... Let the liberals claim whatever they will: every intelligent person can see today that over the last few hundred years an act of conquest has been executed against our homeland. This conquest was not executed by the sword, but rather by means of migration and of the Jewish natural increase. Our Hungarian ancestors conquered this land by the sword, but have lost considerable portions of it to those who migrated here, who, together with their descendants, have filled the land as a consequence of their extraordinary fertility.

Honorable Upper House! I would like to add a few practical conclusions to the theoretical concepts I have spoken of here with regard to the elements of the Jewish problem. First, I must stress that the Christian Church shall never concede its mission to Jewry.... When we accept a soul into the bosom of Christianity, we do not desire it to be accepted into a certain club, but rather to adjust itself to the Christian entity. He who joins the Church of Jesus in the hope of achieving certain benefits shall be disappointed, for when our Lord Jesus founded his church, he promised neither benefits nor recognition nor assimilation, but merely said: "Bear my cross and drink of the cup I have drunk from."

An additional comment: it is astounding to see how little sorrow or soul searching the Jews display in this matter. They view the entire affair as a kind of legalistic process which can be solved by means of the smooth tactical tongues of brilliant attorneys. Judaism seeks in this a kind of formal justice, having profoundly convinced itself that the suffering the Jews have undergone has befallen them despite their innocence. The Jews believe that they suffer because of the stupidity, the wickedness, and the jealousy of mankind, while they remain—innocent, pure, and upright!

Not at all! As long as the idea of Jewish righteousness is based on the aforesaid approach, the Jewish problem will not draw even a single short step nearer to its solution. By this erroneous approach, Judaism manages to convince itself that it suffers because of the guilt of others, despite its own innocence, and it would solve its problem by means of active or passive resistance. The only thing the Jews attain by this approach of theirs is that their opponents find their own hostile attitude justified, the polarity thus becoming ever stronger. I therefore warn the Jews once again to set aside in advance their passive or active resistance. To do so, they need the traits of concession, humility, and modesty.... It has long been known that because of evil, the good, too, suffer. This is true of the Jews, as well.... May the good bear their suffering with bowed heads, not because of their own guilt, but may they note: what kind of a blessing is it for them to have among them those who suffer in vain. The suffering of the innocent is a particularly suitable backdrop for atoning and acting well.

I accept the proposed bill.[17]

The subject of anti-Jewish legislation was put on the agenda of the Synod of Catholic Bishops. Cardinal Seredi reported on the stand taken by his church's delegates in the debate on the proposed bill:

> Regarding the proposed bill, which strives to limit the function of Hungarian Jewry in public and economic life, and to channel it into smaller frameworks, the Cardinal and Bishop of Csanad in the Upper House of the legislature expressed a very proper Catholic opinion with special regard to the converted Jews.[18]

A comparison of Ravasz's speech with that of another participant in the debate, Gyorgy Pronay, who was not a man of the cloth, is most interesting:

> The main responsibility [for the anti-Jewish legislation] rests on the spirit of Judaism, which has courted internationalism, denying nationalism and the national genius. This spirit is destructive, yet for decades Judaism has been applauding it, large sections of the Jewish populace actually living off it.... There undoubtedly exists a connection between this spirit and the vast majority of the Jewish public. Part of the Jewish population is aware of this fact, and this is the source of the great tragedy which leads to the indictment of innocent Jews together with the guilty ones. In fact, all Jews will suffer at the hands of this legislative proposal.[19]

The two speeches have a common denominator: they each place the responsibility for the anti-Jewish legislation squarely upon the shoulders of the Jewish population, and they each mention and even justify the generalization leading to the suffering of innocent Jews as well.

The bill was adopted on May 29, 1938.

The act limited the participation of Jews in the free professions to 20 percent. At first glance it would seem as if the instructions of the act were in no way limiting, in light of the fact that the Jews made up only about 6 percent of the population. Yet it must be taken into account that many and various occupations such as the military, the civil service, the railways, the postal service, etc., had already been completely, or almost completely, shut to the Jewish public. Even living conditions compelled the Jews to concentrate on certain occupations to a far greater degree than their relative portion of the populace would dictate. Besides the direct harm done by the act to thousands of families, it struck indirectly at the entire Jewish population. Most of this population had for several generations considered themselves Hungarian in all respects, and now this anti-Jewish act appeared, overturning their Hungarian patriotism while presenting them as undesirable aliens whose presence on Hungarian soil was barely tolerated—all this in addition to imposing legal limitations upon them.

The Eucharistic Convention

During the final stages of the parliamentary debate on the anti-Jewish act, Hungary basked in the warmth of international appreciation as expressed by the Catholic church, which held a eucharistic convention in Budapest. All the important figures of the Catholic world participated in this convention. There were scores of bishops from all over the world, and Pope Pius XI was represented by his personal representative, Cardinal Pacelli, who, less than a year later, was to become Pope Pius XII. Besides members of the priesthood, high-ranking secular guests from every corner of the world—guests involved in the activities of the Catholic church— took part in the convention. Ceremonial prayer services and impressive masses were held in the great cathedrals and open squares of Budapest, the capital, with throngs of celebrants participating. Budapest took on a festive air and the Catholic church impressed the public with mass ceremonies attended by tens of thousands, perfectly organized, pompous and majestic, exploiting the best of church knowledge and tradition. Special trains at low rates transported tens of thousands of believers from all over Hungary. The postal service issued special stamps in commemoration of the occasion. The atmosphere prevalent at the convention reflected the Christianity of Hungary and the pious, Christian, religious fervor of the Hungarian people. This Christian religious fervor did not limit itself to Catholic church frameworks; it had its influence upon the congregants of the other Christian churches and became characteristic of the entire Christian population of Hungary. Prime minister Imredi appeared at the convention and delivered one of the central speeches. His topic was "Christian Love":

> It was God's idea for the bread of love, coming out of the Last Supper on its world-conquering journey, to live in our midst by virtue of the bonds of His love in this world of ours, the creation of the hands of God.... Love radiates from God, it is the gift of God, it coexists here in our world with us, and it also spreads throughout the world. This love now faces its sublime task: it must rebuild the home of love. For the sake of the success of this work of construction, we must combine the divine concept expressed in Creation with the additional divine concept which created the Cross and the sacrifice of the Last Supper. In the concept of love we must discern a practical plan of operation of which St. Paul sang the most sublime hymn and in the name of which we strive for our rebirth. Love is an eternal

concept and a practical platform, our task being to build with it a strong, unconquerable fortress of courage. This is our historical task.... Time is pressing. We must harness ourselves to the execution of this work of Love, and the sooner the better.[20]

The minister of industry, Geza Bornemissza, was another participant in the convention. The subject of his speech was similar to that of the prime minister. He said, among other things,

The honoring of God and love of one's neighbor are the two elements of Jesus' doctrine. The ropes of neighborly love unite all, large and small, ignorant and erudite, poor and rich, tightening the links between them. The concepts of neighborly love and human cooperation bestow, from a social viewpoint, security in life and security at work; they also guarantee a just distribution of living resources needed to maintain life.... For this reason the church has always attempted to fill social life with the unifying force of neighborly love. The early Christians presented the most exalted examples of love and brotherhood. Medieval Christian regimes also determined the rights and obligations of the various social strata on the basis of Christian love.... We must apply the spirit of Christianity in all walks of economic life, so that our interpersonal relations be guided by a spirit of love and social justice, rather than by the love of profit.

To realize these ambitions government and society must cooperate. The government's Christian love guarantees human hearts tranquillity and soothes the most serious wounds of mankind.[21]

These two love-filled speeches, by the prime minister and his minister of industry, were delivered two days before the final ratification of the first anti-Jewish act, after it had been thoroughly discussed in Parliament, in the Upper House, and in their committees. These debates were widely covered by the media. In addition to impoverishing thousands of Jewish families, the debates concerning it provided an opportunity to express and incite hatred toward Jewry in general and Hungarian Jews in particular. A crowd of tens of thousands of believers, which had gathered to be indoctrinated by its leaders, attended this respectable and sanctimonious ceremony, ready to absorb the message they would utter. The crowd did indeed hear a definition of love and its praises. It may be assumed that they took these words to heart, and that some of the audience began to wonder. Those very leaders who spoke so enthusiastically in praise of love, were—together with their colleagues—the very people who, at the very same time, were actively engaged in besmirching the Jewish populace. These two diametrically opposed approaches—love of Christians on the one hand, and hatred of the Jews on the other—might have generated a certain degree of confusion concerning the nature of the concepts of love and hate. But, even if confusion did arise to any extent in the hearts of the believers as a result of the contradiction in their leaders' approach to the subject of love, the standpoint taken by the heads of the churches quickly enabled them to relieve themselves of any uncertainty.

The secular heads of state appeared on the speaker's podium at the eucharistic convention together with the leaders of the church. The latter had already expressed their opinion of the Jews on the occasion of the debate in the Upper House; now they also spoke up at the eucharistic convention.

The minister of industry did not merely hint in his speech at the existing cooperation between church and state: "the government is beginning to deal with social ills in accordance with the spirit of the great Popes and on the basis of Christian love. It is assisted in this execution of its responsibilities by the understanding and aid of the church and its institutions." The decisive significance of the expression "to deal...in accordance with the spirit of the...Popes and on the basis of Christian love" is sufficiently clear in light of the declared position of the church leaders in the Upper House. Quite correctly the minister relied on the example set by "medieval Christian regimes," which functioned "on the basis of Christian love." It was well known that those regimes were hardly based on social justice, and the attitudes toward their fellow human beings served as shining examples to be followed by the Hungarian government.

After these remarks by the minister of industry, the ranking bishop, Gyula Glattfelder, rose to express his agreement with the stand taken by the minister and his appreciation of the minister for his participation in the convention:

> The fact that a government member is participating in this convention demonstrates that the ancient traditions are very much alive in our land, and in perfect condition. Nothing in our land is secular; even things which would seem to partake of a secular nature—such as trade, industry, machines, and mechanics—are all interlinking with the most sublime goals.[22]

The close relationship displayed by the government Jew persecutors and the priesthood sheds light on the ideological background to an event that took place in Budapest while the convention was in session. A group of priests marched along one of the avenues of the capital and, upon arriving at the national headquarters of the Arrow-Cross party, dipped their flags in honor of the residents of the building.

The concluding speech at the eucharistic convention was delivered by
Cardinal Seredi. He, too, spoke of love, and ended his speech by saying,

> If we love God, we shall certainly love our neighbors, that is, our
> brethren, both individually and in general, all together, just as we love the
> various strata of our society, just as we love the various people and nations
> of the world.
>
> We shall thus, my dear brothers, be consistent in these two loves of
> ours, in order that the hymn always rise up, everywhere, from every mouth,
> in proper respect: Jesus triumphs, Jesus rules, Jesus commands![23]

It is evident that the "love of the peoples and the love of the nations"
mentioned by Cardinal Seredi excluded the Jews at this critical and tragic
moment in their history in Hungary.

It has already been noted that the highest-ranking guest of the convention was the personal representative of the pope, Cardinal Pacelli.
Pacelli was known to be an intelligent, considered, and cool politician,
well versed in the subjects in which he was engaged. It cannot be doubted
that a diplomat of Pacelli's stature was well aware of the anti-Jewish
legislative process that was in motion in the Hungarian Parliament at
the very moment of his sojourn in the Hungarian capital. It might be
supposed that in the name of Christian kindness and mercy, and as the
personal representative of the deputy of the founder of the religion of
love on earth, he might take advantage of the opportunity and raise his
voice against the evil being perpetrated before his very eyes.

But Pacelli preferred to ignore the hate and fanaticism that resulted
in the anti-Jewish legislation and, instead, made pointed mention of the
"wonderful atmosphere of love, the contribution of Christianity," that
prevailed during the convention period:

> This eucharistic convention has been held under conditions of love pangs.
> ... We shall not settle for spreading the message of love; rather, we shall
> rather spread throughout the world the doctrine of love in action. This
> love stems from our feelings, from the throbbing of our hearts and from
> our far-seeing determination. From this determination of ours—which is
> apparent only before God—there must develop day-by-day love-filled ac-
> tivity, which must succeed in overcoming the pettiness, conflict, quarreling,
> and egoism of both great and small.... Our love of God serves as a foun-
> dation stone of our love of our neighbors. Our love of God revitalizes it,
> directs it, grants it nobility, and encourages it to carry out heroic deeds.
> This neighborly love—this wonderful Christian contribution to the world—
> which cannot be expressed either in figures or in literature, exists every-
> where and makes its sublime contribution to the solution of the raging
> problems of social distress, and we shall be worthy of it only if our en-

couragement of love is from now on the alpha and omega of our entire existence.[24]

Pacelli made no attempt to clarify the nature of the "example of love in action" he discerned in the Hungarian capital and the like of which he desired to "spread throughout the world."

Even if Pacelli made no direct mention of the Jews, he did refer to them indirectly:

> Jesus conquers! He who so often was the recipient of the rage of his enemies, he who suffered the persecutions of those of whom he was one, he shall be triumphant in the future as well. . . . As opposed to the foes of Jesus, who cried out to his face, "Crucify him!"—we sing him hymns of our loyalty and our love. We act in this fashion, not out of bitterness, not out of a sense of superiority, not out of arrogance toward those whose lips curse him and whose hearts reject him even today.[25]

(He is quoted in the very same publication as attacking the Communists and mentioning the pope's warning against this danger.)

Pacelli relied on his audience, realizing that hints would suffice and that he had no need to specify the identity and names of those foes of Jesus who had cried out to his face, "Crucify him!" He was sure that his audience understood him well.

Pacelli's comment that toward the foes of Jesus "we act in this fashion, not out of bitterness, not out of a sense of superiority, not out of arrogance" was tinged with more than a little cynicism. How else is one to interpret his ignoring the sufferings of those persecuted?

The appearance of the heads of state and church before the participants in the eucharistic convention, and the speeches they made, prepared hitherto untrodden paths in the field of Hungarian Christian relations with their Jewish neighbors. Even before the eucharistic convention and before the anti-Jewish legislation, hostile statements made by leaders of church and state regarding the Jews were not uncommon. Nevertheless, after the adoption of the anti-Jewish act, discrimination against the Jews took on a seal of official approval. The motives behind this legislation were very far from the "comprehensive love" the eucharistic convention spoke so much about. This can only indicate that the speakers at the convention intended to hint unambiguously to their listeners that this "comprehensive love" was not to include the Jewish population.

In the Wake of the Act's Adoption

The adoption of the first anti-Jewish act did not result in the solution of "the Jewish problem," it did not remove the Jewish topic from the public agenda, and it had no noticeable tranquilizing effect. The atmosphere was saturated with antisemitic emotion.[26]

The leaders of the Christian churches contributed not a little to the repeated discussions and debates that the Jewish topic was subjected to in various public arenas. They addressed the Jewish topic again and again in public discussion. They generally dealt with the subject from two points of view—the limitations imposed by the act upon the Jews; and the damage done by the legislation to the validity of Jews' conversions to Christianity, as well as the corresponding harm done to the Christian churches.

The following excerpts show clearly that, with regard to the first viewpoint, the representatives of the churches supported the government unreservedly; they justified the government's action and even encouraged the government to continue with the anti-Jewish legislation and to entrench it even more deeply. With regard to the second consideration, however, the priesthood raised its voice in protest against those legislative definitions that, in its opinion, violated both church autonomy and the sanctity of the conversion process.

The Reformed church held a national convention of its Society of Spiritual Leaders. The convention took place in the town of Debrecen, the stronghold of Hungarian Calvinism. Participants included the head of the Hungarian Reformed church, Bishop Laszlo Ravasz, and many other church leaders from all parts of the country, as well as several from abroad.

A guest lecturer from England, Conrad Hoffmann, the secretary of the World Missionary Movement to the Jews, spoke of the reasons for antisemitism. The speaker proved to be generous to the Jews in stating that they were not the only ones responsible for antisemitism: "The Jews alone are not to be accused of antisemitism. Christians, too, must suffer pangs of conscience regarding antisemitism, for they have not been successful in converting the Jews to Christianity."[27]

References to the converts were ambivalent. On the one hand, Christianity claims that the way to Christian faith is open to everyone, and that one's racial origins are powerless to prevent one from taking the route to salvation that Christianity offers. On the other hand, however, accepting "the new Christians" into Christian Hungarian society clashed with the outlook of the members of that society. A further complication was introduced by the opinion prevalent at the time, both among church leaders and among the leaders of secular Hungary, that Hungarianism and Christianity were one and the same indivisible concept.[28]

Well aware of this problem, one Bela Papp, a spiritual leader from the town of Vac, spoke up at the convention: "With regard to our desire that the Jews become good Christians, we must not assume that every Jew who converts to Christianity will also become a good Hungarian, just as we would not want every Negro, Turk, or Chinese who converts to become Hungarian as well."[29]

In this way the speaker found an elegant escape from the obligation imposed upon him by Christianity with regard to his attitude toward converts. It was impossible to prevent the converts from joining the believers in Christianity, for once they had converted they were Christians in every respect, but it was possible to block their progress toward membership in Hungarian society.

It should be noted that the speaker based his concept of blocking the progress of the Jews upon their racial origins. This racist concept was expressed by a man of the cloth, at a convention of spiritual leaders, in the presence of the head of his church. The speaker also added that "the Christian churches should view Judaism as idolatry leading away from Jesus."[30]

Bishop Laszlo Ravasz summed up the convention discussions. He, too, referred to Judaism in a similar vein, declaring, "We shall never cause the Jews joining us to feel that they are persons of the second class, of inferior standing."[31] The bishop's message came over clearly: as long as Jews refrained from joining the bishop's faith, and remained Jewish, they were second-class persons, of inferior standing. The bishop succeeded in expressing succinctly the conceptual basis of the Hungarian government's anti-Jewish legislation: the Jews were justifiably being discriminated against, since they were inferior to Christian citizens of the state.

A short time later the Evangelical church held a district synod. In his speech the head of the church in Hungary, Bishop Sandor Raffay, referred to the anti-Jewish legislation, saying,

> I shall not deal with the question of the degree of need for this legislation. Neither shall I enter into a debate on the question of the extent to which the one-sided and egoistic behavior of the Jews brought about this legislation. . . . But for the sake of truth, it must be stated that this legislation is not as cruel as it seems at first glance.[32] The legislation interests us only insofar as it causes many of our believers spiritual suffering and gnawing anxiety. . . . Those in our midst who seek the tranquillity of belief in Jesus Christ we regard with understanding brotherly love, for such is the requirement of the Gospel of Jesus Christ.[33]

The ideas expressed by the heads of the two Protestant churches were similar. Their reference to "understanding brotherly love" was aimed at converts only. The head of the Evangelical church had no good words to say of the Jews except for the statement that "the legislation is not cruel." This was the spirit in which he interpreted, it would seem, the "requirement of the Gospel of Jesus Christ."

The bishop of the Evangelical church in Transdanubia, Bela Kapi, sent a Shepherd's Epistle to all the priests in his district, in which he, too, dealt with the anti-Jewish legislation: "Our church happily congratulates the government on its efforts aimed at introducing a Christian spirit into our economic, cultural, and social lives, and we willingly offer the assistance of our forces in carrying out this corrective activity." Further along in his epistle, he criticized the fact that "along with the numerous constructive regulations in the act limiting the activities of the Jews, there is a deficiency whereby state institutions have usurped the authority to decide upon the validity of the conversion of certain converts to Christianity." Nevertheless, the epistle ends with a declaration: "Our Evangelical church looks with Christian spirit upon the anti-Jewish legislation and the problems accompanying it."[34]

The Catholic church did not stand idly by, observing its Protestant sisters at work. At a synod held with the participation of the Catholic populace in the town of Ersekujvar, Bela Bangha, a high-ranking priest, made his appearance. In his speech he, too, referred to the fear that the act might violate the sanctity of Christian conversion. The speaker showed his understanding of the considerations of the legislators on this point, wondering if every case of conversion indicated a substantial change for the better in the life of the convert, a change that might bring about his spiritual purification:

> The problem is a difficult one, for the act of conversion in itself does not guarantee the simultaneous onset of a desire for a spiritual assimilatory process.... On the other hand, it would be a big mistake for us not to take sufficiently into account the revelation of a frank desire for such assimilation being expressed in the very act of conversion. It would likewise be an ignoring of justice. We must not adopt such steps as do not regard conversion itself as of sufficient importance, steps that may lead to a confrontation between church and state on the question of the interpretation of the concept of Christianity. Such a confrontation is liable to take place in our Christian state.... Even if there do exist certain difficulties in finding a solution to this problem, the legislator must act in such a way that, on the one hand, he succeeds in rejecting efficiently those undesirable elements which have penetrated the realms of economics and society, while on the other, he must not harm people who have for many

years now been following innocently and truthfully in the footsteps of Jesus.[35]

An impressive expression of the support of the Catholic church for the anti-Jewish legislation was revealed in a press item reporting a Synod of Catholic Bishops. The synod was held in the cardinal's palace in Budapest, with the participation of representatives of the two branches of the Catholic church in Hungary: the Latin branch and the Greek one. Cardinal Seredi chaired the conference. The newspaper reports that, regarding the Jewish question, the synod ruled as follows: "The Synod registers with satisfaction the fact that the Royal Government of Hungary strives to defend the interests of the Christian public in face of Jewish spiritual domination. Furthermore, the Synod expresses the opinion of the Catholic church concerning the sanctity of Christianity regarding converts." The paper adds that the Synod of Bishops referred the content of its discussion to the "most authorized state institutions."[36]

The protocol of the session reported by the press reflects the bishops' honest anxiety concerning both the converts to Christianity and the status of the church; at the same time, it also reflects their negative attitude toward the Jews against whom the proposed act was directed. The cardinal reported at the session that in discussions he had held with the prime minister and with the minister for religion and education, he had pointed out the basic deficiency of the proposed act in classifying certain converts as Jews. The cardinal had even expressed his opinion that "the legislation should be based on elements of justice and on the concept of loving one's neighbor," emphasizing that he considered it "very important to limit the activity of the Jews and to remove the Jewish spirit from the public and economic domains, as well as from additional walks of life." The reasons for this struggle were "the same reasons which led the church in our homeland to oppose bitterly the liberal outlook ever since the granting of full recognition to the Jewish religion."[37]

The cardinal raised ideas concerning the general substance of the act, stating that "justice and injustice are served in confusion in so general a bill, and it would be preferable for the bill to base the limitation of Jewish activity on an individual basis." The cardinal was worried by another aspect of the bill:

Whether we classify the Jews as a religious community or as a race, this legislation may provide a dangerous precedent if the treatment of Jews in our homeland is applied to people of other races as well, or to those of other religious communities.... Nevertheless, it is necessary to take additional measures against the Jews. We must uproot decisively all those phenomena that Judaism has introduced into our economic, our social, and our public lives, as well as into our legal system.

The bishops taking part in this discussion expressed their fears that the sanctity of conversion to Christianity might be violated by the proposed legislation, and spoke up in defense of those in their congregations who had nothing whatever in common with "the Jewish spirit." Furthermore, they brought up the problem of the offspring of mixed marriages.

Especially noteworthy in the discussion of the synod of bishops was the fact that no one spoke up against the very idea of anti-Jewish legislation. On the contrary, their support of the legislation was made very clear. "The Bishop of Szekesfehervar stresses that the synod of bishops was unanimous in its desire to put an end to the Jewish destructiveness." He was supported by the apostolic delegate of Rozsnyo, who also demanded "that additional, very firm steps be taken to remove the Jewish spirit, steps that will effectively prevent the spread of the ideas of the Social-Democrats, of the Freemasons, and of the Communists." To conclude the debate it was decided that two bishops would meet with the prime minister and put to him the stand of the Synod of Bishops.[38]

Thus, we have before us the clear and uniform opinion of the three great churches of Hungary as it was expressed by their leaders. Since these opinions were phrased and expressed by the men at the pinnacles of the church hierarchies, and considering the authoritarian atmosphere prevalent in the churches, it is very likely that the priesthood at all levels viewed these expressions of opinion as statements of policy that were to be followed, and in the light of which their flocks were to be led.

It should be noted that the opinions of the church leaders as expressed by them and as adduced above were not voiced during debate in any particular forum and were not stated under conditions of extreme stress. These were opinions expressed by respected leaders and voiced under the tranquil conditions of church conventions. The views of the church leaders as they were published in the various media presented to members of the government, of Parliament, and of the Upper House, as well as to the priesthood and the general public, a clear picture of their attitude toward the Jewish problem and of their approach to the anti-Jewish act. The bodies entrusted with this legislation were given a clear signal of approval for their past activities. With regard to the future, they received a green light to continue with the legislation, as well as encouragement from the highest spiritual authorities in Hungary to broaden the base of the legislation and to deepen it.

The Second Anti-Jewish Act

In mid-November 1938, less than six months after the adoption of the first anti-Jewish act, Imredi announced his intention of pressing for the adoption of further anti-Jewish legislation:

> Our country has an extremely delicate problem which we have to meet, just as we meet all our problems. I am speaking of the Jewish problem. ... We must reexamine the standpoints which guided us up until now, so as to find a solution enabling us to restore the leadership of the Christian elements in this country.... both in the press and in economic life.[39]

The formal excuse exploited by the prime minister for the additional anti-Jewish legislation was that "with the liberation of land from South Slovakia and its restoration to Hungary, the relative number of Jews in the population grew larger." Imredi hinted here at the beginning of the dismemberment of Czechoslovakia, which had begun in the fall of 1938 and had resulted in a gain of 1,040,000 new residents for Hungary, including eighty-seven thousand Jews.[40] This Jewish increment made almost no difference in the percentage of Jews in the entire population of Hungary, and so it is unlikely that this was the real motive driving the government to additional, stricter anti-Jewish legislation. It is more likely that Imredi was aware of the mood prevalent in Hungary, including the vehement antisemitic emotions rife among the Hungarian masses. Imredi had no intention of being outdone by the masses.[41]

Imredi approached his legislative goal energetically. A committee appointed by his party to prepare the details of the proposed act convened promptly. He participated, as did the minister of law who also served as the national chairman of the party, as did high-ranking officials in charge of the practical preparation of the proposed act.[42]

The bill was tabled in Parliament on December 23, 1938. At the time Parliament was recessed for the Christmas vacation, and so was convened especially for this purpose. While presenting the bill Imredi remarked cynically that he was presenting the Jews with a Christmas present.[43]

The basic idea of the second anti-Jewish act was that from then on, one's Jewishness would be determined not according to one's religious beliefs but rather according to one's racial origins. The ministerial explanation attached to the bill stated, "A person belonging to the Jewish denomination is at the same time a member of the Jewish racial community and it is natural that the cessation of membership in the Jewish denomination does not result in any change in that person's association with the racial community."[44]

The proposed bill intended to reduce still further the percentage of Jews active in the various fields. Contrasting with the 20 percent fixed in the first anti-Jewish act, the second anti-Jewish bill fixed a maximum of 6 percent for Jewish activity. This percentage was approximately equal to the percentage of Jews in the general population. The act aimed at bringing about a changing of the guard in the realms of economics and culture, in favor of the Hungarian middle class. "The object of the bill is that capital in Hungary should work under Christian direction," announced Imredi.[45]

At a session of the parliamentary committee, Kornel Kelemen read out a declaration in the name of the opposition and in the name of his party, the independent National Christian party: "For the sake of defending the Hungarian race we are prepared to vote for any bill serving the good of the nation and its future."[46]

The chairman of the United Christian party, Count Janos Zichy, made mention of his antisemitic past, saying that he "has been fighting for forty-four years against Jewish domination. The Clerical People's party once was an object of general hatred, merely because it attempted to prevent the Jewish question from becoming a general problem." The speaker went on to criticize the proposed act for determining which of the converts to Christianity would be considered Christian. "According to the Christian view, every convert is a Christian." He admitted the difficulty in applying this view in practice within the framework of the act under consideration, for then "thousands and tens of thousands will come begging to convert."[47]

Another speaker at the committee session, Lajos Makray, announced that he was basing his views on that of the church and on the Catholic outlook:

> While it is true that the proposed act does not violate Catholic principles, yet it violates the concept of purification of the soul which underlies conversion. . . . I have nothing against the proposed act itself, and thus it would be preferable to make those changes in it which would enable its adoption without any doubts or pangs of conscience.[48]

The atmosphere of antisemitic incitement continued while the proposed bill was debated. The people saw that the vast majority of those who were opposed to some paragraph or other of the proposed bill—

mainly concerning the converts to Christianity—did not avoid expressing their antisemitic opinions. "There is no question but that we have to expel the Jews from economics, from culture, and from politics. No matter how strong the idea of 'general love of mankind' is in our midst, we have to safeguard Hungarianism against the surplus economic and cultural spirit of the Jews," one of the speakers, one Janos Szeder, stated. His statement reflected the viewpoint of most of the participants in the debate.[49]

No wonder, then, that during the debate on the proposed bill there took place a murderous attack on the worshippers at the central synagogue of the Neologic congregation on Dohany Street in Budapest. On February 2, 1938, a Friday night, as the congregation was coming out of the synagogue, hand grenades were hurled at them. One person was killed, and twenty-two wounded. The investigation pointed to the Arrow-Cross party. It is reasonable to assume that the prevailing hate-filled atmosphere, largely nourished by the antisemitic expressions voiced both in the parliamentary debate and elsewhere, contributed considerably to preparing public opinion for the attack.

A few days after the grenade attack in Budapest, Imredi appeared at a party convention in the town of Szekesfehervar. As could have been expected, he spoke of the Jewish question without touching on the attack on the worshippers. "Christianity is not a mere slogan, but rather an innermost experience. During the most recent decades a foreign spirit has taken over various fields of Hungarian cultural life, and as we strive to restore to ourselves these positions, we have need of a healthy Hungarian spirit."[50]

The United Christian party held a meeting in which the members of its factions in Parliament and in the Upper House took part. After the discussions the following resolution was adopted: "In accordance with its already-existing program, the Party welcomes the adoption of the aims of the anti-Jewish legislation and records happily the amendments accepted by the prime minister in accordance with the Party position."[51] The amendments refer to the problem of the converts.

For reasons irrelevant to the scope of this paper, the regent of Hungary, Admiral Horthy, decided to dismiss Prime Minister Imredi. A noteworthy, piquant detail is that the direct excuse for his dismissal was the revelation that Imredi's father had been Jewish. When rumors began to circulate in Budapest about Imredi's Jewishness, he tried to deny them, but when Horthy placed before him documents testifying to his Jewishness, he was forced to accept the verdict and resign.[52]

In Imredi's stead the regent appointed Count Pal Teleki as prime minister on February 16, 1939. He had served as minister of culture and education in Imredi's government.

Teleki was a professor of geography and was considered an intellectual. In cartography he had won international acclaim and status. He had been one of Horthy's "men of Szeged" who had brought about the counterrevolution of 1919. He had served as prime minister from July 1920 to April 1921. During his term of office Hungary had passed its "numerus clausus" act, which imposed limits on Jewish youth with regard to university study, while during his second term of office as prime minister, he had the second anti-Jewish act adopted, as we shall see below. As Katzburg puts it, "thus he symbolized the continuity of Hungarian anti-Jewish policy throughout the period."[53]

Katzburg states further:

> His anti-Jewish ideology was based on the broad historical and social conception of a scholar, combined with a deep inner conviction and fundamental religiosity. These characteristics, together with his considerable personal prestige, added weight to his views. Dezso Sulyok describes Teleki as a "deep rooted antisemite, the most unaccommodating anti-Jewish politician of the Trianon period. In his quiet, contemplative, and soft manner, he stood up against the Jewish national minority more decidedly than anyone else." Teleki's antisemitism was further buttressed by his racial ideology.[54]

The historian Macartney describes Teleki as "a most dedicated Catholic.... In his philosophical outlook on society and politics, the barb of nationalistic roughness was removed by his delicate and profound Christianity.... Oppression and injustice were opposed, according to his outlook, to the laws of humanity and of Christianity."[55]

As a member of the Imredi cabinet, Teleki participated in the preparation of the proposed second anti-Jewish act. He composed the ideological basis that was attached to the bill. As he himself says, he was the most radical member of the Imredi government on the Jewish question.[56]

In one of his speeches in the Upper House he dealt at length with his theoretical views of Judaism and the problem it was causing the Hungarian people. In his opinion, the Jews

> are a racial group living according to a tradition thousands of years old. Consequently Jewish thought has remained unique and closed to its environment.... We can speak of a race, but I put the stress on the four-thousand-year-old Jewish tradition. Their closed lifestyle still exists, and is unlikely to change, not even by means of conversion. This is not a matter of mere religion, but rather one combining religious and national aspects.

The religion is merely one of the components of the entirety, and though their religion may change, much of their original world of thought remains. ... Assimilation is especially difficult for us, for Christian society has already absorbed that world of thought which Judaism brings with it from the Orient and from the Occident—mainly in the economic field, though also in other walks of life, especially theater, the press, and other fields shaping public opinion.[57]

These words of commentary come through clearly in the ministerial explanation added to the proposed second anti-Jewish act, which was apparently composed by Teleki himself.[58]

Teleki spelled out his practical approach to the Jewish problem less than a fortnight after his appointment as prime minister. On February 28, 1939, Teleki appeared at a rally of the Urban Christian party for Hungarian Life, which controlled the Budapest municipality, where he was elected party leader.[59]

Teleki began by recalling memories of his first steps in politics, which he took

under the tutelage and influence of Karoly Wolf. We left Szeged together with Gombos, our leader, the regent, all united in order to carry out a certain task in which we are still engaged. ... We feared that after the initial enthusiasm, after the first Christian reaction to the war and to Communism [he was referring to the white counterrevolution and the White Terror], we would return to the situation which was prevalent before the World War. But this is not so. It turned out that the war and the economic crisis which followed it were mere symptoms of the great spiritual crisis the world is experiencing.

Our present Christian reaction is not a reaction to the World War, but rather our reaction to the liberalism and materialism of the nineteenth century and of the early twentieth century. This approach of ours is connected with the fact that we are at present engaged in our final struggle against Judaism. A final struggle, but not an easy one. The struggle will not end within three months or even six months, not even within a year or two. It is a great and drawn-out struggle, whose dimensions suit the matter it is intended to deal with. ... This struggle may perhaps involve difficulties, and we must state this openly, for if the Christian populace is unaware of this fact, it will be unable to withstand the burden of the struggle. ... Over the past twenty years we have undergone some difficult periods, but we have never despaired, we have never given up. We have remained united under the banner of Karoly Wolf; we have continued our struggle and have never forsaken the banner.

Our plan is as follows: to persevere in our struggle for the Christian idea, and in the end we will triumph!

> Our hopes for victory are especially bolstered up here in our capital city, for this is where our strength was first fired by the strength of the enthusiasm and charismatic personality of our leader, Karoly Wolf.[60]

Teleki left no doubt in the hearts of his audience that he intended to outline his policy regarding the Jews and the Jewish problem in accordance with the blunt, antisemitic example set by Karoly Wolf. And so he did.

At that same rally Teleki was warmly praised by his predecessor, the former prime minister, Imredi:

> Teleki's words have made a deep impression on our hearts, for he is one of the most veteran fighters for the Christian idea. . . . I know that in Count Teleki's personality such a fighter for the Christian idea takes over the scepter of leadership as will, by his force of will and his perseverance, bring these ideas to fruition. The request I make of all those present here is that they serve as Teleki's faithful men-of-arms, just as they have been the faithful men-of-arms of the Christian-national idea over the past twenty years.[61]

The change in premiership had no effect upon the legislative process instituted in the Imredi period. The second anti-Jewish bill was placed before the parliamentary committee, approved by thirty-six votes to twenty-six, and brought before the parliamentary plenum for debate.[62]

The minister of law, Andras Tasnadi-Nagy, presented the government view on the subject of anti-Jewish legislation:

> It seems to me that no topic has been the subject of such comprehensive and thorough public debate in such broad circles as this one. The broadest circles of society, of their various strata, various associations and organizations, have considered it. . . . Ever since the month of November the press has dealt daily with this topic in its editorials, in articles composed by experts. Certain papers have even instituted special columns to discuss this topic.
>
> There is need for a strong decision to put this matter in order, not only for the welfare of the nation, but also for the welfare of the Jews.[63]

The minister of law went on to deny allegations that the source of the anti-Jewish legislation was "foreign influence":

> Contrary to this view, I point out not only the Hungarian movements of 1919 but also the adoption of the "Numerus Clausus" Act, which took place during Count Teleki's previous term of office as prime minister. That legislation was, in fact, the initial step in the present legislation. I also note the founding in 1895 of the parliamentary People's party. Among the

important goals of that party the idea of limiting the activity of the Jewish spirit and the desire to oppose Jewish domination were preeminent.

He objected to the accusation that the present legislation contained "antisemitism per se and a brutal lack of humanity."[64] This law is the first step in the defense of the Hungarian race, while economically it is merely an extension of the anti-Jewish act adopted last year. . . . We must introduce a Hungarian spirit into our economic lives, and these lives must be dominated by the Christian spirit."[65]

The Debate in the Upper House: The Stand of Church Leaders

After the proposed law was adopted by Parliament, it was sent over for debate in the Upper House, and was considered there initially by a "joint committee." The speaker of the Upper House, Laszlo Gorgey, said that "the spirit of the Hungarian race lives in this proposal; it solves the most important existential problem of Hungarianism, opens a new page in the relations between Hungarians and Jews, and ensures a national Christian lifestyle."[66]

The first spokesman in the debate was Cardinal Justinian Seredi, the leader of the Catholic church in Hungary. In his opening remarks he referred to the problem of the converts, saying that had the proposed act dealt only with blocking the Jews, he would have related to it as a legalist, by virtue of his position as a member of the Upper House. However, since Christianity was entangled in every stage of the proposed act, he would relate to it as a representative of the church, for the very people the law applied to were not only Hungarian citizens but his congregants as well, his Christian brethren: "If we are speaking of a Christian Hungary—and we do believe that our country is Christian—it is thus self-evident that Christian concepts should be reflected in our legislation." For this reason he did not view favorably the fact that the proposed law distinguished between one Christian and another.

The cardinal went on to voice several practical proposals, the adoption of which would be aimed at preventing the Jews from streaming to Hungary, infiltrating the country's borders, and receiving citizenship. The cardinal added, "It is not sufficient to make use of the law to block those Jews who should be blocked. It is also important to do away with the phenomena which the Jews introduced into our public lives in the economic and social fields, and to liquidate that Jewish spirit because of which the government has seen fit to table the proposed bill." The cardinal stressed that he was making his comments in the name of the Synod of

Catholic Bishops, a body that had no desire to cause the government and the state any difficulties whatever. He also saw fit to voice his comments "so that present-day or future readers of the proposed bill will be able to read that the Synod of Bishops has based itself on the grounds of righteousness and love."[67]

The next speaker was Bishop Gyula Glattfelder, bishop of Csanad. In his speech he elaborated on the concept of "spirit over matter" and spoke critically of the fact that the proposed law did not sufficiently recognize the purifying power of Christianity. Consequently, it did not recognize the converts as absolute Christians.

The bishop mentioned favorably and picturesquely the veteran anti-semites who had used to be active in the Clerical People's party: "those who strove to restore Christianity to its pristine glory were busy with the Jewish problem at the same time as today's policymakers were still babes in arms."

Glattfelder went on to mention what he called "the Jewish spirit":

> Even those values and topics viewed by the Hungarian nation and by the Christian religion as sacred and worthy of adoration, Judaism regarded as objects to be bargained over.... Since the proposed law aims to restore the balance, we must accept it. The condition in which Christian society finds itself requires emergency treatment.
>
> We must respect the public need, yet we must be careful not to let emotions of hatred or injustice overwhelm this special legislation. Therefore: if anyone compares this legislation with the acts of the early Popes and church princes and with the severe restrictions they, too, imposed on the Jews—he had better note the substantial distinction between imposing restrictive decrees out of prayer and tears and doing so to the accompaniment of gypsy music and indecent language, for the distinction is not merely one of style.

The bishop criticized the law's attitude toward the validity of the conversion of certain converts, as reflected in the opening paragraph of the proposed law:

> Though we accept this proposed anti-Jewish bill, yet under no circumstances can we agree to the tendency to cause Christians harm. A law denying Christianity severely damages the faith of a believing Christian.
>
> Every defensive act aimed at preventing unworthy elements from penetrating the inner sanctum is acceptable to us. Nevertheless, in a Christian country there is no way to divest Christians of the validity of their Christianity. We cannot agree that the conditions of converts and assimilationists be worse than those of the Galician mob [Jews who had migrated during the last few generations from Galicia].

The bishop stressed once again that he had searched in vain for recognition of the influence and superiority of the spirit in the proposed
law: "The regard for jobs, wages, and percentages cannot ensure a Christian spirit in public life or in the press. If we remove the Jews from the
editorial boards of the newspapers, but the destructive Jewish spirit remains there, it will be a most painful scandal."[68]

The bishop's criticism was aimed at the aforementioned first paragraph, in which he demanded amendments. Regarding the proposed law
in general and regarding his attitude to its proponents, he said, "The
honorable prime minister may rest assured that he enjoys the full confidence of the Upper House.... The only conclusion to be drawn is that
since the proposed bill is supposed to ensure the life of the Christian
public in this state room, it should be adopted in general, while the first
paragraph of the proposed bill should be opposed."[69]

The next speaker was Bishop Laszlo Ravasz, head of the Hungarian
Reformed church. Just like his predecessors, he, too, criticized the first
paragraph of the proposed bill and its definitions, which were liable to
cause harm to the converts. He focused on the significance of the assimilation of the Jews and on the purifying spiritual value of the assimilatory
process. His overall approach to the proposed law resembled that of his
predecessors: the law was to be supported.

> There exists a Jewish problem which must be solved, while taking care to
> minimize the harm done to Hungarian Christians and ensuring them max-
> imal advantages.... The proposal is based on the only right and acceptable
> point of view: we are talking of the problem of our struggle against the
> Jewish spirit. This topic may find its solution within the lengthy and com-
> plex process of assimilation ... and so a law must be formulated to speed
> up the assimilatory process and neutralize all those factors which are liable
> to interfere with this process. Consequently we must adopt the law in its
> entirety, for rejecting it may bring about an even worse situation than we
> are in at the present time, a situation extremely difficult for the nation, for
> the Jews, for the administration, and for us all. We must avoid bringing
> about such a situation in which the ramifications of this bill, proposed so
> as to free us of the focused and corruptive effects of Judaism, will be weaker
> than the harm it will have caused all those ex-Jews who have become as
> us in their souls and in their Hungarianism.[70]

The representative of the Evangelical church and its highest-ranking
official in Hungary, Bishop Sandor Raffay, repeated the main points
already made by his colleagues, the heads of the other Christian churches.
He, too, spoke in favor of assimilation and against the stipulation of the
proposed law, according to which even after conversion, the convert

might still be regarded as a Jew. He repeated Glattfelder's suggestion that outstanding intellectuals be awarded privileges similar to those enjoyed by outstanding athletes, such as Olympic champions. Yet, despite his criticism, he too—like his predecessors—undertook to vote for the bill because he was

> convinced that its rejection might well put us, nationally speaking, in a most unpleasant situation . . . and worried by the fact that despite the tablers of the bill being desirous of taking steps in favor of the Hungarian Christians, they are causing Christians harm, for they have ruled that converts remain Jews in the future as well, and not only the converts themselves but their offspring, too. Any person who converts to Christianity becomes a Christian. The concept of "returning to Judaism" should be removed in its entirety from the proposed bill. . . . The most important question is not "who is Jewish" but rather what can be done for the Christian nation.

He announced that he would appreciate it

> if the law were to stipulate that from now on no Jew will be allowed to obtain Hungarian citizenship; furthermore, if the law were to forbid mixed marriages between Christians and Jews. . . . I willingly accept the proposed bill in its general form, in the hope that the government takes into account those proposed amendments worthy of its consideration.[71]

Thus did the heads of the Christian churches, the spiritual leaders of some 98 percent of Hungarian Christians, make their voices heard on the topic so fateful for the Jews of Hungary. Their speeches speak for themselves, and testify to the character of their speakers.[72]

The minister of law, Tasnadi-Nagy, represented the government in defending the proposed bill. He described the basic need for the proposed anti-Jewish law by referring to the views of men of stature, citing statements made by the late Bishop Ottokar Prohaszka and by the priest Bela Bangha on the Jewish question.

The minister of law expressed his agreement with "the wonderful statement by Glattfelder, that there really exists a Jewish spirit and that the Christian society maintains its right to restore the equilibrium. . . . It is high time the Jews felt the existence of this problem, but for some reason they have not paid it any attention."[73]

The minister denied Glattfelder's assumption that the proposed bill had been prepared with a lack of sensitivity or lightheadedly, claiming that he could

> say with a clear conscience that neither he nor anyone else of those who brought the proposed bill before the legislature was influenced by any

negative feelings or by hatred. On the contrary, he feels the pain of all those hurt, but the confrontation is not between individuals; the nation, too, must be considered, and the proposed bill serves the future of the nation.

Therefore, the minister of law rejected the opinion that the proposed bill was un-Christian, was not based on the love of all creatures. "In the name of divine and man-made laws, I ask that the proposed bill be adopted."[74]

Prime Minister Teleki, too, participated in the debate; his speech includes two points worthy of special mention. Like his minister of law, Teleki ensured his audience that in tabling the proposed anti-Jewish law he "was not guided by any desire to persecute the Jews or by feeling of hatred or of sadism, or any other similar emotion." The prime minister went on to deny the allegation that the proposed bill was presented under foreign influence: "I do not feel that this is so. No foreign mentality guided me in this context. My view is based upon the elements of a purely Hungarian outlook, and this applies to me not only today—it was the case twenty years ago as well, long before these attitudes developed outside the borders of Hungary."[75]

Two exceptions from among the members of the Upper House must be mentioned. Count Gyula Karolyi resigned his membership in the Upper House in protest against the proposed legislation. Lorant Hegedus was utterly opposed to the proposed legislation because in his opinion "it contradicted both the Christian approach and the national viewpoint. From both of these points of view the proposed bill is a retreat."[76]

Among the rest of the members of the Upper House, some supported the bill wholeheartedly, even demanding that its language be rendered stricter in various places. Most of the members accepted the proposed bill as it had been tabled. There were also those who only paid lip service to their liberalism or to their religious outlook, but ended up voting for the bill.

The fate of the first paragraph of the bill, concerning the definition of a Christian, remained in the balance. A confrontation developed between the government and the Parliament on the one hand and the Upper House that opposed several declarations of paragraph 1 on the other. The debate on this paragraph underwent various metamorphoses in the different committees: a joint committee, a formulating committee, and then, once again, a joint committee.

Consequent to the opposition of the Upper House, the proposed law was brought back for reconsideration by the joint committee. The atmosphere prevalent at the renewed sessions of the committee was similar to that which had dominated the discussions of the same committee two weeks earlier. Once again bishops Glattfelder, Ravasz, and Raffay took part in the debate. They repeated the reservations they had expressed two weeks before regarding the converts to Christianity, but nevertheless supported the adoption of the legislation after making a number of amendments to its first paragraph. These amendments were intended to lighten the burden of the converts and to broaden the base of those converts who would be exempted from the restrictions of the anti-Jewish act.

Ravasz, faithful to his beliefs, voiced the opinion that "Christianity's ability to reshape human lives is so decisive that even a person who is completely Jewish according to his origins can assimilate entirely within a certain period of time." Ravasz added that despite his displeasure at various aspects of the bill regarding the converts, "the Upper House will not be doing the nation good service if it refuses to adopt the bill."[77] The other two bishops spoke in a similar vein.

The minister of law expressed his appreciation of the bishops and of all those who were striving to settle the disagreements between the Parliament and the Upper House so as to enable the law to be adopted by both sections of the legislature. The committee's proposals were sent back to the plenary session of the Upper House, and it began to debate them on April 15, 1939.

Once again the bishops, the heads of the churches, spoke. Cardinal Seredi, who stressed once again that he was speaking in the name of the Synod of Catholic Bishops, said that he perceived in the solution of the Jewish problem a national interest as well as the legitimate self-defense of the nation:

> "I declare that in our treatment of the Jewish question I perceive an act of justifiable self-defense, and for this reason the state is entitled to limit the existing rights of its citizens, even those of its Christian citizens.
>
> The concept of imposing limitations on the Jews is acceptable to all. Part of the Jewish population—disguised as the press, art, literature, poetry, and music—has cast doubt upon values sacred to Christians. They have done so with the silent acquiescence of the other Jews and despite the constant protests of Catholics.... Even if imposing limitations upon the Jews means a certain denial of rights, the present bill should not be defined as 'a law of punishment.'[78] The influence of the Jews must be curtailed, for they have sinned much against Christian Hungary.... We must ascribe the responsibility to the liberal regime which facilitated the Jewish tricks, despite the constant protests of Catholic Hungarians." Seredi accepted the proposed law in general.[79]

Bishop Raffay, too, spoke at that session. He stated that life had dictated the need for the proposed law. "The Jews themselves are one of the factors leading to the need for this legislation." He also pointed out the limitations of the proposed bill: " 'There are people who converted to Christianity decades ago, but the proposed law classifies them, too, as Jews.' He would prefer that the road to assimilation not be blocked. He accepted the proposed legislation with certain reservations, and welcomed the committee's amendments concerning the converts."[80]

The disagreements, however, were not settled, and paragraph 1 of the proposed bill became an obstacle to its final adoption. In light of the stand taken by the church leaders and their supporters in the Upper House, a self-evident difference of opinion developed between the two parts of the legislature. This difference of opinion threatened to develop into a constitutional crisis, and under certain conditions could even have led to the dispersing of Parliament and the calling of early elections, a year before they were scheduled (May 1940). An increase in the strength of the extreme right-wing parties was expected in these elections. Neither the premier and his party nor the church leaders wanted that. Thus Teleki made a special effort to prevent the conflict between the two houses, and tried to convince the Upper House to accept the proposed bill in its original form, as it had been approved by the Parliament, without the committee's amendments.

Prime Minister Teleki reiterated his view that the complaint that the proposed legislation had been influenced by "foreign ideologies" should be rejected. Nevertheless, he referred to the importance of race and of blood, declaring,

> I support this position, both scientifically and socially. I have been furthering it, both in lectures and in writing, for over twenty years, i.e.: I took this stand long before it became possible to attribute it to the influence of any external factor.
>
> Certain racial characteristics are liable to become dominant to such an extent that in cases of mixed marriage, these dominant characteristics appear at the expense of the weaker side. Anyone having a knowledge, any knowledge, of biology and the other natural sciences is aware of these facts, the validity of which is indisputable.

The prime minister agreed with Cardinal Seredi that Christianity has an assimilating effect, and claimed that the proposed law

> reflects the opinions, the outlooks, and the needs of the population as these have been formulated over decades, and serves merely as a remedy to prevent the poisoning of the body of the nation. The change perpetrated

by Judaism in the body, the character, and the thought processes of the Hungarian nation involves the greatest of dangers; this change is felt even in the thought processes of the Christian elite, which is unsullied in the purity of its blood.

The prime minister, too—like the head of the Catholic church before him—referred to the denial of the rights of a large body of citizens. To justify this denial the prime minister made use of the very same reasoning as was voiced by the head of the Catholic church:

> Though it is true that the proposed bill does entail a denial of rights from many points of view, nevertheless, considering the vital interests of the entire nation, this is nothing but justifiable self-defense against the deep penetration of a foreign body into the national body....I have stated explicitly that this is not persecution, but merely self-defense....The expectations of Christian society, that this bill be adopted, are unambiguous and absolutely justified.[81]

Later on Bishop Ravasz also took part in the same debate. At first he stressed that it was necessary to adopt the proposed bill because

> its rejection would leave the urgent problem unsolved, and not solving the problem would cause harm not only to the entire nation, but to Judaism as well....We must ask: do we have the right to entrust the economic administration and spiritual direction of Hungary to a population group, the complete assimilation of which is doubtful? Has it become so Hungarian and so Christian that it should be permitted to take part in the leadership of the nation in the economic and spiritual spheres?
>
> In general, we must state that despite its numerous values, despite its spiritual superiority, and despite its brilliant intelligence, the spirit of the Jews is nothing but a rootless, alienated, and decadent spirit.

The bishop boasted of his antisemitic past, and made it clear to his audience that

> as early as 1917 he had determined his stand on the Jewish question and his views had not changed since.[82]...The fact that Judaism differs from Hungarianism racially and religiously, with regard to its future and with regard to its historical past, is immutable. The alien nature of the Jewish spirit is the result of all these. Christian culture and national life must take this fact into consideration.

The bishop took advantage of the opportunity to dispatch a strongly worded warning to the Jews:

> In Western democracies there is unbridled incitement on the part of the Jews against all those states which adopt anti-Jewish laws, including Hun-

gary. I ascribe considerable significance to the fact that Hungarian Jewry will reject this defense of itself.... I repeat once again, that those democracies, too, will one day face the Jewish problem. If they have Jews, they will have a Jewish problem. The two have always gone together.[83]

In conclusion the bishop addressed the converts to Christianity: "There is a consoling and calming force accompanied by humility and a modesty of spirit. If one suffers innocently, by this suffering of his he weakens those very elements in the proposed law which are a possible result of human weakness."[84]

Regarding the bishop's statement, it should be noted, first of all, that his view of the Jews—racially, spiritually, etc.—and that of the prime minister are very similar, and, secondly, that he viewed the suffering of the converts as "innocent suffering." This is not valid for the Jews.

In his rebuttal the minister of law referred to Ravasz's statement, and expressed his astonishment at Ravasz's willingness to accept the proposed law only in general. "According to his statements about Judaism, he could have been expected to adopt the proposed law in all its detail, in its original form."[85]

Bishop Glattfelder spoke again later on in the debate. He spoke not only in his own name and in the name of the bishops, but appeared this time as the spokesman for the Upper House. "The Upper House has proved that it is not interested in quarreling either with the government or with the Parliament, and so it has adopted, in general, the proposed law." He requested the House to adopt the amendments as they were formulated in committee. "Assimilation must be permitted. Christianity has the power to shape the character of man, to develop his soul, and to bring about assimilation. Acceptance of Christianity, Christian education, and a Christian environment are of such influence that no doubt can be cast upon their value."

He related how, in 1895, as a young student, he was an eyewitness to an aroused mob denigrating the cardinal and spitting on him as he stepped out of the Upper House, for he had opposed the full emancipation of the Jews:

> "Today, too, excitement is rife, but let us not be afraid of the thunderings and the storms, for even after the most violent storm the skies clear up—and then we shall rejoice and be happy, for we will have seen that our conscience is clear and that our soul is undamaged. I pray for the unbelievers, as well, and they must understand the viewpoint of the Christian church: Christianity is not our uniform, our symbol, our boy scout garb—it is a spiritual renewal, revelation, Jesus' mystic mercies, and thus it is

immeasurable mathematically; it must be believed in." He said that the committee's amendments satisfy him absolutely and he requested that they be adopted.[86]

The minister of law spoke once again, saying that in contrast with the opinions expressed considering the possibility of assimilation, he relied on the views of great men, including the famed late Hungarian bishop, Ottokar Prohaszka, in stating that assimilation is impossible. The minister even referred to the insulting of the cardinal mentioned by Glattfelder: "The dastardly event which occurred to the cardinal forty-five years ago merely demonstrates that it was not a Hungarian spirit which prevailed in the land at the time. For this reason it is important for the Hungarian spirit to prevail in Hungary."[87]

The Upper House adopted the proposed bill with the committee's amendments and referred it back to the Parliament. The amendments to paragraph 1 of the bill were intended to increase the number of converts to whom the law would not apply.

A parliamentary committee considered the Upper House's amendments and expressed its disapproval of most of them. One of those who rejected the amendments was Mihaly Kolozsvari-Borcsa, who, relying on statistics, claimed that the amendments would enable tens of thousands of converts to circumvent the law, and pointed out "the harmful influence the Upper House amendments might have on the Christian nature of the press."[88]

The Parliament reconvened and debated the question without delay. The chairman, Janos Makkai, said that the proposed bill, as prepared by the Parliament, had the support of over 90 percent of the population. He indicated that adopting the Upper House amendments would result in the problem not being solved.

A representative of the ruling party, Imre Molnar, made his party's opinion clear: "The conception and birth of the proposed bill express the common desire of the entire nation; they were not brought about by a single party."

Another representative of that party, Domonkos Festetics, denied that the government had imposed the rejection of the Upper House amendments upon the party. He expressed his rage at "the forming of the impression that we are quarreling and debating the number of degenerate, valueless Jews, whereas we should be discussing serious topics. I do not accept the proposed amendments because in my opinion anyone born a Jew with Jewish ancestors is a Jew."

The Parliament voted to reject the alterations proposed by the Upper

House to paragraph 1 of the proposed law, adopting in their stead a few amendments of lesser significance.[89]

In light of the disagreement between the two houses, the chairmen of the Parliament and of the Upper House had to summon a joint committee of reconciliation. In the discussions of the joint committee, held on April 26, 1939, Bishop Glattfelder was one of the speakers for the Upper House. He opened by pointing out that the Upper House had no intention of preventing the adoption of the bill:

> It will suffice to note that among the members of the Upper House there are those who, forty or fifty years ago, focused the nation's attention—both orally and in writing—on the fact that the strengthening of the Jewish spirit was not to be tolerated.... We announce openly that every word uttered in the Upper House was intended solely to free converts to Christianity from the limitations of this bill. All steps taken by the Upper House were aimed at achieving this goal. All the Christian churches agree that every resident living in this country who has accepted the Christian religion is entitled to enjoy all the rights of citizenship. This concept is a very old one for us; it has been a foundation stone of our political regime ever since the days of St. Istvan.... All the Christian churches are united in their view that one's adherence to Christianity confirms one's links with Hungarianism. No one can possibly be interested in nullifying ideas proposed by the Parliament, ninety-five percent of which are acceptable to the Upper House, because of a miserable misunderstanding between the two houses. No one can be interested in such a situation—except for the Jews. Therefore, we must strive to find the denominator common to the views of both sides.[90]

Bishop Ravasz, too, voiced the opinion that

> there is no difference in national feeling, in good will, and in self-sacrifice between the two Houses. Why, then, are we to assume there is no possibility of the two legislative bodies getting together? ... In accepting the amendment to paragraph 1 as proposed by the Upper House, it is as if we are expressing our appreciation of the Hungarian genius for its assimilatory ability and of Christianity for its regenerative, remedial force. We must do everything we can to reach agreement.[91]

The conceptual difference that led to the disagreement between the two houses was expressed clearly and succinctly in the summary made by the chairman of the joint committee of reconciliation, Janos Szeder: "The proposed bill, as worded by the Parliament, casts a doubt upon the possibility of Jews assimilating and even denies the concept of assimilation as a possible solution of the Jewish problem. The stand of the Upper House contradicts this view, and views assimilation and intermingling in a positive light." In his opinion, it was important to adopt the proposed bill as prepared by the Parliament in order to provide a satisfactory solution to the problem.[92]

Cardinal Seredi and bishops Glattfelder and Ravasz were among the delegates of the Upper House in the subcommittee.[93]

Seredi proved reconciliatory, and announced that by virtue of the reasoning voiced during the debates of the committee of reconciliation he himself tended toward a compromise. He was even taking into consideration the good will shown by the Parliament in its willingness to reach a compromise in light of the efforts at mediation made by the minister of law. For these reasons he accepted the proposals of the subcommittee. He took "into account the fact that this difficult problem has caused considerable anxiety in our public and social lives, and has threatened to lead our political lives into crisis. A solution to the problem adopted in a tranquil atmosphere will provide both our country and our political lives with the required calmness." The cardinal did not miss this opportunity to utter his declaration, with its predictable content and style, making it clear that "he, and all the members of the Upper House together with him, without exception, had spoken up in defense of their Christian brethren when they had presented their amendments to the proposed bill as it had been referred to them by the Parliament."[94]

After the adoption of the compromise amendments, the proposed bill was very similar to the Parliament's original proposal. The amendments enlarged to some extent the group of converts to Christianity to whom the law would not apply. The Hungarian legislator heaped compensation for this concession upon the shoulders of the Jewish populace, as the historians have said: "But to balance this concession the economic restrictions on Jews were increased."[95]

The amendments proposed by the subcommittee were approved by the joint committee of reconciliation by 149 votes to 59, and were referred to the Parliament.[96] The law was adopted on May 4, 1939, made public on August 22, 1939, and included in the Law Code under the heading "Law to Limit the Expansion of the Jews in the Public and Economic Domain."

The law did considerable harm to the Jews of Hungary. Its main effect was economic. According to the minister of law, some twenty thousand jobs previously occupied by Jews would now pass into Christian hands. In the opinion of certain economists, between sixty and seventy thousand breadwinners lost their positions as a result of the second anti-Jewish law. Including their families, some two hundred thousand people were harmed.

The law caused other damage, as well: to the right of the Jews to vote, to their employment in the civil service, to their acceptance into the universities, to their membership in professional organizations, to their activities as newspaper editors, publishers, and correspondents, for example. Jews were forbidden to acquire lands or forests, except at public auctions, and even then only by special permit. The authorities were entitled to compel Jews to sell or lease their lands.[97] The number of Jews permitted to be employed by various industrial plants was fixed at 6.2 percent, their relative weight in the general population. Considering the fact that various sectors of employment (such as the army, the police, and most of the government service) had been almost completely closed to Jews for a long time, while other occupations were now closed to them by the anti-Jewish legislation, it is clear that the livelihoods of a very large number were liquidated, while many were even reduced to starvation.

I have made a special point of citing excerpts from speeches made during the parliamentary debates, despite many of these statements being mere repetitions of speeches made earlier. The detailed description of the legislative process has been adduced in order to cast light upon the atmosphere generated in Hungary in those days and upon the attitudes of those whose roles were central in generating that atmosphere.

It is interesting to note the unanimity prevailing between secular government members and legislators and the church leaders, members of the Upper House. Both groups described the exclusion of the Jews from economic, social, and cultural life as justified self-defense. Both groups stressed the danger inherent in the spirit of Judaism to Christian superiority and to the Christian Hungarian nation. One group would speak of "poison," the other of "corruption," their intention and the consequences were the same. Just like Prime Minister Teleki, the bishops, the leaders of the churches, voiced their descriptions and theories of the Jewish race, upon which they based the justification for their demand to remove people of the alien Jewish race from their community—to place them outside the camp and outside the law. Both groups made considerable efforts to make their hostile and condescending attitude toward the Jews and Judaism heard and seen, and both groups agreed that in the anti-Jewish legislation they saw a significant Christian step, executed in the spirit of Christianity, the perpetrators of which were worthy of being blessed for their efforts. They complimented one another and made their opinions known in public. They were in full agreement all along. The only area in which they disagreed was with regard to the converts to Christianity and the time period during which their Christianity held validity.

The link between the speeches of 1939 and the deeds of 1944 is not coincidental.

Extra-parliamentary Activity during and after the Debate on the Second Anti-Jewish Act

In light of the great interest in the legislative process that the general public showed, the debate on the second anti-Jewish act did not limit itself to the four walls of the legislature. Both during the parliamentary debate and after it, various public figures referred to the legislation and commented on it from different points of view. Just as the church leaders took an active part in the preparation of the law during the legislative debating, so they also expressed their views of it outside the legislature, both orally and in writing. This widespread public preoccupation guaranteed that the second anti-Jewish act remained central in public interest after it was adopted, members of the priesthood thus playing a major role in the cyclic, long-winded public treatment of the law and the public interest in it.

It is interesting to listen to the speeches delivered on the subject of Jewry and Judaism and to study publications concerning the proposed bill issued during the debates and after they were over. The material adduced below is only a small portion of the material produced during that period.

At an advanced stage in the discussion of the second anti-Jewish law, in a speech delivered in the town of Cegled on April 24, 1939, at a rally of ruling party members, the director-general of the ministry of law, Istvan Antal, referred to the delays in the Upper House:

> Our party has been a right-wing party ever since the days of the Szeged revolution in 1919, and is the heir of the right-wing, racial political movements and organizations struggling against the radical left with its attendant phenomena for the formation of an exclusive political and economic government by members of our Hungarian race. . . . The disintegrating leftist forces are at present waging a weak, last-ditch battle despite the general confusion on their ranks. The drawn-out, complicated struggle going on in the legislature over the proposed anti-Jewish law is one of the signs of this last-ditch battle. The twelfth hour has arrived for the completion of the anti-Jewish legislation, for otherwise the Christian masses will be so dis-

appointed that there is no way today of foretelling the possible outcome of such a disappointment.[98]

This speech seems to indicate that the Christian masses had been tensely following the stages of the debate. They were justified in deducing from the tone of the participants in the debate that the solution to many problems of life in Hungary was linked to the completion of the anti-Jewish legislation. Not completing the legislative process would be tantamount to depriving the Christian masses of the solution they yearned for, and so, in the speaker's opinion, their disappointment and outburst of rage would be justified.

In the Catholic periodical *Egyedul Vagyunk* (We Are Alone) there appeared at the beginning of 1939 an article analyzing the Jewish character. The magazine saw fit to introduce the writer of the article in the following way:

> This courageous and clear exposition is written by a Catholic priest, one of the outstanding members of the teaching staff of the Theological Institute of Kalocsa,[99] the young instructor, Dr. Andor Szorenyi. Szorenyi was engaged in Rome for three and a half years in the study of Oriental languages and of the Holy Scriptures, and in 1936, at the age of 28, he arrived at Kalocsa. It is difficult to find so learned an expert as he in the Old Testament and in Jewish literature.

Szorenyi wrote:

> The wandering Jew is the terrible symbol of the Jewish nation, the race persecuted throughout the world.... Gold served as his homeland, and with the help of the vast amount of gold he has amassed at home, he controls various peoples. However, despite his bulging pockets he remains alien and hated everywhere. People do speak with him, while mocking him. They are even willing to suffer his presence for a certain period of time, but in the end murderous persecution breaks out against him with powerful force.
>
> I base my description of the nature and characteristics of this wandering Jew upon the Holy Scriptures, the Talmud, and their official book of regulations, the Shulhan 'Arukh.... Judaism is a race, and Judaism is a people. True, Judaism does have a special religion, which in modern terminology may be defined as a national religion, but beyond this the Jews are a race and a people, and they retain their racial characteristics even if they convert to another religion.... Judaism has always been a material nation, adhering to materialism and living for earthly sensuousness and physical pleasures. It was the role of Providence to lead Judaism toward revelation. Judaism has never thought of the World to Come, and from this point of view the Old Testament is incomplete, for it does not include

the revelation in its entirety. It is unfit to include it, for we only received the entire truth and the light in the New Testament, from Jesus.

In the desires of their imagination the Messiah appears as one coming to distribute to them earthly benefits and physical happiness. True, among them there have appeared pure souls as well, such as—for example—the Virgin Mary, John the Baptist, and others who awaited the Savior. But most of these followed Jesus only after he performed miracles, revived the dead, brought cures for physical afflictions, and distributed bread to the hungry. However, when spiritual nourishment and purity of the soul were on the agenda, they quickly abandoned him and even crucified him.

Their materialistic outlook became more awkward when they turned from a blessed people to an accursed one—at the same time as they denied Jesus the Savior. They adhered inflexibly to their old errors of thousands of years, and fossilized themselves in the terrible spirit expressed in the Talmud, the doctrines of which are nothing but a monstrous distortion of the moral and legal system of the Old Testament. The line characteristic of the Talmud is that it confuses and distorts the concepts of Godhood, angels, evil spirits, the soul, sin, life after death, and of numerous similar concepts. Instead, the Talmud instills unbridled materialism and earthly-materialistic achievements at the head of its hierarchy of values.... Ever since they were granted civil rights in various countries, the Jews set themselves a goal—to achieve the aims the Talmud set before them: imposing Talmudic values and the spirit of Judaism on the nations of the world and, similarly, imposing an unrestrained Jewish government over the other people.

There may indeed be some Jews who are not familiar with the Talmud and who do not speak their language, but the Jewish spirit, thousands of years old, lives in them as well, and Talmudic morality prevails over their outlook, for an exaggerated interest in materialism is the basic component of their souls and their lives. It is sufficient for us to think of Marx and Trotsky, of Znuviev, of Bela Kun, and of the horrible names of their compatriots. Let us think of those controlled by an obsession with gold— the princes of the world of finance, the leaders of the secret cells of the Freemasons, wealthy industrialists and traders, and Shylocks. Only then will my statement be comprehensible, for the most important characteristic of Judaism has been and continues to be brutal materialism.[100]

The priesthood did not merely express its opinions in writing. It was also active among the public. In a small town in the Budapest area, local elections were being held. The list of candidates of the antisemitic right was organized by the Catholic priest, Dr. Geza Decsey. The right bloc included, among other groups, the Christian party and the National-Socialist party. The central point of the right bloc platform was the removal of the Jews from the municipal power centers that were controlled, as it were, by the Jews. The press column reporting the success of the antisemitic bloc bears the headline,"The Christian Citizens of Pestszenterzsebet Say: Finally We Can Walk Upright in Our Town." After the elections, the priest announced, "I must note that our victory is the result both of human effort and of divine assistance and desire to support our struggle, for we believed that this triumph would surely come—merely the first step in our activities."[101]

It is interesting to read the letter composed by a country Catholic priest, in which he expressed his opinion of the Jews. The priest's letter found itself a suitable publisher: the daily newspaper of the Arrow-Cross party, which published it as an editorial. The ideas expressed by the country priest are very similar to ideas expressed again and again by the leaders of Hungary's churches during the debate on the anti-Jewish legislation. The outstanding difference is the degree of sophistication in the presentation of the subject. Whereas the church leaders succeeded in enveloping their ideas in a reserved and cultured style, as befit their status, the very same ideas were expressed by the country priest in a rough and vulgar style.

The priest himself testifies that his ideas stemmed partially from the literary heritage of the rector of the Catholic University of Sciences at Budapest, Dr. Jozsef Trikal. This is what he wrote of the Jews:

> Their roots are not embedded in any nation, which is why they have a supercilious sense of supremacy over all other peoples. They are not related to other peoples, and so they do not like any particular nation. . . . Like a chameleon, so they, too, come to resemble externally the people around them, but internally, in their hearts, they feel scorn for everyone. Their hatred for all who are not their kin is expressed in literature, in theater, and in art.[102]
>
> In places where priests are murdered, the educated are slaughtered, and churches are burnt—that's where the Jew is to be found. Even if no Jew is actually there in a physical sense, his presence is represented there by his venomous literary works. Like naked spirits they drift all over the world, and by means of their filthy moral concepts, their distorted philosophy, and their base artistic schools, they spread their revolting ideas. Their sullied views corrupt the world.
>
> This people of the ghetto are seated on the thrones of rulers and tighten their pressure around the neck of the Christian world. They do not want the Christians to become Jewish. Never! On the contrary, they do desire them to become corrupt and filthy. They want to immerse them in sewage pipes and to rob them of their character, their honesty, their faith, and their trust in God. . . . Today even the government is compelled to recognize the fact that has been clear for a long time to any intelligent person: Judaism

is not a simple religion, it is a race! Blood! Blood which will never be able to deny itself, even if it is immersed in all the baptismal fonts of every Christian church.[103] ... Who would rule that the state is obliged to assimilate into itself everyone who has converted to Christianity, and even to grant him all those privileges which are the right of scions of the nation, sons of the national race? Why must we assume that every two-faced, scheming Jew who has succeeded in deceiving the Christian church and has converted is entitled to have the nation recognize him as a citizen of equal rights?[104] A Jew remains a Jew, for Judaism is a race.

The fact that today there is anti-Jewish legislation throughout the world and not only in our land proves clearly that only the Jews are to blame for this.[105] If they were humble, honest, and decent, if they were unwilling to betray for financial gain everything sacred to us—there would be no anti-Jewish law in Hungary. By erecting the barriers of economic limitation before the unrestrained jealousy of the Jews, we are protecting our dear nation and the pure bride of Jesus the Nazarene: the church.[106]

Not long before this article appeared, the Synod of Catholic Bishops was discussing the question of Jews converting to Christianity and their motives in doing so. A daily newspaper carried excerpts from a Shepherds' Epistle written in Latin, which Cardinal Seredi had sent to the Catholic priesthood: "At the present time many Jews are turning to us and asking to be accepted into Christianity. It is reasonable to assume that their present troubles are what has encouraged these people to try to ensure for themselves and for their children not only eternal happiness but also earthly happiness." After this introduction the cardinal instructed the priests concerning the way they should relate to the Jews turning to them seeking "earthly happiness" by means of the church.[107]

In the records of the session of the Synod of Catholic Bishops held some three weeks after the appearance of the newspaper report concerning this Shepherds' Epistle, we read more explicit statements:

> The Jews expected certain concessions from the proposed [second anti-Jewish] act under discussion at present. This hope aroused so strong a stream of potential converts that certain honorable bishops had to take special measures in connection with those would-be converts, in order to be convinced of the authenticity of all those who would convert.[108]

In a similar vein the Evangelical bishop of Transdanubia, Dr. Bela Kapi, referred to the would-be converts. With reference to the anti-Jewish law he "warned his congregations to accept into their midst only those who desire to be accepted into the church because of the soul-felt religious convictions they profess."[109]

This suspicious treatment of the would-be converts was a direct result of the general attitude toward the Jews and their character.

Premier Teleki appeared at the general assembly of the United National Christian League toward the end of the debate on the second anti-Jewish law. He declared to his audience that his desire was strong to act in accordance with the views of his old friend and mentor, the late Karoly Wolf:

> Making amends for past inaction and restoring the ruins resulting from nineteenth-century materialism are the practical significance of the National Christian idea in political activity. The Christian political way requires filling with content the frameworks which political life has succeeded in setting up. Yet it is not enough to legislate laws. Christian society must unite in order to exploit the opportunities opened up before it by this legislation.[110]

The minister of justice expressed a similar opinion at a party convention in the town of Hajduszoboszlo: "We are convinced that it is incumbent upon Hungarian Christian society to be the lords of Hungary in all walks of cultural and economic life. Now that the anti-Jewish law has been passed, the way has been opened before us to enable us to take immediate control of life in Hungary in general."[111]

The Evangelical church appointed a bishop in the Tisza River district, Zoltan Turoczy. Upon taking office the new bishop declared that "he is not hiding the fact that he holds right-wing views and that he stands strongly upon a national political base. He even believes that in the present period of national renewal God holds exalted things in store for the Hungarian nation."[112]

It is interesting to note that while the bishop placed his hopes in the renewal of national forces, the prime minister, in a speech he delivered three days after the bishop took office, foresaw a brighter future for the Hungarian nation by means of refreshening the Christian forces at the expense of the Jews:

> We are striding down the right road to render this state more Hungarian and more Christian, for today many Christians are occupying positions of the kind that until now were under Jewish control. And so we bear witness to the renewal of the nation, and I am convinced that in the future we shall make good progress along this path, for we have sufficient manpower to enable us to establish a Christian economic life.[113]

At his installment Turoczy presented his political identity card. He defined himself as "right-wing." Definition of the term "right-wing," as it was understood at the time, is offered by an expert, Prime Minister Teleki:

> Our party has borne the flag of the constructive idea of Christianity and nationalism without change and without tiring from the days of Szeged up until today. We knew how to initiate and develop active *right-wing* policies after the collapse of the Red regime. We knew this from the very first moment of our activity and we also knew how to base these policies on those active elements inspired by *right-wing* Hungarian concepts at all times. This is our national concept. Another concept is our integration into the European community in which we live and to which we have to attune ourselves.[114]
>
> We do not need to announce a plan of action at this stage. Our program has been made clear many times: enacting social laws, agrarian reform,[115] and anti-Jewish legislation. We shall proceed and act along this line.... We are faithful servants of the aforesaid concepts, and our party is a stronghold of the concept of *right-wing* Hungarian development. In the name of these concepts we defend this land for the national Christian spirit against all harmful concepts.[116] (emphasis added)

In addition to presenting his political identity card, Bishop Turoczy also clarified his faith in the substance, the goal, and the role of Christianity:

> To this day people have a mistaken opinion of Jesus the pacifist and of the pacifistic church. To this day they view the roles of Jesus and his church as being active behind the front lines of life, as international sanitation workers, as collectors of the injured in life's struggle, who bandage them, cure them, and comfort them—or bury them.
> Such an approach is nothing but a distortion of the truth!
> Jesus himself announced that he was bringing strife to this world. When he ascended into Heaven he imposed on his representatives an order for total conquest, worldwide, and thus he sent them to take up their roles. Had the church not been a fighting church, Christianity would never have attained the position it enjoys today.[117]

We can only guess the conclusion that the bishop's congregation must have drawn when their spiritual leader told them he was "right-wing" and spoke of a "renewal of nationalist forces" and of a "fighting church."

The anti-Jewish legislation was extremely popular. Just after the law was adopted, Teleki dismissed Parliament and announced the holding of new elections. These took place on May 28 and 29, 1939. The government was returned to power with a stable majority of 187 seats out of 260. The elections were characterized by a clear electoral shift to the right. The strength of the Social-Democratic party dropped from eleven seats to five. This party, together with the Liberal party, which also lost some of its strength, expressed its opposition to the anti-Jewish legislation. In contrast, the antisemitic Arrow-Cross party gained strength, going from thirteen seats to forty-five. The right-wing, antisemitic leanings of the ruling party were strengthened as well.[118]

The unrestrained antisemitic invective had found its way into the hearts of the Hungarian populace, which expressed its opinion in the elections. One of the main elements of these diatribes was the juxtaposition of a positive Christianity against a negative Judaism. Various groups joined this antisemitic wave. Christian piety was a basic component of the views espoused by various antisemitic groups, including the Arrow-Cross party.

Accordingly, we read the following news report:

> Within the framework of the thanksgiving prayers held at the close of the harvest season, a crowd of 5,000 celebrated the triumph of the idea of the Arrow-Cross. A procession of believers advanced to a flower patch, focusing on a field altar decked out in flowers, set up in the open. As part of the prayer service Odon Jaszovary, head of the Papal Office, delivered a sermon: "We see in our time the realization of the awful curses laid on the Jews, who moved away from the true faith, as they wander from one place to another over the entire earth without a homeland." Elderly pious women sang devotedly and with tears in their eyes: "Our Mother is a happy woman," while the youth of the Arrow-Cross party, dressed in green shirts, knelt devoutly as the holy bread was presented during the prayer.

The newspaper goes on to say that the traditional honey cakes sold at such events "were made this time in the shape of the Arrow-Cross and were in great demand."[119]

In the town of Pestszenterzsebet was held a cornerstone-laying ceremony for the Reformed church. A Member of Parliament representing the Arrow-Cross party, Kalman Hubay, said in his remarks,

> The Hungarian rebirth is based on two stable foundation stones: the one—an awareness of the Hungarian race linked with a profound social emotion, and the other—the undistorted, true Christianity of Jesus. Hungarian life may be compared to the wild rose growing freely from Hungarian soil and climbing on the Cross of Jesus standing at the side of the road. The rose is intertwined on the Cross and embraces it. Were we to remove the rose from Jesus' Cross, it would surely wither. Similarly, the rose of glorious

Hungarian life cannot come to full bloom if it is removed from the Cross of Jesus.[120]

Every year the Catholic church held a summer university at the town of Esztergom, the seat of the cardinal, for its intellectual following.[121] The 1939 summer session was opened by a lecture by Cardinal Seredi, who stressed that "this is the sixth time the gates of the summer university open in Esztergom. The role of the summer university is to set clear guidelines for the intelligentsia of Catholic society in the most important and pressing problems of our era."[122]

Another lecturer at the opening session was Professor Janos Ivanyi. He lectured on "The Meaning of the Old Testament." The speaker argued with the Nazi approach, which denied the value of the Old Testament literature.

According to him the modern attacks directed at the Old Testament are based on three erroneous assumptions. The first error is the view that the Old Testament is the natural product of the Jewish spirit. The second one is the identification of modern Judaism, its religious outlook and culture and mental approach, with the people and culture of the Old Testament. The third error is the view that Judaism and Christianity are equal heirs to the ancient Jewish faith.

On the contrary, the lecturer stated, "The writings of the Old Testament are the creation neither of human hands nor of a human brain. They do not reflect the Jewish genius.... Only foolish faith can relate this excellent literature to the creativity of the valueless Israelite nation."[123]

The lecturer went on to deal with the people of Israel from the point of view of the Old Testament. Contrary to the view of the new German ideology, and with special reference to its theoretician, Rosenberg, he stated that the idea that modern Jewry was identical with the nation of the Old Testament was to be rejected:

> Those who hold this opinion overlook the fact that they are being nourished from the world of thought of the very same Jewry they are so desirous of getting away from. Here they ignore the fact that their concept, the concept of racial purity and blood purity, was introduced into a legal codex for the first time in history by the very same hated Jews they try so hard to keep away from their own racial compatriots because of their identification with them—all with a considerable degree of justice.[124]

The material adduced here is a random though representative selection of utterances made by secular public figures and by priests concerning the nature of the Jews. The resemblance between the various utterances is so great that no further detail is necessary.

The Demand for Additional Anti-Jewish Legislation

As early as the debate on the second anti-Jewish law, certain right-wing circles voiced their opinion that the anti-Jewish steps included in the current legislation were inadequate. The following are extracts from an editorial that appeared in the Arrow-Cross party organ:

> We have declared on innumerable occasions that we do not view this additional anti-Jewish law as a final solution to the Jewish problem.... We are interested in a country which will be rid of Jews. The concept of a country rid of Jews is not a barbaric concept, but rather a basic condition for the existence of proper public life.
>
> The anti-Jewish bill at present being debated will surely make it possible for the more cunning of that race to escape the application of the law. But when our country is established, based on the views of Hungarianism—and this will indeed come to pass, if not today then tomorrow, and surely in the very near future—then all their attempts will be found to be useless, for in the Hungarianistic country there will be no Jews of special status. The Arrow-Cross will strike at each and every Jew to an equal degree.[125]

The pressure applied to the government grew stronger. There were even elements in the ruling party and in the government itself that pressed for additional, comprehensive anti-Jewish legislation. Balint Homan, the minister of culture and education, handed over to the regent, Horthy, a memorandum he had prepared in which he claimed, "We should draw all the consequences from the new European development," and accordingly recommended a more radical line on the subject of anti-Jewish legislation, "to put an end to solutions by compromises." In their stead he proposed enacting legislation "based on racial principles."[126]

Another member of the ruling party, ex-Premier Imredi, criticized the faults of the law, especially in economic matters, claiming that "high-level positions vacated by Jews were not being handed over to the real guardians of the Christian economic forces ... and government officials and politicians—hired by Jewish money—were being appointed to a high percentage of these positions."[127]

An independent member of Parliament, Ferenc Rajniss, demanded the legislation of a third anti-Jewish act, and demanded of the government a report on the implementation of the second anti-Jewish act.[128]

A representative of the Arrow-Cross party, Karoly Marothy, urged the final solution of the Jewish problem and asked the government to make the appropriate preparations for the expulsion of the Jews from Hungary. Another representative of the Arrow-Cross party, Matyas Matolcsay, claimed that for the past year and a half no Jewish land had been transferred to Christian farmers, despite the fact that the Jews possessed half a million *hold* of land (1 *hold* = about 5.7 *dunam* = about 1.4 acres).[129]

In his reply the prime minister said that

> in light of the numerous evasions of the law, the second anti-Jewish act being too cumbersome, he, too, was aware of the law's limitations. Yet he regarded negatively the idea of adopting laws on any subject whenever this is felt necessary, although in view of the faults of the existing legislation he desired to have a clear, basic law adopted which would simplify the entire subject. Thus, in the very near future this task would be completed, and Parliament would then become aware of the far-reaching effects of the reprocessed law.[130]

Despite the prime minister's reply and despite his announcement that he would respond to the request and legislate an additional anti-Jewish law, the representative of the Arrow-Cross party, Zoltan Mesko, demanded, less than a week later, "that the legislation of the third anti-Jewish law be speeded up, and that all business be transferred to Christian hands."[131]

This last demand was put especially to the minister of trade and industry, Jozsef Varga, during the debate on his ministry's budget. The minister calmed the questioner, explaining in detail the steps he had already taken and those he would yet take to meet the questioner's demand. He mentioned the regulations already promulgated and those he was about to promulgate to carry out the idea of Christianizing trade. On a practical level, both sides spoke of preparing a list of merchants, both wholesalers and retailers, who alone would be permitted to market basic products:

> The retailers have already been selected by us in almost every area; furthermore, we have completed the list of wholesalers who will be permitted to engage in the sugar trade. Regarding other products, the preparation of the lists is progressing. The wholesalers we have selected are all Christian, without exception. In the marketing of sugar and oil in 90 percent of the cases the Christianizing of the trade has been completed. We shall continue to develop trade in this direction at an accelerated rate of speed. In the very near future I shall publish appropriate regulations, and in this way we shall speed up the trade Christianizing process to a very great extent.

The minister also told of the large loans that had been made to Christian storekeepers and of the goods that had been put at their disposal at comfortable rates of interest.[132]

The subject was not removed from the parliamentary agenda. During the debate on the budget of the prime minister's office, the premier was asked by Karoly Marothy, a member of Parliament from the Arrow-Cross party, "to implement the anti-Jewish act more strongly." Another member of this party, Gabor Vajna, demanded that the government take strong steps against the press owned by the Freemasons and the Jews. And another member of the same party, Count Miklos Serenyi, demanded the total eviction of the Jews from Hungary.[133]

The prime minister was clearly angry at the accusations leveled against him and his government, accusations that seemed to indicate that he and his government were not sufficiently firm in carrying out the laws that had already been adopted, that they were not working hard enough to prepare additional anti-Jewish legislation, and that their dedication to the anti-Jewish campaign was not as strong as that of members of the Arrow-Cross party. He took offense at being criticized for no reason at all, as if he were insufficiently devoted to the antisemitic cause. He claimed,

> From my experience I know that whenever my government and I initiate anything, the opposition begins to apply its pressure: they claim that the government does not intend to complete the endeavor it has undertaken. They act as if they had initiated the matter under discussion ... this is what has happened in connection with the anti-Jewish legislation. As soon as I pointed out that we were about to advance along this line and that we were preparing for additional legislation, the pressure began immediately.

The prime minister's dissatisfaction with the extremist antisemitic Arrow-Cross party for its attempt to usurp his lead and his initiatives in persecuting Jews is evident.

With regard to implementing the laws which had already been adopted, the prime minister apologized that this did not progress at the rate he would have preferred:

> The situation is that many difficulties in implementing the laws are cropping up. One of these difficulties concerns the knowledge of languages. . . . Very few of our youth know any foreign language. Here we have the case of *Pester Lloyd* [the government's semiofficial organ in the German language]. It is the only Hungarian paper to appear in a foreign language, and when I send them my speeches, it often happens that I myself have to translate them if I want the speech to appear in its original meaning. Thus we in

Pester Lloyd have to employ Jewish newspapermen who know German. On the other hand, in such places of work as have no particular problem, we have enacted drastic changes.[134]

To prove his claim that he and his government had not been negligent in implementing suitable steps against the Jews, the prime minister cited data indicating the reduced number of Jews in various positions. In his speech he also announced the imminent promulgation of additional regulations aimed at making the lives of the Jews more difficult, even in those areas not included in the anti-Jewish legislation itself. Like the premier and the minister of trade and transport, other ministers and their ministries promulgated stringent regulations concerning Jews and did their very best to make their lives more difficult. While making their announcements regarding their activities, they voiced—in Parliament and outside it—their credo concerning the need to keep the Jews out of various positions, and to reduce their *lebensraum* to the greatest extent possible.[135]

While the leaders of the country were planning how to render their attack on the Jews more effective, the Evangelical bishop of Transdanubia, Dr. Bela Kapi, delivered a kind of pledge of allegiance to the government and its work, saying that "with regard to the relations between his church and the state, he had full faith in the government of Count Pal Teleki."[136]

The head of the Reformed church went even further. In the summer of 1940, when there was no longer the slightest doubt regarding the nature of the Nazi regime in Germany, Bishop Ravasz stated in a speech he delivered in his central church at Calvin Square in Budapest, "I am convinced that the worldwide struggle in which the German nation is at present engaged is basically a religious struggle.... I am convinced that this struggle will be followed by a deeper awareness of the redeeming and liberating God."[137]

It should be noted that the bishop's flattering declaration about Hitler's war was delivered at a time when Hitler and Stalin were allies, and not during the period when Nazi Germany was at war with the Bolshevik regime and was defending, as it were, the Christian culture of Europe.

A no less unambiguous statement was made by Bishop Janos Vasarhelyi, the administrator of the Reformed church in Transylvania, in March 1941, before the outbreak of Russo-German hostilities. After the transfer of the northern part of Transylvania to Hungarian rule, the church held a convention to consider its own organizational structure in light of the new situation. Participating in the convention were the minister of agriculture, who represented the prime minister, and Bishop Ravasz, head of the Reformed church in Hungary. Bishop Vasarhelyi thanked Horthy, the regent of Hungary, for his efforts to restore Transylvania to the Hungarian homeland, and added, "We thank duly our great allies, Hitler and Mussolini, who, wisely and strongly, paved the way for the realization of Hungarian justice."[138]

The enthusiastic comments uttered by the church leaders regarding Germany, Hungary, and the heads of their two governments were certainly interpreted by their audience as granting legitimacy to the acts committed by these governments and by those supporting them. As shown above, the antisemitic line occupied a dominant place in the activities of these two regimes.

"The History of the Jews in Hungary" was the title of the lecture delivered by Bishop Raffay. The lecturer led his audience along some thousand years of Hungarian history in order to show that the Jews had always been the objects of adverse decrees. The bishop extolled the memory of "King St. Laszlo, who was the first to impose decrees on the Jews. The decree he imposed on them in 1092 was a decree for the protection of the race, for it prohibited the marriage of Jews to Christians." While citing the detailed list of antisemitic decrees promulgated during the various periods, the bishop expressed his dissatisfaction with the fact that over a period of time the Jews had caused "numerous complications":

> King Lajos the Great was the first to take severe steps against the Jews; he expelled them in 1360. However, when the national economy faltered, four years later, he invited them to return to Hungary.... When the Jews returned to Hungary, they demanded the return of their homes. This demand of theirs caused, of course, numerous complications, and as a result Jews and Christians came to live alongside one another in certain streets, and in homes which were owned jointly by members of the two religions, they even lived side by side.

In this way the bishop went on to list the various periods in Hungarian history when decrees were imposed upon the Jews. He concluded his speech with the following comment: "For as long as Judaism has existed, there has also been a Jewish problem; the age of antisemitism is the same as the age of Judaism."[139] Raffay's message in his talk was that the current situation was not without precedent, given the way the Jews had lived their lives in Hungary during the thousand years that Christian Hungary had existed. The present situation was merely the natural and direct continuation of the ancient Hungarian tradition. In other words, the roots of the legitimacy of the negative treatment afforded the Jews are to be found in the historical Hungarian past.

Raffay's statement to the effect that the Jews were different from the other citizens of Hungary was strengthened tangibly by a regulation promulgated by the office of Laszlo Endre, the deputy governor of the district of Pest—the largest and most central of the districts of Hungary— some three weeks after Raffay's talk. Endre's regulation obligated the Christian storekeepers in the district to mark their shops with a sign:

> "A Christian-Hungarian Shop."
> This order by the deputy governor caused great rejoicing throughout the district ... for unfortunately there still are Christian merchants and craftsmen who maintain their relations with the Jews. What now remains to be done is to take steps against those Christian clients who are not ashamed to do their shopping in stores owned by Jews.[140]

The Third Anti-Jewish Act

The second anti-Jewish act did not deal with the question of mixed marriages between Jews and Christians. The third anti-Jewish act was intended to amend this omission. The churches were decidedly interested in this legislation, especially with regard to the converts to Christianity.

The Synod of Catholic Bishops held its half-yearly meeting in the fall of 1940, and considered the proposed third anti-Jewish bill. The bishop of Kalocsa, Gyula Zicsy, suggested,

> Now that the prime minister has announced his intention of bringing before the legislature the third anti-Jewish bill, the Synod of Bishops requests his Holiness the Cardinal to ask the premier if the proposed bill includes stipulations which might violate church positions. ... His Holiness the Cardinal considers it important that Catholics be made to suffer no more from the denial of their rights. It is extremely important that the Synod of Bishops take a uniform stand lest the government think the Synod of Bishops is not united. We are protecting those of our faith alone, and not the Jews.[141]

At the spring session of 1941 the cardinal reported on his meeting with the prime minister, during which

> he stressed the desire of the Synod of Bishops that the proposed bill not make it more difficult for the Christian citizens of Jewish origin, but rather make it easier for them. ... The prime minister stressed for his part that the new law would be clearly defined. The cardinal himself requested that the wording of the law be clear so that those to whom the law was intended to apply would not be able to evade it without being punished for doing so.[142]

After his meeting with the cardinal, the prime minister was able to draw the conclusion that even if the paragraph in the proposed bill encountered church opposition, the bill itself was guaranteed, in general and on principle, not to come up against church disagreement, since the cardinal had already expressed his agreement and support for this new bill, and the government accordingly continued its preparations to present it to Parliament.

Laszlo Bardossy was appointed prime minister of Hungary in place of Teleki, who committed suicide.[143] He presented his government to Parliament on April 24, 1941. He referred briefly to the question of mixed marriages, confirming the need for legislative steps to prevent assimilation.[144]

In the speech he delivered in the town of Bekescsaba, the chairman of the ruling party elaborated on the subject:

> The two anti-Jewish acts already adopted have achieved extremely positive and practical results, but we note a great many evasions of the law. If the law is lacking, we must amend this.... We must try as hard as we can to enable our fellow Hungarians by race to live their lives in racial purity, and so the government will be presenting a bill over the next few days, which will prohibit marriage between Christians and Jews.[145]

The bill was presented to Parliament on June 30, 1941. The introduction to the bill mentions the Marriage Act of 1895, and claims that "that law did not yield good results. Mixed marriages had a definitely detrimental effect upon the evolution of our national soul. They brought into a position of influence that Jewish spirit whose harmful effect we have seen."[146]

The Marriage Act of 1895 granted the Jewish community of Hungary equal rights. The priesthood was the spearhead of the camp that opposed that liberal legislation.[147] The 1941 government, in preparing to enact a marriage act, based its stand on that of the church and the priesthood in 1895, which vehemently opposed the bill that awarded the Jews equal status in their marriages. The legislation tabled in Parliament was worded in the hostile spirit of the priesthood of almost fifty years before. The government, however, went beyond the vision of the priesthood, and proposed that certain Jewish converts to Christianity be considered Jews as well. This proposal revealed the existence of a disagreement between government and priesthood, the government even succeeding in arousing the fury of certain Christian circles. The representative of the United Christian party spoke out furiously against the possibility of "Hungarian citizens who no longer have anything to do with Jews" being cast out of Hungarian society, and of the possibility that "people who behaved as radical antisemites will be driven back to Jewry."[148]

The bill was adopted by the Parliament on July 2, 1941, and was placed before the Upper House. The first speaker was Cardinal Seredi, who opposed the bill. He began his speech as follows: "I would like to stress that my opposition to the bill does not stem from my taking into consideration the good of the Jews, but is rather a matter of principle: the bill places stumbling-blocks before the sanctity of Catholic marriage." Cardinal Seredi was offended by the fact that the bill under consideration forbade marriages not forbidden by church law, that is, marriages between Christians and converts or between Christians and the descendants of converts classified as Jews by the bill. The cardinal viewed this situation as coercion detracting from one's freedom of action, and so expressed his opposition to the bill.[149]

Seredi was followed by the representative of the Reformed church, who expressed his own opposition to the bill as well, and explained that

> he had voted for the first anti-Jewish act because he was convinced that there was a Jewish problem which was to be solved by displacing the Jews in the various economic sectors. Similarly, we had to take from them their considerable influence in directing the cultural life of the nation, for this is one of the important existential problems of the Hungarian nation.

Concerning his voting for the second anti-Jewish bill, the bishop explained that the period was a preelection one, and rejection of the bill might have led to an undesirable deterioration: "However, the present bill is more harmful to Christians than to Jews. ... I admit it is right to state that a person born Jewish does not improve substantially by converting to Christianity, yet the Churches are unable to agree that a person born Jewish remains Jewish forever, even if he accepts Christianity."[150]

The delegate of the Evangelical church, Bishop Kapi, expressed his fear

> that the bill, though presented for positive reasons, will not achieve its aim, and might even cause harm to the sanctity of married life, harm to the nation and also to Christianity. ... According to the outlook of the Evangelical church, marital ties are not merely a matter for the church, but also for the state, and the state has the right to make suitable arrangements in the matter of marriage. But here we see that the state, by virtue of its legislation, takes up its position at the entrance to the churches and declares: I permit these marriages, but I forbid those. ... Such a confrontation between church and state cannot serve the state's interests. ... This legislation clearly does not harm the Jews, but rather those Christians who will once again be compelled to consider themselves Jewish. This bill is merely a tool in the hands of the Jewish-missionary concept, for those Christians harmed

by the bill will have no choice but to fall back among those people from whom they had already detached themselves, they and their forefathers.[151]

A former prime minister, Istvan Bethlen, also expressed his opposition to the proposed bill. He was unable to accept the paragraph in the bill "which views children of mixed parentage as Jews. . . . They are Christian to the same extent that they are Jewish, and all that can be said of them is that racially they are of mixed blood. Yet besmirching them as Jews degrades them." Bethlen went on to propose the adoption of a positive approach to children of mixed marriages. They must be allowed to marry only Christians, and then within a few generations it will be possible to approach

> closer and closer to that purity of race the proposed bill sets as an ideal. This is the correct way to solve the problem, for in this way we shall gradually limit their Jewish blood, and in this way we shall create pure-blooded Hungarians, and not contribute our Hungarian blood to enlarge the number of Jews to be treated as citizens of a lower rank.

He was not willing to agree to the adoption of such a step, for "even in Germany children of mixed marriages are treated with more understanding than in the bill under discussion."[152]

In light of the opposition, the bill was sent for discussion to a sub-committee, where slight changes were inserted in paragraph 9 of the bill, which defined the Jewishness of the children of mixed parentage, and the subject was returned to the plenum of the Upper House for debate.[153] The church leaders elaborated on their opposition to the bill, expressing their anger at the harm done to the converts and their offspring. Cardinal Seredi made the following statement:

> In the recent past I have made my opinion known even in delicate situations so as to place myself on the side of truth and justice. . . . The divine founder of the Catholic church instructed his church to preserve the way of truth and to avoid following erroneous paths. . . . I hereby solemnly declare that my attitude to the proposed bill reflects that of the Synod of Bishops and the spirit of the Catholic church. . . . Thus, while the bill under discussion is supposed to be counteracting the Jewish spirit, it adheres faithfully to just that spirit. This bill would seem to support the concept of marriage arrangements adopted in 1895 according to the demands of the liberals and of the Jewish Freemasons, against the adamant opposition of the Catholic masses in those days.
>
> Had this bill prohibited marriages between Jews and Christians, I, too, would have supported it. But the bill does not distinguish between real Jews and those Jews who have already become Christians. This bill, which

is presented to the Christian legislature of Christian Hungary, harms mainly Christians of Jewish origin. This bill will drive them back down to Judaism forever—them, their children, and their posterity—and in so doing will increase to a considerable degree the number of Jews in our midst.... We attribute to divine Providence the fact that our nation has made its home in the Carpathian Mountain basin, and so we are obliged—in the name of the same divine Providence—to protect constantly the immunity and the spirit of the nation, and I oppose the trend which predominated in ruling circles in the nineties of the last century: to view the integration of the Jews as a very desirable step. Regarding this bill, had its provisions not harmed the sanctity of Christian marriage, I would have voted for it.

Seredi added, "My opposition to the proposed bill does not stem from my interest in Jewish welfare. I oppose its very principles."[154]

Bishop Ravasz said that his desire was to lessen the suffering of Hungarian Christians, and in this he was merely expressing his basic views—and those of the vast majority of the members of his church:

According to the bill, a Christian of Jewish origin is prohibited from marrying anyone who is not Jewish, for the ex-Jew is liable to have a detrimental influence on the morality of the non-Jewish party.... There can be no baser plot against a person, one of whose parents abandoned the Jewish religion, and he himself was educated under the auspices of the Christian church, became a good Christian and a Hungarian—and now he is about to be forced to return to the place he and his forefathers left. This is the greatest possible insult, the most painful punishment.

The bishop declared that he was not prepared to give up

those Hungarians whose blood is about fifty percent Hungarian blood, as long as the chance exists for all their blood to become purified and Hungarian...even the legislations of Nuremberg and Italy do not represent the approach demanding the expulsion of people of mixed blood in order to improve by this means the protection of those of 100 percent pure blood. There has been only one national leader to act in such a fashion. This was Ezra, the leader of the Jews in the days of the return to Zion. The Holy Scriptures relate that the Jews had married into all kinds of peoples during their exile, and Ezra expelled from Israel, mercilessly, every woman and every child born of these marriages.

From a national viewpoint one must not disqualify those marriages which ensure the supremacy of the Christian spirit and Christian morality—merely because the blood of one of the parties is not entirely pure. Driving these away by force and pushing them into the clutches of non-Hungarian life cannot be resolved with the doctrines of Jesus, as they do not serve the interests of the nation.[155]

Bishop Kapi, the representative of the Evangelical church, spoke in a similar vein:

> This law limits the independence of the church. . . . According to the outlook of the church, the act of conversion to Christianity turns the convert into a Christian, and so it is natural for the church to defend her believers. The church makes sure they find their place in Christian society as Christian citizens enjoying equal rights; similarly, the church ensures they are not limited in any way when they decide to marry. . . . The state should be interested in creating and maintaining firm relations with the church, in educating its sons in the Christian spirit, and in filling their souls with a sense of justice.
>
> Those to whom this law is a heavy sentence—what are they to do? Shall they degenerate back to the place their ancestors left a long time ago, and wither there?[56]

The minister of justice, Laszlo Radocsay, spoke for the government in defense of the bill. In the main he agreed with the representatives of the churches. He disagreed with them with regard to the degree of assimilation required of the descendants of mixed marriages in order for them not to be considered Jewish any longer and to be deemed fit to enter the Hungarian Christian community. He spoke as follows:

> At the end of the last century special Jewish literature and art began to develop, material which was spiritually foreign to the Hungarian public. This development reached such dimensions that there remained no choice but to perceive the danger inherent in it. Theatre, the arts, the press, music—all were saturated with this foreign spirit. An extremely dangerous culture had been created, to which it was impossible to relate calmly. . . . The Jewish control of our economy endangered our nation less than these intellectual assaults which were directed against the very soul and culture of the nation. For this reason we have to put an end to this unsuccessful attempt at assimilating the Jews, a process which lasted fifty years and from which no positive result could possibly evolve—and so we have to adopt the path of stopping the assimilation.
>
> That descendant of a mixed marriage, having grown up and lived in a Christian environment, having been born a Christian and so growing up in a Christian atmosphere, has undoubtedly been completely assimilated, for Christianity has a vast assimilatory force. This bill is based on the assumption that the descendant of a mixed marriage who has reached so advanced a state of assimilation will not be considered Jewish when he comes to marry. The bill draws the borderline in such a way that when he comes to marry, a descendant of a mixed marriage who was born a Christian and whose parents were Christians when they married, will not

be considered a Jew. Nevertheless, we must protect ourselves from any further blood dilution.

It would seem that the minister of justice was motivated by this defensive obligation when he specified his objection to recognizing the Christianity of certain converts for the purposes of the definition in the bill under consideration.[157]

The joint subcommittee adopted the final version of the bill on June 23, 1941, and after its confirmation in the legislature it was published officially on August 8, 1941.

The material cited above indicates that the differences between the stand adopted by the churches and that of the government were limited to certain groups of converts. The areas of disagreement between the two sides were restricted to details of secondary importance. On the other hand, government and church held similar views on the principles that were the basis of the legislation. Both sides expressed their sorrow at the mistake that had occurred when the Jewish religion was granted full recognition in 1895, and proclaimed the purifying influence of Christianity in contrast to Judaism. The style affected by the church leaders in their speeches was no less abrupt and insulting to the Jews than the style of the secular government representatives. When the leaders of the priesthood stood up to defend the status and Christianity of the converts, they expressed their fear of "the degeneration" of the latter back to Judaism. The chairman of the Neologic Jewish community in Budapest spoke up against the insult directed at Jews and Judaism by these expressions: "as if Jewry, the Jewish religion, which was both the first to declare monotheism and was the cradle of Christianity, is of such a low category that adherence to it implies regression."[158]

While the debate on the bill was going on and after the bill was adopted, the expression *"fajgyalazas"* (shaming the race) was adopted by wide circles in Hungary. The expression was not a new one, especially since the Nuremberg legislation, which included the phrase *"Rassenschande"*—but after the Hungarian legislation it was commonly used by all. According to the legal definition, any sexual connection between a Jew and a Christian woman—except for prostitutes—was considered "shaming the race." The expression rapidly made its way to articles in the press, speeches, and popular antisemitic songs, alongside other expressions referring to the occupations the "Jewboys" enjoyed, such as evading taxation, spreading false, evil rumors, etc. These songs were sung by wide circles on many occasions, and in this way the concept came to enjoy wide popularity and distribution.

Thus historians view the act:

Karsai:

The Race Protection Law had only a little influence on the material situation of Hungarian Jewry. The Jewish population of Hungary regarded mixed marriages with a lack of enthusiasm, and from this point of view the law caused no special problems. On the other hand, from a moral viewpoint the law had an extremely debasing effect. The debates in the legislature, especially in Parliament, provided an opportunity to level accusations against the Jews and to attack them violently. Among those who exploited this opportunity, extreme right-wing members of Parliament were the most conspicuous: members of the Arrow-Cross party and the Imredi faction. The former discussed at especially great length the degenerate moral level of the Jews, with specific reference to their extramarital sexual relations and their illegitimate births. According to the speakers, Jews were involved in between 60 and 80 percent of these cases.[159] These sensational debates and speeches were widely reported in the press and of course had their effect on the attitude of the Christian population toward the Jews.

Katzburg:

But beyond its humiliating effect on every Jew as an individual and on Jewry as a community, the law had an implication which was more far-reaching, and, in the light of later events, fateful for Hungarian Jewry. This law gave legal sanction to the principle of the segregation of Jews as an inferior race. In this respect the Race Protection Law can be regarded as a major step in the process of the exclusion and elimination of Hungarian Jewry. Noteworthy in this connection is a comment by the Nazi publicist Kurt Ammon: "[With this law] the last word in the Hungarian Jewish question has not yet been said, but nevertheless the Law is an important step toward the final solution, which should be sought only by settling the Jews outside the country."[160]

Braham:

By far the most devastating effect of the law was psychological and propagandistic. Whipping up the hysteria that had been associated with Hungary's entry into the war against the Soviet Union shortly before,[161] the law served as a vehicle for the exacerbation of the anti-Jewish psychosis connected with the "holy crusade against Judeo-Bolshevism." It prepared the ground for the acceptance by Hungarian public opinion of the draconic measures that were to be adopted during the German occupation.[162]

The Labor Battalions Act

The atmosphere prevalent in Hungary from the late 1930s on hardly contributed to the creation of a situation where Jews would be armed and serve in the army. On December 2, 1940, the Jews who were serving in the army were expelled from their units and stationed in units belonging to "labor battalions."[163] A decree promulgated in April 1941 provided the formal basis for the separation of the Jews from the other recruits. In their new units men of rank were not allowed to wear the symbols of their rank, even if these indicated officer status. The regent confirmed the decree, provided it would not apply to those officers who had served in World War I and earned medals of high distinction.

Separating the Jews and concentrating them in special units enabled the commanding officers of these units to treat their men any way they chose. In most cases they treated them brutally, and life in most of these units was no different from life in the death camps.

Upon Hungary's joining the war against Russia, and upon the Hungarian army pushing forward into the conquered territories in the Ukraine, the labor battalions, too, were sent outside the borders of Hungary. The torturing of the defenseless Jews reached indescribable proportions. The exact number of victims murdered brutally by their guards in the Ukraine will apparently never be known, but people in the know assume the number is somewhere between fifty and sixty thousand. Adult men and youths representing the best of Hungarian Jewry were put to death in all kinds of bizarre fashions. Several of the commanding officers of the units had received a secret order before they left Hungary to "bring their battalion home in an attaché case." In other words, it would be sufficient to return the list of those who survived after the liquidation of those serving in the labor battalions.[164] In many units the officers of the labor battalions understood that when the Jews in their hands were destroyed, the officers would remain "unoccupied" on the Ukrainian front. Since service in the Ukraine was not performed enthusiastically by many of the officers and men of the Royal Hungarian Army, and since the date of their return to Hungary depended upon the liquidation of their unit, the officers, sergeants, and the staff of each unit competed against one another as to who would contribute more to hastening their return home.

After the labor battalions became established, the government was not satisfied with operating them merely by regulations; the government wanted to base the entire organization on legal action to be taken by the legislature. The minister of defense, Karoly Bartha, presented an appropriate bill to Parliament on June 19, 1942, and—according to a comment made by a member of Parliament—"it was accepted with pleasure by every single member of the House." The debate on the bill once again provided an opportunity to deliver antisemitic speeches in Parliament.

While the debate was in progress, a proposal was made to concentrate all Jewish women, children, and the elderly in ghettos, paralleling the concentration of the men in labor camps surrounded by barbed wire.

The proposed bill was adopted by Parliament and moved along to the Upper House. In presenting the bill the minister of defense said that the law would apply to all those defined as Jews according to the Marriage Law of 1941. Concerning the importance of the law, the minister of justice said the following:

> Let us not forget our bitter experience in World War I, and let us not make such great concessions in the field which comprises the greatest threat. . . . It will be catastrophic if within the army framework there will be those who do their destructive mischief, as they did in 1918. Now, on the other hand, in light of the set of anti-Jewish laws we have legislated, they will act so strongly that their actions will dwarf their previous deeds. I am neither able nor desirous of accepting the responsibility for such a situation, and especially now, with our forces engaged in their most difficult struggle against an enemy whose political leadership is almost entirely in Jewish hands.[165]

When the subject was debated in the legislature, the labor battalions had already been in existence for over a year and a half, and everyone was aware of the brutalities those serving in them had suffered. Nevertheless, the representatives of the Christian churches did not speak up against the murder of innocent recruits, a phenomenon that had become commonplace. Instead, Bishop Glattfelder preferred to give vent to his philosophical thoughts on his favorite topic, "The Superiority of the Spirit over Matter," and indirectly succeeded in linking his topic with the proposed bill and with the harm it would cause the converts to Christianity:

> I, and many more like me, whose outlook includes the basic principle of the superiority of spirit over matter, cannot accept calmly the possibility that this topic be decided on the basis of materialistic views. We shall never ignore our spiritual values, the influence of divine mercy, and the formative power of sanctity. This is the subject being considered within the framework of this problem.[166]

The bishop went on angrily and vehemently to deny the suspicion that in defending the converts he was actually defending the Jews. In his speech Glattfelder once again made use of the motif he had raised earlier: he who classifies converts to Christianity as Jews insults them.

The bill also dealt with the premilitary service of the youth, known as Levente. The bill proposed that the authorities separate the Christians from the Jews in these premilitary units as well. Here, too, the rules of the separation were supposed to be based on the definition of a Jew which was part of the Marriage Act of 1941. Glattfelder protested against this as well:

> If we remove from the premilitary units the youths who grew up with a Christian mentality and in a Christian atmosphere, and were never aware of their Jewish origins, and if we compel them now to join the camp of the Jews, and this law forces them to sew onto their clothing the Jewish yellow patch—this will indicate a lack of consistency on the part of the Upper House.[167]

At the Synod of the Catholic Bishops, too, no notice was taken of the suffering of tens of thousands of Jewish recruits to the army, the bishops preferring to limit their anxiety to "matters of the spirit." The bishop of Kalocsa, Gyula Zicsy, reported to the Synod of Bishops that he had received complaints "that in the Jewish labor camps the converts are made to work on Sundays as well, and they are not given the opportunity to participate in church ritual."[168]

The law was adopted on July 31, 1942.

The Jewish Religion Status-Lowering Act

Following the enforcement of the anti-Jewish acts of 1938, 1939, and 1941, the formal-legalistic situation that came about was illogical. While the Jews as individuals suffered from the restrictions placed upon them by the anti-Jewish legislation, the decrees, and the supplementary regulations, Judaism as a religion enjoyed a status equivalent to that of the great Christian religions. It will be recalled that after a long and difficult struggle the status of the Jewish religion was in 1895 rendered equal to that of the Christian churches, and it became "an accepted faith," a status preferable to its previous status, that of "a recognized faith."[169]

Balint Homan, the minister of religion and education, who presented the bill to Parliament, gave fitting expression to the existing anomalous situation:

> This bill has no more than declarative significance. It comes merely to grant legal form to the situation already existing in actual fact. This condition of internal contradiction has come about from the fact that the religious community whose members' rights have been limited by previous legislation enjoys the status of a preferred religious community. The pre-

sentation of this bill to Parliament is merely the natural conclusion to which the anti-Jewish legislation must lead.[170]

The bill known as "Determining the Status of the Israelite Religious Community" was presented to Parliament on December 17, 1941.[171] In the ensuing debate in Parliament voices insulting Judaism were heard, as well as severe criticism of the spirit that had facilitated granting the Jewish religion a status equal to that of the Christian churches in the 1895 legislation. A representative of the Christian party claimed,

> Jewry took rapid control of our economic power, but was not satisfied with that. With the aid of liberalism, the Jews put their hands on our spiritual power as well. Who is it who dares claim that in the prevalent Hungarian atmosphere the value of Judaism is equivalent to that of Christianity? And so, since there is no way to compare the activities and contributions of the two religions, by granting full rights to the Jewish religion, Judaism was actually given precedence, and a great injustice was done to the Christian churches.... When the Christian party accepts the bill hereby proposed, we view it as a confirmation of the correctness of the stand taken by its predecessors [the Catholic People's party, founded in the 1890s, which fought a long and stubborn battle against granting Judaism the status of "accepted religion"]. At this opportunity our party requests that the Hungarian legislator not settle for the adoption of this proposed bill, but rather not stop until all those laws legislated during the aforementioned struggle against the churches ... are erased from the Hungarian codex of laws. Christian Hungary desires to advance along the Christian path with Christian ideas, and these ideas should be included in Christian legislation.[172]

In describing the debate concerning the proposed bill, Katzburg wrote,

> An opportunity was provided for attacks on Judaism. Some did so from a Christian dogmatic point of view; others in more coarse terms, directing their attacks against the Talmud, demanding that recognition (preferably toleration) of the Jewish religion should be subjected to an examination of the tenets of Judaism. An Arrow-Cross party deputy opposed the recognition of Jewry altogether and instead proposed that Jews be placed under strict police control; another deputy of the same party demanded that Jewish pupils be segregated in schools and that the Jews be herded into ghettos.[173]

After consideration in an appropriate subcommittee, the bill was passed to the Upper House. Since the bill contained no attacks on the Christian faiths, it aroused no opposition among church leaders. On the contrary, this bill matched their view that granting the status of an "accepted religion" at the close of the nineteenth century had been a fundamentally mistaken act. It should be recalled that while the debate was raging on the proposed second anti-Jewish law, Bishop Glattfelder expressed himself in this vein, praising those members of the Upper House who forty or fifty years before had already fought against the strengthening of the spirit of Judaism and had raised their voices against the granting of equal status to the Jewish religion and to the Christian faiths.[174] When the government began to lower the official status of the Jewish religion, it acted in such a way that satisfied the church, which had demanded such a step, and had awaited it for over forty years.

The act was adopted on July 29, 1942.

It inflicted great damage on the Jewish communities. It ruled out any government support for Jewish educational institutions or participation in the salaries received by the rabbis. The set of anti-Jewish laws that preceded this legislation severely impacted the livelihood of many Jews. This hurt, poverty-stricken population—which had previously borne part of the expenses of the Jewish community—now became a heavy burden on the rapidly emptying Jewish public coffers. And so the Jewish community found itself damaged two or three times over, with the loss of government participation in its expenses, a considerable reduction of the income collected from the Jewish community, and a growing number of people dependent upon community generosity.

Moreover, denying recognition of the Jewish religion struck hard at the public status of the Jews. The act pulled the rug out from under the most important achievement of the Jewish public since it had existed in Hungary. This denial also struck at the self-confidence of the Jewish community—already showing signs of weakening—which had for many years viewed itself as possessing equal rights to those of the other religions and as constituting an integral part of the Hungarian homeland.

The Jewish Estates Expropriation Act

On March 3, 1942, Miklos Kallay was appointed prime minister.[175] About a week after his appointment he appeared at a convention of his party, the ruling party. The chairman of the party, Bela Lukacs, who introduced the prime minister, described him as "the man who would lead the nation in the path of the 'Szeged idea,' based on the conception of defense of the Hungarian race." Lukacs went on to request that "he lead us along the road to the full realization of the concept of right-wing policy in the Christian spirit."[176]

In his very first speech, Kallay laid out the internal and external policies of his government. With regard to foreign policy he stated:

The first thing I must say is that the government I hereby present is a cabinet of war, for we are participating seriously in the war. It is a most fateful war, which will not only decide the fates of individual nations, whether they will survive or cease to exist; the fate of the entire human race will be decided in this war. For us the decision was made long ago. This is no temporary decision; neither is it an opportunistic one; for we took up arms in support of Germany and Italy before they became world powers. We would neither have been worthy of our Hungarian name nor fitting heirs to our forefathers' heritage, had we not joined the camp fighting against eastern barbarism, had we not stood firm when it became necessary to defend Christianity, when we await the realization of our lofty Hungarian ideals. We belong, without reservation, at the side of our allies, Germany and Italy, and we must take action on the battlefields of Russia, for our Hungarian pride does not permit us to allow others to fight our war. This struggle against Bolshevism is what shall determine the framework of tasks to be undertaken by this government.

In his speech Kallay repeated some half a dozen times that Hungary was at war with the Soviet Union, and spoke of the sacrifices the Hungarian nation would have to make for the success of its struggle.

With regard to internal policy the premier touched briefly on various problems, spending considerable time on the Jewish question while announcing that "within a week a bill will be presented for the total expropriation of estates belonging to Jews." His words were applauded noisily, his audience uttering sounds of encouragement:

The Jews are antisocial beings, both as a community and each and every Jew as an individual. If we look at the balance of Jewish activity in any country, we shall always arrive at the conclusion that, in the long run, they have been detrimental.... and even if we succeed with difficulty in overcoming the damage they caused us in 1918, we will yet be unable to be sure of overcoming them. And so, this bill speaks merely of amending the social injustice caused us as a result of the activity of Hungarian Jewry. ... Therefore my outlook on the Jewish question is extremely simple: we must perform any task which serves the interests of the nation. Any step serving to advance us in this direction must be carried out without mercy and without considering any other factor. The Jewish problem is a problem of the entire nation.

Displacing the Jews economically is a basic condition for the economical progress of the Hungarian nation, and practically speaking, I am about to deal with only a single topic—the problem of the Jewish-owned estates. From this viewpoint my position is enviable, for I need only carry out what I proposed when I was the minister of agriculture in Gombos's government: the total and immediate expropriation of the estates belonging to Jews. As in the past, today, too, I want to make it clear that I have no intention of touching any land, even a single parcel of land owned by a Hungarian, as long as it is possible for me to make use of lands owned by Jews ... and so, in the very near future I shall direct the party and Parliament to facilitate the transfer to Christian hands of all those estates owned by people to whom the anti-Jewish legislation applies.[177]

Kallay went on to announce that the Jews whose estates would be expropriated would be recompensed in such a way that any large-scale flow of compensation into the economy would be prevented—for such a development might have a negative effect on the national economy. The practical significance of this announcement was that the government would compensate the owners of the expropriated estates by means of nonnegotiable bonds bearing interest at the rate of 3.5 percent, which would be frozen for thirty years. According to the proposed law, the expropriation of the estates could take place even before the sum of the compensation was determined.[178]

At the end of his speech, the chairman of the party congratulated the prime minister, promising him that "the members of the party would be united in their faithful support of the prime minister and of the trail he blazed in his speech: the way to build a Christian, right-wing Hungary."

Less than a week later Kallay appeared in Parliament, presented his government, and once again stressed that the government was a war cabinet. The general line of his speech in Parliament resembled that of the speech he had delivered a week before at the party forum. Again and again he analyzed Hungary's participation in the war at the side of the Axis forces, the subject cropping up in various contexts in this speech no less than twenty-four times. It would seem that Kallay himself noted his obsessive stressing of the subject, commenting,

There may be some who think it unnecessary to revert to this subject so many times. However, for as long as I fill this office I shall indeed repeat it again and again. . . . In telegrams I have exchanged with the leaders of our allies I have stated in connection with our foreign policy that we have pursued a consistent foreign policy for over twenty years, a policy based on Hungary's unchanging orientation. The unambiguous significance of this orientation is that, in accordance with its historic tradition, our nation fights against the Asian danger of Bolshevism, thus playing the role of defender of Christianity. A further meaning of Hungarian orientation is loyalty: loyalty and an obstinate support of our great allies and friends, the Axis powers, together with whom we struggle for a more decent world and for a new Europe. . . . Just as our place is alongside Germany and Italy today on the battlefield, so it will be tomorrow, too, when peace negotiations take place, at the negotiation table where the decisions for the future will be made.

We have come into this war with our full might, with all the military power at our disposal. We shall support our army with our entire economic effort and with our entire capability. I have already declared that we have come into this war because of ideals, because the Hungarian people fight against Bolshevism with all their might. We must take part in this struggle with all our strength because this war will decide the fate of our nation— survival or cessation. And so once again I beg of you: starting today, starting now, please view this subject as the most central and most important problem of our country and of all our actions.

Another central topic in Kallay's speech was the expropriation of the estates belonging to Jews:

The ministry of agriculture is involved in all kinds of problems, but with your permission, I will not deal with them at present.... I assume you read today in the official newspaper that all the estates of more than 500 *hold* belonging to Jews are, from today, in a state of deep freeze. This deep freeze includes all their equipment, both their living equipment, i.e., the animals, and their inert equipment.... We have no intention of carrying out the expropriation of the estates by word of mouth or by all kinds of biological definitions. The proposed legislation will be carried out on the basis of the law for the Protection of the Race, and it is obvious that the legislation hereby proposed will not recognize all the exemptions which were granted to certain Jews within the framework of the second anti- Jewish law.

Incidentally, I must also announce that I have confiscated all the forests which were in the hands of Jews. We are talking of more than half a million *hold* of forests—in addition to all the other estates, whose combined area itself comes to more than half a million hold.... We shall expropriate all the lands in return for bonds, we shall not pay cash for the expropriated estates. The prime minister also mentioned the role of the minister of justice, "who will, in the most immediate future, present a bill for the expropriation of the estates of the Jews."

Kallay also referred to Jewry in general:

I shall not discuss the Jewish problem in order to clarify the question of whether Jewry is a race or not. I am of the opinion that we have already passed this stage, and that it has been clearly demonstrated that Jewry is indeed a race.... This is natural and self-explanatory, and I am unable to think of Jewry in any other terms than as a race.[179]

The first speaker after Kallay was the chairman of his party:

Hungarian policy has been based for the past decade on the idea of protecting the race, on the ideas of Christianity and nationalism known as "the Szeged idea."... The various governments recognized the unique justice of this concept, upon which this party is based and this government relies, and which has always believed in the right-wing, Christian concept of protecting the race.... We have engraved this national concept on the pages of history of Hungarian life at a time when many European states were still going astray in the channels of false democracy, and sought their happiness in the spirit of the international idea. This Christian idea did not spring up out of the depth of the hearts of such broad circles in any country other than our own, as has happened in our land, as has happened to us, when we were called upon to found everything on the solid basis of the Christian idea and Christian morality.

After congratulating the premier on his alliance with the Axis powers, the speaker began to discuss internal matters: "The premier's announcement of the expropriation of the estates of the Jews is welcomed by the members of the Party and by Hungarian circles of a right-wing outlook." He went on to say that the prime minister's opinion on the role of the Jews caused him much satisfaction; he wanted "to continue to march along the path upon which we marched our first march last year when we adopted the law of Protection of the Race. We must continue this way, thus ensuring the absolute social isolation of the Jews."

The prime minister's speech was debated that same day and the following. Most of the participants in the debate expressed their satisfaction with the premier's approach to the Jewish problem and encouraged him in his work. Moreover, the speakers welcomed the prime minister's clear, unambiguous stand regarding Hungary's firm support for Germany and Italy in their struggle against Bolshevism.

Count Bela Teleki, a representative of the Transylvanian party, announced that

> full coordination must be achieved between foreign policy and internal policy. Our fate will be decided in this war, and we have the opportunity to lay the foundations for a greater, richer Hungary.... Our full cooperation with the Axis forces, based on full mutual trust, is the only policy capable of concentrating the entire nation under the banner of war. The residents of Transylvania are ready to suffer deprivation, for they know that this suffering is for their own good.

Bela Imredi, the former prime minister, spoke for his opposition party, expressing his happiness at the premier's announcement that "this war is our war.... Indeed, this struggle is being waged between conflicting outlooks, and we must find the common denominator between our ancient Hungarian heritage and the new spirit permeating Europe. This new spirit is striving to serve nationalistic concepts."[180]

On the following day, the representative of the Christian party expressed his admiration of Hungary's prime ministers, past and present, saying that "the people must work together in doing a good deal for the sake of a greater, independent, and Christian Hungary.... With honesty and loyalty we are participating in the struggle against the Bolsheviks on the side of our allies." The remaining speakers uttered similar statements.

In his reply, Kallay repeated the main points he had made previously, adding, "for as long as the war lasts we must limit our legislative work to those most important and urgent cases. My proposal relating to the expropriation of the estates belonging to the Jews is an example of this sort of legislation."[181]

Even before the debate was over in Parliament, Kallay won the support and encouragement of his district of origin, Szabolcs. The national council of Christian craftsmen held a convention in the capital of the district, Nyiregyhaza. The honorary president of the organization, member of Parliament Kalman Bertalan,

> praised the prime minister's eternal credit in the victory of the concept of race protection.... Kallay was among the very first in the district of Sabolicz to speak of the idea of protecting the race, and he fought for the victory of the Christian, socialist, and nationalist concept as far back as twenty years ago. He was the person who began to fight for the political concept of protecting the Hungarian race during a period when the powerful Jewish liberals controlled the souls of the people.... Kallay, who was one of the first fighters for the concept of protecting the race, now brings this idea to its culmination in the expropriation of the estates of the Jews.... In his first act Kallay proved he had won the victory of the concept of protecting the race for everyone.

The resolution adopted at the convention stated,

> We believe and we know that by means of his judgment, his strong hand, and his firm resolve the prime minister shall succeed in advancing the Christian idea and social development even in this period of war.... In humility, in brotherly love, in dedication, and in appreciation we congratulate his Excellency and his family, and call upon God to bestow His plentiful blessings upon his work and his deeds.

The local paper devoted an appreciative column to the resolution, and it was quoted in a national paper. It congratulated Kallay for "his first act as prime minister being in the spirit of the concept of protection of the race—expropriating the estates of the Jews. This is not the first time that Kallay stands firm in support of the Christian and social concept of protecting the race. He declared his position while he was still governor of our district."[182]

About a month after the debate in Parliament the enlarged national council of the ruling party convened, with the participation of some thousand delegates from all parts of Hungary, members of the party faction in the legislature, and the provincial governors who were party members. Kallay delivered the main speech at the convention.

In this speech he dealt once again with the subjects that had come up for discussion in his previous appearances at the party forum and in Parliament. With regard to Hungary's participation in the war—a topic he mentioned more than a dozen times—he said,

> We shall sacrifice for it whatever we are required—in effort, in wheat, and in blood....I declare openly that I accept the responsibility for this war, for I know the goal we are fighting for, and I even know what the future may have in store for us if we lose....If we do not triumph, there shall be no homeland, there shall be no Hungarian people, there shall be no religion, there shall be no prayer "Our Father who art in Heaven," we shall not have our daily bread, and evil will rule over the face of the earth.

Kallay appealed to the emotions of his audience and said, "Our soldiers are doing their duty so courageously and so successfully that the German High Command has seen fit to express its thanks to them, and it has done so not only in a run-of-the-mill Order of the Day, but also in messages it has sent us."

Concerning the expropriation of Jewish estates the prime minister reminded his audience that this was actually an old proposal of his, from the days when he served as minister of agriculture in the Gombos government. He repeated his view that in return for the confiscated lands the government would pay in bonds, adding, "We cannot allow the enormous sums of compensation; the Jews will have to find their way to undesirable forms of investment: hoarding merchandise, raising prices, and similar negative activities."

Kallay seems to have been encouraged by the agreement his antisemitic steps met in the Hungarian public, and announced additional new steps:

> The bill ensures that anyone leasing his field to a Jew will be entitled to cancel the lease....A most important component of the bill is that which states that Jews will in the future be forbidden to settle in the countryside. A Jew whose lands are confiscated will not be permitted in the future to retain more land than the area occupied by his home, together with a small garden, the maximum area being 2,000 square meters.

Kallay even sang his own praises with regard to his practical approach to solving the Jewish problem, and was warmly applauded.

I permit myself to say, that of all those who have held the position I hold today none has treated the subject with the same decisiveness and the same precise definitions as I. I know that further steps must be taken against Jewry. I know that the Jews must be removed from most walks of Hungarian life. I am also aware of the fact that this removal must be executed, not slowly but at an accelerated pace. . . . I know how fast this task must be carried out. I feel I have shown you how fast I work by raising before you such proposals as no one in a responsible position in this country ever dared even dream about, as recently as one month ago.

The Kallay Proposal for the Expulsion of the Jews from Hungary

In the speech he had delivered before the enlarged national council of the ruling party, Kallay brought up an idea that surprised his entire audience:

As long as we are dealing with the Jewish question, I had better put my own standpoint before you. . . . I know there is no final solution to this problem other than the removal [Kallay used the term *kitelepites,* which may also be translated as "expulsion," "exiling," "uprooting"] of the Jews, who number 800,000 people. . . . In the meantime, the Jews must be removed from each and every socially and nationally important position— until such time as the final solution becomes feasible.[183]

In this part of his speech Kallay made use of two expressions that became catastrophic for the Jews during World War II—"the removal of the Jews" and "the final solution." With regard to "the final solution," we shall give Kallay the benefit of the doubt and assume that he used the expression without the significance and the inverted commas that were added to it at a later stage. However, this is certainly not so with regard to the idea of "removing the Jews." This was the first time in the modern history of Hungary that a person at the very pinnacle of the executive pyramid publicly announced plans to expel all the Jews from Hungary. Such opinions had been expressed previously, but not by so prominent a personality. It should be noted that Kallay hurled the idea of expelling the Jews into the political and public life of Hungary about two years before the German invasion of that country.

The idea was absorbed, began to spread rapidly, and was referred to on a practical basis by various factors, both in Parliament and outside it. It may be assumed that when the time came for the expulsion of the Jews in 1944, the idea of uprooting hundreds of thousands of citizens from their homes had already lost most of its strangeness.

Kallay was ahead of his time, even ahead of the Germans.

As part of the debate on the bill expropriating the estates, which was held at the end of May, a deputy representing the ruling party referred to the idea of exiling the Jews that Kallay had brought up:

> The prime minister has announced that the Jews should be exiled from Hungary. Since the bill before us concerning the expropriation of Jewish property is limited to a single sector, the agricultural sector, we should—in the spirit of the concept of exile as proposed by the prime minister—prepare a series of regulations to comprise a suitable method of expropriating all valuables owned by the Jews.[184]

The debate in Parliament continued into the beginning of June. One member of Parliament spoke of the ideological link between the expropriation of land and the expulsion of the Jews: "Land is not a normal trade item; land is our living space, a part of the Hungarian homeland. Hungarian land and the Hungarian nation are the components of the Kingdom of St. Istvan. The proposed law is an integral part of the program aimed ultimately at the exiling of the Jews from the country."[185]

Other members of Parliament referred to various aspects of the treatment accorded the Jews within the framework of the discussion of the proposed bill and while referring to the prime minister's various speeches. One Parliament member suggested broadening the prime minister's proposal to forbid Jewish settlement in the villages; he demanded "that the prohibition on Jews purchasing real estate not be limited to the villages, but rather expanded to include the towns as well." Yet another Parliament member referred to what Kallay had said about Jewish lessees: "Let us speed up the solution to the problem of the estates in the hands of Jewish lessees."[186]

Another speaker referred to the process of expropriating Jewish pharmacies, and proposed that "just like the compensation procedure in return for expropriated land, so we must see to it that the pharmacy owners be recompensed in bonds."[187]

Yet another speaker came to what he felt was the self-evident conclusion to be drawn from the confiscation of Jewish-owned land:

> The Jews, who are at the present time busily losing their property and becoming proletarians, comprise a real public danger, since they are involved with the simple, ignorant folk who tend to believe everything. For this reason it is not enough to expropriate Jewish lands and property. After the expropriation, a suitable regulation is to be enacted, one which will rule that all the Jews are to be gathered in a closed area.[188]

It should be noted that the idea of exiling the Jews was deliberated outside of Parliament as well. The Hungarian ambassador to Germany,

Dome Sztojay—who was to become Hungarian prime minister after the German invasion of March 1944—expressed his opinion later in 1942 that "it would be right for the government of Hungary to exile a considerable portion of the Jewish population to occupied sections of Russia." Sztojay spoke of between one and three hundred thousand Jews who were to be exiled immediately.[189]

The bill was received favorably by Parliament. The minister of agriculture even complimented the opposition for not having expressed any ideological opposition to the proposal.[190] One of the speakers, Count Gyorgy Apponyi, did express his reservations regarding the idea of the government offering valueless compensation for the expropriated estates, but he, too, expressed his agreement with the idea of expropriation: "According to the outlook of Christian morality, the right of the individual to property ends where it comes into conflict with the public interest. The right of expropriation exists in every civilized state, but compensation for the confiscated lands must be paid in accordance with the full and true value of the lands."[191]

Yet another speaker who took part in the debate during that session referred to the problem of expropriation without suitable compensation, asserting, "Let us not worry about certain regulations violating the rights of the individual, for the ancient Hungarian constitution presents us with many examples of this kind. We are living today in a period which obliges us to apply new approaches in place of all kinds of outdated laws, which do not adequately meet the needs of the nation."[192]

It wasn't long until a certain member of Parliament even came up with an ideological justification for expropriation without appropriate compensation. "According to the Hungarian constitutional outlook, the source of private property is the holy crown of the kingdom, which represents the general public at its highest level. This is especially true when dealing with real estate. In certain cases the holy crown may have its ownership rights restored."[193]

The bill was adopted by Parliament on June 10, 1942, and sent to the Upper House.[194] There it was considered without delay, the House being united in its positive approach toward it. The bill was weakly opposed by one member of the Upper House, himself a landowner, who expressed his anxiety that the confiscation of Jewish estates without paying suitable compensation might serve as a precedent:

One of the important elements of our constitution has been the procedure whereby in every case of expropriation, the recompense has been determined by an independent court of law. This deviation from the accepted procedure arouses anxiety that in another period and under changing circumstances the regime may apply this method to other people's estates as well.[195]

The minister of agriculture expressed his appreciation of the Upper House for its matter-of-fact approach to the bill. "We do not disagree on the outlook which determines that land belonging to the Hungarian homeland must remain in Hungarian hands."[196] The Upper House adopted the bill with minor amendments on June 15, 1942.

The historian Katzburg refers to this bill in the following way: "The significance of the law was chiefly political. Hungarian Jews regarded the right to own real estate as a symbol of their civil equality. The ban on land ownership removed one of the last remnants of Jewish emancipation."[197]

The position adopted by the church leaders—especially by those of the Catholic church—calls for special consideration. Contrary to their actual and decisive involvement in the debates on the earlier anti-Jewish bills—especially on the first three bills—this time the leaders of the Christian churches, members of the Upper House, stood out by not participating in the debate on the proposed law. In light of their declared antisemitic views, as these had been expressed in every one of their speeches delivered during the consideration of the anti-Jewish legislation both in the Upper House plenum and in its subcommittees, one cannot be surprised that they did not object to the robbery being carried out in the guise of legislation, though there may have been additional reasons for their silence.

It is reasonable to assume that the fact that the heads of the priesthood ignored the subject resulted from their awareness of the meaning of the expropriation of the estates. The churches were among the largest landowners in Hungary.[198] At the same time, one of Hungary's most serious problems was the poverty that was instrumental in the degeneration of her agricultural workers, who had no land of their own and who numbered some three million at the time. Most of this huge population lived under the severest conditions, their status not amounting to much more than that of the vassals of earlier centuries. They lived on the lands of their masters and labored exceedingly hard for a minimal wage. The path to improvement of their conditions, their status, and their education was almost completely blocked, and they had no real hope of improvement. After the events of 1918–1920 the leaders of Hungary realized that it was necessary to find a way to improve the conditions of this population stratum. Plans were laid for a necessary agrarian reform, but these remained embryonic and never reached the stage of actual implementation.

Whenever the question of agrarian reform came to be of public interest, the Catholic church—itself the owner of huge estates—felt itself threatened, and devoted time and thought to repelling the challenge. Upon the government's preparing a bill on the topic in the early 1920s, the Synod of Catholic Bishops referred to it in this way:

> To whatever extent a fair division of lands is desirable, a far-reaching agrarian reform is equally dangerous, because it opposes the concept of the right to possess private property, it lessens the fruits of labor, it furthers the existence of a revolutionary atmosphere, and strikes at the foundations of cultural institutions. The Synod of Bishops is able to participate in a national campaign aimed against the danger inherent in excess.[199]

The bishops thus determined their basic stand relative to the idea of "agrarian reform." From a study of additional protocols of sessions of the Synod of Bishops, the bishops would seem to have adhered to this stand of theirs for the ensuing twenty years during which the subject periodically came up for discussion.[200] The bishops expressed their desire to assist the government, but stipulated conditions for their assistance:

> To further the existence and happiness of the nation, the church is willing to make sacrifices to the greatest extent possible. The cardinal, however, has especially stressed that the church is unwilling to endanger its institutions, for their survival is of supreme national interest.... If and when it is proposed that certain lands belonging to the church be distributed in order to facilitate the establishment of small farms, the church will be willing to do so, but only on condition that the leases be drawn up between church and state, and not between church and the lessees. In this way the church will be sure that the leasing fees will actually be paid her.[201]

The Synod of Bishops also announced that it would "be willing to support a Land-Lease bill, on condition that the rights of the church as a landowner are preserved, and that the church receives full compensation for its agreement to the leasing."[202] At another session the bishops expressed their opinion that it was "desirable for some body to be set up to make all necessary arrangements while guaranteeing Catholic interests."[203]

The bishops' debates and resolutions indicate their awareness of the importance of owning land and their knowledge of how matters could be arranged in such a way as to guarantee Catholic interests. They knew how to word their stipulations in order to ensure their ownership of the lands even after they were leased—in return for appropriate compensation, the responsibility for the actual payment being the government's.

Those same bishops, headed by the cardinal, remained indifferent and could not find a single word in favor of "the idea of the right to possess private property," when the property under discussion belonged to Jews. Similarly, they were not perturbed by the possibility of the existence "of a revolutionary atmosphere and of harm done to the foundations of civilized institutions" in the wake of the distribution of the lands that had been taken from the Jews.

In this light, there would seem to be more than a little cynicism in the speech Seredi delivered about a year after the Expropriation of Jewish Estates Law was adopted, at a nationwide Catholic convention held in Budapest:

> We respect everyone's right to his privately owned property, which he acquired either courageously or industriously, or which he inherited from his forefathers who acquired it either courageously or industriously. According to the doctrine of Jesus we fearlessly demand the enforcement of justice in the mutual relations between individual and collective.[204]

In the cardinal's opinion, "justice according to the doctrine of Jesus" would seem to be powerless to come to the defense of Jewish property.

One of the immediate results the government expected of the agrarian reform was the availability of plots of land on which the homes of agricultural and industrial workers were to be built. In this way the government hoped to appease to some extent the rage of the manual laborers who, despite their rigorous labors, benefited but little from this labor, making no progress whatever toward a better future. The prime minister referred both to this problem and to the opportunities inherent in the expropriation of Jewish lands.[205] A member of Parliament referred to the subject as well, stressing the necessity of a solution for the problem: "The solution of the problem of distributing the plots for the construction of homes should be viewed as one of the most important and urgent matters."[206]

And so the minister of agriculture expressed his willingness to ascribe urgency to this problem. In his summation and reply to the debaters he said, "First and foremost, I shall devote special attention to the solution of the problem of plots of land for construction and to the furthering of this matter."[207]

Since the general public considered the solution of the construction lot problem more immediate and simpler to execute than the comprehensive solution of granting agricultural land to millions of landless agricultural workers for cultivation, it also aroused more hope and expectation in public opinion. The government, with a considerable degree of justification, expected the distribution of lots to the needy for construction to function as a safety valve, releasing to some extent the pressure of that public opinion. In light of the fact that the premier announced explicitly, "I shall not touch any Hungarian land. . . . as long as it is possible for me to use the land belonging to Jews,"[208] it may be possible to assume that in addition to their traditionally hostile stand regarding the Jews and Judaism, church leaders considered the confiscation of Jewish estates to be useful—that is, the more problems solved by means of the lands expropriated from the Jews, the smaller the number of accusing fingers to be pointed at the churches, the owners of giant estates, for not participating in the effort to relieve the suffering of millions of their landless and homeless congregants.

Another fateful topic raised in the prime minister's speeches was, as already noted, the idea of exiling the Jews from Hungary. It is interesting to follow the reaction of the churches to this proposal. This reaction was voiced indirectly, but the intent of its message was unmistakable.

Two weeks after Kallay's announcement of the plan for a final solution to the problem of Hungary's eight hundred thousand Jews by means of their expulsion, Cardinal Seredi appeared at a ceremony held in the town of Nagyvarad on the 750th anniversary of the canonization of one of Hungary's first Christian kings, St. Laszlo. Seredi chose the topic of "the obligation to obey the laws of the state" as a central motif for his speech:

> We are to learn from our king, St. Laszlo, that as Christians we have to strive for sanctity in all walks of life, and we even have to achieve that sanctity. In order to achieve our goal, we must adhere to our faith according to the example he set us. . . . We must ascribe to the will of God not only religious laws, but also those of the state, and so we are obligated to obey them to the best of our conscientious awareness. We must view them as obligating us, just as our king, St. Laszlo, did.
>
> The truth is that not only was the great king conscious of Jesus' commands—"Render unto Caesar that which is Caesar's, and unto God that which is God's"—he also spread the doctrine of the apostle unto the nations: "Everyone must be loyal to the authorities, because authority is of God." And so, one who resists the authorities is resisting God, and those who do so merely bring harm upon themselves. It is thus important that you be faithful to the regime not only for fear of punishment, but also because of the command given by your conscience.
>
> In light of this it is self-evident that if we desire to be good Catholics and loyal Hungarians, we have to accept the fact that not only the laws of the church obligate us conscientiously. Our homeland, too, is entitled to legislate obligatory laws, and indeed has such laws. The law of the

church has been clear since its very founding, ruling that the rulers of nations are entitled to pass laws which obligate their subjects from a conscientious viewpoint, for their laws are the logical result of the obligation to further the interests of society.... And so, the churches protect the interests of their states even more efficiently than the state authorities themselves can do.[209]

As already noted, the fact that the Seredi speech followed that of Kallay so closely is what renders the Seredi speech as significant as it is. Regarding the obligation of obedience to secular authority, Christians were instructed by the founder of their faith: "Render unto Caesar that which is Caesar's"—the conclusion being, "one who resists the authorities is resisting God." The cardinal did not categorize the obligation of obedience; neither did he express his reservations at brutal announcements made by the chief authority, announcements which I believe are opposed to the laws of both humanity and God.

Seredi even succeeded in ascribing to the ancient Hungarian king and his deeds a dimension of immediacy by adding a number of biographical details concerning him:

Pope Celestine III included him ceremoniously among the saints of Christianity 750 years ago. His knightly Christian behavior—a trait he developed for himself as king of Hungary—established him as an ideal character worthy of emulation, not only in the eyes of those who succeeded him on the throne of the Hungarian kingdom, but also in the eyes of all Christian Europe, who viewed him as its leader, both spiritually and militarily. For this reason the leaders of the Crusades—who had organized themselves for the liberation of those places which were sanctified by our Lord Jesus and which were then under the rule of the Turkish idolators—turned to King St. Laszlo and invited him to be their supreme commander.

We, his descendants, have made a pilgrimage to his town in order to express our admiration of him. Yet let us not forget that this expression of our admiration will be of value to the beloved, holy king, only if each and every one of us does his very best to live in accordance with his exalted example.... The life of St. Laszlo is so overflowing with religious and patriotic themes that each and every one of us can learn a great deal from him, and we all can advance in the footsteps of the examples he has set for us.[210]

In this fashion Seredi succeeded in ascribing immediacy to the leader of the ancient Crusades, an immediacy that managed to capture the hearts of his audience. It will be recalled that in his speech in Parliament of

March 19, 1942—less than two months before Seredi's speech—Kallay referred to Hungary's war against Bolshevism as "a renewed Crusade." "In accordance with its historical tradition our nation wages war against the Asian danger of Bolshevism and fulfills in this way its role as the defender of Christianity."[211]

The parallel is clear: the Turks parallel the Russians, and idolators parallel the Bolsheviks.

And Seredi presented the king, the Crusader leader, as a character worthy of emulation. Indeed, the achievements of that king were emulated by Seredi's contemporaries; in fact, the latter surpassed the original. That king was the first Hungarian monarch to enact legislation against the Jews. This occurred in 1092, at a national conference held in the province of Szabolcs.

> A convention of the holy synod took place, headed by Laszlo, the faithful Christian king of the Hungarians, with the participation of the bishops, the heads of the monasteries, and the priesthood throughout his kingdom, with the approval of the entire nation. They conferred about the strengthening of Christianity. The synod adopted the following resolutions: prohibition of marriage between Jews and Christians; confiscating the tools of a Jew working on Sunday or on a Christian holy day in a way insulting to the Christian spirit; and prohibiting the owning of a Christian slave by Jews.[212]

Appealing to the tradition of St. Laszlo was, in a way, the closing of a historic cycle. As the historian Venetianer defined it:

> The prohibition of the owning of a Christian slave was in itself a severe economic blow at the Jews, for it denied them the opportunity of cultivating their lands. . . . This limitation already contained the seeds of the economic shift which compelled the Jews to abandon agriculture and to turn to other economic fields.[213]

Despite the long period of time intervening between the decrees of the eleventh century and those of the twentieth, the similarity between them is great: the reasoning behind the anti-Jewish decrees in both cases was the desire "to strengthen Christianity"; the church leaders participated in the adoption of the anti-Jewish resolutions; the decrees were adopted "with the approval of the entire nation"; and they forbade mixed marriages. With regard to the prohibition of Jewish occupations, the twentieth-century decrees were far harsher than those of the eleventh century. This applies, too, to Jewish ownership of land. While in the eleventh century denying Jewish ownership of land was the logical result of the decrees, in the twentieth century the aim of taking over Jewish land was not even disguised. Seredi recommended that his believers "follow the examples set for us by the ancient king." It would seem that Seredi's statement that "we are to ascribe to the will of God...the laws of the state as well" included Kallay's ideas of confiscating estates and the planned expulsion. The conduct of the Hungarians in the summer of 1944 proves that the words spoken by Seredi in the spring of 1942 were well received.

A short two days after the Seredi speech the Reformed church held its General Reformed Convent Congress with the participation of the head of the church in Hungary, Bishop Sandor Ravasz. At this congress as well, the idea was voiced that it was necessary for members of the church to carry out loyally government decisions. The main trustee of the church, Jeno Balogh, delivered the central speech, spoke of subjects of immediate concern, and said,

> Hungarians belonging to the Reformed church bear the yoke of carrying out national and church roles, and they do so with devotion and with steadfast resolution. The Hungarian nation, in cooperation with her great allies, is fighting in this world-embracing war for important values. We must fight this defensive war of ours for exalted moral values, which in their importance surpass any material value—we fight for our religion and our faith, we fight against the denial of God, which has become established, has developed, and has become a great and organized power.
>
> The Reformed church collaborates with the government in all those areas which are aimed at improving the conditions of those millions of deeply rooted Hungarians, living in villages and working on agricultural farms. Within the framework of our creative policy there already exist useful, beneficent enterprises aimed at strengthening the Hungarian population.[214]

The speaker did not explain the nature of the "useful, beneficent enterprises" aimed at "improving the conditions" of the agricultural laborers, but the hint was supposed to be well understood by the listeners since it was uttered during the last stages of the debate on the law for the expropriation of Jewish estates.

The idea expressed by religious functionaries, that the obligation of obedience to the secular authorities was a religious obligation, served to strengthen the position of the secular rulers of the state. And so it is not surprising that the minister of propaganda, Istvan Antal, voiced a similar opinion. At a eucharistic convention at the town of Szentes he lectured on the subject "Catholicism and Public Life." He spoke of the roles of the leader and the led, and said:

The leaders must remember at all times that they are to exercise the power entrusted to them according to the laws of God and the exalted principles of justice, love, and freedom. On the other hand, those led are to be conscious of the fact that their obligation of obedience to the legal leaders is in accordance with the laws of God.... The most brutal, barbaric, and horrible regime ever to rise to power in human history threatens Christian Europe from the east. By virtue of the flood of its cohorts, by virtue of its untapped material power and its rude brutality, Asiatic Bolshevism strives to subjugate Christian Europe, which has cultivated its culture in the spirit of Jesus' cross.

We are to build a social order based on the laws of Jesus, viz., freedom, justice, mutual social responsibility, human respect, and, in short—Christian brotherhood and solidarity in the spirit of the doctrine of Jesus.[215]

As the war dragged on, disgust with and fear of communism were increasingly voiced, as was the identification of Judaism with communism. Sometimes this identification was merely hinted at, sometimes stated explicitly. From the prominence accorded the struggle of communism against Christianity, one could clearly conclude that communism was not at war with Judaism. On the contrary, communism and Judaism were capable of coexisting harmoniously, at one and the same time:

The minister of propaganda, Istvan Antal, came to the town of Szombathely as the guest of Bishop Jozsef Grosz.... In his speech he pointed out the fact that we have to face up to the red danger threatening us from the east. Together with our great allies we are participating in this struggle being waged for European culture and for the Christian way of life.[216]

The bishop of Szekesfehervar, Lajos Shvoy, spoke less obscurely. He was explicit where the minister of propaganda had been implicit. In a Shepherds' Epistle he published on the occasion of the 1943 Lent, he pointed an accusing finger at those he considered responsible for the outbreak of war, and went so far as to reveal to his readers the motives of those who lit the fire of war:

Ignoring the Gospel of our Lord Jesus—just as heretic philosophy and international Jewry have done for decades—is what has led the Christian nations to this point.... Heretic Bolshevism and its new idolatry are waging a life-and-death struggle against the Christian outlook, their goal being to wipe Christianity off the face of the earth.

The bishop proved optimistic about the results of the struggle: "A new world and a new society will come about as a result of the difficult birth pangs of this struggle, and the glory of victory will belong to the eternal King of all generations: the Lord Jesus Christ."[217]

With regard to the Jews the message was clear: they have no place in that "new world and new society" to be established after the war was over, for they were among the initiators of the war against Christianity.

With the adoption of the anti-Jewish legislation in the summer of 1942, the anti-Jewish legislative process came to an end, but this did not mean that Jewish suffering was over. For about a year and a half, from the adoption of the anti-Jewish laws of 1942 until the German invasion of 1944, the various government ministries came out frequently with new regulations, operative instructions, and decrees that were aimed at creating the practical frameworks for the implementation of the anti-Jewish laws. A considerable portion of the implementation of the anti-Jewish legislation was entrusted to the local authorities: provincial, municipal, and village councils. Most of these did their best to embitter the lives of the Jews and did more than was required of them by the central government. Not in vain did Kallay praise the village notaries for "their loyalty and their efficiency," while announcing the increased authority of the local councils.[218]

The local authorities, who were most active in implementing the expropriation orders against the Jews, called upon the local population to cooperate with the government, and they responded willingly to this call, as in the following example.

As the dissection of Czechoslovakia began, in the autumn of 1938, territory from the south of that country was annexed to the north of Hungary. The Hungarian authorities set up public committees to examine and reorganize the occupation permits held by the tradesmen and craftsmen in the new territories. The Catholic periodical *Uj Elet* reported in its first issue of 1943 on the good results of this reorganization:

> The excitement aroused by the publication of the instruction issued by the prime minister's office, making mandatory a renewed examination of the occupation permits of tradesmen and craftsmen, calmed down some time ago.... This instruction enabled the local population to take an active part in carrying out these changes. In each and every district a local committee was set up to express its opinion of the possessors of permits. The authorities were represented on these committees by a single delegate, all the other committee members representing the various strata of the local populace. These committees well reflected the opinion of the public in the relevant district.
>
> According to the data just published, out of 22,847 possessors of permits 6,220 were Jews at the time of the return of these areas to our Hungarian homeland.... During the reconsideration, the permits of 3,748 Jews and of 79 Christians were canceled.... It is a wonderful fact that so many

Christian tradesmen and craftsmen have been so rapidly integrated into our economy, after removing so large a number of Jewish merchants and craftsmen within the framework of the changes taking place.... According to the data of June 1941, 3,119 permits were issued to Christian craftsmen and tradesmen to replace the 3,748 permits taken from the Jews, and the Christians have already initiated their economic activity.[219]

A number of points in this list are noteworthy—first, the expression "the excitement... calmed down": the prolonged processes of inciting against the Jews and choking off their livelihood had been normalized, and was treated as self-evident. Though they may have aroused some excitement at the time of their implementation, as time passed by the public learned to regard them as normal, and "the excitement calmed down."

Second, except for the lone government representative, the committees—which stole the bread from the mouths of thousands of Jewish families—were made up of representatives of the people. The compiler of the article cited above was justified in stating that "these committees well reflected the opinion of the public." Third, the Catholic periodical did not stop with a report of the activity of the committees. It also expressed its undisguised joy at what it defined as the "wonderful fact" that the Christian tradesmen and craftsmen, who had replaced the Jews removed from the sources of their livelihood, had integrated themselves so rapidly into the Hungarian economy.

It was not only the merchants and craftsmen who stressed their Christianity and attempted to make the most of it; academic professionals did the very same thing: "The Hungarian Catholic Doctors' Association and the Evangelical Hungarian Doctors' Union appealed to their members to hang in their clinics the uniform symbol of Christianity—the cross.... to ensure their constant acting and speaking in accordance with the demands of the Christian world of thought."[220]

The prime minister spoke of the nature of the "Christian world of thought." On his visit to the town of Ungvar, Kallay said,

We are pioneers, pioneers of Christian thought.... We Hungarians have always been the bearers of European culture and we are also the first to fight for the national Christian revival.... We have to open our eyes, we have to make doubly sure of what goes on in this land during this rough period. We must not be satisfied with having removed the Jews from various positions; it is insufficient to have removed the influence of Jewish capital. It is most important for us to be rid also of the influence of the Jewish spirit.

The chief functionary of the Greek Orthodox church, Jeno Ortulay, spoke in the name of the local population after the prime minister's speech. In the name of the hosts the Greek Orthodox Bishop Sandor Sztojka thanked the prime minister.[221]

Three days after his visit in Ungvar, Kallay took part in a meeting of the council of his party, where he delivered the main speech. He touched on most of the immediate questions facing Hungary, and voiced a kind of interim summary of the seven months he had been premier:

> No change has taken place in our foreign policy, and the meaning of this continuity of foreign policy line is our unquestioned loyalty to our struggle alongside our allies. We shall be prepared to make sacrifices to ensure the continued existence of this alliance, even over and above those sacrifices which are obligatory within the framework of this loyalty.... Neither have we changed direction in our internal policies; indeed, it would have been impossible for us to change direction, for the direction we follow is that which guarantees the survival of an independent, right-wing, Christian Hungary.
>
> I hereby inform you that the minister of finance will prepare a bill dealing with the imposition of a property tax on the Jews. We have no choice but to bear the special expenditures connected with our war efforts and it is only natural that we impose the main portion of those expenditures upon those who, over the last few decades, have taken control of a considerable part of our national property. For my part, I shall do the utmost to increase the level of this tax to its maximum.
>
> The housing shortage is one of our social problems. In this field, too, the Jews enjoy a considerable advantage, this phenomenon rendering more tangible their antisocial attitude. This problem, too, I would like to solve in accordance with the outline I have drawn up, and I would also like to assist in finding suitable housing for those Christian circles who have difficulty in this. I shall use all my power to ensure that the important positions are put into Christian hands as soon as possible.
>
> Let Jewry engrave on the tablet of its heart: the Jews must give up all hope! Never again will there be here conditions like those which prevailed under the last regime, a regime which would compel us to return to the Jews their confiscated lands. Our national Hungarian consciousness shall never deteriorate to such a nadir.
>
> And here I want to clarify a certain point: with regard to our treatment of the Jewish question I am prepared to take all the steps aimed at supporting the political, economic, and moral needs of the nation, to respond to them and to further them. On the other hand, I shall not be prepared to tolerate a situation whereby now, in their defeat, the Jews do even more to poison the atmosphere and engage in their destructive activities than they did when they were strong.[222]

Kallay's repeated calls to the nation to contribute to the war effort so as to defend Christian values did not go unheeded. In the very same issue of the newspaper that carried the Kallay speech cited here, there appeared an article that emphasized the importance of marking "the Day for the Treatment of the Recruits":

> The churches participate in the war effort. This is self-evident, for in this war the fate of the church and of the altar shall be decided: will their fate be as it has been in the kingdom of Stalin, or will it be as it is in those sections of Europe called "Christian"? . . . One of the astoundingly human features of this war is the priests who—together with Mountain Hunter units—climbed to the very highest of summits, and the priest-paratroopers who landed in their parachutes on the island of Crete [these descriptions fit the priests who served in the Nazi army].
>
> Our priests, too, are located in the fields of battle near Voronyezs and along the Don River. But for our churches this is not enough—they have been contributing to the war effort in the spirit of Jesus Christ, the Peace Maker. . . . This is the correct way to act! "The Day of Caring for the Recruits" is one of the most encouraging features of Hungarian Christianity.[223]

It was clear that from the beginning "the treatment of the recruits" was not meant to apply to Jewish recruits, nor did it include them. The "caring" of the Jews was determined by the person who was the master of life and death of tens of thousands of recruits along the Russian front: General Gusztav Jany was the commanding officer of the defeated Hungarian Second Army. Many of the labor battalions in which the Jewish recruits served had been dispatched to the fields of battle in the Ukraine and most of these had been attached to Jany's Second Army. Jany, more than anyone else, was personally responsible for the torturing and murdering of tens of thousands of young Hungarian Jews. After the war he was executed as a war criminal.

After his return to Budapest Jany came to the offices of the Red Cross to express his thanks to the organization for its activities on behalf of his soldiers. He spoke of the importance of helping one's fellow man and of assisting the suffering. "The special value of these characteristics is inherent in their stemming from love of Jesus and their being permeated with Christian love."[224]

The ministry of propaganda dedicated its new abode in Budapest: "In the framework of a moving traditional church ceremony, the Apostolic Prelate, Zsigmond Mihalovics, sanctified the building and prayed to God to bestow His blessing of abundance upon the new edifice, upon its workers, and upon the work which would be carried out within its walls."[225]

The minister of propaganda spoke:

Hungarian propaganda bases its methods upon the ideal contained in the concept of Jesus and upon the concept of a homeland.... This true, noble, and pure propaganda is merely a desire to preserve in the hearts of men that exalted moral level and to strengthen in their souls those exalted human characteristics.... The church of Jesus has been maintaining those exalted human characteristics for two thousand years, in the fullness of their exalted purity.... Hungarian propaganda is guided by two principles: our country must remain Hungarian forever, and the glow of the Cross of Jesus will never fade over Hungary and in the souls of the Hungarian people.[226]

When the minister spoke of "the desire to preserve in the hearts of men that exalted moral level and to strengthen in their souls those exalted human characteristics," he chose to shut his eyes to the existence of a group of people in Hungary, half a million strong, who did not benefit from the existence of those characteristics in the souls of the leading circles in the state.

Shutting one's eyes was the principle guiding Cardinal Seredi as well, when he gave voice to his idea at a national Catholic convention:

We Catholic Hungarians strive to further a better future for Hungary. ...We demand justice, both for the individual and for the entire public. We adamantly reject the allegations leveled against us from beyond our borders to the effect that various rights have been denied to our national or religious minorities.... There has never been anything like that in our country.[227]

Conclusion

At the onset of the anti-Jewish legislative process, the Jews of Hungary were citizens enjoying equal rights—at least in theory, if not in practice.

Six years sufficed to take up this group of people and place it outside the public domain. Most of the Jews' civil rights were denied them. Their livelihoods and their institutions were discriminated against. Their security was undermined. Physical assaults against Jews in the streets became normal events, and the shattering of windows in Jewish homes and shops occurred night after night—and the regime did nothing to protect them. On the contrary, the regime encouraged those attacks, in which thousands of Jews lost their lives.

A short time after Hungary entered the war against Russia, in July 1941, the Hungarian authorities hunted down "foreign" Jews in Hungary's northeastern provinces. Some thirty or thirty-five thousand Jews were arrested and about eighteen thousand of them were expelled from Hungary, into the Kamenets-Podolsk region of the Ukraine, where they were murdered.

In the town of Ujvidek, in the area annexed to Hungary from Yu-goslavia, the Hungarian security forces engaged in "a hunt for partisans." On January 21–23, 1942, the Hungarian army and police force concentrated about three thousand Jews[228]—men, women, and children—and led them toward the frozen Danube River. The security forces opened fire upon them. Those who were not killed by their fire froze to death in the river.

We have already noted the tens of thousands of Jews killed by the soldiers and officers of the Hungarian army during their service in the labor battalions.

In the spring of 1944, as the Red Army crept nearer and nearer to the borders of their country, Hungarians began to sense the Communist giant encroaching on them. Decades of propaganda had succeeded in implanting the fear of communism as the incarnation of evil on earth into the Hungarian public. An integral part of the anti-Communist propaganda was that the Jews were a fifth column, the pioneers of the Communist camp dwelling inside Hungary, while their Communist allies threatened the borders of their country from without.

A newspaper report told of a mass conference in the town of Kiskun-Felegyhaza, held ten days before the invasion of Hungary by the Germans: "The speakers proved objectively, in an unbiased and unprejudiced manner, the absolute identity of Judaism and communism. They also pointed out ways to fight against them."[229]

Of the importance of the war against these hazards we hear, at that time, from the bishop of Eger, Bela Czapik, who was the third most powerful official of the Hungarian Catholic church: "I still maintain the rank of captain which I earned in the Hussar unit. I do not give up my rank, and if problems arise, the bishop of Eger shall once again put on his uniform."[230]

In light of the growing outside pressure, the cooperation between the government and the churches was maintained, and even improved. The authorities found a symbolic way to thank church leaders for their support of the regime. The regent of Hungary granted his archbishop, Cardinal Justinian Seredi, the coveted medal of excellence, the great Cross of the Fraternity of St. Istvan.[231]

This medal of excellence was awarded to only one church leader of the Catholic church. But it must be remembered that while the debates on the steps to be taken by the state against the Jews—"the pioneers of international communism"—were in full swing, the leaders of the churches consistently maintained their three-way solidarity. All three expressed at every opportunity opinions identical in their support of the steps proposed by the regime. Therefore, the awarding of this medal of excellence to the leader of the greatest of Hungary's churches can be viewed as an expression of appreciation to the leaders of the other two churches as well.

The stands adopted by the churches vis-à-vis the Jews were identical. Furthermore, they strongly resembled—if they were not identical with— the position taken by the leaders of the regime regarding the Jews. The official organ of the Catholic church prided itself in that the Hungarian legislator imbibed his ideas from articles appearing in previous editions of the publication. During the debate on the second anti-Jewish act, on April 20, 1939, *Magyar Kurir* wrote,

> While Jewry begs (like a beggar extending his hand) for a sense of broth-erhood among the Hungarian public, it is unwilling to bend even a finger in order to return to the Hungarians those positions it, in its impudent and ruthless arrogance, grabbed control of.... The Jewish question has not yet been solved, and its very existence is stifling and poisonous.... Many im-portant legislators have adopted our rulings, even as our minister of law has adopted them in referring often, openly and lengthily, to what we wrote in earlier issues.

The Hungarian people were well aware of the position taken by its leaders, and its hatred of the Jews who were identified with international communism grew ever stronger—as did its fear of the Red Army ap-proaching the borders of its country. In the spring of 1944 the banners of that army were flying on the northeastern slopes of the Carpathian mountain range, within sight of the Hungarian border. The triangle— the regime, the church, and the people—stood firm in a united front in its opposition to the Hungarian Jewish population, and this population, in turn, found itself helpless, isolated, shunned, debased, beaten, and robbed—at the focal point of waves of hatred, on the most fateful day in its history of hundreds of years, the day of the German invasion of Hungary, March 19, 1944.

3

1944

Introduction

The German invasion of Hungary on March 19, 1944, aroused no opposition among the Hungarian populace. Jozsef Darvas describes the situation in the following manner:

> The conquest of the country was carried out quietly and aroused no attention. On Sunday morning [March 19] SS units took control of the important government buildings and other key points.... Those Hungarians whose lives were not endangered by the conquest regarded events with complete indifference. As far as they were concerned, the word "conquest" was completely meaningless, for the Germans had been here before as friends and allies. As far as they were concerned, nothing had happened. A few Hungarians even rejoiced: "The end has come of Jewish sedition, of Jewish betrayal of Hungarian interests, of their violation of Hungarian honor and of their provoking of our glorious ally."
>
> Most of the populace of the capital behaved as if nothing has taken place. The masses paraded through the streets, giggling merrily.... Here and there they would stop, watch the military convoys and the steel-helmeted soldiers standing stiffly on the military vehicles, next to their machine guns. Many laughed joyously and waved at the soldiers. Had they had flowers in their hands, they would certainly have tossed them at the soldiers.... The residents of the capital accepted as self-evident the fact that the representatives of a foreign power were entitled to arrest thousands of citizens, concentrate them and thrust them into various prison cells until these quickly filled up to overflowing. The arrests were carried out by a Gestapo unit stationed in Budapest. The unit had no need to overcome organized resistance forces. All it had to do was to arrest those who were not of their supporters. Everything transpired quietly. The only exception was Endre Bajcsy-Zsilinsky [a Hungarian statesman of a liberal persuasion], who drew his pistol in face of the Germans who broke into his home. The Germans shot him and dragged him, bleeding, from his home.
>
> As far as is known, these were the only shots fired that day in Budapest.[1]

The Hungarian people thus viewed the German invasion as a step taken by a friendly power, aimed at strengthening the vital link between the two nations. As a newspaper put it a few days after the invasion:

The Hungarian nation has been living for hundreds of years in the Danube Basin, sharing the fate of the Germans. Even after they blocked the waves of aggression approaching us from the east, the two nations were still threatened by common dangers, and both spilled their blood in their struggle for European culture and stood together in the defense of the eastern gates of Europe. This historical tradition is the source of the unreserved spiritual friendship prevailing between the German people and the Hungarian people. The Hungarians view the German soldiers who have come to us through the traditional spectacles of friendship and armed brotherhood. Their arrival grants Hungarians peace of mind.[2]

The forces hostile to the Jews that had existed in the Hungarian population reawakened as the Germans invaded and gave tangible expression to their antisemitism. As Zandberg put it,

In those days various types of fascists sprang up like mushrooms and filled the city streets with their frightening uniforms; they were dressed in a black suit, or black trousers, a dark green shirt and a black tie. A large symbol of their party, the Arrow-Cross symbol, glistened on their shirt collars.... These people stood out everywhere and at every opportunity. They organized parades and rallies, and exploited every chance to curse and denigrate the Jews in the streets and other public places. When they realized that the police were not interfering with them, they began to strike at the Jews physically as well.[3]

In the other words, the reins were loosened.

The attitude of the Hungarian people toward the Jews was expressed during the first six weeks following the German takeover of Hungary, when no less than thirty-five thousand denouncements against the Jews were made to the German authorities.[4] In other words, the antisemitic incitement of decades bore fruit, and not only did the Hungarian nation adapt easily to its new situation; it also did its best to assist the new regime in its persecution of the Jews.

After the end of World War II, a Hungarian statesman and writer made an analysis of the attitude of the Hungarian populace toward the Jews. His findings were as follows:

If during the persecutions a Jew was to have knocked randomly on any door, the odds were that he would have been handed over to the authorities; in exceptional cases he could hope the door would be slammed in his face and no denouncement be made to the authorities, but he had just about no chance at all of being offered refuge, even temporary refuge.[5]

Thus, Laszlo Endre, who was appointed director of the interior ministry after the German invasion and was directly responsible for organizing the expulsion of Hungarian Jewry, reflected the approach of the Hungarians toward the Jews. A report of a speech he made on the radio at the end of March 1944 states,

> Laszlo Endre rejected the approach which claimed that the Jewish question had once again been placed on the agenda as a result of international events. He drew attention to the fact that the entire Hungarian population, being interested in maintaining its racial purity, has been pressing for a solution to this problem for twenty-five years. Hungarian antisemitism is not a political fad, it is not an imitation of new political ideas. The people have learned the hard way the great harm they have suffered because of the ever-growing Jewish influence. They have not learned this lesson over the past year or two. This people was the first in Europe to learn it from direct experience.... We express our unreserved faith that Jewry is an undesirable element for the Hungarian people in every way: morally, spiritually, and physically. With this awareness, we have to seek out the solution which removes Jewry from Hungarian life totally and absolutely.... The spiritual and physical liberation of the state from the Jews is undoubtedly in the interest of the Hungarian nation, and we shall certainly carry this out.[6]

As already noted, this attitude toward the Jews was the natural continuation of the antisemitic atmosphere and relationship that had prevailed in Hungary during the period preceding the German invasion.

We find additional evidence for this continuity in the composition of the new government. With the German invasion of Hungary, Prime Minister Kallay was removed from his position, and the Hungarian ambassador to Berlin, Dome Sztojay, was appointed in his place. Yet many government members remained in their posts. Over the coming weeks, a number of provincial governors and deputy governors were replaced, but no substantial change took place in the civil service or in local government. The leaders of the new regime and their German overlords relied on the existing civil service to carry out the letter and spirit of the policies of the new regime.

The loyalty of the rulers, the administration, and the people of Hungary to the antisemitic ideas of the invading Germans helps make comprehensible a step that otherwise might be considered unusual. It might have been expected that upon their invasion of Hungary the Germans would entrust the formation of a government to the Arrow-Cross party, as this party had voiced over a period of years its full identification with Hitler and his policies vis-à-vis the Jews, and had often expressed its hope that the day would come when these policies would be carried out in actual practice in Hungary as well. Despite this stand of theirs, the invading Germans did not enable them to participate in the government in any role at all.[7] However, there was really no need of this. The Germans were fully aware that they could rely on the loyalty of the regime even without the participation of the Arrow-Cross party, and the government for its part knew that the civil service and the local government would carry out the policies that had for many years been the ideological basis of the Arrow-Cross party. The executive level was composed mostly of people of political beliefs that suited the ideas of the Arrow-Cross party, even if formally they were not members of it.

And so, as we shall see, the Germans entrusted the execution of the expulsion to the Hungarians, who did not disappoint them. Moreover, we shall encounter various Hungarian antisemitic initiatives that were more evil and more brutal than even the Germans had expected.

The previous section described the government-people-church/priesthood triangle, the three sides of which came out in support of each other during the period of the anti-Jewish legislation. After the German invasion, too, this triangle continued to exist, and—like the government and the people—the church/priesthood also viewed the new situation thus created as the natural extension of the situation prevalent in Hungary in the past. The bishops, it will be recalled, fought against the depriving of Christian converts of their rights during the period of the anti-Jewish legislation, and they did so while expressing their negative opinions of Jews and of Judaism. Their attitude toward the topic of the expulsion of the Jews was reminiscent of the way they acted during the period of anti-Jewish legislation. The German invasion changed nothing at all in this respect.

It is clear from the discussions held by church leaders with political figures, and from the correspondence between them, that if the expulsion of the Jews was objected to on occasion, this was nothing more than lip service. On the contrary, in studying how they dealt with the topic, one fairly regularly encounters expressions and comments whose nature was such that their very use led the government to harden its position relative to the Jews whose expulsion had been decreed.

The Expulsion

One will recall that it was the government that acted to serve the Germans, while the regent, Horthy, who remained in office even after the German invasion, had nothing to do with the Jewish question. At a government session convened on March 29, 1944, the prime minister announced that the regent had "guaranteed the government a free hand concerning the anti-Jewish regulations and that he is not interested in bringing any influence to bear on this subject."[8]

In the wake of the German invasion, many decrees were imposed upon the Jews. The following are but a few examples. All shops belonging to Jews were closed down, but the shopowners were required to pay their Christian workers salaries even after the shutdown. A moratorium was declared on all debts Christians owed Jews. A Jew who owned real estate and who had rented his property to a Christian had no right to end his lease. Jewish pharmacy owners had their permits canceled and were forbidden to engage in their trade. All publishing licenses in Jewish hands were canceled. The continued existence of Jewish organizations was forbidden. The libraries and archives belonging to such organizations were confiscated in favor of the Hungarian Institute for Jewish Studies. It was forbidden to publish papers compiled by Jews. Jews were forbidden to visit public bathhouses or parks. Jews were required to declare all their property, except for furniture and household utensils whose value was no more than ten thousand *pengo*. They were required to hand over to the banks their jewelry and any gold coins that were in their possession. The Jews were forbidden to open their safes in the banks, but had to declare their contents. All bank accounts belonging to Jews were frozen, and the amount the Jews could withdraw from their accounts was limited to a thousand *pengo* per month. Jews were compelled to sell their racehorses. A yellow slip was attached to the bills of sale, thus facilitating identification of the source of these horses.[9]

Jews with telephones were required to disclose special details concerning themselves and their loyalty to the regime. Lawyers' permits were canceled. All the Jews still working in the civil service, for local government, or in any other public institution were dismissed from their posts. Jews were forbidden to engage in any work related to the theater, the cinema, or the press. Jews were forbidden to travel outside their areas of residence.[10]

The Jews were required to return to the authorities the food coupons in their possession, and the authorities then issued them special food coupons—colored yellow. While exchanging the food coupons, the authorities drastically reduced the amount of food allocated to Jews. The monthly sugar quota was fixed at three hundred grams [about ten ounces], no addition being given to children, nursing mothers, or pregnant women—unlike what was customary with the non-Jewish population. In addition, Jews were prevented from acquiring certain foodstuffs at all. Specifically, Jews were forbidden to purchase animal fat and were required to make do with three hundred grams of sesame oil per month.[11]

Incidentally, in this context the director of the interior ministry, Endre, commented piously, "From now on the Jews will be able to live in accordance with the laws of their race and their nation. By us not making it possible for them to use pig fat, we have made it possible for them to cook using sesame oil—thus helping them observe the precepts of their religion."[12]

These and many other decrees were imposed upon the Jews of Hungary within a very short period of time. Hardly a day went by without some new decree being made public, but the significance of all of these dwindles in comparison with the decree of the yellow patch. At its March 19, 1944, session, the government decided upon "an identifying mark for all the Jews." The practical significance of this government decision was that all Jews of either sex above the age of six years were required to bear on the left side of the breast of their outer garment, in prominent fashion, a six-pointed yellow star about four inches square. This requirement was obligatory in the public domain, that is, whenever they left the privacy of their homes.

The formal explanation found in the protocol of the government session was that

> for reasons of public security and for improved efficiency in defense of the fatherland, it is desirable that it be possible to identify the Jews—upon whose loyalty one cannot rely. Marking the Jews in the aforesaid fashion will render the supervision of their activities and conduct much simpler. Furthermore, it will be possible to remove them from those areas where their presence may endanger the interests of the defense of the fatherland.[13]

In fact, the official explanation was not identical with the actual aim of thus marking the Jews, which was preparing and facilitating their concentration and expulsion from Hungary.

The semiofficial government newspaper, which appeared in German, evaluated these decrees and their effect in an editorial on April 1, 1944:

> If our government takes steps against the Jews, a foreign race in our midst, and shuts the gateway to those positions from which they can cause damage ...it does not do so out of hatred or revenge, and certainly not in order to turn them into martyrs, but rather only in self-defense.
>
> It is thus certain that whatever we have done until now in this field must be considered a courageous step granting the people of our country a sense of security.[14]

Endre's declaration appears in the same issue:

> The government has decided to solve the Jewish problem once and for all according to a uniform and comprehensive program.... The steps taken

until now are only the beginning of the final solution of this problem in Hungary.... The special designation of the Jews is merely a necessary step of active self-defense, for the events of the past few months have demonstrated that the inciting Jewish spirit has brought about tangible damage to the opinions of the innocent Hungarian populace.[15]

In order to render more efficient the task of concentrating the Jews and deporting them, the government appointed another director-general of the interior ministry in addition to Endre. This official's sole function was to deal with the Jews. For this purpose Laszlo Baky was selected. He already had experience in dealing with Jews: he had served under Horthy in the White Terror period of 1919–1920.

On April 7, 1944, Baky sent a secret memorandum to all bodies dealing with the Jewish question. This memorandum contained operative instructions concerning the concentration and deportation of the Jews:

> The Royal Hungarian Government will shortly purify the state of the Jews. I order this purification be carried out on a regional basis. To this end the Jews must be concentrated—no distinction on the basis of sex or age is to be made—in concentration camps to be set up for this purpose.... The concentration of the Jews is to be carried out by the gendarmerie or the police in charge of the area being purified. The German security police will be present in the regions being purified, and will serve in an advisory capacity. Special attention must be paid to our full cooperation with them.
>
> The Jews will be transported by train, in the manner usual with prisoners.... All government agencies will be placed at the disposal of the gendarmerie and the police.... Police and gendarmerie units in adjacent regions will coordinate activities among themselves, to ensure the common and simultaneous execution of the purification activities.

In this memorandum there appear further instructions connected with the expulsion of the Jews, such as how to determine concentration areas, how to organize an efficient system of expropriating Jewish property, how to treat this property, and additional technical matters. The memorandum concludes, "This instruction of mine is extremely confidential. The various agencies and the commanding officers of the units are responsible for ensuring that none of the contents of this memorandum become known to anybody before the time fixed for the beginning of the purification."[16]

Concentrating the Jews in ghettos began in the northeastern districts of Hungary, in Ruthenian Sub-Carpathia, a short time after the dispatch of Baky's instructions. The concentration and deportation of the Jews moved on from one district to another according to a preplanned schedule, in which Budapest was to be the last district from which the Jews were to be expelled.

A description of the suffering of the Jews in the ghettos and in the camps in which they were concentrated is not within the scope of this work. Yet it should be noted that the physical and mental torture suffered by the candidates for deportation while still in the ghettos accounts for the fact that when the deportation trains arrived to transport the Jews to their final destination, most of the Jews boarded them on the assumption that this new destination would be an improvement over their intolerable conditions in the ghetto.[17]

The first deportation train left Hungary on May 15, 1944. During the ensuing seven weeks 437,000 Jews were expelled from Hungary.[18]

The Hungarians were anxious to expel their Jews, and they pressed the Germans to allocate a larger number of trains for this purpose in order to complete the task as quickly as possible:

> General of the SS Winckelmann had informed the Hungarian government that he could not supply a sufficient number of wagons to carry out the deportation of the Jews.... Eichmann was ready to grant no more than two trains per day. Laszlo Endre, the delegate of the Hungarian government, wanted six trains per day. The Nazi commander-in-chief declared himself unable to spare so many wagons and locomotives for this purpose, but finally, they arrived at a compromise of four trains per day. In order to counterbalance this, Endre, taking into account the number of Jews concerned and wishing to speed up their deportation, ordered each trainload of 45 wagons to consist of 4,000 persons, instead of the normal 1,600–1,800 that were customary on military transports.[19]

While visiting the sites where the Jews had been concentrated prior to their dispatch, Endre himself intervened in the matter of crowding the Jews into the train coaches. At the town of Paks, for instance, "after there were already sixty Jews in each of the carriages, he gave a personal order that each Jew raise both arms, thus making it possible to crowd into each coach an additional twenty Jews."[20]

On June 16, Endre sent the prime minister a memorandum in which he wrote, "the agencies under my authority have received instructions to act humanely and according to the spirit of Christianity both while separating the Jews and while transporting them to work outside the borders of the country."[21]

What he concealed in his memorandum Endre revealed when he took part in the government meeting five days later, on June 21. He made a detailed report of his operations and once again referred to "the spirit of Christianity": "The general principle in connection with the transportation to camps and the deportations was that everything should be done in a humane way and in accordance with the Christian spirit." In order to explain this concept to his audience, Endre went into some detail: "Lunatic asylums, sanatoria, hospitals, convalescent homes, and other places suitable for hiding Jews have also been combed out."

Endre did not forget the Jews languishing in prison and the young Jews who had been incarcerated in institutions for young offenders, making sure that they, too, boarded the deportation trains: "The situation as regards public security has been stabilized, and the typically and characteristically Jewish intellectual crimes have ceased.... After the deportation of the Jews, the Christian inhabitants have endeavored to settle down to a new life."[22]

On the day the first deportation train set out, Endre delivered a speech at a ceremony dedicating the Hungarian Institute for Jewish Studies. He made reference in this speech to respected authorities: "The popes, as well as our own ancient and saintly kings, legislated draconian laws and imposed severe decrees upon this parasitic race. Thus, no one can complain that we are not acting in accordance with the spirit of Christianity when we enact draconian regulations against the Jews so as to protect our nation."[23]

Others, too, joined Endre in stressing that his own actions and those of his government were carried out in the spirit of Christianity, for its sake and for its benefit.

The induction ceremony of a new provincial governor was graced by the arrival of the interior minister, Andor Jaross, to the town of Szombathely. Before the ceremony itself, a ceremonial prayer service was held in the town cathedral. The local bishop participated in the ceremony as well as the new governor, who declared that "the struggle in our country between various outlooks and beliefs has been decided. Only a firm right-wing policy based on Christian and national morality is the correct policy."[24]

In his visit to the town of Nagyvarad, Jaross spoke of St. Laszlo, one of Hungary's ancient kings, as an example of fighting for those values in whose light life is to be lived:

> We must learn anew the historic value of the ancient king.... There exists an historic analogy in that our king, St. Laszlo, too, brandished his sword against the dangers which threatened from over our eastern border....
> Today, too, there exists a threat to Central Europe. Eastern bolshevism is threatening every square inch of our soil.
> There can be neither Hungarian security nor a future for Hungarian history as long as Stalin's bolshevik empire is perched on the eastern slopes

of the Carpathian mountains....We shall also close accounts with our internal enemy, if once again he dares raise up his head. In 1918–1919 and in previous years Nagyvarad was viewed as a fierce fortress of Jewish liberal capitalism. Today I see before me a new Nagyvarad. I see here a nationalistic Nagyvarad whose streets no longer have any Jews....The city has solved this problem, and it was with a feeling of relief that I realized that its solution suits the demands of our generation. Yet the problem has not yet been solved in its entirety. We must remove from the blood cycle of the nation all toxic material and any possibility of blood poisoning.[25] Taking into consideration the entirety of the problems, the government of Hungary is proceeding step by step.[26]

Imredi, too, claimed that "the separation of the Jews must be carried out in accordance with the requirements of Christian morality."[27] "Together, firmly and decisively, we are carrying out our task in a Christian spirit and with no hatred,"[28] declared Endre at the close of a lightning tour of thirty-four towns in Hungary. He repeated, "The new instructions are not dictated by hatred or a lack of consideration."[29]

The German Nazis based their doctrine upon their faith in the superiority of their race. The Hungarian Nazis, including Endre, used this idea, yet adjusted it to the situation in Hungary. They stressed the superiority of Christianity to Judaism. Below are excerpts from Endre's lecture, broadcast over the government radio as part of the lessons from the Academy of Outlooks:

During thousands of years of human history, ever since the founding of Christianity, never has such a confrontation taken place between two contradictory outlooks as the ferocious struggle taking place at present between Judaism and the nations of Europe. This struggle did not originate in this war. It has been going on ever since Judaism appeared on the stage of history. Judaism, in its hatred, removed itself from other peoples....The books of the Talmud, replete with blind hatred for the non-Jewish nations, have replaced their ancient sacred books...and in accordance with the instructions of the rabbis of the Talmud they live earthy lives full of earthy rejoicing and earthy pleasures. They are busily organizing their world government and achieving unlimited advantages with the aid of their superior economic status.

Endre went on to describe how Jewish capitalists financed the Bolshevik revolution and how they took control of the League of Nations. He also ascribed the French Revolution to the Jews, who were also guilty—in his opinion—of the outbreak of World War I and of the dissolution of the Austro-Hungarian monarchy:

Judaism made special efforts to replace Christianity and to upset the foundations of the central Christian powers, for they were her greatest enemies.

We and the Jews live in two completely separate worlds. The Jew seeks God's land on this earth in hoarding property, in hedonism, and in controlling others. We, on the other hand, seek God's land in the next life. ... Our moral concepts are so different from one another that we are unable to judge their actions according to the scale of the laws we have created for our brethren and our flesh.[30]

On another occasion Endre succeeded in expressing the idea of the inferiority of the Jews and their faith in a more concise fashion, in a single sentence: in the Pecs ghetto five thousand Jews were concentrated prior to their expulsion. They were forced to stand at attention in rows under the summer sun. Endre arrived with gendarmes and reviewed the panic-stricken Jews. In ridicule and scorn he repeatedly asked them, "And why doesn't Jehova, your famous God, work a miracle now?"[31]

Thus the voice of Christianity reached the ears of the Hungarians from the mouths of such government ministers as Endre and his colleagues. They spoke in the name of Christianity, and no priest voiced other opinions. Even if there were Christians whose opinions differed from those of the government representatives, these opinions never reached their destination: the ears of those who performed the expulsion—the Hungarian population.

Who Carried Out the Expulsion?

On a visit to Hungary in 1983 I met with a high-ranking government official. After hearing of my plan to study the subject dealt with herein, he said, "My dear sir, can't you find any other topic to deal with in connection with Hungary? After all is said and done, we Hungarians were not hostile to the Jews, we were not interested in deporting them, and we certainly did not carry out the expulsion—the Germans did so."

With regard to the first part of his statement, we have already seen in this volume the Hungarians' alleged nonhostile attitude toward their Jewish neighbors. We shall now consider the second part of the high-ranking official's statement: the attitude of the Hungarians toward the deportations and the role they played in carrying them out. Hungarians with a conscience feel today that the expulsion of the Jews from their country is not a chapter that glorifies their historical heritage. The attempt of the official to ascribe responsibility for the deportation of the Jews to the Germans is thus understandable. In various Hungarian publications on this topic that have recently been printed, mention is made of the "expulsion of the Jews by the Germans."

We shall thus have to examine the facts as they come to light within the available material dating from the period under consideration. The following is an excerpt by Levai from his book, *The Black Book:*

> Owing to their insignificant numbers, the Nazis were practically unable even to supervise the deportations, let alone to carry them out. The marking of the Jews with the Star of David, their "round-up" into ghettos and concentration camps, were made possible only by the fact that the gendarmerie—though well-acquainted with the situation and numbering some 20,000 men—could everywhere be sure of the aid of the local police. Even then the procedure could not have been carried through if the Christian population had shown resistance.[32]

The following excerpt is from the Operational Instructions memorandum dictated by Endre:

> "In the execution of the action against the Jews in the Gendarmerie District of Kassa, the Germans will proceed to Munkacs in 10 cars with 8 officers and 40 soldiers on 10th inst.... Hungarian interests will be represented by Lieut.-Col. Vitez Ferenczy, Attorney Medgyesy, and Detective Inspector Koltay.... Immediately after their arrival the German committees will contact our committee. Members of our committees are requested to display courtesy and tact, to give information and explanations required, to render all assistance with regard to accommodation and food, and, where necessary, to place an interpreter at the disposal of their German counterparts."[33]

> The first step was taken, therefore, by the Nazis on May 11, when they sent eight officers and forty soldiers to Munkacs. With the aid of this force they carried out the total destruction of Hungarian Jewry from one end of the state to the other.[34]

After completing its task in a given province—that is, after deporting the Jews of that province—the German force would move on to the province next in line for the deportation of its Jews, and so on to additional provinces. In this way it was present in each province, where it advised in the execution of the deportation.

On June 21; 1944, Endre reported to the government:

> "In every province, prior to the deportation of the Jews, we met with the commander of the province, the governor of the province, the representatives of the police, and the gendarmerie. They received detailed instructions either from Director-General of the Interior Ministry Baky or

from me. A representative of the German security police regularly took part in these meetings as well."[35]

Carrying out the deportation was the task of the police and the gendarmerie, who acted under the auspices of the interior ministry. Officers of the German S.D. also took part in planning the operation.[36]

According to another description based on contemporary documents,

> Eichmann's main office was in Budapest, but within a short period of time he set up ten delegations in other towns. Nevertheless, his unit, from a numerical point of view, remained insignificant. In his Budapest office there were, besides Eichmann himself and six arbitrators, another ten people and twenty guards. Throughout the state the entire team numbered some two hundred persons.... The German occupational regime could clearly function only if it could rely absolutely upon the Hungarian civil service. Without the assistance of the various ministries, of the provincial and the municipal administration, as well as that of the police, the gendarmerie, and the army—without all this help the entire Nazi occupation machine would have become incapable of operating within a few days.... The gendarmerie happily undertook to organize the deportations with the direct or indirect aid of the civil service.[37]

There are indeed slight differences in the reports as to the number of Germans involved in the deportations and the technical organization of the team that operated under Eichmann, but the sources agree with regard to the small number of the Germans as compared with the enormous operation of deporting hundreds of thousands of people:

> The entire police-administrative setup connected with organizing the removal of the Jews from their property, their ghettoization and deportation was local and not German. The situation we behold in Hungary is more than what is customarily termed "collaboration." Here we have local initiative in preparing and totally carrying out the deportation, in many cases with enthusiasm.
>
> The testimony of most survivors and all existing contemporary literature—not just that of Jewish origin—is united in the evaluation that not only did most of the Christian population view calmly the removal of the Jews, but it even participated willingly in the entire process, including the final expulsion.... Most of the population viewed the deportation of the Jews calmly or even with joy at the Jewish tragedy.[38]

There exists a document that supports the assumption that the Germans relied upon the Hungarian authorities for the deportation of the Jews, while the Hungarian authorities relied upon the broadest sections of the government apparatus. The document was written on May 26, 1944, by a German described in the document itself as "a special expert" sent to Budapest to report from there to Berlin on the progress in carrying out the deportation program. The expert, a high-ranking political advisor, Von Thadden, classified the document as "highly confidential." He wrote it in his own handwriting in only seven copies, each of which was numbered.

He described the process of rounding up the Jews and deporting them from the various provinces of Hungary. Regarding Budapest he wrote,

> It is believed that it will be possible to begin with the work in Budapest proper toward the middle or end of July. For this, a one-day action on a large scale is planned, which is to be carried through with the aid of strong forces of the provincial Hungarian police, of all special units and police training schools, as well as by making use of all Budapest postmen and chimney sweepers, who are to act as pilots. All autobus and streetcar traffic will be suspended for that day so that all means of transportation can be used for the deportation of the Jews.[39]

Referring to the expulsion of all the Jews of Hungary, the compiler of the document wrote, about ten days after the beginning of the expulsion, "It may be assumed that the process of deporting all the Jews will end no later than the beginning of September."[40] The German special expert could not imagine that the Hungarians would succeed in completing the operation (except for Budapest) by the beginning of July.

We have the testimony of a gendarmerie officer named Bodonyi who took an active part in the deportation of the Jews. He was in command of one of the units engaged in placing the Jews on the deportation trains and crowding them into the wagons. He was captured after the war and interrogated concerning his activities. The following is the interrogation as written down by the intelligence officer of the U.S. Army who interrogated him:

> Q: Many attempt to defend themselves saying that while loading the Jews on the trains German officers or SS soldiers were present, and they were the ones giving the gendarmerie their orders. Do you know of any such case and if your answer is positive—where and when was it?
>
> A: I know of no case where Germans were present. Even if there is a possibility that people dressed in civilian clothes whom I did not recognize, who came together with His Excellency Baky or with the Director-General of the Interior Ministry Endre, were Germans—they never interfered in our work arrangements.
>
> Q: Does this mean that the loading of the trains with hundreds of thousands of Jews who were to be murdered, and all the brutality accompanying this act, was the glorious project of the Hungarian gendarmerie?
>
> A: It was our job to carry out the instructions.[41]

On this topic we also have the testimony of the two Germans who headed the German occupation apparatus in Hungary: Veesenmayer, the German ambassador to Hungary and Hitler's personal representative, and Winckelmann, supreme commander of the SS and German security police in Hungary.

At the trial of the Hungarian war criminals, the following dialogue took place between the president of the court and Veesenmayer:

Q: What would have happened if the Hungarian government had decided that it was not prepared to meet the German demand concerning the deportation of the Jews?

A: It would not have taken place. The fact is that nothing happened when Horthy announced that they would not continue with the deportation.[42]

Q: In other words, you claim that if the Hungarian government had replied negatively from the very beginning, it could have achieved a situation where the Jews would have continued to live after the German invasion just as they had lived before it? Do you claim that in this case Germany would not have taken any steps of a compulsory nature?

A: They would certainly have tried to apply pressure, but they did not have available the forces with which they could have carried out their threats.

Q: How can you make such a claim when the forces they had sufficed to take absolute control of Hungary?

A: The conquest lasted a very short time, and the first divisions were taken out a few days after they had entered Hungary. We must also take into account that the deportation was not a military task, but rather a police one, and such forces, if they were available, were of a very small number.

Q: Were the Germans unable to bring here for this purpose adequate police forces?

A: I think not. Furthermore, these forces would have had to know Hungarian and to be familiar with the country and the people.

Q: And in Poland, for instance, with whose aid did they solve the Jewish problem? Were they able to transfer adequate German police units there?

A: I was never in Poland, but I consider it a completely different type of territory. It was the first country we conquered, and we occupied it absolutely. Poland had no government; it was ruled by a German administration. A German administration operated there with many departments, which extended everywhere.

Q: Nevertheless, under these conditions you were able to solve the Jewish problem thoroughly, as you described its solution to yourselves. Why were you unable to do the very same thing in Hungary as well, with its smaller area?

A: 1944 is considered to have been a year of crisis.

Q: In other words, at that time you did not have unlimited German forces available?

A: No, at that time it was already impossible to bring forces of such size here.[43]

At the war criminals' trial, when Winckelmann, the supreme commander of the SS forces encamped in Hungary, was asked: "Were the Germans able to carry out the deportation even without the aid of the Hungarians?"—he replied: "I am certain the German authorities would not have applied any compulsory means. When Himmler gave me his instructions he noted that he was not interested in this topic."... Winckelmann even adduced evidence in support of his claim by saying that Germany was interested in avoiding at any cost a clash with the Hungarians. Germany ascribed supreme importance to being able to exploit Hungary as a transit area for her armies.[44]

Regarding the nature of the Hungarian performance and the dedication of the Hungarians to furthering the deportation of the Jews, we have the testimony of a front-ranking Nazi leader, Goebbels. In an internal memorandum he sent to Nazi party activists on August 2, 1944, in which he reviewed the "Jewish Problem" and its solution in Hungary, he wrote, "The deportations were carried out in the shortest period of time, with amazing perseverance and obstinacy. A vital factor in the success of the operation was the fact that the steps against the Jews were found acceptable by most of the Hungarian nation."[45]

The dedication of the Hungarians to the idea of expelling the Jews and the belief in that idea did not come about suddenly, on March 19, 1944. This dedication had roots that ran deep, branched out in a complex fashion, and were firmly anchored in the reality of the lives and beliefs of the Hungarian masses. The historian Reitlinger, in referring to this full Hungarian collaboration, has indicated the circumstances supporting their devotion and has estimated that the unreserved cooperation on the part of the gendarmerie would never have been possible had the churches in Hungary raised their voices against antisemitism.[46]

Yet another reference linking the two matters reads as follows:

Because of the preceding quarter of a century of counterreactionary and antisemitic government, and most of all, because of its poisonous propaganda in which the churches, especially the Catholic church, had played a role of the first importance... the police were saturated with hatred of the Jews; they regarded antisemitism as a natural way of life; they did not feel remorse, pity, pangs of conscience; they regarded themselves as the vanguard of Christendom: so they were taught in the school and in the church.[47]

A Hungarian priest, too, was of the opinion that the churches could have restrained the gendarmerie and the police from abetting the deportation of the Jews:

> The gendarmerie and the police were trained in a religious spirit to view obedience to the church as an obligation. This spirit, in the past, permeated all of Hungarian society. Had all these people who took a direct part in the deportation of the Jews been informed that neither they nor their families would be permitted to partake of any sacred ceremony, their transgressions would not be forgiven them, they would not be eligible to receive the final sacraments in case of death, and their newborn children would not be baptized; furthermore, had they been aware that the churches would be locked in face of their guilt, and even the church bells would cease to ring—all this would have generated a severe crisis in those people engaged in the deportation day by day. Had the churches adopted such a position, they would have caused great embarrassment, both high in governing circles and down among those carrying out their instructions—the officials and the train workers.... I am sure that many people who assisted with the Jewish expulsion would have announced that they were unwilling to take upon themselves the dispatch of their neighbors to their deaths, for since the churches would regard such activity negatively, the deed they were being asked to perform by the authorities would be simply an "act of Cain," and they would be unwilling to act on the same moral level as Cain. Their consciences would be sensitive to the horrible aspect of their deeds.[48]

But the churches did not make their voice heard on behalf of the persecuted. On the contrary, the persecutors were able to understand that their actions were considered desirable by the church. Their government, too, acted in accordance with the requirements and expectations of the churches, as we shall see below.

On May 31, 1944, the Hungarian minister of law sent the interior ministry of his own government a draft of a proposed bill aimed at removing the Jews from all walks of Hungarian public, cultural, and economic life. The bill deals with various defined topics and maps out areas from which it would become obligatory to remove the Jews. The bill, however, does not stop there; it adds,

> The ministry is hereby empowered, above and beyond and in addition to the areas defined in this law, to enact regulations and take such steps as will lead *to the absolute removal of the Jews from the public, the cultural, and the economic life of the state by means of all the additional steps it finds appropriate for the national good.* [49] [The emphasis above and in the following three paragraphs is added.]

The wording of the bill regarding the removal of the Jews from the various walks of life is an almost precise excerpt from the statement made by Cardinal Seredi on this subject and adduced in the previous chapter. At a session of the Synod of Catholic Bishops reviewed in detail by the press, the cardinal stated that he ascribed "great importance to limiting the activity of the Jews and *removing the Jewish spirit from public and economic areas, as well as from additional walks of life.*"[50]

During the debate on the second anti-Jewish law in the Upper House the cardinal said, "It would also be important *to eliminate the features they have introduced into our public life in economic and social areas and to eliminate the Jewish spirit.*"[51]

Further along in the debate on the very same legislation the cardinal stated, "The concept of *limiting the activity of the Jews is acceptable to all.... It is necessary to reduce the influence of the Jews.*"[52] It will be recalled that the bishops and heads of the Protestant churches expressed themselves in a similar vein.

The cardinal and his colleagues could observe in 1944 that their preaching and the ideas they had voiced as early as 1939 must have fallen on attentive ears.

A village priest interviewed by a newspaper in the summer of 1944 gave accurate expression to the thinking of the average Hungarian Christian at that time:

> I state categorically that church history and tradition have always negated Judaism.... The Jews—the people and their priests—murdered our Lord, the Messiah, on the cross, in the most despicable and horrible manner. There in Pilatus's court they made their historic declaration: "May his blood be upon our heads and upon the heads of our offspring." ... Ever since the Jews crucified Jesus, they have been the foes of Christianity. May the Jews be expelled from Hungary, and then the church, too, will be able to breathe more freely.[53]

And so in the summer of 1944 the Hungarian people strove to act in the spirit of this village priest and his superiors, and carried out what the historian Cohen defines as follows: "The most rapid rate of deportation in the history of the Holocaust was rendered possible only by the ideological and psychological preparation of the masses for just such a possibility, over a period of a generation."[54]

Priestly Activity

The three Christian churches took an interest in the plans and activities of the government on the Jewish question. They approached the government at various dates during the summer of 1944 and made their opinions known on the steps adopted by the government and their possible ramifications. The leaders of the priesthood were extremely consistent, acting in accordance with the precedent they had set during the debates on the anti-Jewish legislation. They raised their voices on behalf and in defense of their flock of Jewish converts to Christianity, completely or nearly completely ignoring the plight of the Jews. In many instances they even justified the persecution of the Jews, thus assisting in fanning the flames that were consuming Hungarian Jewry. Moreover, I will describe how, in the vast majority of their appeals to the government, the church leaders stressed that their interest was limited to the Jewish converts alone, and in many cases they added, in passing, expressions besmirching the Jews. There are very few cases where their appeals included a general protest against the deportations, without special emphasis that their intervention was on behalf of the converts alone.

It should be noted that a few days after the German invasion of Hungary, the leaders of all the churches knew about Auschwitz and about what was perpetrated there; furthermore, they knew that Hungarian Jewry was to be deported to Auschwitz. In an interview held in the mid-1980s, Jozsef Elias, who in 1944 was a young priest serving as the secretary of the Good Shepherd organization affiliated with the Reformed church, related that four days after the German invasion, on March 23, precise details of the German plans were known in the offices of the Apostolic Nuncio in Budapest. These details included the yellow star decrees, the rounding up of the Jews into ghettos and concentration camps, and their deportation to the gas chambers and the crematoria. According to Elias, the Vatican itself was almost certainly the source of this information. The receipt of such detailed information in the offices of the nuncio preceded all the decrees made public at a later date by the Hungarian authorities; Elias dates it from the day the Sztojay government took office. Elias wrote down whatever he knew and passed the information along to all the bishops of his church.[55]

From statements made by the priest who served as Cardinal Seredi's personal secretary in 1944, Dr. Tamas Zakar, it would seem that Seredi, too, informed the bishops of the Catholic church of all he knew on the subject of the deportation of the Jews.[56]

Moreover, Cardinal Seredi and Bishops Raffay and Ravasz, the heads of the Protestant churches, received on May 15 or immediately thereafter precise information concerning Auschwitz. This information was included in the Vrba Report, known also as the Auschwitz Report.

The report is named after its compiler, a young Jew named Walter

Rosenberg, who had been expelled from Slovakia to Auschwitz and who had escaped from there after a stay of nearly two years. Subsequent to his escape, he began to use the name Rudolf Vrba in order to evade numerous German attempts to recapture him. Vrba was accompanied on his escape from Auschwitz by his friend, Alfred Vetzler, who subsequently went about under the name Josef Lanik. They escaped from Auschwitz on April 10, 1944, and after much suffering, innumerable hazards, and much courageous initiative, they managed to reach the town of Zsolna in Slovakia on April 24. On the following day they informed the stunned leaders of the local Jewish community of happenings at Auschwitz.

Vrba, a young man with a sharp eye and an analytical mind, served in the camp in a minor administrative role. His position enabled him to move about relatively freely throughout the camp, and in this way he succeeded in gathering the data he included in his report at a later date. Vrba calculated that some 1,750,000 Jews had been murdered in Auschwitz since his arrival there in June 1942.

He told of his observations, which had led him to the conclusion that frantic preparations were being made in Auschwitz for the arrival of a large number of new victims, to be absorbed speedily and efficiently even under considerable pressure of time. He related that up until the end of 1943 the victims had arrived at the train's final station, from where they had been transferred in trucks to the gas chambers and the crematoria. At the beginning of 1944 the Germans began to work feverishly on extending the train tracks to the gas chambers themselves. This extension of the tracks rendered the operation of Auschwitz considerably more efficient. Vrba calculated that since only in Hungary, of the entire German occupation area, did there remain a large Jewish population, the German preparations at Auschwitz were intended for the rapid absorption of Hungarian Jewry. One of the main objects of his escape was, he said, to warn the Jews of Hungary and their leaders of the fate awaiting them.

The Vrba Report consisted of thirty-eight pages typed in German, containing a detailed description of Auschwitz and its operation, written in a cold, dry, and down-to-earth style. He told of the location of the camp, its equipment, how its commanding officers and guards operated, the selection and murder systems, and the operation of the gas chambers and the crematoria. He reported how the victims who were to be exploited in compulsory labor before their murder were processed and tattooed. Vrba told of the extraction of gold-filled teeth from the mouths of the dead and of other commercial uses the Germans found for the corpses of the murdered. To his report he added sketches.[57]

The report was immediately sent to Hungary to be distributed, and was handed over to an employee of the Protestant church's Good Shepherd organization for translation and printing. These tasks took a few days, and the report was delivered in Hungarian to the heads of the Christian churches between May 10 and 15, just when the first deportation train left Hungary.[58]

In light of the above information, it may be assumed that the church leaders were well aware of the existence and significance of Auschwitz from the very first days of the German invasion. Even if the initial information lacked precise details of Auschwitz, the Vrba Report filled in whatever was missing, and from mid-May, when the report reached their hands, their knowledge of the subject was extremely detailed.

We must examine the deeds and statements made by the church leaders during this vital period, in light of this fact.

Seredi's first appeal to Sztojay after the German invasion concerned the yellow Star of David, and was made on March 28, three days prior to the publication of the regulation rendering wearing one obligatory. In his appeal to Sztojay, Seredi expressed his dissatisfaction with the fact that Jewish converts to Christianity were also to be obligated to wear the yellow star, but did not discuss the significance of the decree for the Jews and its expected effect upon them. As Levai puts it,

> The Prince Primate did not, in this instance, protest against the anti-Jewish regulations, but raised the following objection: "The six-pointed star is not the emblem of the Jewish race, but of the Jewish religion. Consequently the display of it is, in the case of Christians, a contradiction and constitutes a renunciation of faith."[59]

After the promulgation of the decree, Seredi appealed to Sztojay:

> The Roman Catholic priests, monks, and nuns [of Jewish origin] were exempted from the terms of the previous anti-Jewish measures. There are certain individuals whose view it is that the stipulations of the more recent anti-Jewish measures and particularly [of the regulation requiring the wearing of a yellow star] refer to these persons as well. I, for my part, cannot believe that individuals who have done their utmost for their country and who, by virtue of their vocation, are members of the clergy, can be regarded as coming within the scope of these regulations or that they should be subjected to such scorn. May I be permitted to request your Excellency to issue a statement clarifying the position and to state categorically that the persons indicated above are exempt from the terms of the recent anti-Jewish regulation. Should instructions to this effect not be forthcoming, I shall, to my greatest regret, find myself compelled to forbid the representatives of the church to wear the six-pointed star. Were they to do so, this

would have to be regarded as a renunciation of faith and cannot on this account be permitted. I am sure that Your Excellency will appreciate the justness of my request and will take the necessary and wise steps to remedy this untenable state of affairs."[60]

Seredi's firm stance bore fruit, and a few days later, on April 5, the government published an amendment to the previous regulation, exempting from the obligation of wearing the yellow six-pointed star all those whose exemption had been demanded by Seredi.[61]

That very day Sztojay replied to Seredi, "Allow me to draw your attention to the decree...published in today's issue of the *Official Gazette*, modifying the terms of the decree promulgated in respect of Jews wearing a discriminating emblem. Article 1 of the decree includes all those provisions which Your Excellency felt to be necessary."[62]

This correspondence shows that from Seredi's very first appeal to the government subsequent to the German invasion, he laid his cards on the table and revealed that he was interested in the converts alone. Even more important is the fact that the cardinal's decisive stance produced results and convinced the government to retreat from its earlier public position, despite the fact that it had already been published.

On April 23 Seredi met Sztojay and presented him with a document containing the stand of the Catholic church regarding the situation that had come about in Hungary as a result of the German invasion. In the introduction to his letter Seredi demanded liberty and justice for all: "We have no right to limit the right of citizens to life, to personal freedom, to freedom of worship, to work, to earning a livelihood, to ownership of their property, and to human dignity, to upright and honorable lives with neither justification nor a court verdict."[63]

The excerpt cited above can be understood to mean that he intended to defend the rights of the Jews as well. There are, furthermore, additional excerpts from this letter that can apparently be interpreted in this spirit. Yet the rest of the letter and the written summary of Seredi's practical demands persuade the reader that the visit was meant to protect the interests of the converts. He wrote as follows: "I refer to those regulations already promulgated or those which are to be promulgated in the near future which, with no legal basis, cause harm to Hungarian citizens, my Catholic brethren. These regulations expose them to scorn for no reason."

After the lengthy introduction containing, as noted above, ideas about the importance of the morality of the regime, Seredi summed up his practical demands in five points:

I herewith insistently request the Royal Hungarian Government of Christian Hungary, a government consisting entirely of Christians, to consider the baptized Christians, even though they be of Jewish origin, and distinguish them from the Jews, as they, by the act of their baptism, have already distinguished themselves.

I present five demands:

[1] The regulations concerning those of Jewish faith should not be applied to Christians.

[2] Those of Christian faith should not be represented in the same Council as those of Jewish faith [the Jewish Council was established the day after the German invasion of Hungary]. The whole organization of the Jewish Council is rooted in the Jewish religion and it is not right that Jews should have power over Catholic priests or monks, or over Christians in general. Nor should they enjoy judicial authority over these, with which they might, should they happen to be biased, harm those who, for the greatest part, followed the call of their conscience and renounced their Jewish faith.[64]

[3] Christians should no longer be obliged to wear the Star of David. ... The exhibition of this sign by Christians is tantamount to apostasy, against which the dignitaries of the church protest most solemnly.

[4] I further request that those Catholic priests, the aged and the infirm, and in general those baptized who fall under the stipulations of the regulations concerning Jews, should be allowed to employ non-Jewish domestics [in the decree promulgated by the government on March 29, the employment of non-Jewish servants in Jewish households was prohibited].[65]

[5] I further have to draw attention to the fact that in many cases, when the property of a parent who is considered a Jew is confiscated or the head of the family is forbidden to work, children, to whom the stipulations of the Jewish laws do not even apply, are deprived of their fortune.

Hoping that neither Your Excellency nor the other Christian members of the Royal Hungarian Government will disown their Christian co-religionists.[66]

This presentation of five points dealing explicitly and solely with the demand to interpret leniently the regulations apparently applying to the Jewish converts to Christianity shows that in the cardinal's appeal to the prime minister, the Jewish question remained outside the scope of the cardinal's interests. Sztojay understood the significance of Seredi's appeal—an indication that the suffering of the Jews did not bother the cardinal.

Sztojay's May 3 reply reflected the understanding that had developed between the two, and dealt solely with the topics involving the converts. Sztojay agreed that the converts need not be represented by the Jews in their council. He promised that the minister of the interior would prepare appropriate legislation to facilitate the establishment of a special council to be made up entirely of converts. This council, he intimated, would represent the interests of the converts before the authorities. Until such time as the technical and legislative details setting up this council would be completed, the converts were to be represented by a convert serving on the existing Jewish Council and heading a subcommittee to be set up for the converts. The legislation being prepared by the interior minister would even allow the converts to protest in case the Jewish Council acted against them dishonestly or took exaggerated steps against them.

With regard to the converts being required to wear the yellow six-pointed star, Sztojay reiterated his stand—that the emblem did not represent any religious belief. It was merely an administrative device set up by the authorities, which was intended to facilitate the treatment of those to whom the anti-Jewish regulations applied, "and the government will not object to the Jews of Christian persuasion wearing a cross on their clothing in addition to the Star of David."

Concerning the employment of Christian domestics in the homes of converts, the government would be willing to take into consideration the priests and others employed by the church. The government was even ready to permit the employment of Christian domestics by families whose children were Christian, even if one of the parents was Jewish.

Regarding the expropriation of property belonging to the head of a Jewish family whose children were Christian, Sztojay wrote as follows: "The Royal Hungarian Government would take care that such property would receive due consideration in accordance with the existing legislation when the time came for the future of such property to be decided."[67]

As for the Jewish problem in general, Sztojay noted, "It is impossible to jeopardize the life and future of 13 1/2 million Hungarians for the sake of one million Jews."[68] Sztojay did not deem it necessary to explain to Seredi in detail just how the survival of Jews would jeopardize "the life and future" of the Hungarians, and how their destruction would guarantee them. It would seem that he was not worried about the possibility of Seredi asking him that question.

On May 10, Seredi wrote to the prime minister once again:

I must again repeat my demand for discrimination between converted Jews and Jews adhering to the Israelite faith. This applies especially to cases in which Christians of Jewish origin are to be housed with Israelites in the same flats, houses, ghettos, labor camps, etc.... This at least we owe our Christian coreligionists. Furthermore, they have to be assured of freedom of religion. It must be made possible for them to leave their domiciles in order to fulfill their religious obligations and, should the need arise, priests must be permitted to visit them. Care should be taken that their moral life is not endangered. Most of all it must be prevented that they, as a consequence of indiscriminate deportation, suffer loss of life. . . . Therefore I respectfully request the Royal Hungarian Government that, bearing in mind its historical responsibility, it should cause steps to be taken by Hungarian and non-Hungarian authorities alike to prevent such deportations.[69]

Here Seredi no longer made any pretense of intervening on behalf of the Jews.

Yet the Jews were mentioned in Seredi's epistle. That is, in his afore-mentioned letter to Sztojay he referred one by one to the five points he raised in his memorandum of April 23 and to Sztojay's reply of May 3, and dealt in the main with matters of minor significance and with a repetition of matters dealt with in the past. He even requested that the gendarmes and the police be informed that Christians obliged to wear a yellow star might display a cross on their clothing, in addition to the Star of David, "in order to avoid unnecessary bother." When Seredi came to the Jewish question, however, he displayed considerable decisiveness and adopted an uncompromising attitude. He wanted to be given sub-stantial guarantees that Christians would under no circumstances be rendered subordinate to any Jewish authority in the framework of the Jewish Council. He stressed his request that if any problems should arise in this regard, they be dealt with efficiently by the authorities.[70]

As we have noted, nowhere in the letter is there any sign that the fate of the Jews occupied the cardinal to any degree. The letter is dated May 10. Five days later the trains began to set out for Auschwitz, and even then, when the deportations were under way, Seredi was interested mainly in his personal prestige and his church's status in his contacts with government leaders. The following is an excerpt from the letter he wrote and distributed among the Catholic bishops on May 17:

Previous Royal Hungarian Governments used to inform me in advance of proposed legislation and regulations of interest to the church, to its insti-tutions, to its rights, to its faith, and to its moral laws, or to church personages, so that I would be able to make my comments. . . . However, in the present situation preliminary notices are no longer given to me. . . . In the vast majority of cases I am able to make comments only after the promulgation of the regulations. . . . I must state that it is neither my fault nor that of the Synod of Bishops, that in my exhausting and difficult talks with the appropriate authorities, and mainly with the prime minister, I did not succeed any better when I rose to defend righteousness and, in partic-ular, the rights of our Catholic brethren.[71]

Seredi thus concludes this stage of his treatment of the subject by professing innocence of any guilt.

The Protestant churches were active at the same time, and they, too, gave preference in their dealings with the government to the status of converts to Christianity and the violations of that status. Their appeals resembled those of the Catholic church, and on occasion the wording of the appeals made by the various churches was completely identical.

From a document of the Evangelical church dated the second half of July, which summed up the steps taken by the Protestant churches on this issue, we learn of the following relevant steps: on April 4, at the same time as the appeals of the heads of the Reformed church and its various provincial centers were lodged, the leadership of the Evangelical church appealed in identical letters to Prime Minister Sztojay, to Interior Minister Jaross, and to the minister of culture and religion, Dr. Istvan Antal. In these letters three demands were made "regarding Jews of the Christian faith":

> [1] They should be exempted from the requirement of wearing the discriminating emblem.
> [2] They should be permitted to employ in their homes Christian domestics.
> [3] They should not be subject to the authority of the Jewish Council. The church requests that a separate council be established for the converts.[72]

According to yet another source, at the same time as the step just described was taken, on April 6, Bishop Ravasz presented the prime minister with a memorandum containing requests for consideration of Christians who were partners in mixed marriages.[73]

The prime minister's reply was sent on May 10. In it he turned down the request contained in paragraph 1 of the church memorandum, yet added that "the government has no objection to the converts wearing on their clothing a cross, in addition to the yellow six-pointed star." Regarding the employment of Christian domestics in the households of mixed couples, "the government is prepared to permit such employment if one of the couple is a Christian, even if he is of Jewish origin, on condition that the children of that family are Christian."[74]

Even before the prime minister's reply had been received, the Evangelical church made yet another appeal, on May 5, in an additional memorandum to the head of the Royal Hungarian Government, in which it requested that the Jews of the Christian religion not be housed in the ghettos together with the Jews of the Jewish faith. Since this memorandum remained unanswered, the church presidency sent yet another memorandum, on May 26, to the head of the Royal Hungarian Government, in which it adopted the following position:

[1] The appointment of a convert to membership in the Jewish Council is not an acceptable solution to this problem.

[2] All those who, together with their children, converted before their children were seven years of age, should be considered non-Jews.

[3] The presidency protests against the transfer of these people to the ghettos.

[4] If, nevertheless, the government should insist on the converts moving into the ghettos, the church presidency requests that Christian priests be permitted to visit members of their flock in the ghettos.

[5] The presidency warns the government against expelling the Jews beyond the borders of the state.[75]

The first four paragraphs in this Evangelical church appeal deal with requests for consideration of converts. The fifth paragraph refers to the Jews as well.

On May 19 a representative of the Jewish communities informed Bishop Ravasz, the head of the Reformed church, that the deportations had begun and that according to the most reliable information available "there was no return from such a journey." It should be recalled that the Vrba Report was at this time in Ravasz's possession. Ravasz turned to the Evangelical bishop, Kapi, and the two Protestant churches prepared a joint memorandum to the government. The memorandum reached its destination on June 21, over a month after the Jewish appeal to Ravasz, owing to the fact that the nine bishops resided at different places and their signatures had to be obtained individually.[76]

The Protestant bishops were in no hurry. Hungary is not a large country, and a journey of a number of hours suffices to reach every corner. The movements of the bishops and their messengers were not restricted, and they could move freely. The telephone and mail services functioned normally. Nevertheless, the collection of the nine signatures took a month. It should be noted that throughout the month of signatures the deportation trains from Hungary fed the Auschwitz ovens over ten thousand Jews every day.

Reading the memorandum raises the question whether it would have been preferable had the memorandum never been written and delivered to its destination. The encouragement of government activities contained in the memorandum far exceeds its defense of the Jews—in a document intended to serve as a defense of the Jews. It contained the following:

The solution of the Jewish question is a political task. We are not dealing with politics now. The execution of this solution is a great work of administration. We are not experts on that. . . . We do not wish to aggravate Your Excellency's political position; we even wish to promote the solution of the great task you took upon yourself.

As bishops of the two Protestant churches we protest against devout members of our congregations being punished only for being considered Jews from a racial point of view. They are being punished for a Jewish mentality from which they, and in many cases their ancestors, have solemnly disconnected themselves. Their lives, as regards Christian spirit and morality, are not considered in the least.[77]

With such defense the Jews were in no need of prosecution. The deportations went on until the last of the Jews, except for the Jews of Budapest, had been deported.

In the summer of 1944 there appeared yet another official Christian factor which took an interest in the ways in which the Jewish question was being solved: the pope's personal representative in Budapest, Nuncio Angelo Rotta. Like his colleagues, the heads of the Hungarian Christian churches, he, too, took a special interest in the fate and the safety of the converts, expressing himself accordingly on various occasions before various government agencies.

Rotta met Sztojay on March 23 and March 30. On April 18, he held yet another discussion with the prime minister, while, on April 27, he visited the deputy foreign minister, Arthony-Jungerth. In a memorandum he delivered to the Hungarian government on May 15, he summed up his discussions with the government leaders. Like his colleagues, Rotta, too, spoke in general terms of the lack of justice characterizing the solution of the Jewish question; like them he focused his attention upon the special injustice done to the converts in being treated no differently from the Jews. He wrote:

On many previous occasions the Apostolic Nunciate has brought to the notice of the Hungarian government those provisions of the new anti-Jewish decrees which it considers unjust, especially the failure to discriminate between baptized and Israelite Jews. . . . The Apostolic Nunciate considers it to be its duty to protest against such measures. It once again appeals to the Hungarian government not to continue this war against the Jews beyond the limits prescribed by the laws of nature.[78]

In the covering letter attached to Rotta's protest, the following, appeared:

I regard it as my duty to present this note of protest and again to demand that the rights of the church and its flock be respected. The fact that persons are persecuted because of their racial origin is in itself a breach of the laws of nature . . . but to pass anti-Jewish laws without taking into consideration that many Jews have, through baptism, become Christians, is a serious offense against the church.[79]

In its reply the government stressed its explanation of the question of the converts, relying on the anti-Jewish legislation that had been in force for the past few years.

This reply did not satisfy the nuncio, so, on June 5, he once again addressed the government in a memorandum in which he refuted the government's arguments concerning the application of the anti-Jewish legislation to the converts. He expressed his anxiety for the spiritual well-being of the converts in concentration camps, and wrote, "In some places the authorities have gone as far as to hinder the priests in giving these unfortunate children of the church the consolations of religion." In the conclusion of his memorandum he made three concrete demands:

[1] All Jews are to receive humane treatment.

[2] Baptized Jews are to be exempted from anti-Jewish legislation, at least those Jews who, with regard to the date of their conversion, are above all reasonable suspicion [i.e., those converts who converted long before, and so could not be suspected of doing so merely to try to escape the treatment given the Jews].

[3] The Royal Hungarian Government is asked to take urgent steps to put a stop to the deportation of Jews and to permit the spiritual care of the unfortunate Christians.[80]

On June 30, the government replied to the nuncio, claiming to have considered his appeal seriously:

The Royal Hungarian Government . . . does not reject out of hand the arguments advanced by the Apostolic Nunciate, especially insofar as these refer to the baptized Jews. Taking this line, the Royal Hungarian Government has examined the recent note submitted by the Apostolic Nunciate and would herewith like to give a résumé of its point of view:

A special branch of the Jewish Council will in future represent the interests of the converted Jews in Hungary. Until the articles of this council have been approved, Mr. Sandor Torok [a converted Jewish journalist] will represent the converted Jews in the Provisional Executive Committee. All steps have been taken to ensure that the activities of this representative are suitably supported.

The memorandum repeats the government's claim that Hungarian Jewry was not being deported:

A large number of Jewish laborers has been placed at the disposal of the German government. The fact that these laborers took their families with them to Germany was due to the consideration that it would be better not to part these families, as these Jews can be expected to get through a great amount of work. . . . Instructions have been issued to ensure that converted Jews and their families are accorded precedence among the workers, whose retention in the country is made imperative by economic and industrial considerations.[81]

The nuncio visited Sztojay once again on July 6, and told the prime minister, "You yourself see what the theory of racism leads to. People born as Christians and those who have been living Christian lives for the past thirty to forty years are now being subjected to the same unfair treatment accorded the other Jews."[82]

According to the nuncio, the failure of racism, as put into effect by the Hungarian government, was that it overran its boundaries and affected Christian believers negatively. This would seem to indicate that had the government seen fit to limit its racist activity to people of the Jewish religion only, he would have reacted differently.

Sztojay took notes of his meeting with the nuncio. His notes show that the nuncio's major topic of interest was the fate of the Jewish converts. It should be noted that the nuncio did protest in general terms against the brutality evinced toward all those suffering from racial persecution, both Jews and converts alike, yet most of the conversation between the two concerned the converts. Sztojay illuminates an interesting angle of the nuncio's attitude toward the entire Jewish population:

Concerning the separation of the Jews from the rest of the populace, I commented that this matter is important, for in a life-and-death struggle such as the one the Hungarian nation is currently engaged in with Bolshevism, the Jews exude a negative influence. They are defeatists and favor our enemies, in spite of its being clear that were Bolshevism to be triumphant, Hungary would be inundated.

The nuncio agreed that there is indeed a Jewish danger, and that it is vital to eradicate this danger, but stressed that this must be carried out while taking into consideration Christian morality and church rights. . . . The nuncio repeatedly stressed that nothing should be done to limit the church's freedom of movement, for then he would be obliged to inform the Holy Father of it, a step which would undoubtedly leave an undesirable impression.[83]

In mentioning "Christian morality" the nuncio put himself into the same camp as Laszlo Endre, the man responsible for the deportations, who had repeatedly stressed in his reports to the government and on various other occasions that he was carrying out the deportation while guided by the "spirit of Christianity."

As already noted, the nuncio was especially interested in the fate of the converts. The nuncio's attitude did not escape the prime minister, who was shrewd enough to understand that if he made concessions in connection with the converts, the nuncio would no longer be an obstacle to his disposal of the Jewish question. At the government session held on July 13, a week after his meeting with the nuncio, Sztojay delivered personally a semiofficial letter to his interior minister, Jaross, in which he included a request:

> As you know, the Apostolic Nuncio paid me a visit on the 6th of this month and made several requests.... One of these requests was that the government exempt various converts from the obligations of the anti-Jewish regulations. At that meeting I informed him that there is a good chance I will be prepared to treat his request most cordially, and if he gives me a list of the people involved, I will take the steps necessary to exempt from the application of the anti-Jewish laws.
>
> Enclosed please find the list, together with my request that you urgently examine these cases and give instructions to exempt from the application of the anti-Jewish laws those whose names are included in the list.
>
> It would seem to be unnecessary to emphasize that our speedy and positive response to this modest request of the nuncio will have a desirable effect upon his attitude toward us, a result which will indirectly improve the position adopted by the Holy See toward us—an apparently desirable development in the present situation. I will appreciate your informing me of the results of your consideration of the matter.[84]

From these meeting with the leaders of the churches and with the nuncio, the government succeeded in clarifying the stand of the important Christian factors in Hungary—strong opposition to any harm done to the converts and to the church, and agreement with the government regarding the necessity to "remove" the Jews. For the sake of style, they sometimes added a comment on "lack of justice," "boundaries dictated by natural law," "unnecessary brutality in execution," and so forth. Even if the Hungarian government had desired to take note of the protests of Christian leaders, it would have been unable to do so because such protests were simply never made.

Here are additional instances of so-called church intervention.

An Evangelical priest from the town of Mohacs wrote on June 30 to the national head of his church after the deportation of three families of his flock:

> Strangers by virtue of the blood flowing in their veins, yet close to us spiritually, members of our flock who have converted and joined us are suffering from an approach which not only contradicts our Evangelical

outlook, but also opposes our 900-year-old Hungarian-Christian past....
Until now they lived in the ghetto together with the other Jews, and bore
their fate with true Christian resignation.... As for me, both as a Christian
and as a Hungarian, I accept without reservation the methods adopted by
the exalted governmental authorities.... I do not wish to become the
spokesman for all the Jews of Mohacs, for other than my own flock I have
never had any connection with any of them. I am aware that Jewry has
been a foreign limb on the national body, and that it has been obligatory
to remove it. I have no objections to this, merely to the execution.... At
this stage I limit my protest to my own brethren only.

Here the priest provided the names of those three families and continued, "I was never a friend of the Jews, but I am both a brother and
a friend of those who have joined me in Jesus. On this basis I undergo
mental suffering together with my beloved flock."[85]

The bishop of Csanad, Hamvas, wrote to Seredi on July 15, 1944,

The honorable prime minister's promise that the Jews of the Christian faith
will not be expelled from Budapest is extremely calming. For this achievement I am especially grateful to Your Holiness. But what about the fate
of those who have already been deported from the towns and provinces?
Members of my flock from Szeged and Mako have already been deported.
We should demand their return. Similarly, we must insist that the deportation of converts from the towns and provinces where the deportation
has not yet been completed be stopped.... The honorable prime minister
also wrote that Christians of Jewish origin will reside separately in the
future and will be able to live according to the tenets of their religion. But
will they have the opportunity to earn a livelihood?[86]

The special interest displayed by the priesthood and the heads of the
churches in the problems of the converts, while almost completely ignoring the Jewish tragedy, did not escape the attention of an expert on
the Jewish question. SS General Winckelmann wrote to his superior,
Himmler, on July 13, "Last week such incidents occurred here as would
elsewhere have given rise to much anxiety. The nuncio and Cardinal
Seredi registered constant protests with the regent concerning the Jews
of Budapest. The fact that in this context all their anxiety was for the
converts alone stems undoubtedly from the very nature of the church."[87]
There exists the testimony of a person who in the summer of 1944
was involved in a daily, practical sense in the "solution of the Jewish
question," the Hungarian minister of the interior, Jaross, who stated in
his interrogation after the war was over,

The leaders of the priesthood made declarations on behalf of the converts
only. Cardinal Seredi requested that they be exempted from the obligations

of the anti-Jewish legislation, while Reformed Bishop Ravasz himself, in a speech delivered in the Calvin Square Church in Budapest on Good Friday, stated that "the Jews are now receiving their punishment from God for having crucified Jesus."[88]

Ravasz was not the only bishop who thought along those lines and expressed himself accordingly. In mid-May 1944, the Jews of the Debrecen area were concentrated in the city of that name, in eastern Hungary. Rumors spread through the ghetto that due to the advance of the Red Army and the threat it posed to Hungary's eastern border, the authorities wanted to evacuate the Jews from the area of the expected battle. It was thought that the Jews, as a factor disloyal to the regime and supportive of the Bolshevik enemy, might betray the Hungarian army attempting to block the advance of the Red Army. The rabbi of the Jewish Status Quo community of Debrecen, Rabbi Meir Weiss, asked to be received by Reformed Bishop Imre Revesz. At their meeting the rabbi proposed that since the bishop was familiar with the Jewish community and knew of its loyalty to Hungary, he might be willing to guarantee that the Jews would not perform any hostile acts against the Hungarian army. In this way the reason for removing the Jews from their homes and from the town would fall away, and perhaps the authorities would agree to leave them in the Debrecen ghetto.

Revesz replied that if he were able, he would save the converts. As for the Jews: since at the time of the trial and crucifixion of Jesus the Jews took upon themselves and upon their seed the curse of the Messiah's spilt blood—he was unable to be of assistance to them.[89]

The Shepherds' Epistles

Some time after Seredi received the Vrba Report in mid-May, he commented to his secretary, "I have prepared the outline of a draft of a Shepherds' Epistle, which I shall discuss with the bishops."[90]

And so, the archbishop sent copies of the epistle to the bishops of Eger and Kalocsa, as well as to those of Szekesfehervar, Csanad, and Gyor.[91] The only recipient who reacted to it in a substantial and fundamental manner was Czapik, the bishop of Kalocsa, who was second in the hierarchy of the Roman Catholic church in Hungary. Czapik's letter to Seredi provides insight into the attitude of the highest-ranking church leaders toward the mass murder of Hungarian Jewry, and toward its perpetrators and its participants. The letter provides a kind of ideological guideline to the Shepherds' Epistle of the Catholic church, as it was later worded by Seredi:

We must mention the deprivation of the rights of the Jews only in a general fashion. While it is true that everyone is aware of the horrors, and everyone knows what happens to them at their final station, it would not be right to put this before the public in writing. We, at any rate, are not permitted to do so.... We will be criticized, because the epistle presents the Jews only as persecuted beings who are suffering, without mentioning the fact that many of them sinned against Hungarian Christianity while none of their community ever reprimanded them for this.

We must avoid going into great detail on the question of the deprivation of Jewish rights—as I have already noted above. Such details would be the first source which could be interpreted as an admission of the facts. Let the Synod of Bishops not do this!

Those passages dealing with the deprivation of Jewish rights should be reworded, it being preferable for us to defend the natural laws of God and to stress our dissatisfaction with the violation of these laws. With all due respect and appreciation, I am opposed to the suggestion that we criticize the government publicly and that we break off all contact with them.[92]

Czapik's comments can be summed up in three sentences: the bishops should not make public what is happening to the Jews; what is happening to the Jews at the present time is nothing but appropriate punishment for their misdeeds in the past; the leaders of the church should maintain correct relations with the government.

The final wording of the epistle was done by Seredi. It is dated June 29, 1944. Between the idea of preparing such an epistle and its actual writing, the Jews of Hungary endured six fateful weeks, and by the date the epistle was actually written the vast majority of the Jews had already been deported from the towns and the provinces.[93]

The epistle is an interesting document and worthy of study. In his introductory remarks the cardinal presents the virtues of the 2,000-year-old church and the privileges of the heirs and followers of the church fathers, the bishops, who have always spread their protection over the oppressed, and even defended slaves. They have always supported the poor and assisted those of the lower classes. The Hungarian Synod of Bishops, during the thousand years of its existence, has also spread the wings of its protection over the poor and simple who suffered persecution. After the epistle elaborates on the subject of church generosity, it reaches the middle of the nineteenth century. Here the epistle describes the sacrifice made by the church in liberating the vassals, despite the great damage this act caused. The cardinal told of the generosity of the church in the age of the agrarian reform and of its contribution in this respect, and described the church's struggle on behalf of human dignity, freedom of religion, the right to possess property, and so on. All this is done while quoting freely from the Bible and mentioning the humane approach adopted by various popes.

In dealing with his own era, Seredi devoted a lengthy passage to a condemnation of the Allies for bombing of the cities of Hungary and causing damage to peaceful citizens. Even the idea spread by the Nazi propaganda machine about the evil Allies who parachuted booby-trapped toys from their airplanes in order to strike at innocent children found its way into the epistle.

At this point Seredi went on to mention deeds being carried out in Hungary that were liable to bring down the wrath of God upon their perpetrators: "These steps have reduced and even negated the natural rights of a certain section of our society, including even the rights of those who accept the holy faith we accept—all because of their origin."

The first half of the sentence quoted above was intended to imply a defense of the Jews, but in this central sentence the word "Jew" does not appear, and it may be reasonably assumed that this omission was deliberate. The fact that in the second half of the sentence Seredi mentions "those who accept the holy faith we accept" should prove who it was that the church and the Shepherds' Epistle proposed to defend.

However, the epistle does indeed go on to mention the word "Jew":

We do not deny that a number of Jews exercised a wicked, destructive influence upon Hungarian economic, social, and moral life. It is also a fact that the others did nothing to protest against their coreligionists in this matter. We do not doubt that the Jewish question must be solved in a legal and just manner. And so, we do not voice any opposition to the steps which have been taken against them until now in the economic field in the interests of the state. Similarly, we lodge no protest against the eradication of their undesirable influence. On the contrary, we would like to see it disappear. Nevertheless, we would be neglecting our moral roles in the church, were we not to speak up against the damage to justice and the harm to Hungarian citizens of our own Catholic faith, who are being harmed only because of their racial origin.

For this purpose we have tried, both orally and in writing, to spread the wings of our protection over our neighbors, citizens of Hungary, and over those of our faith who have been harmed by the regulations recently made public. We have requested that these regulations be canceled or amended.... As we rely upon the Christianity and humanity of our government ministers, we do not despair nor have we given up hope, despite the fact that our achievements to date have been few and inadequate. Thus, we have not made any declarations until now, though in the meantime we have taken all possible steps to achieve our aim.

Nevertheless, we now perceive in amazement that despite our efforts and all our discussions, our pressure on extremely important matters has been almost fruitless. For this reason we are formally denying any responsibility for the results.

Seredi concludes his epistle: "Pray and work for our friends, all Hungarian citizenry, and especially for our Catholic brethren, for our Catholic church, and for our beloved Hungary."[94]

It should be noted that traces of Czapik are distinctly noticeable in the final wording of the epistle. Seredi accepted his suggestions and went even further: not only does the epistle not include any details of brutality toward the Jews; it completely ignores this brutality. A general reference was the only indication of certain unpleasantnesses the Jews had been encountering of late. The terminology adopted by the two most prominent personages of the Hungarian Catholic church is fascinating. They both used the legalistic term "deprivation of rights" to mean, in practice, the murder of almost half a million people. In accordance with Kapi's counsel, Seredi was extremely cautious in choosing his words, and preferred to write euphemistically.

The question of the purpose of the epistle should be examined in light of what it included and what was omitted from it.

The document includes some two thousand words. It is very doubtful if the population, visiting the churches in the heat of a Hungarian summer, was capable of following such a drawn-out reading, of concentrating on its content, and of absorbing its significance, especially since it was written in an archaic, medieval style that made it all the more difficult for its audience to concentrate. Its lengthy introduction and historical review certainly led the listeners to wonder about its relevance to the difficulties of their daily lives.

With regard to its content, as soon as the epistle begins to discuss current affairs, its language becomes obscure, and the average listener certainly had difficulty understanding its meaning. Only on a single topic did the epistle use clear, unambiguous language—in besmirching the Jewish population, a topic to be discussed below.

Seredi refers to his discussions with the authorities in his diplomatic, enigmatic style, saying, "Indeed we registered sporadic successes." In other words, Seredi termed a success the fact that as a result of his intervention elderly converted priests would henceforth be permitted to employ Christian domestics, as well as the fact that in the future Jewish converts would be permitted to wear a white cross on their clothing in addition to the yellow six-pointed star. Seredi modestly describes his successes as "few and inadequate," yet the very use of the term success in describing the events of those days is a clear sign of a lack of sensitivity.

As noted above, in contrast with the obscure language employed throughout most of the epistle, Seredi's style becomes clear when he speaks of the topic that was the real reason for the document's being written: the Jewish question. Yet, instead of defending them, Seredi's clear style attacks and condemns the Jews: "We do not voice any opposition to the steps which have been taken against them until now in the economic field." Every Hungarian was aware of the nature of the economic steps taken against the Jews: expelling them from their homes in the presence of their Hungarian neighbors, throwing them out of their shops, removing them from their lands, and robbing their property in broad daylight. These were "the economic steps which have been taken until now"—the steps to which there was no opposition. Those Hungarians who eyed Jewish property greedily now enjoyed the implicit support of the leader of their church in their thinking: "We do not deny that a number of Jews exercised a wicked, destructive influence upon Hungarian economic, social, and moral life. It is also a fact that the others did nothing in protest against their coreligionists in this matter." Seredi, together with Kapi, divided the Jewish population into two parts, each part being worthy of punishment—one because it behaved badly, the other because it did not protest. Seredi's approach in his epistle reflects his consistency. More than five years before the tragedy of 1944, while debating on the second anti-Jewish bill, Seredi had declared, "Part of the Jewish population casts doubt upon those things sacred to Christians. They do so with the acquiescence of the other Jews."[95]

A Catholic listening to the cardinal saying, "we lodge no protest against the eradication of their undesirable influence. On the contrary, we would like to see it disappear" could rightfully deduce that both his government and the heads of his church believed it desirable that the unwanted influence of the Jews disappear. In facilitating the disappearance of their influence, the facilitators made the Jews themselves disappear. And even if there were some differences of opinion between church and state over the technical steps employed by those facilitating the disappearance of the Jews in the execution of their duties, there was complete agreement between the two sides with regard to the importance of the disappearance itself.

One way or another, the job was done, and Hungary remained clean, purified of those Jews with "the wicked, destructive influence." The foremost church institutions justified, at least a posteriori, a deed for which the Hungarian people were ready as a result of the many years of incitement provided by their leaders, including the leaders of their churches.

What did the Shepherds' Epistle omit? It omitted any reference to accepted moral standards; it omitted any call for an examination of current events and contemporary leaders on the basis of the religious precept "Thou shalt not kill."

On the other hand, the Shepherds' Epistle contains the declaration that the Synod of Bishops relied on "the Christianity and humanity" of the government ministers. In Seredi's considerations, his sense of obligation to collaborate with the authorities[96] was stronger than his basic human emotion, which would have obliged him to save the innocent from their murderers.

The Protestant churches, too, prepared a Shepherds' Epistle in the summer of 1944, and there is a strong resemblance between their epistle and that of the Roman Catholic church.

The Protestant churches suggested to Seredi on a number of occasions that all the Christian churches adopt a common stance in their talks with the government. In order to achieve this cooperation between them, Ravasz declared that "for the defense of the interests of Christians of Jewish origin, he is willing to cooperate with the Catholic church." The Catholic priest who heard this declaration reported it to Seredi, but the latter did not respond to this appeal, just as he refrained from responding to other appeals. When he did respond, his reaction was negative.[97]

In light of Seredi's rejection, the bishops of the two Protestant churches prepared a Shepherds' Epistle to be read out in their churches. The epistle is dated "the last Sunday of the month of June," that is, June 25. It is to be noted that, in contrast with church documents prepared in the summer of 1944, this document was exceptional in that it lacks the usual emphasis that the appeal was being made on behalf of the Jewish converts to Christianity. Nevertheless, the epistle does refer to the memorandum which the nine Protestant bishops had presented to the government a few days earlier, in which the demand to prefer the converts was prominent. The Shepherds' Epistle strongly condemns the action taken by the government and demands unequivocally that an end be put to the deportations, the torture, and the brutality accompanying them.[98]

Yet this epistle, too, like Seredi's, was composed after considerable delay, after the deportation of most of Hungarian Jewry outside of Budapest. Like the Catholics, the Protestants also refrained from publicly depicting the government as serving a foreign power in the murderous policy it was following.

The church leaders did not inform the government of their intention to appeal in Shepherds' Epistles to their faithful, but the government learned of it nevertheless.[99] The postal system was instructed to delay the dispatch of Seredi's epistles, but some of these were packed in parcels and so reached their destinations. Despite the tone of the epistle—hostile to the Jews—the government feared for some reason the possibility of the epistles being read out in churches throughout the country, and appealed to the church leaders to consider canceling their reading. The government sent Minister Istvan Antal to meet with the cardinal, who was staying at his summer home in Gerecse. The meeting took place on June 6. Antal tried to persuade the cardinal that no good could come of reading the epistle, hinting that the reading might have "undesirable consequences" both in Hungary and abroad. I assume he was indicating the possibility of the Arrow-Cross party taking power under German auspices.

Despite Antal's points not being well reasoned, and despite the fact that his threats, under the circumstances at the time in Budapest, were vain threats, Seredi hurriedly retreated and agreed in principle to postpone the date upon which the epistle was to be read out, while postulating three conditions: first, the prime minister would guarantee officially that the violations of civil rights would cease; second, the converts would be exempted from all the decrees applying to the Jews—more specifically, they were not to be expelled from the country in the future, and the prime minister would do everything possible to have those already deported returned; and lastly, the church authorities would be entitled to inform their believers that they were negotiating with the government over the Jewish question, and that some success had already been achieved.

Antal accepted the first two conditions and realized it would be better if the cardinal and prime minister discussed the third condition between them. On the following day, July 7, Seredi instructed his bishops and priests by telegram to postpone reading out the Shepherds' Epistle until further notice.

The next day, on July 8, the prime minister, accompanied by three members of his government, visited Seredi in Gerecse. The cardinal, together with two archbishops and two bishops, received them. The prime minister handed the cardinal a document in which he referred to the previous correspondence between them concerning exemptions for the converts from the anti-Jewish decrees. The prime minister was now happy to inform the cardinal that certain steps, which until then had been mere thoughts, would now be put into effect on behalf of the converts, to lighten their burden. The prime minister summed up his position in five points:

1. The government had set up a council to protect Christians of Jewish origin. This council would function separately from the Jewish Council.

2. The government had checked into the complaints of brutality against the Jews, and found that in most cases the complaints were groundless, while in other cases they were exaggerated. The government had punished those responsible for this unseemly conduct, and would prevent repetition of such cases.

3. The deportation of Budapest Jewry had, for the time being, been canceled.

4. If at any time in the future the Jews of Budapest would be deported, the Jews who had converted to Christianity would be permitted to remain in Hungary.

5. The relatives of priests—parents, brothers and sisters and, in the case of Protestant priests, wives and children as well—would be exempted in the future from the requirement to wear the yellow Star of David and from all the other decrees accompanying the wearing of this emblem.[100]

The government seems to have understood just what the churches expected of it. Three of the points concern advantages to be awarded to the converts, while the two remaining points concern the Jews and the converts equally. In return for the prime minister's promises, Seredi agreed to refrain from reading the Shepherds' Epistle in the churches.

A study of this agreement reveals an interesting situation. The second point was nothing but a lie, and was recognized as such by both sides, each of whom was aware of the fact that the other realized that such was the case.

As for the third point, the government simply deceived the church. As we shall see, the government had decided on the day before the premier's meeting with the church leaders to stop the deportation of the Jews. There was no connection between this decision and the contents of the epistle. In other words, depicting the cessation of the deportation of Budapest Jewry as a response to the cardinal refraining from having the Shepherds' Epistle read out in church was only a pretense.

That same point should be read in light of the condition written into the following point, that if the deportations were renewed, it would be the Jews of Budapest who were to be deported, while the converts would remain in the city. The church leaders accepted this point, which meant, essentially, Jewish blood in return for saving the converts and refraining from reading the epistle. It should be noted that the prime minister met with Seredi in Gerecse a mere two days after he met with the nuncio in Budapest.[101] The impression he received from the papal representative was still fresh in his mind, and he surely deduced that the idea that conceding the safety of the converts would render it easier to deal with the Jews would be acceptable to the cardinal as well. Seredi and his colleagues did not disappoint him.

From a practical point of view, the parties concluded that on the evening of July 8 and the morning of July 9 an announcement would be made on the state radio in the following wording: "Cardinal Justinian Seredi, Prince Primate of Hungary, wishes to inform all parish priests that the general pastoral letter entitled 'Successors of the Apostles' and dated June 29 is intended for the information of the clergy only. This being the case, the letter is not to be read out to the congregations."[102]

Instead of the Shepherds' Epistle, on Sunday, July 16, the priests were to read from the pulpits an announcement agreed upon by Seredi and the prime minister:

Cardinal Justinian Seredi, Prince Primate of Hungary, in his own name as well as the name of their Excellencies, the Hungarian Synod of Bishops, informs the Catholic congregations that he has repeatedly intervened with the Royal Hungarian Government on behalf of the Jews, especially those who have been baptized, and is continuing his negotiations in this direction.[103]

The fate of the Protestant pastoral letter was very similar and perhaps identical with that of the Catholics. The government minister, Istvan Antal, visited Bishop Ravasz on July 11, told him of the arrangement reached between the government and Seredi, and proposed wording a similar arrangement with the Protestant churches. It was agreed that on July 16 the priests of the Protestant churches would read out the following announcement in their churches: "The leaders of both Protestant churches have repeatedly intervened with the competent Government authorities regarding the Jewish question and especially with reference to the baptized Jews. Their endeavors in this respect are continuing."[104]

In this way the pastoral letter affair came to its inglorious end. During the period under discussion the ovens of Auschwitz functioned more than at any previous or subsequent time.

It is interesting to follow the government's energetic action taken to prevent the Shepherds' Epistle from being read out in public. It is surprising that leading government figures attributed so much importance to these letters, that they took part in pressuring the church leaders, and made use of various devices to have the letters shelved. Had they reached their destinations, it is doubtful if they would have attracted much attention, and it is almost certain that no activity whatever would have resulted from them.

The government feared the epistles because it ascribed to the churches—rightfully—considerable influence over their believers. The government's error was in ascribing to the church leaders the desire to use their influence on behalf of the Jews. It is not difficult today to imagine what the churches could have achieved had they put into effect the potential of their ability to influence the people.

In other words, preparing the epistles took between a month and a month and a half, whereas shelving them was a far more rapid process and took place even before the letters themselves had been made public. One possible explanation for this is that the preparation of the epistles was intended only to calm the consciences of their writers, those who had been able to help and to save Jews but had refrained from so doing. When they encountered the first obstacle in the path of making the epistles public, their writers desisted from the rest of their initiative, and the subject of pastoral letters ended in roaring silence.

It was roaring silence in more than one sense: when the priests were about to put into effect what little was left of the Shepherds' Epistles, and prepared to read the cardinal's announcement, the loudspeakers in the churches suddenly went silent—with Seredi's approval.[105]

Yet the silence in the churches was not absolute. When the Jews had been expelled from the town of Veszprem, and the city was then *Judenrein* (cleansed of Jews), the residents of the town were invited to a thanksgiving ceremony in the Franciscan church. The announcements that appeared throughout the town read,

> With the help of Divine Providence our ancient city and province have been liberated from that Judaism which sullied our nation. In our thousand-year national history, this is not the first time we have been freed from some scourge which had befallen us. However, no previous event can compare in its importance with this event, for no previous foe threatening us, whether by force or by a political takeover, had ever succeeded in overcoming us to the extent that the Jews had succeeded, with the aid of their poisoned roots which penetrated our national body and took hold of it. We are following in the footsteps of our fathers in coming to express our thanks to our God who saves us whenever we are in distress. Come and gather for the thanksgiving service which will take place on June 25 at 11:30 A.M. at the Franciscan Church.

The local branch office of the Arrow-Cross party signed the fliers and distributed them.[106]

The German ambassador, Veesenmayer, reported the thanksgiving prayer service at the Franciscan church to his superiors in Berlin: "The arrangements for organizing the service were agreed upon by the leader of the Arrow-Cross party in Veszprem, Dr. Ferenc Schiberna, and the local Franciscan priest, without the involvement of the Catholic bishop. When the bishop heard of the planned thanksgiving ceremony, he expressed his opposition because 'those deported included some converts.' "

As a result, Dr. Schiberna discussed the matter with the bishop, who then agreed to hold the thanksgiving prayers on condition that the Te Deum prayer not be recited and that the Arrow-Cross party men would not appear at the ceremony in uniform. "The Arrow-Cross men rejected these conditions, and the service was held before an overflowing church. The Arrow-Cross men appeared at the ceremony in their uniforms."[107] In other words, other voices replaced the pastoral letters.

A Quarter of a Million Budapest Jews—Trapped

The deportation of Hungarian Jewry was an operation unprecedented in its efficiency, in its brutality, and in the lack of any humane reaction on the part of any sector of the Hungarian population. Its uniqueness stands out even more clearly when one takes into consideration the fact that it took place during that stage of World War II when the war had already entered its decisive phase, and the oppressive regimes in various European lands were drawing rapidly to their collapse. It is thus simple to comprehend the expressions of anger and condemnation voiced by statesmen and leaders in the free world regarding the leaders of the Hungarian regime. They even threatened the latter with reprisals for their deeds. At the government session held on July 5, 1944, the deputy foreign minister spoke of the heavy pressures being brought to bear on him: "The representatives of the neutral states in Budapest are protesting to me unceasingly on this subject." He even mentioned the demand voiced by public opinion in the Anglo-Saxon countries "to apply sanctions to Hungary; one of the suggestions made was to bomb Budapest and obliterate the government buildings."[108]

In addition, the military situation of the Axis powers, which was deteriorating rapidly on all fronts, compelled the Hungarian government to devote some thought to its future actions. On June 19–20 the Japanese navy had suffered a defeat near the Mariana Islands. The Russians were sweeping ahead rapidly on all fronts. And in the west, the allies had liberated Cherbourg on June 26.[109]

The new situation encouraged Horthy to reconsider the passive approach he had adopted ever since the German invasion. He invited himself to the June 26 government session, which convened as the Crown Council and discussed the matters on its agenda with Horthy in the chair. He told of the pressure being applied to him from various directions, and claimed that public opinion ascribed to Endre and Baky the brutalities carried out against the Jews. Therefore he demanded they be dismissed from their positions. With regard to the deportation of the Jews, his tone was less decisive:

> I would like the deportation of the Jews to be stopped. The deportation is merely a cruel solution and does not coincide with the Hungarian character. Yet if the government feels that the Germans demand the deportation to continue and are unwilling to give in, and we are under obligation on this matter, then I will not permit the Hungarian gendarmes to engage in the deportation process. In this case, the Germans themselves will have to carry out their plan, using the troops they have here.[110]

Horthy's demand to put an end to the deportation, which was not sufficiently decisive, did not lead to that result; the deportations went on in accordance with the original plan until the last Jew had been expelled from the cities, the towns, and the villages, including even the suburbs of greater Budapest.

The seeds of doubt had, as we have noted, already been sown in the hearts of the ministers, but nevertheless the deportations went on. There was need for a dramatic shock to stun the members of the government so that they would resolve to put an end to the deportations. Such an occurrence derived from a telegram sent by Veesenmayer to Ribbentrop on July 6, in which Veesenmayer tells of his meeting with Sztojay, which had taken place two days before, at which Sztojay had read out to him

> in absolute secrecy three telegrams deciphered by Hungarian counterintelligence. The telegrams had been dispatched from Bern, Switzerland, by the Ambassadors of England and America, and they contained a detailed description of the fate of the Jews deported from Hungary.... They therefore propose to bomb and to destroy the final train stations reached by the deported Jews. Furthermore, they propose to bomb the train tracks linking Hungary with these stations. The telegram also contains a proposal to carry out spot-bombing of all Hungarian and German centers in Budapest and of all agencies collaborating with them, and marks precisely the streets and building numbers where these centers and agencies are located. Another telegram contained a list of the names of seventy Hungarians and Germans described as the main parties responsible for the deportations.

Sztojay attempted to make an impression upon me, and so explained to me that this threat does not frighten him, for in case we are victorious, the threat will then be meaningless, whereas in the opposite case his life will at any rate be forfeit. Nevertheless, it was possible to see that the telegrams had a very strong effect upon him. He even mentioned the telegrams at the government session and—as I have since heard—they had an appropriate effect there as well.[111]

On the following day Sztojay informed Veesenmayer of the government's decision to stop the deportations.[112] The Jews of Budapest, about a quarter of a million persons, remained in Hungary at that time. This Jewish population knew nothing of the government decision. On the contrary, everything pointed to their having to follow the same path taken earlier by their brethren from outside Budapest.

During the month of April a rumor had spread through Budapest, according to which the Jews of the capital were to be collected up in ghettos, just as the other Jews of Hungary had been gathered before them. In light of these rumors, Radio BBC announced from London that if this did take place, England would alter its policy of bombing Budapest. Until such time only industrial sites and other targets of importance to the Axis powers' war effort would be bombed. But if the Jews were evacuated from the various sections of the capital, even the residential quarters in the evacuated areas would be included among the targets of the British air force. The Hungarian officer in charge of anti-aircraft defenses protested, for the same reason, against the intention of concentrating the Jews in a ghetto in Budapest.

In light of the new situation, Endre developed a new system of gathering the Jews up without concentrating them in a ghetto. On June 15, the mayor of Budapest promulgated a decree requiring all the Jews of Budapest to move into certain buildings, the names of which appeared in the list attached to the decree. These buildings were marked with a large yellow Star of David near their entrance, and were termed from then on "Jewish buildings." Before the decree was made public, the Jews of Budapest had lived in 21,250 apartments. The list of buildings intended to become "Jewish buildings" included no more than 2,681 apartments, slightly over 12 percent of the number of apartments held by Jews previously. The quarter of a million Jews were to carry out their move into this reduced area within eight days, and the entire operation was to come to an end by 8:00 in the evening of June 21.[113]

The move caused the Jewish population great suffering. Finding living space in the Jewish buildings was an almost impossible task, despite the efforts made by the Jewish leadership to assist and to guide those who had been evicted from their homes. Wagon and truck drivers took advantage of the opportunity they were offered and raised the price of transporting those few belongings that the Jews were permitted to take with them.[114]

Hardly had the evicted persons managed to place their belongings in their new living quarters when a new decree descended upon them: the curfew decree. This was made public by the chief of the Budapest police on June 23, and went into effect that very day. In general, people wearing the yellow Star of David were forbidden to be outside their living quarters. Exceptions to this rule were those who had to leave their homes for vital purposes such as medical attention and shopping. These sallies were limited to the three hours between 2:00 P.M. and 5:00 P.M., and the quarter of a million Budapest Jews were imprisoned in their homes for twenty-one hours a day. That decree also forbade the Jews to accept visitors to their homes or to hold conversations through windows that opened onto the street.

In every Jewish building the owner or janitor was required to prepare in triplicate a list of all the Jews in the building, in which apartments they lived, their sex, and their age. The janitor was to hang one copy of this at the entrance to the building or in some other suitable place. He was to keep two copies, to be shown to the authorities or handed over to them whenever this was required. The Jews were forbidden to visit the homes of Christians, public parks, or esplanades. They were also forbidden to travel in the city trolley cars, except for the last carriage.[115]

These and many additional decrees aroused the Jews' fear of what the future might hold in store for them, for they viewed these decrees as a preliminary stage of their deportation. The Germans did not accept gracefully the idea that the quarter of a million Jews of Budapest might escape them, many of these Jews being educated and cultured, others still considered wealthy despite having lost their possessions as a result of the regulations. The Germans found faithful allies among the government ministers and the high-ranking officials in Hungary. The Jaross-Imredi-Baky-Endre group agreed with the Germans, and did whatever it could to thwart the government decision and carry on with the deportations. Jaross told German Ambassador Veesenmayer on July 9 that "despite the regent's stand, he was prepared to go on with the de-Judification of Budapest, even if he had to do so indirectly."[116]

Interior Minister Jaross did not conceal his opinion from his colleagues in the government, and at their meeting of August 2 he made a proposal both practical and indirect, which would facilitate the continued deportation of the Jews:

There are at present in Budapest approximately 280,000 Jews. . . . The number of converts to Christianity in Budapest may be estimated at 20,000. The idea he proposed was that by giving in on the question of deporting the converts, it might be easier to expel the Jews. . . . The technique of such an expulsion would be as follows: the Jewish candidates for deportation would be transferred from Budapest to camps located outside the capital, from where they would be deported. . . . The prime minister views the situation as follows: in another week or two the deportation of the Jews will be resumed. In his opinion, it simply will not do to leave so large a number of Jews in Budapest.[117]

Jaross knew that he had nothing much to fear from Horthy's pro-Jewish feelings, for at the very same session of the Crown Council in which he expressed his opposition to the deportation of the Jews, he expressed another element as well. Over and above Horthy's taking pity on the Jews, he was perturbed that events were taking place in Hungary without his knowledge and perhaps even against his will. Horthy had been brought up on the concepts of the Austro-Hungarian monarchy. Before World War I he had served for years as the military aide to the old emperor, Franz-Josef, and believed that all those subordinate to the head of the hierarchy owed him absolute allegiance. Horthy believed that he was the one to make decisions in his kingdom. Reality, however, was stronger than his beliefs. In the spring and summer of 1944 events took place without his knowledge or consent. Horthy expressed his annoyance in a conversation that he held on July 4 with Veesenmayer, who reported on his talk with Ribbentrop:

Two evenings ago I had a lengthy two-hour talk with the regent, at his request. He began by saying that he requested of the Fuehrer to begin urgently removing the Gestapo from Hungary in order to restore Hungarian sovereignty, as he had indeed been promised. He is in a very difficult situation. He feels he is merely a pawn in the hands of others, and that he is not in control of what takes place in his own country.[118]

For the restoration of Hungarian sovereignty Horthy was prepared to pay a suitable price, and some time thereafter did not hesitate to propose an exchange: the deportation of the Jews in return for the withdrawal of certain German units. The protocol of the August 10 government session reads:

After obtaining the consent of His Excellency the Regent, the Royal Hungarian Government is prepared to declare that in order to bolster up the economic war effort, it will place at the disposal of the German Reich, from August 28, 1944, all those Jews: [a] serving in the labor battalions and whose families are already in Germany (some 50,000–60,000 persons); [b] with a criminal record or those who are dangerous to the public.... In return, the Hungarian government requests permission to carry on with the solution to the Jewish problem. Therefore, it would appreciate it if— for the sake of friendly German-Hungarian relations—the German security police, and especially the unit commanded by *Obersturmbahnfuehrer* Adolf Eichmann, be returned to Germany."[9]

Horthy was less perturbed by his anxiety for the welfare of the Jews than he was busy searching for an efficient way to be suitably rid of his uninvited guests, the Germans. What he had to say at the Crown Council session expressed his fears for his status and authority being reduced, as well as his anxiety for Hungary's good name in the international community. His negative attitude toward the Jews had not changed. In the summer of 1944 he spoke about the Jewish question with his confidant, Baky, who had served under his command in the days of the White Terror,[120] and said to him,

Baky, you are one of my old Szeged officers.... Now the Germans want to deport the Jews. I don't mind. I hate the Jews and the Communists. Out with them, out of the country! But you must see, Baky, that there are some good Hungarian Jews too, like little Chorin and Vida [wealthy industrialists, converted Jews. Chorin was the chairman of the National Union of Factory Owners in Hungary between 1933 and 1941]. Aren't they good Hungarians? I can't let them go, can I? But take the rest, the sooner the better!"[121]

One of the researchers of the period describes Horthy as a person who "had ... Christian humanistic values."[122] As a matter of interest it should be noted that even Hitler noted the Christianity of Admiral Horthy and his wife. Horthy tells in his memoirs of the friendly attention Hitler paid him and his wife, noting that on the occasion of one of his visits to Berlin their polite host made sure that there was a crucifix in the room assigned to Mrs. Horthy, who was a Catholic.[123]

It is to be noted that the Vrba Report reached Horthy at the end of May or at the beginning of June 1944, and thus it is clear that he was aware of the fate awaiting those whose "removal from the country" he recommended so convincingly.[124]

Thus, Jaross and his colleagues who strove to continue the deportations even after the government had resolved to end them knew on whom and what to rely. It is no less significant to stress that Jaross, like Horthy, distinguished between Jews and converts as candidates for deportation. This is evident from Horthy's consent to the arrangement the government proposed in its August 10 session as well as from his conversation with

Baky. It has already been shown that this distinction was paramount in the government's discussions with the leaders of the churches. It remains to be shown that the entire government made this distinction when considering the Jewish problem.

The impression reached from statements made by various personages is that the government resolution of early July to put an end to the deportations was neither absolute nor final. In mid-July, Himmler's confidant, Hottl, spoke with one of the leaders of the Arrow-Cross party, Vajna (who filled the post of interior minister in the Szalasi government after October 15), and quoted one of Himmler's remarks to him: "The solution of the Jewish problem is not merely a Hungarian problem, but rather a pan-European one. And if the Fuehrer decided that the Jews must be removed from Hungary he will not stand by idly doing nothing in light of what is now going on in Hungary. These steps go against his will."[125]

On July 18, the Hungarian government sent an informative dispatch to the foreign delegations in Budapest in which it stated,

> The following alleviations in the treatment of Jews were approved: 1) No more converted Jews will be sent abroad.... All Jews baptized before August 1, 1944, will remain in the country but will be separated from non-Jews.... These rules will not only apply to the converted Jews living in Budapest, but also to those in the provinces.[126] A revision is promised in respect of the converted Jews already sent to Germany for labor purposes. ... The deportation of Jews for labor purposes will take place in the future only with particular regard to the laws of humanity. The Red Cross will be granted the right to carry out inspections.[127]

This dispatch reflects the government's consent to the demands made by the church leaders to give the Jewish converts preferential treatment in comparison with that given the Jews. It would seem to indicate that the deportation of Jews might once again become feasible in the future.

In a telegram sent by the German foreign office on July 27, 1944, to the German embassy in Budapest, the foreign office urges the embassy to inform it of the date set for the deportation of the Jews of Budapest. Ambassador Veesenmayer's reply, sent two days later, indicates that he had already acted on his own initiative:

> In the conversation I had with Sztojay three days ago, I urged him to begin immediately and with no delays to expel the Jews in the direction of the Reich.... Sztojay mentioned that he was in a government crisis which he desired to resolve speedily, after which he would request the government's consent to renew action against the Jews. He expressed his hope that the

separation of those whom he called Christian Jews—those who had converted prior to January 1, 1941—would be completed in a few days. I
replied to him . . . that first of all and without any delay fifty thousand Jews
should be expelled to camps outside the capital city, in order to deport
them at a later date to the Reich.[128]

Indeed, in his telegram dated August 14, 1944, Veesenmayer informed
the foreign office in Berlin that the Hungarian interior minister had informed Eichmann of the government's resolution to propose to the regent
that the deportation of Budapest Jewry begin on August 25. "All the
technical preparations for the action against Budapest Jews have been
made."[129]

The intention to renew the deportation was floating in the air. Not
only the Jews were worried about this; the representatives of the neutral
countries in Budapest viewed it as very possible that the deportations
were to be renewed. The Apostolic Nuncio and the Swedish ambassador
thus visited Deputy Prime Minister Remny-Szneler on August 21 and
handed him a memorandum in their name and in the name of their
diplomatic colleagues, the representatives of Portugal, Switzerland, and
Spain:

> The envoys of the neutral states represented in Budapest have been ac-
> quainted with the fact that the deportation of the Jews still remaining in
> the capital is about to take place. They all know what this means, even
> though it has been described as "labor service."
>
> It is the human duty of the representatives of the neutral countries to
> protest against these actions. . . . The representatives of the neutral coun-
> triess herewith request the Hungarian government to forbid these
> cruelties.[130]

Since experienced diplomats sensed the impending deportations, it is
not surprising that the Jews, imprisoned in their homes and nourished
by rumor, viewed the restrictions imposed upon them as the preliminary
steps leading to deportation. And if they still had a spark of hope, the
new prime minister of Hungary smashed their illusions.

On August 23, Rumania executed a 180-degree reversal by requesting
and obtaining a ceasefire with the Soviet Union. Rumania broke off
relations with Germany and turned her armaments against the Germans,
on the side of the Red Army. This dramatic shift that took place in
Hungary's eastern neighbor forced Hungary to act, and, on August 29,
Horthy appointed General Lakatos as prime minister in place of Sztojay,
and entrusted him with three assignments: to restore Hungarian sovereignty to whatever degree possible, considering the German presence; to
put an immediate end to all persecution of the Jews; and to prepare for

Hungary an armistice agreement to be put into effect at the appropriate time.

The first and third assignments do not fall within the scope of the present work. As for the second, Lakatos reached an agreement with the Germans whereby the Jews of Budapest were to be removed from the capital, and gathered together in concentration camps outside the city, where they would have to work for their livelihood. The Jews, of course, were not informed of this arrangement. On the contrary, the Jews heard that in a speech delivered on the radio, Lakatos had said that he knew that the task of removing all the dangerous elements living among the Hungarians—members of a foreign race although they spoke Hungarian—had not been completed, and that they still endangered public life and especially Hungary's righteous struggle. He calmed the public, saying that there was a desire to guarantee in every way the spiritual and economic supremacy of those of the Hungarian race, and that this would be carried out in accordance with noble Hungarian thought, in a humane fashion and in accordance with the obligations in the agreements reached and in light of the demands made by the lofty goals before them.[131]

Except, perhaps, for the last sentence, which could be interpreted in mutually contradictory ways, the rest of what Lakatos had to say was merely a literal repetition of what Hungarian Jewry had become accustomed to hearing through the long years of their persecution. If the Jews had based any hopes on the appointment of Lakatos as prime minister, this speech dashed them completely. The most they could expect was that when their removal as dangerous elements was carried out, they would be treated in accordance with what he had defined as "noble Hungarian thought," and so forth, the meaning of which they had become familiar with over a period of years. With regard to their daily life, the personnel changes in the government led to no change whatever. All the prohibitions and decrees remained valid.

Thus the summer of 1944 found the Jews of Budapest in a state of constant fear of the future, as well as anxiety for the fate of their relatives who had been deported from the cities and provinces of Hungary. The threat of deportation continued to hover over them until autumn, when the Red Army completed its encirclement of the city. It is therefore no wonder that the Jews of Budapest tried to hang on to whatever seemed to extend some little hope—including conversion to Christianity.

Their naive hope that conversion would serve as a life-saver was based upon the rumors they had heard concerning the preferential treatment the government was to give the converts in the event that the Jews of Budapest were to be deported. As we have noted, these rumors had some basis in fact. And so, while between early January and March 19, 1944, the offices of the Jewish community in Budapest had received 176 statements of the intention to convert, during a single month following the German invasion, 788 such statements were received.[132]

The offices of the Budapest rabbinate were flooded with such statements, the result being that rabbinate officials had to work around the clock—and were still unable to cope with the administrative work involved in dealing with these statements of intent. Rabbi Dr. Zsigmond Groszman complained that he was unable to meet with all those who wanted to convert, and especially that he was unable to hold an intimate conversation with them: "This is not a religious movement; the vast majority of those who desire to convert state this openly. They want to improve their chances of survival and believe that by converting their situation will be better."[133]

The conversion movement lasted during the months of April, May, and June and was accelerated during the first half of July. On July 11 a public announcement by the mayor of Budapest was promulgated, calling for all those who had lived previously in the cities and provinces of Hungary, outside the municipal jurisdiction of Budapest, and had been baptized before August 1, 1944, to bring a document proving their conversion to the offices of their churches in order to be registered in the offices of their churches in Budapest. The final date for registration was fixed for July 17 at 5:00 P.M.[134]

The mayor's public announcement provided support for those who believed there was a chance that conversion would facilitate their survival—and thus created an increased stream of would-be converts to the churches.

If it is true, as some scholars would have it, that several church leaders suffered pangs of conscience as they saw in 1944 where their antisemitic incitement in previous years had led,[135] they were now given the opportunity to atone to some degree for their deeds in the past. The laws of the church require a certain period of preparation for all would-be converts, but if such a period was not feasible because of the existing conditions, Seredi could have relied on a certain paragraph in his church's regulations. Chapter 752, paragraph 2 of the Catholic church's lawbook states, "An adult in danger of death, with no way of enjoying thorough instruction in the principles of the Catholic faith, can be converted without delay."[136]

There is not a shadow of doubt that it was possible at the time to apply this paragraph to the Jews of Budapest, thus enabling church authorities to extend their protection to those fleeing for their lives. But the church leaders did not choose to act in this fashion. Not only did they not extend a helping hand to those in need of succor, but they even set up impassable barriers at the entrances to their churches, and the flight of those fleeing was blocked by the high priests of religion.

Seredi published in the Roman Catholic church's official newspaper instructions requiring the priests to consider carefully the true intentions of candidates for conversion. Seredi's instructions were promulgated on July 24, some two weeks after the announcement by the mayor of Budapest regarding the registration of converts, at a time when the confusion of the Jews was at its peak and approached hysteria. They stated:

> The rites connected with the sacrament of baptism are to be strictly adhered to. The period of dogmatic instruction laid down is to be prolonged, as now, in view of the growing number of candidates for conversion, it is more necessary than ever for the priest responsible for the baptism or his deputy to ensure that the applicant not only possesses the dogmatic knowledge required, but also yearns for the Church of Christ from the bottom of his heart and has sincere intentions. The sacrament of baptism can only be administered after the conscientious observance of a term of probation, and only to those of whom it can be certain that they seek not only the possession of a certificate of baptism, but mainly the regenerating force and redeeming grace of Christ, that is to say to those who will not only augment the number of so-called registered Christians, but who wish to be a part of the community of the Church of Christ.[137]

Seredi was not operating in a vacuum. It is reasonable to assume that Seredi's act and the views of his flock regarding the would-be converts had a mutual effect: on July 19, just a few days before the publication of Seredi's instructions in the newspaper, a citizen—a retired high-ranking official—visited the office of the archbishop in Budapest and held a conversation with its director, a prominent priest. She had come to warn of the ominous phenomenon of Jews of no internal convictions coming to convert, and warned the church not to accept them into Christianity. She related that the tenants of a certain building had resolved to convert "out of fear and out of individual interests, for they hoped that their conversion would obtain various advantages for them."

On the following day she summed up her visit in a letter:

> In the future the Jews must be prevented from violating Christianity and desecrating its sacraments. . . . I would be violating my own conscience and would view myself as being a partner to the plot, were I not to inform you of its existence. . . . In my humble opinion, such deeds could have been prevented by making an appropriate announcement in the press, drawing the attention of those in charge, for the betrayal of Christianity will lead

both to the church being punished and to strong reprisals by the state authorities.

Allow me to add that insofar as I am guided by a sense of obligation and considering the present dangerous situation threatening both my church and my homeland, I permit myself to send a copy of this letter to his Holiness, the Cardinal-Archbishop, most supreme Prince of our Church.[138]

We do not know if His Holiness actually read the copy of the letter that was sent to him, and we need not assume that the most supreme Prince of the Church was in need of civilian encouragement in order to publish his announcement in the press. Yet the juxtaposition of dates—of the writing of the letter and of the promulgation of the announcement—as well as the complete agreement of the head of the Catholic church hierarchy with a simple daughter of the church is indeed a coincidence.

The Evangelical church acted similarly. On July 10, Bishop Kapi instructed the priests of his church in the Transdanubia region as follows:

Our church must adhere to its basic views. According to these views our church does not deny its missionary obligations regarding the Jews as well. On the other hand, the church is not willing to become a pawn in the hands of those trying to take advantage of it in order to attain individual and selfish goals. Regarding those who come to be baptized we must insist on a minimal period of instruction of sixty hours spread over a period of six months. This period is also a trial period. I reserve the right to decree an additional trial period if necessary.[139]

A few days later the general directorate of the Evangelical church considered this question. In its resolutions, it called upon its priests to bestow favor upon veteran converts at present in distress. They were to be visited on every occasion, both in the ghetto and outside it; they were to be provided with the various church publications, and so on. But as for those who were trying to convert at the present time, the brochure calls unambiguously for an uncompromising hard line to be adopted in fixing the conditions for conversion, as in Kapi's directive.

The two circulars are almost identical, and this emphasizes the uniformity of opinion on the subject between the religious leader and the lay leadership of the church. "The period of instruction is at least sixty hours, spread out over half a year. This period is also a trial period. The bishops' right is hereby reserved to decree a trial period lasting even more than half a year."[140]

The period required for the conversion of Jews was treated by the churches as if those who sought sanctuary with the church had all the time in the world at their disposal.

Against this background one must interpret the protest made by the general secretary of the Evangelical churches in Hungary against the letter he had received from the general secretary of the Evangelical church in Germany. The latter referred to a publication that appeared in the city of Dresden on July 14:

> From this publication it would seem that the Evangelical priests in Budapest are performing a considerable number of conversions to Christianity. I find it difficult to believe this rumor and actually refuse to believe it, especially in light of the terrible events of our time, when the responsibility for their occurrence rests on the shoulders of the Jews, those very Jews against whom our Father Luther already adopted so strong a stand. Taking this fact into consideration, I cannot imagine any priest in any church being ready to convert to Christianity even a single Jew.
>
> I would greatly appreciate receiving your clarifications on this point as soon as possible.
>
> I thank you in advance for the trouble you have so kindly taken. With the blessing of a fellow-priest and with a "Heil Hitler."
>
> Your faithful admirer, Father Voigt.[141]

In light of the consistency of his church with regard to the Jews and their sufferings, the suspicions voiced by the German priest hurt his Hungarian colleague, and he hastily replied as follows:

> As for your letter taking an interest in the Jewish question, I speedily inform you as follows: it is indeed true that a fever of conversion has broken out among the Jews of Budapest. The storming of the church offices in order to obtain a certificate of baptism is so great that these offices hardly manage to fill their regular functions. There is no question here of them repenting. By conversion the Jews merely desire to save their lives.
>
> The Hungarian Evangelical church is not prepared to compromise on the Jewish question. We accept into the six-month preparatory course only those who are married to an Evangelical-Aryan spouse.
>
> Accepting other Jews into the church is absolutely forbidden. Two priests, who out of flightiness baptized Jews at their request, have been suspended from their posts. For decades now the Evangelical church has been extremely careful on the Jewish question. The duration of the preparatory period is almost a year, and so the Jews have preferred to turn to the Roman Catholic church, which has not put any obstacles in their path and settled for more convenient conditions. The Catholic church takes

a liberal approach on this matter; nevertheless, ten days ago a directive of
the Catholic church came out, adopting the Evangelical approach.'⁴²

The approach of the church leaders won public support. The following
is a contemporary editorial of a newspaper: "It is evident that the mass
turn to conversion at the present time is motivated by a desire to obtain
material and social advantages." The newspaper quotes faithful Christians expressing their bitterness at the Jewish invasion of their churches:

> Where is the modern Jesus to drive these peddlers out of our sacred
> churches? ... Why must we suffer, in that by virtue of the invasion of all
> these new Christians our churches will turn into inferior, stinking syn-
> agogues? Why must we suffer a situation in which those who have grown
> up on Christianity and live lives of deep faith in the Christian spirit are
> forced to find themselves outside their churches, so that in the pews of
> those very churches those very Jews engaging in their dark and dismal
> businesses are able to find comfort? ... The priests must not allow these
> bloodsucking peddlers to manage their business at the expense of the priests
> in the sacred temples of God. They must pray to Jesus who in his time
> drove the peddlers out of the House of God with a whip.'⁴³

The thought that certain priests did indeed convert Jews to Christianity
with irresponsible haste served as a convenient battlefield for intrachurch
bickering. The importance of the subject required that it be discussed
before a high-ranking government authority—the minister of religion and
culture. Raffay, who was interested in putting a stop to the criticism of
his church, reported to the minister on July 24, 1944, that there were
no grounds for the complaint lodged by a Catholic priest that in a suburb
of Budapest Evangelical priests baptized Jews in contravention of the
standing instructions. Raffay announced that after a thorough examination of all the documents, "it was ruled that the baptismal ceremonies
had been carried out in accordance with the standing instructions." The
protocol reporting on the examination of the subject states, "The church
regulations concerning the baptism of Jews are maintained fastidiously
by the priest's office, including the particularly severe instructions recently
added."¹⁴⁴

On another occasion, in the autumn of the same year, priests of the
Reformed and Catholic churches lodged yet another complaint against
an Evangelical priest for baptizing Jews with insufficient preparation.
The Evangelical church was not prepared to appear in the eyes of its
sister churches, the Catholic and Reformed churches, as showing mercy
to Jews. The consideration of the allegation occupied the Evangelical

church and reached the desk of its leader. A final memorandum dated October 3, 1944, of over a thousand words, demonstrates at length that the allegations were groundless, and that the Evangelical priest was innocent of all wrongdoing.[145]

As already noted, the memorandum was composed at the beginning of October. The Red Army had crossed the Hungarian border on September 23. By October 7 its front lines were at the gates of Szeged, the second-largest city in Hungary, which fell into Russian hands three days later, on October 10, after a short battle. With the conquest of Szeged, the vanguard of the Red Army crossed the Tisza River. There was no further natural barrier on their way to the capital of Hungary, and the Red Army advanced toward Budapest, meeting with no resistance.

In other words, the churches and priests in Budapest had their own order of priorities. Even while the old world order was collapsing about them and, while the Bolshevik threat was approaching the gates of their capital city, thereby realizing their worst fears, they had the time to justify their actions in face of suspicion of aiding Jews. There was full agreement between the plaintiffs and the defendants—the suffering of the Jews and their efforts to escape were to be ignored.

The survival of the Jews of Budapest in the spring and summer of 1944 is to be viewed in light of the events described above. Their survival did not result from the efforts of the church or from its desire to help, but rather—as noted above—from the situation at the various fronts, which deteriorated extremely swiftly as regards the Axis forces, who strove to the best of their ability to stem the tide of the Allied forces driving in on them. Doubts began to assail the hearts of the rulers of Hungary. The war had reached the homes of a million inhabitants of Budapest, who had suffered over the summer from almost daily Allied bombing. Airplanes appeared over Budapest by day and by night, unimpeded by any resistance, contrary to the promises they had heard from the Nazis over the years. All this played a part in the hesitations of the rulers of Hungary, and encouraged them to settle for the sacrifice of almost half a million Jews, who had lived in the towns and provinces of Hungary, and whom they had already managed to deport.

It is reasonable to conclude that the decoded telegrams described above played a weighty role, ruling in favor of putting an end to the deportations and not renewing them. It may be said with certainty that the survival of the Jews of Budapest in the summer of 1944 is not to be attributed to the churches. These were at best indifferent.

Hungarian Initiatives

In setting out to execute its anti-Jewish policies, the Hungarian government enjoyed the support of the population of its country. The Hungarian
public expressed its support by its various actions, as well as its proposals
aimed at rendering Hungarian liberation from the Jews more efficient
and at making life more difficult for the Jews being expelled. Here are a
few examples of such initiatives, in addition to those mentioned above.
Among the initiators were both organizations and individuals.

Even the Germans noted the enthusiasm with which various Hungarian
circles brutalized the Jews under their control, above and beyond the
level decreed by the authorities. This was apparently the background for
the oral appeal made by the German embassy in Budapest to the Hungarian foreign office. This appeal was summed up in a memorandum on
August 12, during one of the stages in the drawn-out negotiation regarding the renewal of the deportation of Budapest Jewry, at a time when
such a step seemed reasonable to the Germans:

> The German Embassy is honored to direct the attention of the Royal
> Hungarian Foreign Office to the fact...that it is desirable that the Hun-
> garian authorities guarantee to whatever degree possible the humane treat-
> ment of the groups of Hungarian Jewish laborers being sent to work in
> the Reich. In the opinion of the German commanders of these labor groups,
> it is very desirable that the laborers be provided with food for the duration
> of the trip, which takes a considerable time.
>
> May we thus request that the relevant Hungarian institutions be per-
> suaded to devote special attention to the trains being provided with food
> for the duration of the journey.... The German Embassy will be grateful
> if the appropriate institutions look into an existing problem: that the equip-
> ment the laborers traveling to Germany take with them and the food
> provided for them not be expropriated from them by the Hungarian border
> police. This has occurred in the past, possibly because the police were not
> properly instructed. It is extremely important that such expropriations
> cease.[146]

Hungarians in no way connected with the deportations offered their
own vehicles—horses and wagons—to speed up the removal of the Jews
from their areas:

> In every town and in every village the local population accepted the steps
> taken for the de-Judification of their settlement with open support and
> undisguised rejoicing. They regarded very favorably the execution of the
> government's instructions in this respect. Everywhere the local population
> assisted in furthering the actions taken by the authorities. In most places

the people placed at the disposal of the authorities, and at no cost whatever, vehicles to speed up the removal of those who, by their very presence in the immediate vicinity, detracted from the ability of the Christians to survive.[147]

At the official ceremony marking the beginning of the campaign to destroy Jewish books, the official in charge of the campaign, the commissioner of communications, Mihaly Kolozsvari-Boresa, delivered a speech, saying:

> In this solemn act, the end has come upon an unhealthy process which has lasted fifty years.... The Jewish spirit succeeded in making its influence felt by a large portion of the Hungarian reading population through the agency of Jewish publishers, printing houses, and literary institutions. The fact that day after day my office receives hundreds of reports of Jewish books being found in many and various locations proves that we have exposed the jungle which had existed in this area.[148]

The Royal Hungarian Club of Vehicle Owners turned on May 13 to the minister of the interior and requested "the wise guidance of his Excellency is solving a juridical problem the club members were faced with, as a result of two government directives which seem mutually contradictory." The writer claimed that according to a certain interpretation, one of these directives could be understood as forbidding the continued membership of Jews in the club, while from the other directive it would seem that the Jews were allowed to continue as members of the club. The club passed the matter along for the decision of the highest relevant authority: the minister of the interior.

Yet the club did not wait for the minister's reply. In accordance with the atmosphere prevalent in the summer of 1944 it took its own decision. Along with the question, the club also presented the minister with the solution it had arrived at:

> We are honored to inform His Excellency that until we receive clear instructions we are demanding that our members produce documents testifying to their origin. The names of all those who, according to their papers, are considered Jewish will be removed from the register of club members, even without introducing any amendment of the club's regulations.[149]

The eagerness of the Hungarian populace to make life insufferable for the Jews sometimes took on so grotesque a form that it would have been amusing had it not taken place against so tragic a background. In early May, a local newspaper raised the question whether the Jews were to be permitted to own dogs:

The eight hundred thousand Hungarian dogs are of considerable national economic value.... The pedigreed dogs have value as exports and as imports. A pedigreed dog is worth between 400 and 500 *pengo*, and on occasion even more. Our dogs are thus property worth many millions.

● In this respect we have put the question to the ministry of agriculture: are the Jews permitted to own dogs? The relevant department replied as follows: for the present we know nothing of any directive explicitly prohibiting the possession of dogs by Jews. However, since the Jews are obligated to declare their property and possessions of value, this directive can be interpreted in such a way as to obligate the Jews to declare any pedigreed dogs of great value.... At any rate, the dog tax directive, to be promulgated in the near future, will deal with this aspect of the problem as well.[50]

The ministry of industry admonished the mayor of Budapest for not complying with the directive concerning

shutting of shops belonging to Jewish craftsmen and selling products manufactured by others [opticians selling spectacles].... Since the National Association of Christian Opticians has complained to me that my aforesaid directive has not been executed in Budapest to this day, I hereby request the mayor of Budapest to see to it that the aforesaid directive is carried out, to see to the quality of its execution, and to report to me accordingly on the execution of my instructions.[51]

In other words, there were Christian opticians who carefully saw to it that the municipality obeyed its instructions.

A citizen wrote to the mayor of Budapest and proposed a way to deal properly with the Jews:

The Jews must not be expelled from Budapest, for their presence here provides us with anti-aircraft defenses. Likewise, they must not be gathered into a ghetto, for then we may be destroyed while the ghetto may survive. survive. On the other hand, I would like to suggest that in apartment houses the Hungarian Christians should live on the ground floor and the lower floors of the buildings, while the Jews will live on the upper floors. During air attacks, they must be forbidden entry into shelters. They must remain in their apartments, and must be prohibited from opening doors and windows while the air attack is in progress.

Electricity to the homes of the Jews should be cut off. In this way they will no longer have any way to use the radio sets they have hidden, and which they use both to transmit and to receive. They must also be prohibited from using pocket flashlights, for they might use these to signal enemy aircraft.

If these ideas of mine are put into practice, a much smaller number of Hungarians will be harmed and many more Jews will perish. After all is said and done, every Hungarian is duty-bound to strive to attain these goals.[152]

Support for this kind of thinking can be found in the newspaper article written by a Catholic monk and printed in a Catholic periodical in the summer of 1944. It said, "The Christian doctrine of brotherly love is not violated by what is being done at present with the Jews. On the contrary, it is realized by means of these deeds."[153] That is, the priest supported the steps taken by the authorities.

The monk could have found support for his view in the appeal made by high-ranking priests to the Hungarian population to support the state authorities. Thus, a senior official of the Greek Orthodox church wrote to the priesthood and to the public in a Shepherds' Epistle:

> His Excellency the regent, in his role as the commander-in-chief of our army, has given his order. Hungarian soldiers are bound by the bonds of war to defend our nation and our European culture against Bolshevism, which strives to destroy it all.
>
> May your pure Hungarian heart, the defender of Jesus and sword of our religious belief, be your weapon in this great struggle. The Holy Ghost shall strengthen your spirit.[154]

In the contemporary Hungarian terminology, the term "Bolshevism" had an unambiguously Jewish meaning, and this was to be opposed.

Two new bishops were consecrated in the spring of 1944. In honor of the occasion the two bishops addressed their flocks. Bishop Jozsef Mindszenty wrote in his first Shepherds' Epistle, "The Hungarian people have always been God-fearing, faithful Catholics, living in accordance with the laws of their faith. The Hungarians have always lived with Jesus above and beyond the way of life of other nations. This is indicated by our laws as well."[155] The bishop did not specify to which of the laws of Hungary he was referring, but it may be assumed that his believers knew what he was talking about.

The other bishop to address his flock was Endre Hamvas:

> When we were lonely and alone after the treaty of Trianon which was forced upon us, our soldiers came out of Szeged in the name of God and under the flag of the Virgin Mary to spread the gospel of the Hungarian resurrection, and if we have indeed reached such a point that by virtue of our adherence to our ways we have been lifted up and have now attained the clouds, we must continue to put our trust in God, who has liberated us from our sufferings in order to maintain forever in our hands our national revival.[156]

Here is a fitting place to recall that in Szeged, under the flag of the Holy Virgin, Horthy and his colleagues began the White Terror twenty-five years before.

In the city of Szeged, the twenty-fifth anniversary of the counter-revolution was celebrated. The deputy mayor of Szeged said at the ceremonial rally, "The Szeged counter-revolution raised up the flag of Christian, popular Hungary, a flag that was borne aloft by Miklos Horthy and Bishop Istvan Zadravecz."[57]

At a convention commemorating the outbreak of the counter-revolution, held at the military academy of Budapest, the minister of trade and transportation, Antal Kunder, participated:

> Those present approached the Catholic or Protestant prayer chapels. The prayer was led by a ranking military chaplain. In his sermon he spoke of the connection between the Gospel and our modern period, stressing that "only unsullied faith in the doctrine of Jesus can guarantee the triumph of our arms."
>
> The minister spoke after him, and described the historical background of the counterrevolution. He spoke at length of the unbridled behavior of "the foreign race that pushed our Hungarian nation toward absolute destruction."

The minister told of Communist activists, whose Jewish names he stressed deliberately, and made sure to add the title *elvtars* (comrade) to their names; the term *elvtars*—reserved for active members of the Communist party—was despised in the Hungary of that time. He told of how they defiled Christian sacraments:

> They took action with the assistance of the foreign race . . . and we stood by helplessly, watching how the foreign race humbled and destroyed everything Christian and Hungarian. . . . But when the time came we rose courageously, ready for self-sacrifice, for the sake of that lofty concept: defense of our God, of our homeland, of our Christianity, and of our Hungarianism.
>
> Our suffering, however, is not yet over. We are once again being called upon to make sacrifices in order to be able to remain Christian and Hungarian. The enemy is the very same enemy, threatening once again our national survival. But today we meet the enemy when we are armed. In our present struggle we are not alone, as we were twenty-five years ago. The Fuehrer of the great German Reich, Adolf Hitler, and his courageous army stand today at our side.[58]

The priests and bishops had solid ground on which to base their hatred. They had before them the image of Bishop Prohaszka Ottokar, who had been active at the beginning of the century until his death in 1927, and was considered one of the founding fathers of clerical antisemitism. With regard to the Jews he freely used poisonous phrases and enjoyed immense popularity, both among the priests and among the general public.

A certain weekly journal quoted at length in the summer of 1944 from the writings of Bishop Prohaszka:

> Jewish morality is anathema to Christian civilization, and this curse will completely obliterate Christian civilization if the latter does not succeed in removing the poison. . . . In the eyes of Jewry, all the Christian nations are enemies, and all means capable of leading to the stifling of the Christian nations are justified in their eyes. . . . It can clearly be seen how, without any pangs of conscience, the Jew sucks the blood of his victim, the victim he has already destroyed.
>
> In brief: there is no such thing as Jewish morality, and consequently Jews have no knowledge whatever of the concept of "moral values." Thus, the main qualities of the Jew are unlimited egoism, crushing his fellow man—pressuring him mercilessly and drinking his blood. A Jew is unable to distinguish between good and evil; in his eyes, any means leading to a flow of money into his pockets are justified, including forging checks, false testimony, or even trading the shirts, trousers, or bodies of young girls. It's all the same in their eyes. . . . May a Hungarian person not defend his life, his livelihood, and guarantee his happiness, his culture, and the Hungarian spirit?
>
> The Christian nations must not give the Jews equal rights; they must defend themselves from them and must constantly get rid of them, at every opportunity and in any way they are able.[159]

And so, in the summer of 1944 Hungary was busily realizing the will of the bishops "to get rid of the Jews." As this task drew to a close outside of Budapest, the Hungarians there became aware of the new situation that had evolved in their immediate vicinity: for the first time since Hungary had been liberated in 1688 from Ottoman occupation, Hungary was *Judenrein*. With the very first wave of emotion generated by their liberation from the "Jewish oppression," the Hungarians realized that the expulsion of the Jews had been accompanied by a positive side effect: there was abandoned Jewish property throughout Hungary, ownerless, available to any outstretched arm. They assumed it was all at their disposal.

The government was aware of the expectations of the people, and thus decided to clarify what it intended to do with the Jewish property. Interior Minister Jaross said,

> I make it clear that all property and valuables which Jewish greed managed to accumulate during the liberal period has ceased to be their property.

All this now belongs to the Hungarian nation.... This property must benefit the entire Hungarian nation. We must inject it into the economic bloodstream, so that every honest and fair working Hungarian will receive his portion.[160]

At the close of part 2 of the present study, we considered the hostile triangle—the regime, the public, and the church—that embittered the lives of the Jews in Hungary. Now, too, in connection with the property, the triangle reappeared. The regime, which inherited the Jewish property, promised the public its part in the booty. These are two sides of the triangle. What was the stand of the third side, the church, in this matter?

The third traditional partner, the church, did not stand idly by; it was not prepared to give up its portion of the spoils.

The priest of the Evangelical mission in the province of Bekes sent a letter on July 25 to the office of Bishop Raffay in which he described the request he had made to the authorities to transfer into the hands of the church the real estate that had belonged to the Jewish community. Raffay's secretary wrote in the bishop's name to the chief provincial priest, pointing out improper administrative steps that had been taken in the process of acquiring the abandoned buildings of the Jewish community. Therefore, he was "unable to justify the request of a permit for the Evangelical church to transfer to its own jurisdiction the synagogue, other buildings, and real estate once belonging to the Jewish community of Bekes, and use it for the purposes of the religious Evangelical community."

Raffay's secretary went on to clarify the substance of this administrative defect, which rendered the church impotent even to ask to inherit this abandoned Jewish property:

Church law rules explicitly that if a certain community is about to bring about any change whatever in its sum total of immovable property, it may do so only in accordance with the permission of the church institutions in charge.... The church in Bekes has acted contrary to the existing regulations in proposing to purchase Jewish property without acquiring a permit from the supreme church authorities. His Excellency is asked to bring this to the awareness of the church in Bekes, so that it may cancel permanently its application to the authorities to acquire Jewish property.[161]

In other words, the bishop did not voice any criticism whatever of the morality of the step, but merely of the violation of the regulations.

In contrast to the priest of Bekes, the priest from the mission of the town of Kiskunhalas found a way to proceed that won Raffay's approval.

In his letter of August 16, 1944, to those in charge of the mission in Kiskunhalas, he wrote,

> Blessed be the reader in the name of the Lord!
> The general leadership of our church has taken its stand concerning the proper form of applications concerning real estate belonging to the Jews. The relevant resolution has been sent to His Excellency as well. The stand taken by the general leadership of the church applies in every case, being the only stand to suit our church's moral level.

Raffay expressed his opinion that, since in Kiskunhalas the mission was to lease from the authorities a villa that once belonged to Jews, no change thus coming about in the list of church immovable property,

> I express no opposition to the way the church in Kiskunhalas is acting, and I express my consent to the creation of the relationship between lessor and lessee, the authorities and the church.
> May the Lord's mercy rest upon us.[162]

In Raffay's letter one cannot but note the efficiency of the church: it successfully formulated regulations by which to take control of the property of those who, only a few months earlier, were the neighbors of the church flock. It had already distributed these regulations to whoever had need of them. This efficiency is noteworthy in light of the fact that only a short time before, the bishops of the Protestant churches required over a month to sign a memorandum they were sending to the government, supposedly to protect the Jews.

As in many other cases, here, too, the church was in the forefront of developments. Others, in various circles, who were interested in participating in the division of the spoils, viewed the church as an example. In most of the applications made to the authorities in this connection, stress was placed on the Christianity or the Christian loyalty of those applying. Here are a number of examples:

A man whose occupation was providing sound amplification and music on special occasions told of his struggle against the Jews who had controlled the area, a struggle that had gone on for years: "In this application of mine, I request no private profits for myself. All my desire is to work for the good of the public, and for this purpose I am interested in bolstering up my company—the only Christian company in this field of business." To attain his aims the man added the names of three Jewish firms that had engaged—until they were closed down—in supplying equipment to cinemas and theaters, and that owned equipment suited to his own needs and those of his business. The applicant also added that those firms were now shut down, and he requested that they be transferred to him with all their equipment and materiel.[163]

"The Commissioner for Leather Works calls upon the Christian shoe dealers in Budapest to inform him in writing within 48 hours of the quantity of shoes they wish to receive from the stock of shoes in those Jewish shops which have been closed down."[164]

A war casualty complained of the dishonesty shown by the heads of his village in distributing the shops the Jews had left behind when they were deported:

> May I note that the regulations make it clear that when distributing Jewish shops, preference is to be given to those whose own shops have been destroyed by bombing; immediately after come those of old, deeply rooted Christian families—especially if these Christians are war casualties....I am a veteran Christian and a war casualty, yet nevertheless I have received nothing.[165]

The Order of St. Domunkos fielded a football team that applied to the official in charge of the distribution of Jewish property:

> Considering the fact that each and every member of our organization is a Christian...we humbly request Your Excellency to deliver to us the equipment of the football team which used to represent the leather factory belonging to Adolf Vidonyi, and which no longer exists....Since we are aware of Your Excellency's generosity and positive attitude to Christian sport and sportsmen, we are sure that our modest request will be met.[166]

If in the small towns faithful Christians and churches took action to expand their activities by making use of abandoned Jewish property, the Catholic church had a problem of another kind in Budapest—from which the Jews had not been expelled. Jews, both as students and as employees, were present in Catholic educational institutions. Under the inspiration of the cardinal and in accordance with his directives, the church acted to solve this problem.

On August 5, 1944, shortly before the school year was scheduled to reopen—on September 1—the inspector-general of the Roman Catholic educational institutions sent out a circular to all the educational institutions under his supervision. "In accordance with the instructions of His Holiness the Cardinal, promulgated on June 28, and in order to facilitate the carrying-out of these instructions, I hereby inform the management of the aforesaid institutions, that a renewed examination must be made of the origins of all people employed by these institutions."[167]

The inspector-general explained how the examination was to be carried out, and stated who had to be examined. He based his instructions on a government directive that appeared in March 1944.[168] However, the document he was referring to, ME 1210/1944, deals with limiting the employment of Jewish lawyers and various professionals employed by the civil service. The document makes no mention of teachers, and so does not require their origins to be checked. But even if the Catholic inspector-general gave the aforesaid government document an extremely broad interpretation, applying to teachers the limitations affecting various professionals, it is still difficult to understand how he included in this examination the technical employees of Catholic educational institutions. The explanation is, apparently, that the inspector-general, relying on the cardinal's directive, as he himself notes, outdid the government itself.

In fact, his directive bore fruit. In the spirit of the demand made by the Catholic inspector-general, an announcement was made by the Catholic university, the Peter Pazmany University of Sciences, on August 11, 1944. The announcement revealed that the university went even further, and checked the origin of its students. The announcement listed the documents a candidate for acceptance had to present to the university institutions. At the top of the list were the documents intended to indicate the student's racial origin. These documents even preceded certification of the candidate's previous education.[169]

The Catholic university's announcement, like that of the Catholic inspector-general, was based on government directive ME 1210/1944, which, as already noted, is irrelevant to the subject. The university correctly assessed the mood of the cardinal and the inspector-general, and in accordance therewith published its instructions prohibiting the acceptance of Jewish students.

On August 23, the Catholic inspector-general sent a circular to the schools under his supervision, instructing them to refrain from accepting Jewish pupils into the first-grade classes of their institutions. As for the higher grades, the inspector wrote to the schools as follows: "Even those pupils who have already been studying at their institutions are not to register automatically. Likewise, they are not to expel them. They are to be registered in separate lists, and until a final arrangement is reached they are to be allowed to study in the institutions they have already been frequenting."[170]

The final arrangement was reached ten days later, when, on September 2, the Catholic inspector-general wrote to the educational institutions under his supervision: "With regard to the circular I sent out on August 23, I hereby inform you that a pupil required to wear a yellow Star of David is not permitted to study in our educational institutions."[171]

It may be assumed that among the 13 million Hungarians there were those with human feelings who took pity on their neighbors when they saw what was done to them, and there may even have been those willing to act to save the lives of their neighbors and their acquaintances had they been encouraged to do so by their spiritual leaders. But in most cases, these leaders conducted themselves otherwise.

In a certain town the gendarmes prepared a list of those suspected of communism and of espionage. In the list appeared the names of many Jews. The gendarmes handed the list over to the local magistrate in order to have it stamped with the town emblem and officially confirmed. The Jews on the list were to be sent to their final destination beyond the borders of Hungary. The magistrate, who was aware of the fate awaiting the Jews on the list, suffered pangs of conscience. He appealed to his priestly confessor for spiritual guidance. His confessor calmed him down: "You need suffer no pangs of conscience for sending these Jews to their fate. They have sinned so greatly that whatever befalls them is actually a light punishment for them."[172]

In light of this priest's attitude, and in light of the many statements made by both political and religious leaders, it is not surprising that one of the bishops, in his letter to the cardinal, described how he had encountered the phenomenon "of Christian believers raising the question in the confession booth: is it permitted to take pity on the Jews? Yesterday I was told by an old religious woman that she had given bread to people who were shut up in the ghetto."[173] The writer added that the woman told him her story in a whisper, fearful that she had committed a serious transgression.

In the midst of a description of the hard-heartedness of the priesthood at its various levels, it is refreshing to recall the great personality of the bishop who wrote this letter—Baron Vilmos Apor, bishop of Gyor. Contrary to most of his colleagues, he acted constantly, devotedly, and untiringly in the summer of 1944 to get the supreme church authorities to work to save Jews. He begged Cardinal Seredi time and again to use his influence to restrain the actions taken by the government, but encountered an absolute refusal. He was deeply tormented by the afflictions and sufferings of those persecuted, and his image shines forth to this day out of the black memories of 1944.[174]

Yet activities like those of Bishop Apor were not common. One of the characteristics of the period, as we have already seen, were the initiatives taken by various secular and religious bodies and by the public. The public approached the authorities with many proposals to render the system more efficient, in addition to making the thirty-five thousand denouncements mentioned at the outset of this chapter. The Germans proposed two deportation trains per day—Endre requested six. The deportees attempted to bring buckets of water into the carriages—the guards accompanying them poured the water out. There is no end to the evil that was revealed. The description of a single event will render the concept of Hungarian initiatives more tangible, and it is representative of them all.

The heads of the town of Soltvadkert, in the province of Pest, invented a system to torture the deportees to the maximum. In this town there had lived, up until the deportation, some hundred Jewish families. Toward the end of June, while the deportation was under way, only women, elderly people, and children remained in the town. Those men who had not met their deaths in the battlefields of the Ukraine between 1941 and 1944 were suffering in compulsory labor camps throughout Hungary. Those helpless people who remained in the town until the deportation reached them were to be sent by train to the provincial capital of Kecskemet—the point from which they would set out for their fateful trip to Auschwitz.

Before the deportees were taken aboard the carriages, the train station workers and townspeople padded the floors of the carriages with a fifteen- to twenty-centimeter layer of whitewash powder. When this powder penetrates one's breathing passages, it causes a terrible sense of suffocation, and when it attacks one's eyes, it causes a terrible burning sensation. This is also true of its contact with one's skin. As the deportees entered the carriages, their foot movements raised up a cloud of whitewash powder from the floors of the carriages, and the suffering they underwent from this powder was added to the tortures stemming from having seventy, eighty, or even ninety people locked up in a single airtight carriage in the burning summer of the Hungarian lowlands.

The enterprising local residents were, however, not satisfied with that. A locomotive was linked to the carriages with the deportees, and, for no purpose whatever, dragged the carriages back and forth with strong and sudden lurches. These lurches raised up additional clouds of whitewash powder and increased the sufferings of those locked up in the airtight carriages.

The unconcealed rejoicing of the townspeople at the game they were playing with their victims reinforced the mirth caused by realizing their wildest fantasies: the removal of their hated neighbors, the Jews. Only after they were satisfied by watching the torments of suffering human beings was the train allowed to proceed on its way.[175]

Conclusion

The last chords in the symphony of antisemitic hatred that had begun to be heard decades before were sounded in 1944. The events of this year demonstrate in retrospect that all the acts of antisemitic incitement, of anti-Jewish legislation, of making the lives of Jews unbearable, of excommunicating them and outlawing them were merely preparatory steps leading to 1944. The year 1944 also brought the Jewish question to the doorsteps of the Hungarian masses. While the anti-Jewish legislation of previous years was carried out in the legislature in the distant capital by members of the superior upper classes, in 1944 every minor official and every gendarme became master of the lives and fates of the Jews. Whereas earlier others took the initiative or carried it out, in 1944 the Hungarian people were given the opportunity to participate personally in the historic events. Thus the number of Hungarians involved personally and directly in the deportations came to many tens of thousands: the gendarmes, the various officials, the wagon drivers who transported the Jews to their concentration points, trainworkers, and many, many others. Everything was done openly, and since the Jews generally lived in various streets in each town, many millions, even if not personally involved in the expulsion of the Jews, were at least eyewitnesses to the terrible scenes enacted before them.

It has been said that "The Hungarians were the most brutal of European nations. Such a degree of bestiality, such a lack of humanity toward the Jews was not shown by any nation in Europe. In this field the Hungarians surpassed even the infamous Latvian people."[176]

Eichmann stated at his trial, "The Hungarians virtually urged us to relieve them of their Jews. . . . Hungary was the only European country to encourage us relentlessly. They were never satisfied with the rate of the deportations; no matter how much we speeded it up, they always found us too slow."[177]

In the words of an oral historian,

> Rumania and Bulgaria had been occupied four years earlier than Hungary and even so, although thousands of Jews had been killed, Rumanian Jews survived at a much higher rate than Hungarian Jews, while the Bulgarian government did not allow the Jews to be deported at all. In the case of the Hungarian Jews the antecedents here sketched resulted in one of the most puzzling tragedies.[178]

This attitude prevailed during the deportation period as well. The priests did nothing to save the Jews. Even if we assume that the priests were convinced that their secret correspondence with the government on behalf of the converts and the draft of the Shepherds' Epistle they had prepared to protect them were acts required of them in defense of those persecuted, we are still confronted by a contradiction: the incitement, the ridiculing of those persecuted, and the rejoicing at their being removed were all done openly, out loud, and even with a thanksgiving service in church. On the other hand, the so-called protesting voice of the priests was missing from all those places where it could have legitimately and almost freely expressed itself. As already noted, even the microphones were put out of order when a declaration was being made that might have been interpreted as giving some support to the Jews, even though this was done only after they had already been deported from the smaller towns and from the provinces.

In contrast to what happened to the Jews, the church came through the summer of 1944 unscathed. As Szenes puts it,

> The Roman Catholic church was strong, free and influential. Even in 1944, during the period of the German occupation of Hungary, the Catholic church had about 5,000 churches and a similar number of priests and pulpits in those churches, which at the time were the only places where the public could gather to hear what was said. In the 660 monasteries some twelve thousand monks and nuns lived and worked. The administration of the church and its institutions, its schools and its social circles operated freely. Church newspapers appeared both in Budapest and in the other towns. While the authorities were persecuting and oppressing all resistance ... the church was completely untouched.[179]

Thus, had the churches and their leaders wanted to act in a humane fashion, they could have done so with the means at their disposal. But the church leaders made use of their power to express their confidence in the acts of the government, and in most of their contacts with government representatives, they besmirched the Jews. This approach was consistent throughout the period considered in this paper, from the end of the previous century. Were the leaders of the priests in agreement with the leaders of the Catholic organization, Actio Catholica? This organization, which was an apolitical federation of all the Catholic organizations, enjoyed the support of the Synod of Bishops. The organization was headed by a leading bishop, and the bishops and other leading priests played key roles in the activities undertaken by it.[180] In an article written by one of the prominent leaders of the organization in 1939, he mentions various prohibitions concerning the Jews enforced by popes and church bodies over the centuries, concluding as follows: "These papal decrees and synod resolutions have never been abrogated. Consequently, all these decrees are valid to this day."[181] Even if there were priests who did not fully agree with the contents of this article and with the opinions of its writer, his spirit undoubtedly hovered over their activities.

Certain Reformed church circles met in the summer of 1946 and again in 1947, and considered the stand adopted by their church and its attitude toward the Jews in the Holocaust period. These circles adopted a resolution recognizing the responsibility of the church for the events of the Holocaust and demanding that the church request the forgiveness of the Jews. Yet this attitude did not reflect the official position of the church, and was even opposed to it. The unambiguous response of the church was handed down swiftly. After the stand taken by these circles was made public, the priests of the Reformed church were called to a general convention held in Budapest. The chairman of the convention, who was also the head of the Reformed church in Hungary, Bishop Ravasz, announced, "The Reformed church has no reason to ask forgiveness of the Jews for what befell them."[182] His statement was received with cheering rounds of applause.

There is thus no reason to be surprised at yet another event that demonstrates the spirit and atmosphere of the period:

> As the lines of Jews were driven in the drizzling rain through the streets of the capital toward the race tracks [where the Jews were concentrated] amid the abuse of their fellow citizens, a little girl of four, whose parents had previously been shot, strayed away from the column. An Arrow-Cross man grabbed the little thing and threw her back into the line with such vigor that she landed with her face on the muddy pavement, lacerating her skin. The onlooking crowd greeted this feat with laughter, roaring its approval.[183]

To sum up: together with the long campaign in which their rights were denied, the Jews were also denied their identity as human beings. Their delegitimation went hand in hand with their dehumanization. The church and the priests were present throughout the delegitimizing process, and the Hungarian legislators enjoyed their support.

Notes

1. The Preparatory Years

1. Jacob Katz, "The Unique Character of Hungarian Jewry," in *Hungarian Jewish Leadership in the Test of the Holocaust,* edited by Israel Gutman, Bela Vago, and Livia Rotkirchen, Jerusalem, 1976, 24. In Hebrew.
2. The spelling of "antisemitism" as a single word is preferable to "anti-semitism." This spelling eliminates the possibility of interpreting the word as indicating the existence of some "semitism" other than the Judaism to which antisemites show hostility. The expression "antisemitism" was coined in the late 1870s to replace "Jew hatred," which certain circles considered uncultured. See Yehuda Bauer, *The Holocaust in Historical Perspective,* Seattle, 1978, 8.
3. The Hungarian expression that was used to describe the legislation against the Jews is "Zsidotorveny." Its literal translation is "Jewish legislation." Since this literal translation lacks the connotation the original Hungarian expression has, I have preferred to use in this book the expression "anti-Jewish legislation," which is closer in significance to the Hungarian original.
4. "The size of the population of Hungary in the seventeenth century may be estimated at three million." *Magyarorszag Torteneti Demografiaja* (The Historical Demography of Hungary), edited by Jozsef Kovacsics, Budapest, 1963, 434.
5. C. A. Macartney, *October Fifteenth: A History of Modern Hungary, 1929–1945,* vol. 1, Edinburgh, 1956–1957, 18.
6. Nathaniel Katzburg, *Antisemitism in Hungary, 1867–1914,* Tel Aviv, 1967, 253. In Hebrew.
7. Ibid.
8. Ibid.
9. Ibid., 12.

10. Ibid., 14–15.
11. Ibid., 16–17.
12. From the introduction compiled by the Hungarian author Mor Jokai to the book by Bela Bernstein, *Az 1848–49i Magyar Szabadsagharc* (The Hungarian War of Liberation of 1848–1849), 1898; quoted in Peter Ujvari, *Magyar Zsido Lexicon* (Hungarian-Jewish Lexicon), 817.
13. Ibid., 987. For the number of Jews that served in the army see also Katzburg, *Antisemitism,* 32, n. 54.
14. Ibid., 33.
15. Ujvari, *Lexicon,* 817.
16. Katzburg, *Antisemitism,* 41.
17. Ibid., 54, 74, 84–86, 171–77.
18. In 1880, there existed throughout Hungary seventy-eight antisemitic organizations. Ibid., 95.
19. Ibid., 55.
20. For the blood libel see Jozsef Bary, *Vizsgalobiro Emlekiratai—A Tiszaeszlari Bunper* (Memoirs of the Investigating Judge—The Criminal Case of Tisza Eszlar), Budapest, 1933; Karoly Eotvos, *A Nagy Per,* n.p., n.d.; Sandor Hegedus, *A Tiszaeszlari Vervad* (The Tisza Eszlar Blood Libel; hereafter Hegedus, *Vervad*), Budapest, 1966; Lajos Marschalko, *Tiszaeszlar: A Magyar Fajvedelem Hoskora* (Tisza Eszlar: The Golden Age of Hungarian Race Defense), Debrecen, 1943.
21. Bary, *Vizsgalobiro,* 48.
22. Ibid., 16.
23. Hegedus, *Vervad,* 67.
24. Ibid., 68.
25. Ibid., 59.
26. Katzburg, *Antisemitism,* 112.
27. Hegedus, *Vervad,* 60.
28. Bary, *Vizsgalobiro,* 114. See also Gyula Verhovay, *Az Orszag Urai* (Lords of the Land), Budapest, 1890, 32–33.
29. Bary, *Vizsgalobiro,* 115.
30. Katzburg, *Antisemitism,* 53. See also Bary, *Vizsgalobiro,* 115–16.
31. Ibid., 116.
32. Ibid.
33. Ibid., 117.
34. Ibid. See also Katzburg, *Antisemitism,* 115.
35. Ibid., 117.
36. Bary, *Vizsgalobiro,* 570.
37. Ibid. It should be noted that the literal translation of the Hebrew word *shohet* (slaughterer) is *metszo,* but there exists another word, *sakter,* which is merely the Hungarian form of the Hebrew *shohet.* In the Hungarian vernacular use is made of the word *sakter* to ridicule that occupation and, by association, those who have need of it. Both Bary and the antisemitic

periodicals, including the clerical one, made consistent and sole use of the term *sakter* throughout the trial and in its wake.

38. Ibid., 576.
39. Ibid., 583.
40. Marschalko, *Fajvedelem*, 206.
41. Hegedus, *Vervad*, 193.
42. Katzburg, *Antisemitism*, 144.
43. Ibid., 141–51.
44. Hegedus, *Vervad*, 128. The archbishop consistently read the antisemitic periodical *Fuggetlenseg*. Marschalko, *Fajvedelem*, 228.
45. Bary, *Vizsgalobiro*, 434.
46. Katzburg, *Antisemitism*, 160.
47. Ibid.
48. Marschalko, *Fajvedelem*, 246.
49. Ibid., 224.
50. Ibid., 235–36.
51. Bary, *Vizsgalobiro*, 603.
52. Marschalko, *Fajvedelem*, 227.
53. Gyula Verhovay, *Alarcz Nelkul* (Without a Mask), 9–10, 54. Marschalko, *Fajvedelem*, 3–4.
55. See Nathaniel Katzburg, "The Struggle of Hungarian Jewry for Equal Religious Rights in the Nineties of the Nineteenth Century," in *Zion: A Quarterly for the Study of Jewish History* (hereafter Katzburg, *Struggle*), vol. 22, Jerusalem, 1957, 119–21. In Hebrew. For sources see ibid., n. 6. See also Jeno Gergely, *A Puspoki Kar Tanacskozasai: A Magyar Katolikus Puspokok Konferenciainak Jegyzokonyveibol* (Debates of Synod of Bishops: From the Protocols of the Conferences of Catholic Hungarian Bishops, 1919–1944; hereafter Gergely, *PPK*), 20–21.
56. Katzburg, *Antisemitism*, 164.
57. Katzburg, *Struggle*, 124, 133–34. The memoranda are in the Royal Archives in Vienna.
58. Ibid., 136, according to an item appearing in a Jewish newspaper in the German language on June 28, 1895: "The priests read out the pastoral letters in their churches, adding some suitable preaching of their own. This preaching was so impressive that it was not quickly forgotten by the believers, who continued to discuss the subject outside the churches as well." Lajos Venetianer, *A Magyar Zsidosag Tortenete* (The History of Hungarian Jewry; hereafter Venetianer, *Zsidosag*), Budapest, 1986, 443.
59. Katzburg, *Struggle*, 136–45. See ibid., n. 56: "In the Upper House the conservative elements were a strong, solid body including 42 Catholic bishops who were members of the Upper House by virtue of their positions; the Protestant sects had 13 representatives." See also Venetianer, *Zsidosag*, 424.
60. Ibid., 442.

61. Katzburg, *Struggle,* 140–41.

62. Venetianer, *Zsidosag,* 446–47.

63. Ibid., 447.

64. Ibid., 450–52. The list appears in the newspaper *Budapesti Hirlap,* June 21, 1908.

65. Katzburg, *Antisemitism,* 187–88, according to the stenographic records of the sessions of Parliament, on March 16, 1898.

66. Prohaszka (1858–1927) was a lecturer in theology at the beginning of the century. From 1905 until his death he was the bishop of Szekesfehervar. He was a talented, tireless, strongly expressive antisemitic activist who wrote and spoke freely. He was a prolific author and the most prominent speaker on any and all antisemitic topics. He inspired antisemites during the 1930s and 1940s.

67. Katzburg, *Antisemitism,* 191–92.

68. Zoltan Bosnyak, *Prohaszka es a Zsidokerdes* (Prohaszka and the Jewish Question; hereafter Bosnyak, *Prohaszka*), Budapest, 1939, 7–9.

69. Ibid., 24–25.

70. Katzburg, *Antisemitism,* 192.

71. The protocol relating to the session of the Synod of Bishops held at the outset of 1939, in light of the parliamentary debate on the second anti-Jewish bill, reads as follows: "The Cardinal emphasized that he considered it extremely important to remove the Jewish spirit from public and economic spheres, and elsewhere. The church was to be motivated in this struggle by those very same ideals that guided it in its bitter struggle against the spirit of liberalism ever since it spoke up against the adoption of the law granting the Jewish religion equal status" (Gergely, *PPK,* 257).

72. Macartney, *October Fifteenth,* vol. 1, 4.

73. "There was a single racial factor in the kingdom that adhered as strongly as possible to the Hapsburg ideal: the Jews. They well understood that any change would be detrimental to them. In a multiracial and supranational kingdom, where the ethnic entities were guaranteed many means of expression, the situation of the Jews was extremely comfortable." Jacob Talmon, "Document and Testimony—the Meaning of the New Antisemitism," in *The Holocaust of the Jews of Europe,* edited by Israel Gutman and Livia Rotkirchen, 125 (in Hebrew).

74. Macartney, *October Fifteenth,* vol. 1, 21.

75. Ibid., 22. T. Ivan Berend, *Valsagos Evtizedek, Kozep Es Kelet Europa a Ket Vilaghaboru Kozott* (Decades of Crisis: Central and Eastern Europe between the Two World Wars), Budapest, 1983, 127–30; N. Katzburg, *Hungary and the Jews: Policy and Legislation, 1920–1943* (hereafter Katzburg, *Hungary and the Jews*), Ramat Gan, 1981, 33–34; M. Nagy-Talavera, *The Green Shirts and the Others: A History of Fascism in Hungary and*

Rumania (hereafter Nagy-Talavera, *Green Shirts*), Stanford, 1970, 24–25; *Encyclopedia Judaica*, vol. 10, 1290–91.

76. For an elaboration on this idea see Katzburg, *Hungary and the Jews*, 35–38.

77. Nagy-Talavera, *Green Shirts*, 25.

78. Macartney, *October Fifteenth*, vol. 1, 23. Horthy (1868–1957) joined the navy at the age of fourteen and worked his way up rapidly. Between 1909 and 1914 he was Franz Josef's military adjutant. In World War I he excelled in a number of naval clashes in the Adriatic Sea, and in 1918 he was given the rank of admiral and made commander of the Austro-Hungarian navy. In 1919 he was appointed head of the counterrevolutionary forces, and on March 1, 1920, he was elected regent of Hungary and granted extremely wide powers. He served as regent until October 15, 1944. He died in Portugal in February 1957.

79. Ibid.

80. Katzburg, *Hungary and the Jews*, 41.

81. Nagy-Talavera, *Green Shirts*, 57.

82. Ibid., 57–58.

83. Ervin Pamlenyi, *A Hatarban a Halal Kaszal: Pronay Naploja* (Death Reaps at the Border: Pronay's Diary; hereafter Pamlenyi, *Pronay*), Budapest, 1963, vol. 2, 136–40; cited from Pronay's book, 92–96.

84. Katzburg, *Hungary and the Jews*, 40.

85. Ibid., 39–40.

86. Elek Karsai and Istvan Pinter, *Darutollasok Szegedtol A Kiralyi Varig* (The Crane Feather Owners from Szeged to the Royal Palace; hereafter Karsai, *Darutollasok*), Budapest, 1960, 213–16.

87. Katzburg, *Hungary and the Jews*, 45.

88. Extracts from the protocols of the sessions of the Synod of Bishops between 1919 and 1944 were collected together in Gergely, *PPK*.

89. Ibid., 74. The Christian Political Organization related to the elections that were supposed to take place on January 25, 1920.

90. Ibid., 320–24.

91. Ibid., 67. This amount supplied the needs of the Catholic church, including all its churches. See table in ibid., 359–60.

92. The leader of the Arrow-Cross party, too, compared the Jews to fleas.

93. Dr. Gyorgy Kis, *Megjelolve Krisztus Keresztjevel Es David Csillagaval* (Sealed in the Cross of Jesus and the Star of David; hereafter Kis, *Megjelolve*), Budapest, 1987, 248–49. The article is quoted in "The Complete Writings of Prohaszka," vol. 23, 354.

94. Macartney, *October Fifteenth*, vol. 1, 30.

95. Before their invasion of Hungary in the ninth century C.E., the Hungarian tribes lived in the region of Etelkoz, in the Don River delta. According to a Hungarian legend, the Hungarian tribes sealed a blood pact among them-

selves. The seven tribal leaders let a little of their blood into a basin, stirred the blood mixture, and each drank of the mixture. The patriotic organization was named after the site and the event.

96. Dezso Nemes, *Az Ellenforradalom Tortenete* (The History of the Counter-revolution; hereafter Nemes, *Ellenforradalom*), Budapest, 1962, 158.

97. Ibid., 156, 157, 159.

98. Pamlenyi, *Pronay*, 301.

99. Gergely, *PPK*, 102.

100. Macartney, *October Fifteenth*, vol. 1, 32.

101. Ibid., 30.

102. Katzburg, *Hungary and the Jews*, 41–43.

103. *Nemzeti Ujsag*, December 12, 1919, 2.

104. Yad Va-Shem Archives, File 12/015.

105. Katzburg, *Hungary and the Jews*, 45–46.

106. Pamlenyi, *Pronay*, 93–95.

107. Gergely, *PPK*, 84. At the session of the Synod of Bishops held on October 27, 1920, the archbishop announced that the appointment became possible after he "made a detailed report to the Apostolic Holy See." The archbishop also thanked the bishop of Eger for his generosity, which made the appointment possible, saying that "the Holy Father has expressed his appreciation of this demonstration of generosity." Ibid.

108. Yad Va-Shem Archives, File 12/015.

109. Pamlenyi, *Pronay*, 93, n. 242.

110. Gergely, *PPK*, 74. While the formal founding convention of the party was held only in December 1919, the Synod of Bishops hastily offered the party its support even before the party itself was formally in existence. Thus the bishops can be credited with an important role in the organization and formation of an antisemitic political party.

111. See p. 4.

112. Gergely, *PPK*, 40. See also ibid., 119–20. At the conference held by the leadership of the professional organization set up by the Socialist-Christian party, it was resolved that "in order to protect the moral and material interests of the organization, it will focus on the framework of that Socialist-Christian professional organization that was founded twenty years ago and has gained considerable experience ever since. In the future, too, the organization will use the term 'Socialist-Christian.' " The conference also declared that "only a government based on Christian foundations is able to save Hungary from total destruction. . . . The professional organization will support the incumbent government as its actions are guided by Socialist-Christian concepts." *Nemzeti Ujsag*, November 13, 1919, 2.

113. Gergely, *PPK*, 40–42. The intraparty changes occasionally took place as a result of the direct intervention and influence of church functionaries. See also Nemes, *Ellenforradalom*, 151–54.

114. *Nemzeti Ujsag,* December 30, 1919, 3. See also Nemes, *Ellenforradalom,* 154.

115. Ibid., 150.

116. Ibid.

117. *Nemzeti Ujsag,* December 30, 1919, 2.

118. Ibid., December 4, 1919, 3.

119. Yad Va-Shem Archives, file 12/015. The poster was undated, but its content indicates that it was quite probably distributed before the elections of January 1920, as part of a propaganda campaign.

120. As above, n. 119.

121. In comparison, in the debate on the first anti-Jewish bill on May 24, 1938, Bishop Ravasz compared the Jews to "parasites climbing on the host plant, entrenching their roots in it in order to be able to subsist at its expense." See Part 2, pp. 86ff.

122. Dr. Miklos Kmosko, *Zsido Kereszteny Kerdes* (A Jewish-Christian Problem), Budapest, 15–16. The pamphlet was published without a date. From its contents it seems to have been published before the 1920 elections.

123. *Nemzeti Ujsag,* December 30, 1919, 2.

124. *Lexicon Magyarorszag Tortenete* (The History of Hungary), vol. 2, Budapest, 1964, 368.

125. Nemes, *Ellenforradalom,* 165.

126. Yad Va-Shem Archives, File 12/015. The poster was undated. Its general contents indicate that it was published soon after the January 1920 elections.

127. Gergely, *PPK,* 76. The date of the protocol is August 22, 1919.

128. Ibid., 123–24, 157–58.

129. Ibid., 27, 132, 144.

130. *Nemzeti Ujsag,* December 12, 1919, 1.

131. Ibid., December 30, 1919, 1, 2.

132. See ibid., n. 68.

133. *Nemzeti Ujsag,* December 6, 1919, 1.

134. Ibid., December 11, 1919, 1.

135. Yad Va-Shem Archives, File 12/015.

136. Gergely, *PPK,* 27.

137. Istvan Haller, *Harc A Numerus Clausus Korul* (The Struggle around the Numerus Clausus; hereafter Haller, *Numerus Clausus*), Budapest, 1926, 41–43. For the Numerus Clausus, see also Katzburg, *Hungary and the Jews,* 60–79.

138. Haller, *Numerus Clausus,* 52, 54.

139. Ibid., 58.

140. Ibid., 67–68.

141. Ibid., 83.

142. For Father Zakany's attitude toward the Jews, see part 1, p. 31.

143. Haller, *Numerus Clausus*, 98–106.
144. Ibid., 106–18, 122–23.
145. Ibid., 134.
146. Katzburg, *Hungary and the Jews*, 63–64.
147. Ibid., 64–79. See also Haller, *Numerus Clausus*, 190–219.
148. See this part, p. 39ff.
149. Nagy-Talavera, *Green Shirts*, 58.
150. Katzburg, *Hungary and the Jews*, 80.
151. Ibid., 84.
152. Nagy-Talavera, *Green Shirts*, 71–72.
153. Katzburg, *Hungary and the Jews*, 85.
154. Nagy-Talavera, *Green Shirts*, 71.
155. See this chapter, p. 17ff.
156. Nemes, *Ellenforradalom*, 154–55. It should be noted that Budapest was a separate entity within Hungary. Nearly a fifth of Hungary's residents resided in greater Budapest. It was the center of heavy and light industry, of trade, of administration, of the press, of the arts, etc. The significance of the activities of the Budapest municipality was felt far beyond municipal limits, and served as an example for the activities of the various towns and provinces of the country.
157. See this part, p. 38ff.
158. Gergely, *PPK*, 102.
159. During Horthy's rule, Sandor Ernszt was active in general politics and in Christian party politics as well. He was the link between the archbishop and the Synod of Bishops, on the one hand, and between the Christian party and most of the Catholic-oriented social organizations, on the other. Most financial support given by the Synod of Bishops to these bodies passed through him. He was one of the leading activists in many Catholic organizations and was even a government member: in 1930 he served as minister of welfare and labor, and in 1931 he became minister of religion and education. At Wolf's party rallies, he generally appeared on the platform together with the chairman, Wolf. See ibid., 118, n. 2.
160. Ibid., 129. Protocol date is October 14, 1925.
161. Ibid., 124. Protocol date is March 17, 1926.
162. Ibid., 195–96. Protocol date is October 19, 1932.
163. Ibid., 210. Protocol date is October 11, 1933.
164. Ibid., 266. Protocol date is October 3, 1939. See also ibid., 13, 14.
165. Ibid., 310. Protocol date is October 16, 1943.
166. *Magyarsag*, April 25, 1938, 4. For comparison purposes note that Bishop Ravasz, head of the Reformed church in Hungary, in a speech he delivered in the summer of 1940, classified Hitler's struggle as a "religious struggle," which, in the end, "will lead in its wake to a deep recognition of God the Redeemer and the Liberator." *Fuggetlenseg*, August 13, 1940, 5.
167. *Magyarsag*, May 10, 1933, 4.

168. Ibid., June 25, 1933, 5.
169. Ibid., July 2, 1933, 4.
170. Ibid., November 4, 1933, 1–2.
171. Ibid., March 5, 1935, 4.
172. Ibid., December 13, 1935, 3.
173. Ibid., January 3, 1936, 3. Cardinal Seredi expressed himself in a similar vein during the debate on the second anti-Jewish bill. See also *Budapesti Hirlap*, April 16, 1939, 3.
174. *Magyarsag*, March 24, 1936, 4.
175. *Uj Magyarsag*, October 7, 1936, 10.
176. The cardinal of Hungary made his residence in the town of Esztergom, and he maintained an office in Budapest. Bishop Meszaros administered the cardinal's Budapest offices between 1919 and 1940.
177. *Magyarsag*, May 13, 1933, 5. For the sake of comparison, note Prime Minister Teleki's speech in Parliament: "Our capital is a beautiful city, but its intellectuals are not. The Jewish spirit that finds its expression at the expense of the Christian public is that which characterizes the intellectuals of our capital." *Pesti Hirlap*, December 4, 1940.
178. *Magyarsag*, November 16, 1933, 5.
179. Ibid., March 5, 1935, 5.
180. The leaflet is quoted in the Jewish weekly *Egyenloseg*, March 24, 1938, 9.
181. *Uj Magyarsag*, November 10, 1938, 5.
182. Ibid.
183. *Magyarsag*, November 19, 1933, 4. Despite the extreme care with which the Numerus Clausus law was applied, and despite the fact that only 5.5 percent of Jewish students were accepted for the first academic year, the percentage of Jews among all the students of the institutions of higher learning rose. This is because the percentage of Jews was lowered, and only the most talented of them were accepted into the university. These students persevered at their studies, with only a few dropping out before completing their degrees. In light of this fact, the Christian students demanded that during the registration for the first academic year the total number of all Jewish students currently registered at all levels of study and in universities throughout Hungary is to be taken into account. *Magyarsag*, January 17, 1934, 4.
184. Ibid., November 29, 1933, 5.
185. Ibid., November 30, 1933, 6; January 14, 1934, 11; January 17, 1934, 4; August 19, 1934, 35.
186. *Zsido Szemle*, October 23, 1936. Quoted from the local paper *Debreceni Fuggetlen Ujsag*.
187. *Magyarsag*, January 14, 1934, 11.
188. Gergely, *PPK*, 187, 210. The Catholic umbrella organization was founded at the recommendation of the pope.
189. *Magyarsag*, November 19, 1933, 4. See also Gergely, *PPK*, 153–54.
190. *Zsido Szemle*, December 1, 1934, 5.

191. *Pesti Hirlap,* May 15, 1934, 8.
192. *Uj Magyarsag,* October 6, 1936, 3.
193. *Korunk Szava* (The Voice of Our Generation), January 1, 1936, 426. The periodical defined itself in its sub-heading as an "active Catholic organ." For the nature of the periodical, its editors, and its links with the Catholic church, leadership, and institutions, see Gergely, *PPK,* 50–51.
194. *Fuggetlenseg,* February 16, 1937, 2.
195. Gergely, *PPK,* 110. The date of the protocol is April 9, 1924.
196. *Magyarsag,* January 17, 1936, 4.
197. *Fuggetlenseg,* February 16, 1937, 2.
198. Ibid.
199. Some 89 percent of the population of Hungary were members of the afore-mentioned two churches. See Gergely, *PPK,* 347.
200. *Pesti Ujsag,* June 8, 1937.
201. Gergely, *PPK,* 200–203, 332–34. The Synod of Bishops often discussed the Actio Catholica organization and its various activities. The topic appears in the collection of protocols more than twenty times.
202. Ibid., 156–57. The date of the protocol is October 25, 1929. The prepa-rations for the establishment of the organization took several years. The Synod of Bishops held discussions on the organization a long time before it actually began operations.
203. Ibid., 24, 186–87. The date of the protocol is October 14, 1931.
204. *Magyarsag,* March 6, 1934, 2.
205. *Actio Catholica Orszagos Elnoksege* (The National Board of Actio Cath-olica), Budapest, undated, 7, 15. There is considerable similarity between the proposal included in the official publication of the national board of an official Catholic organization, Actio Catholica, and the ninth article of the flier put out by the Awakening Hungarians on the subject of boycotting the Jewish press.
206. *Pesti Hirlap,* May 20, 1939, 6. For the sake of comparison see the statement made by the national chairman of Actio Catholica, Cardinal Seredi, above in this part, n. 71.
207. For purposes of comparison, note Hitler's statement: "Both as a human being and as a Christian I read lovingly, with no restrictions, the chapters describing how the Lord grasped the whip and drove out the usurers, the leeches and the fleas, from the Temple. Today, too, two thousand years after that event, I observe with the greatest excitement his great struggle against the Jewish poison. . . . He appreciated the nature of these Jews, and he began to struggle against them." *Virradat,* October 30, 1939, 3 (an extract from Hitler's speech in Munich on April 12, 1922). See also Adolf Hitler, *Mein Kampf* (My Struggle; hereafter Hitler, *Mein Kampf.* The En-glish translation was published by Stackpole, New York, 1939), 298.
208. For purposes of comparison see the debate on the second anti-Jewish bill in the Upper House, during which Bishop Glattfelder spoke admiringly of

former popes and church leaders who enacted numerous anti-Jewish laws. *Nemzeti Ujsag,* April 1, 1939, 2.

209. *Magyarsag,* January 25, 1939, 9.

210. *Nemzeti Ujsag,* July 23, 1939, 26.

211. *Magyarsag,* November 27, 1938, 5.

212. *Reggeli Magyarorszag,* February 13, 1943, 5.

213. Gergely, *PPK,* 276. The date of the protocol is October 16, 1940.

214. John Toland, *Adolf Hitler* (hereafter Toland, *Hitler*), New York, 1976, 319–20.

215. See this chapter, p. 30.

216. Eugene (Jeno) Levai, *Horogkereszt, Kaszaskereszt, Nyilaskereszt,* (The Hooked Cross, the Sickle Cross, the Arrow Cross; hereafter Levai, *Horogkereszt*), Budapest, 1945, 50–53. See also *Magyarsag,* December 2, 1934, 8.

217. *Zsido Szemle,* November 27, 1936, 7.

218. See part 2, 90ff.

219. *Egyenloseg,* May 5, 1938, 6.

220. Pinchas E. Lapide, *The Last Three Popes and the Jews* (hereafter Lapide, *Three Popes*), London, 1967, 123.

221. Levai, *Horogkereszt,* 52.

222. Gergely, *PPK,* 48.

223. Levai, *Horogkereszt,* 54.

224. Ibid.

225. Ibid., 40–53. See also Miklos Lacko, *Nyilasok, Nemzeti Szocialistak, 1935–1944* (The Cross Party Men, National Socialists, 1935–1944; hereafter Lacko, *Nyilasok*), Budapest, 1966, 20–41, 333. Also see Karsai Elek, *Szalasi Naploja* (The Szalasi Diary; hereafter Karsai, *Szalasi Naploja*), Budapest, 1978, 16.

226. Yad Va-Shem Archives, File 16/015. The platform is undated, yet it may be assumed that it was written toward the end of 1937 or at the onset of 1938. Selected excerpts from the platform are quoted in the newspapers of the Arrow-Cross party, *Hungarista Ut,* June 9, 1938, 1–2. The newspaper quotes an earlier publication in *Osszetartas,* April 17, 1938.

227. Marton Himler, *Igy Neztek Ki A Magyar Nemzet Sirasoi* (Thus the Gravediggers of the Hungarian Nation Looked; hereafter Himler, *Igy Neztek Ki*), New York, 1958, 34.

228. Rezso Szirmai, *Fasiszta Lelkek: Pszichoanalitikus Beszelgetesek A Haborus Fobunosokkel A Bortonben* (Fascist Souls: The Conversation of a Psychoanalyst with Prominent War Criminals in Prison; hereafter Szirmai, *Fasiszta*), Budapest, 1946, 249–57. A mimeographed book in File No. 015/22a in the Yad Va-Shem Archives.

229. Ferenc Abraham, *A Szalasi Per* (The Szalasi Trial; hereafter Abraham, *Szalasi Per*), Budapest, 1945, 23. For comparison, Pope Innocent III, 1198–1216, said that the Jews "are to us as dangerous as the insect in the apple, as the serpent in the breast.... They have already begun to gnaw like the

rat." James Morton Freeman, *Centuries of Intolerance: The Record of the Roman Catholic Church and Anti-Semitism* (hereafter Freeman, *Intolerance*), New York, 1947, 22.

230. *Magyarsag*, December 2, 1934, 8. See also ibid., July 8, 1934, 5.

231. A photograph of the poster appears in Andras Torok, *Szalasi Alarc Nelkul: a Szalasi Mozgalomban* (Szalasi without a Mask: Five Years in Szalasi's Movement; hereafter Torok, *Szalasi*), Budapest, 1941. The aforementioned convention was held in December 1936.

232. *Pesti Ujsag*, November 29, 1937, 2.

233. Between the world wars Endre occupied various positions in the civil service, and wherever he was, he made life difficult for the Jews. After the German invasion of Hungary in March 1944, Endre was appointed director of the interior ministry, and was directly responsible for organizing the deportation of the Jews. He carried out his task brutally, and after the war was executed as a war criminal.

234. *Nemzeti Figyelo*, February 27, 1938, 1.

235. Levai, *Horogkereszt*, 70.

236. For comparison, in 1932 a German pastor named Julius Kuptsch published a pamphlet called "Christianity in National Socialism," in which he wrote, "National Socialism is a profession of allegiance to the Sign of the Cross; the crooked cross is the token of the German after the flesh, as God desired him to be according to His Creative Order; the Cross of Christ is the token of the German after the spirit, whom Christ had redeemed. Consequently, the National Socialists carry the Swastika on their breasts and the Cross of Christ within their breasts." Richard Gutterridge, *Open Thy Mouth to the Dumb: The German Evangelical Church and the Jews, 1879–1950* (hereafter Gutterridge, *Open Thy Mouth*), Oxford, 1976, 63–64.

237. *Nemzeti Figyelo*, April 10, 1938, 1.

238. The item was quoted in the semiofficial organ of the Catholic church, *Nemzeti Ujsag*, July 22, 1938, 1.

239. Gergely, *PPK*, 15, 307.

240. *Roham*, April 14, 1938, 1.

241. Ibid., 7.

242. Kis, *Megjelolve*, 173–74. Quoted from the Catholic periodical *Vigilia*, 1975, vol. 3, 193–94. Nyisztor was a well-known personality in the Catholic hierarchy and a leading publicist between the two world wars. He was coeditor of the Catholic-scientific periodical *Magyar Kultura* (Hungarian Culture), which was published with the assistance of a fund set up by the Synod of Bishops. With him on the editorial board was also Bishop Gyula Czapik, who was later appointed bishop of Eger. Kis, *Megjelolve*, 224.

243. Gergely, *PPK*, 49.

244. Kis, *Megjelolve*, 173. Quoted in the Catholic periodical *Vigilia*, 1975, vol. 3, 184.

245. Macartney, *October Fifteenth*, vol. 2, 448.

246. *Kurir,* April 15, 1938, 1.
247. Lacko, *Nyilasok,* 126.
248. Ibid., 127.
249. Levai, *Horogkereszt,* 72. This accomplishment was especially notable since the election laws in that period in Hungary denied the right to vote to many of the supporters and potential voters for the party.
250. One of those who made this claim was Bishop Ravasz. He said that he had voted for the second anti-Jewish law, as shown in *Pesti Hirlap,* July 13, 1941, 3. Prime Minister Bardossy spoke out in a similar vein, as shown in Levai, *Horogkereszt,* 73–74, as did another prime minister, Imredi, as shown in Katzburg, *Hungary and the Jews,* 102.

2. Anti-Jewish Legislation

1. See pp. 191, 192, 196, 200–205, 215.
2. Katzburg, *Hungary and the Jews,* 96.
3. Ibid., 260.
4. *Fuggetlenseg,* February 16, 1937, 2.
5. Katzburg, *Hungary and the Jews,* 97. In March 1938 Imredi was appointed minister without portfolio to deal with economic matters in the Daranyi government. His main task was to carry out the idea expressed by the prime minister in his speech at Gyor. On May 14, 1938, Imredi was appointed prime minister and continued with the procedures instituted for the adoption and application of the anti-Jewish bill. The journalist Sandor Torok, a converted Jew who represented the converts before the authorities in the summer of 1944, was on close terms with Imredi. He said of him, "He was known as a Catholic with a deep religious sense, who had good connections with the cardinal and with the bishops." Sandor Szenes, *Befejezetlen Mult, Keresztenyek es Zsidok, Sorsok* (The Unfinished Past, Christians and Jews, Fates; hereafter Szenes, *Befejezetlen Mult*), Budapest, 1986, 191. Imredi played various key roles in the Hungarian administration in the coming years. In 1946 he was executed as a war criminal.
6. Ibid., 98.
7. Ibid., 258.
8. *Nemzeti Figyelo,* February 27, 1938, 1.
9. See part 1, 36, 38.
10. *Nemzeti Figyelo,* March 20, 1938, 9.
11. See part 1, 21ff.
12. Yad Va-Shem Archives, File 12/015.
13. During the period under consideration the Catholic church was represented in the Upper House by eleven bishops and fourteen priests in various positions. Gergely, *PPK,* 44. According to the numerical relationship among the churches, it may be assumed that the Protestant churches were repre-

sented in the Upper House by about half the number of representatives the Catholics had.

14. Dr. Henrik Fisch, *Kereszteny Egyhazfok Felsohazi Beszedei a Zsidoker-desben* (Speeches by Christian church leaders in the Upper House on the Jewish Question; hereafter Fisch, *Kereszte ny Egyhazfok*), Budapest, 1947, 21–24. Raffay delivered the speech on May 24, 1938.

15. The constitution of the Arrow-Cross party states, "The Jews are not a nation, but a race. They are not able to live within a nation; they are destructive." Yad Va-Shem Archives, File 16/015, 2. Regarding the bishop's claim that "Judaism is not a religion," cf. Hitler's statement: "The Jews have no religion. . . . As a result of their nature, the Jews are unable to maintain religious institutions for the simple reason that they lack all ideals in any form, and do not recognize life after death." Robert Waite, *The Psychopathic God: Hitler* (hereafter Waite, *Psychopathic*), New York, 1977, 98.

16. Cf. as above.

17. Fisch, *Kereszteny Egyhazfok*, 27–40. Ravasz delivered the speech on May 24, 1938. For purposes of comparison, in his interrogation after the war Imredi was asked if as a pious Catholic and devoted Christian, his conscience did not chastise him for the brutality used in the deportation of hundreds of thousands of human beings, including women, infants, old people, and the infirm. Imredi replied, "I bore the cross of responsibility with Christian devotion and I prayed for those suffering." Himler, *Igy Neztek Ki*, 59: "While we were speaking of our redeeming Cross, we did not bear it ourselves, but rather loaded the Cross onto the shoulders of the Jewish people and we crucified our Messiah by the thousands, to such a degree that even the murder of millions in the Holocaust left us indifferent." Claire Huchet-Bishop in the introduction to the book by Malcolm Hay, *Thy Brother's Blood* (hereafter Hay, *Thy Brother's Blood*), New York, 1960, xvi.

18. Gergely, *PPK*, 251.

19. *Az Est*, May 5, 1938, 7.

20. *Nemzeti Ujsag*, May 28, 1938, 2.

21. Ibid., 7.

22. Ibid., 6.

23. Ibid., May 31, 1938, 4.

24. Ibid., 5–6.

25. Ibid., May 26, 1938, 4. Of the attitude of prominent priests to the Jews and their problems one may learn from their statements throughout the anti-Jewish legislative process. Rank-and-file priests expressed their opinion of the Jewish question in a different manner. A procession of priests that marched along Andrassy Boulevard in Budapest as part of the Eucharistic Convention and reached No. 60, the main headquarters and national center of the Arrow-Cross party, unfurled its banners—church banners—in honor of the building and its occupants. Levai, *Horogkereszt*, 70.

26. See part 1, 75, for the impressive increase in the number of Arrow-Cross party members during the aforesaid period. The leaders of that party declared the year 1938 "Our Year."

27. *Pesti Hirlap,* August 26, 1938, 4.

28. During the debate on the second anti-Jewish bill, the minister of justice, Tasnadi-Nagy, said, "When tabling this bill we stressed that a convert is a Christian, but this does not mean that he is also a good Hungarian. Baptism does not turn a convert into a good Hungarian, just into a Christian." *Nemzeti Ujsag,* March 9, 1939, 8.

29. *Pesti Hirlap,* August 26, 1938, 4.

30. This is quoted in the article "The Jewish Problem before a Forum of Reformed Pastors," which appeared in the Jewish community weekly, *Egyenloseg,* November 1, 1938, 3.

31. *Pesti Hirlap,* August 26, 1938, 4. For purposes of comparison, "The people of the Bible appear in the general public eye as accursed idolators, who crucified Jesus.... Their problem can be solved by baptism." Mihaly Kolozsvary-Borcsa, *A Zsidokerdes Magyarorszagi Irodalma* (The Jewish Problem and Its Literature in Hungary; hereafter Kolozsvary-Borcsa, *Zsidokerdes Irodalma*), 22.

32. For the sake of comparison note the statement made by the minister of justice in the debate on the second anti-Jewish bill: "I do not see where in this proposal there is inhumanity and brutality.... Our heart does not contain even a single spark of hatred." *Budapesti Hirlap,* March 8, 1939, 5.

33. *Pesti Hirlap,* November 8, 1938.

34. Ibid., January 22, 1939, 4.

35. Ibid., January 8, 1939, 8. In a book Bangha had published in 1920 he wrote, "We must clean the villages of the Jews. It would be most desirable if the villagers would not see Jews at all." Bela Bangha, *Magyarorszag Ujjaepitese es A Keresztenyseg* (The Reconstruction of Hungary and Christianity); quoted by Kis, *Megjelolve,* 245. Bishop Bangha enjoyed a prominent position in the Catholic church hierarchy, and every so often he was entrusted with central roles by the Synod of Catholic Bishops. See Gergely, *PPK,* 175, 214–21.

36. *Pesti Hirlap,* January 14, 1939, 2.

37. See part 1, 17.

38. Gergely, *PPK,* 256–59. Protocol date is January 31, 1939. According to the Catholic priest Gyorgy Kis, who spoke some forty years after the war, "From the end of the thirties the unrestrained propaganda strove to have the Jews hated. I am sorry to say that even the Catholic press took part in this. The church newspapers and periodicals, intended for the believing population and for church functionaries, adopted Hitler's well-known slogans of the plutocratic, capitalistic, bolshevistic Jewish poison. The hate-filled articles were often written by church functionaries. One of the writers

of articles in the Catholic publication, *Magyar Kultura*, which was, incidentally, the periodical read by the high-level Catholic intelligentsia, boasted during the parliamentary debate on the second anti-Jewish bill that many legislators had adopted, word for word, articles which had appeared earlier in his periodical, together with their reasoning and conclusions, and even the minister of justice referred to them many times." Szenes, *Befejezetlen Mult*, 274–75.

39. *Egyenloseg*, November 17, 1938, 1.
40. This was the "Vienna Resolution" of November 2, 1938, adopted by the foreign ministers of Germany and Italy. Randolph L. Braham, *The Politics of Genocide: The Holocaust in Hungary* (hereafter Braham, *Politics of Genocide*), New York, 1981, vol. 1, 144; C. A. Macartney, *October Fifteenth*, vol. 1, 329–43.
41. At his trial in 1945, Imredi claimed that the Munich agreement, signed by the powers in September 1938, convinced him that Hungary had a chance to liberate itself from the chains of the Trianon Agreement if it adopted pro-German policies in the fields of its foreign and domestic policy. This approach compelled him, he said, to render the situation of the Jews more serious and to enact yet another law against them. Katzburg, *Hungary and the Jews*, 115, 116.
42. *Magyarsag*, November 19, 1938, 3.
43. Nagy Talavera, *Green Shirts*, 147. There is also a somewhat different version. It was the Arrow-Cross party representatives who cried out happily, "It is the most beautiful Christmas present they could have hoped for." Eugene Levai, *Black Book on the Martyrdom of Hungarian Jewry* (hereafter Levai, *Black Book*), Zurich-Vienna, 1940, 14.
44. Braham, *Politics of Genocide*, vol. 1, 154.
45. Katzburg, *Hungary and the Jews*, 119. See also Imredi's statement made in the discussions of the united committee, *Magyarsag*, February 4, 1939, 6.
46. *Pesti Hirlap*, January 24, 1939, 3.
47. Ibid., 4.
48. Ibid.
49. Ibid.
50. Ibid., February 7, 1939, 4.
51. Ibid., February 15, 1939, 2.
52. Macartney, *October Fifteenth*, vol. 1, 327. Despite the embarrassing revelation of his origins, Imredi remained active in Hungarian political life. After the invasion of Hungary by the Germans in 1944, Imredi was even a member of the Sztojay government. He attempted to neutralize his Jewish origins by claiming that his father's mother—who was married to a Jew— had an affair with an Aryan Christian, his father was born as a consequence of it, and so he had no Jewish blood flowing in his veins. After the war, while conversing with his interrogator, an American army intelligence officer, Imredi claimed that he was "a Hungarian nobleman." The inter-

rogator commented on that: "And as a nobleman, you are not ashamed to be carrying around a collection of documents weighing a kilogram and a half in order to prove that your grandmother was bedded by men other than her husband, and that your father was actually his mother's bastard?" Imredi commented on that: "We must accept the facts as facts, even if they are debasing." Himler, *Igy Neztek Ki,* 56–7.

53. Katzburg, *Hungary and the Jews,* 133.

54. Ibid., 133–34.

55. Macartney, *October Fifteenth,* vol. 1, 222–23.

56. *Nemzeti Ujsag,* April 1, 1939, 4.

57. Ibid., 4–5.

58. *Budapesti Hirlap,* March 1, 1939, 3.

59. This party was one of the later incarnations of the Christian party that was founded by Karoly Wolf.

60. *Budapesti Hirlap,* March 1, 1939, 3, 4.

61. Ibid., 4.

62. Katzburg, *Hungary and the Jews,* 131.

63. For purposes of comparison see Bishop Ravasz's speech: "The adoption of this bill will serve well not only the welfare, tranquillity, and security of the state, but will be useful also to those who today protest its adoption so vehemently." Part 2, p. 86.

64. For purposes of comparison see Bishop Raffay's speech: "For the sake of the truth it must be stated that this legislation is not as cruel as it seems to be at first glance," Part 2, p. 96.

65. *Budapesti Hirlap,* March 8, 1939, 5, 6.

66. *Nemzeti Ujsag,* April 1, 1939, 1.

67. Ibid. Seredi's comments in the Upper House reflected the resolutions of the Synod of Bishops on January 13, 1939. Just before the debate in the Upper House there appeared an article in the official periodical of the Catholic church, *Magyar Kultura,* on February 5, 1939. The article was written by one of the editors, Zoltan Nyisztor. Nyisztor writes, "In the field of theater a commercial Jewish spirit has reinforced its positions, and does not allow anyone else to enter into its portals. . . . In the theater they perceived a field open to free and profitable hunting, whereby they succeed in obtaining both money and women. . . . It is from their press that the poison has gone out, despoiling the noble Hungarian middle class and damaging not only their tradition, but even their morality. With their deviousness they have introduced nudity into the life of the Hungarian people, and the concept of beauty queens into the imagination of the Hungarians, and the distorted corruption of virtue into Hungarian blood." Kis, *Megjelolve,* 224–25.

68. For the sake of comparison see a speech he delivered in Stuttgart on February 15, 1933, in which Hitler said that it was the desire of the National-Socialist government "to refill all our culture with a Christian spirit—and not only with politics. We want to burn out with fire the corrupting features

of our theater and press." Norman Baynes, *Hitler: Speeches, 1922–1934* (hereafter Baynes, *Hitler: Speeches*), London, 1942, 370. Karoly Huszar, who was premier of Hungary during the White Terror period and national deputy-chairman of Actio Catholica, said at a mass rally of his organization, "We have to base our entire society upon elements of Christian belief. It is not sufficient to remove the Jews from economic positions; we must introduce into each and every area of life Christian spirit and morality." *Pesti Hirlap*, May 20, 1939, 5.

69. *Nemzeti Ujsag*, April 1, 1939, 1, 2.

70. Ibid., 2.

71. Ibid.

72. For comparison purposes see a speech made by Luther, a diplomat in the German foreign service who spoke in October 1942 with the Hungarian ambassador to Germany, Sztojay. His first demand was "progressive legislation aimed at eliminating all Jews from cultural and industrial life." *The Holocaust: Selected Documents in Eighteen Volumes* (hereafter Mendelsohn, *Selected Documents*), edited by John Mendelsohn, New York-London, 1982, vol. 8, 191. Laszlo Endre, state secretary in the Hungarian interior ministry in 1944, who was responsible for the expulsion of Hungarian Jewry, spoke at the opening of "the Hungarian Institute of Jewish Studies" after the deportation of the Jews from the towns and the villages, and told "of achievements in the self-defensive struggle against Jewry and of the purification of public life from the harmful influence of the Jews in social, spiritual, and economic fields." *Harc*, August 26, 1944, 6.

73. *Nemzeti Ujsag*, April 1, 1939, 2, 3. It seems that the approach taken by the speaker was acceptable to the Hungarian regime. One of Horthy's officers tells in his memoirs that Horthy told him in the summer of 1944, "They [the Germans] want to deport the Jews. I don't mind. I hate the Jews and the Communists. Out with them, out of the country! But you must see, Baky, that there are some good Hungarian Jews too, like little Chorin and Vida [wealthy industrialists, Jewish converts. Chorin was chairman of the National Union of Factory Owners in Hungary between 1933 and 1941]. Aren't they good Hungarians? I can't let them go, can I? But take the rest, the sooner the better!" Macartney, *October Fifteenth*, vol. 2, 283, n. 1.

74. *Nemzeti Ujsag*, April 1, 1939, 3–4.

75. Ibid., 4.

76. Ibid., 3, 5.

77. *Budapesti Hirlap*, April 14, 1939, 4.

78. Seredi's position must be examined in light of the declaration he made a few years before, with regard to "legislation violating rights." At a rally of the Actio Catholica he declared, "I have no doubt that those close to the decision making will never legislate a law which does not harmonize fully with the laws of God and the church. They also will not accept the

existence of such a law, and will not act according to its provisions."
Magyarsag, March 6, 1934, 2.
79. *Budapesti Hirlap*, April 16, 1939, 3.
80. *Budapesti Hirlap*, April 16, 1939, 4.
81. Ibid., 3, 4.
82. As a student of theology at the University of Kolozsvar in 1916–1917, Ravasz became known for his antisemitic publications. Endre Ady, a Hungarian national poet, wrote then of him that "in the Calvinist periodical there appear very wild, antisemitic articles written by someone by the name of Laszlo Ravasz." Szenes, *Befejezetlen Mult*, 45.
83. Bishop Ravasz thus viewed the Jewish question as a universal problem with regard to its location. His colleague, Bishop Raffay, viewed it as universal with regard to its time. "Ever since the Jews existed, a Jewish problem has existed as well, and antisemitism is as ancient as the Jews themselves." *Pesti Hirlap*, November 28, 1940, 4.
84. *Pesti Hirlap*, April 18, 1939, 5.
85. *Budapesti Hirlap*, April 18, 1939, 5.
86. Ibid., April 19, 1939.
87. Ibid.
88. *Pesti Hirlap*, April 20, 1939. In July of that year Kolozsvari-Borcsa received from Hitler a very prestigious medal of excellence, the Cross of the German Order of the Eagle, of the highest rank. The certificate that was added to the notification of the award of the medal of excellence was signed by Hitler. It said that he had won this award by virtue of his "many accomplishments in the field of Christian-Hungarian press." *Fuggetlenseg*, July 22, 1939, 5. After the German invasion of Hungary in March 1944, Kolozsvary-Borcsa was appointed commissioner of journalism, literature, and information. In this job he was responsible for the burning of books by Jewish authors as well as books on Judaism from the public libraries. This was accomplished either by their public burning or by sending them to paper factories to serve as raw material for recycling. *Magyarorszag*, June 16, 1944, 5. After the war he was executed as a war criminal. See n. 31.
89. *Pesti Hirlap*, April 22, 1939, 2.
90. Ibid., April 27, 1939, 5.
91. Ibid.
92. *Budapesti Hirlap*, April 27, 1939, 2.
93. Ibid.
94. Ibid., April 28, 1939.
95. Katzburg, *Hungary and the Jews*, 138.
96. *Budapesti Hirlap*, April 28, 1939.
97. Katzburg, *Hungary and the Jews*, 141–42. The minister of trade and transportation, Jozsef Varga, reported to the parliamentary financial committee about a year and a half after the adoption of the second anti-Jewish law: "The integration of Hungarian Christian elements in mercantile life has

taken giant steps forward during the past year. In the immediate future the reorganization of the marketing of sugar, petroleum, wood for heating, and potatoes will be complete, thereby handing over to Christian tradesmen such commodities as will influence the marketing of other products as well. ...The most important branches of our external trade are already all in Christian hands." *Pesti Hirlap,* October 30, 1940, 7.

98. *Budapesti Hirlap,* April 25, 1939.

99. In the hierarchy of the Roman Catholic church in Hungary, only the status of the cardinal archbishop was superior to that of the bishop of Kalocsa. The bishop of Kalocsa headed one of the three provinces of the Catholic church in Hungary. The state authorities themselves recognized the important status of the bishop of Kalocsa. Gergely, *PPK,* 15, n. 12.

100. *Egyedul Vagyunk,* 1939, vol. 1, 13–19. "Incitement in articles appearing in the Catholic press during this period could not have appeared without the consent of the bishops, or at least without their silent acquiescence." Kis, *Megjelolve,* 16.

101. *Uj Magyarsag,* December 21, 1938.

102. Cf. Seredi's speech in the Upper House on April 16, 1939.

103. Cf. Ravasz's opinion of the Jews being a race rather than a religion.

104. Cf. the opinion expressed by Bela Pap in *Pesti Hirlap,* August 26, 1938.

105. Cf. Raffay's speech in *Pesti Hirlap,* November 28, 1940.

106. *Magyarsag,* January 20, 1939, 1.

107. *Pesti Hirlap,* December 22, 1938.

108. Gergely, *PPK,* 257. The session was held on January 13, 1939. For the sake of comparison, note that in the summer of 1944 many Jews wanted to convert. A priest named Gyorgy Balint expressed his opinion on the subject in a newspaper interview. "Question: Do you believe in the honesty of the intentions of the many Jews now applying for baptism? Answer: Every conversion from one religion to another must stem from the depths of the soul. There exists a vast chasm between Judaism and Christianity. ...And so, the church authorities have always promulgated strict rules regarding the conversion of Jews. Yet these rules were useful only on occasion, for over thousands of years Judaism became so materialistic that if it desires to accept the pure morality, the restraining spirituality, and the tolerant and pleasant way of life of Christianity, it will have to give up its features which are dictated to it by its very blood. The Jew is interested only in this life, whereas Christianity puts its emphasis on life after death. ...The Jews are in need of special heavenly mercy to be able to comprehend Christian morality, and to live accordingly." *Harc,* August 12, 1944, 5.

109. *Pesti Hirlap,* October 6, 1939, 4.

110. Ibid., March 25, 1939.

111. *Fuggetlenseg,* May 16, 1939, 5.

112. *Pesti Hirlap,* May 17, 1939, 8.

113. *Fuggetlenseg,* May 20, 1939, 1.

114. Hungary joined the three-way alliance, Germany-Italy-Japan, about two weeks after the Teleki speech. It may be assumed that he hinted at this imminent development.
115. The agrarian reform meant mainly the expropriation of Jewish estates. The Expropriation of Jewish Estates Law was adopted in September 1942.
116. *Pesti Hirlap,* November 16, 1940, 3.
117. From a pastoral letter in *Pesti Ujsag,* August 24, 1940, 5. For the fighting church see also the Pacelli speech in *Nemzeti Ujsag,* May 31, 1938, 4.
118. Katzburg, *Hungary and the Jews,* 158–59.
119. *Virradat,* July 3, 1939, 2.
120. Ibid.
121. The Synod of Bishops decided to hold a summer university at its session on March 22, 1933. Except for 1938, the year of the International Eucharistic Convention, ever since its founding the university was held every year up until 1939. Gergely, *PPK,* 204, 268.
122. *Nemzeti Ujsag,* July 13, 1939, 23.
123. For the sake of comparison, Cardinal Faulhaber of Munich, in speaking of the Old Testament, said, "This wealth of thought is so unique among the civilized nations of antiquity that we are bound to say: 'People of Israel, this did not grow in your garden of your own planting.' " Cardinal Faulhaber, *Judaism, Christianity, and Germany* (hereafter Faulhaber, *Judaism*), London, 1934, 68.
124. *Nemzeti Ujsag,* July 23, 1939, 24.
125. *Magyarsag,* January 25, 1939, 1.
126. Katzburg, *Hungary and the Jews,* 161. The memorandum was handed to the regent in June 1940.
127. Ibid., 162. Imredi delivered his speech on July 3, 1940.
128. *Pesti Hirlap,* November 10, 1940, 3.
129. Ibid., 4.
130. Ibid., 3, 4.
131. Ibid., November 16, 1940, 3.
132. Ibid.
133. Ibid., November 23, 1940, 3.
134. Ibid.
135. See *Pesti Hirlap,* December 4, 1940, 4; ibid., December 12, 1940, 4; ibid., December 17, 1940, 3; ibid., January 14, 1941, 3–4. See also Katzburg, *Hungary and the Jews,* 158 ff.; Levai, *Black Book,* 24; Nagy-Talavera, *Green Shirts,* 152 ff.
136. *Reggeli Magyarorszag,* October 5, 1939.
137. *Fuggetlenseg,* August 13, 1940, 5.
138. *Pesti Hirlap,* March 30, 1941, 4.
139. Ibid., November 18, 1941, 4. For the sake of comparison, note Laszlo Endre's lecture on Hungarian radio: "This struggle did not begin with this war. It has been going on since Judaism appeared on the stage of history,

and ever since, we and the Jews have been living in two different worlds."
Uj Nemzedek, June 26, 1944, 5. A central figure in the Roman Catholic
church, the director of the College of St. Imre Baboda, expressed himself
in a similar vein. In an article he had published in the book *A New Guide
to Catholic Writers*, which appeared in 1941, he wrote, "The redeeming
blood of Jesus serves as ransom for all and atones for all. The exceptions
to this rule are those who do not long for the blood of Jesus as redeeming
blood, but rather accept the responsibility and the curse for his crucifixion.
... Every one of the Jews is to be punished and to suffer for those injuries
Jewry caused the Christian nations." Kis, *Megjelolve*, 219–20.

140. *A Nep*, December 19, 1940, 5.
141. Gergely, *PPK*, 276–77. The protocol is dated October 16, 1940.
142. Ibid., 279. The protocol is dated March 12, 1941.
143. Hungary signed a pact of eternal friendship with Yugoslavia on February 26, 1941. When Yugoslavia refused to join the alliance of Axis powers,
Hitler informed Hungary that he recognized the justification for the territorial claims Hungary had to the northern provinces of Yugoslavia—in
return for the participation of Hungary in the assault of Yugoslavia. Teleki
was opposed. Bardossy, who was foreign minister at the time, and the
leaders of the army responded to Hitler's call, and the Crown Council, in
its session of April 2, 1941, agreed unanimously to take part in the attack
on Yugoslavia. Teleki committed suicide the following day, and Bardossi
took his place as prime minister.
144. Katzburg, *Hungary and the Jews*, 172.
145. *Pesti Hirlap*, June 10, 1941, 5.
146. Braham, *Politics of Genocide*, vol. 1, 194.
147. See Hegedus, *Vervad*, 60–67.
148. Katzburg, *Hungary and the Jews*, 175. For the law, the way it was adopted,
and its effects, see ibid., 158–83.
149. *Pesti Hirlap*, July 13, 1941, 3.
150. Ibid.
151. Ibid.
152. Ibid.
153. Ibid., July 15, 1941, 3, 4.
154. Ibid., July 19, 1941, 3, 4.
155. Ibid., 4, 5. For purposes of comparison, "The prime aim of the Jewish
religion is the protection of the purity of the race." Hitler, *Mein Kampf*,
298.
156. *Pesti Hirlap*, July 19, 1941, 5.
157. Ibid., 5, 6.
158. Quoted in Katzburg, *Hungary and the Jews*, 181.
159. The deputy-governor of the province of Pest, Laszlo Endre, sent a memorandum on November 5, 1940, to Prime Minister Teleki, in which he
complained that Jews drafted into the work units were making advances

to innocent Hungarian girls who were living under difficult economic conditions, and were persuading them to "take part in immoral activities. There were also features that confirmed the assumption that they did these acts not only because of their natural carnal characteristics, but also because they have deliberately evil thoughts of avenging in this way their forced participation in the labor units." Endre went on to propose the enacting of a law or a regulation to facilitate the castration of recidivist wrongdoers. The prime minister's office sent the memorandum to the ministry of justice with the added comment that the proposal should be included in the third anti-Jewish bill. Karsai Elek, *Fegyvertelenul Alltak Az Aknamezokon* (They Stood Disarmed in the Mine Fields; hereafter Karsai, *Fegyvertelenul*), Budapest, 1962, vol. 2, 237–39.

160. Katzburg, *Hungary and the Jews*, 181–82.

161. Hungary broke off diplomatic relations with Soviet Russia on June 23, 1941, on the day the third anti-Jewish law was adopted. Four days later, on the 27th of the month, Bardossy announced in Parliament the existence of a state of war between the two countries.

162. Braham, *Politics of Genocide*, vol. 1, 195.

163. For the legislation see Katzburg, *Hungary and the Jews*, 201–11.

164. Nagy-Talavera, *Green Shirts*, 182; Oszkar Zsadanyi, *Te Vagy A Tanu* (You Are the Witness; hereafter Zsadanyi, *Te Vagy A Tanu*), 66 ff. Regarding the way they were drafted, Prime Minister Kallay said, "Every Jew of draft age must be drafted into the labor units, regardless of how suited he is to service in this framework." Ibid., 83.

165. *Nemzeti Ujsag*, July 15, 1942, 5.

166. Ibid.

167. Ibid.

168. Gergely, *PPK*, 277.

169. Katzburg, *Antisemitism*, 112.

170. *Nemzeti Ujsag*, December 19, 1941, 5.

171. Katzburg, *Hungary and the Jews*, 187. For this legislation see ibid., 184–90.

172. *Nemzeti Ujsag*, December 19, 1941, 5.

173. Katzburg, *Hungary and the Jews*, 188.

174. *Pesti Hirlap*, April 27, 1939, 5. For another statement by Glattfelder see *Nemzeti Ujsag*, April 1, 1939, 1. The then justice minister, Tasnadi-Nagy, expressed himself similarly in the debate on that bill, quoting at length from a declaration prepared by a parliamentary faction in 1894, demanding the removal of the Jews from all walks of life. "The political aim of the Jews is the undermining of the foundations of Christian society and the economic and moral destruction of Christian nations. The pinnacle of their hopes is the collapse of Christian royal dynasties and houses." The minister added, "We have before us a stunning prophecy which foresaw the Jews joining the destructive and revolutionary extremist movements, and the

prophecy of the destruction of the royal houses is taking place right now before us." *Nemzeti Ujsag,* March 8, 1939, 7. See also Hitler's statement: "The aim of Bolshevism is the destruction of the leadership heading the nation by virtue of its blood ties, and replacing the present leadership with Jewish elements." *Uj Magyarsag,* November 10, 1936, 3.

175. Kallay was a personal friend of the regent, Horthy. At the onset of his public career he was active in local government and, among other things, filled the post of governor in his home province of Szabolcs. He specialized in agriculture and economics, and served as minister of agriculture in the Gombos government from October 1, 1932, to January 9, 1935. In 1937 Horthy appointed him commissioner of irrigation and flooding, and granted him membership in the Upper House. Braham, *Politics of Genocide,* vol. 1, 222.

176. *Nemzeti Ujsag,* March 14, 1942, 1, 2.

177. Ibid., 2–3. In 1954 Kallay published an autobiography in English. From reading the book one gets the impression that Kallay tried to fool the Germans and to make life easier for the Jews. He quotes parts of his speech, adduced herein, and explains to his readers that in referring to the war against communism he actually meant his strong opposition to Nazism. "I really meant by it that because we were Christians we could not be National Socialists, and still less Communists, since both of those ideologies were opposed to religion. . . . Neither could we accept racial discrimination. The reference to Christianity implied all that." Nicholas Kallay, *Hungarian Premier* (hereafter Kallay, *Hungarian Premier*), London, 1954, 73. Kallay's claim presupposes the ignorance or lack of intelligence of his readers. Even if his secret thoughts are perhaps open to speculation, there is no doubt about the energy he expended to further the adoption of the legislative initiatives he presented to Parliament. The facts were clear at the time both to the general Hungarian public and to the Jews. It is true that in 1943 there were doubts as to the political wisdom of Hungary's blind adherence to the Axis powers. But this awakening came about after a series of events that clarified the developing course of the war—most prominent among them, the destruction of the Hungarian Second Army on January 12–14, 1943, on the Ukrainian plains. Kallay was forced to seek a way out of the war he had supported at the time of his appointment as prime minister, when Hitler and his forces were at the pinnacle of their achievements. When Kallay began to seek routes of communication with the Allies in the west, it was convenient for him that Jews were in Hungary. They could serve as an alibi for him, as he himself describes matters in his book. However, there is no reason to doubt the honesty of his intentions and opinions as stated throughout 1942 (see below, n. 222). As for Kallay's interpretation of his earlier speech, one has need of an overly developed imagination to assume that his audience in March 1942 figured that "the eastern barbarism," which Kallay attacked vehemently and against which Hungary

went to war, was nothing but "Nazi heresy." In his numerous speeches Kallay repeats again and again the principle of Hungary's loyalty to her allies and the importance of the struggle being waged against the common foe. In his speeches there were unambiguous undertakings to persevere in the war effort against Communist Russia for the sake of a European victory over the common enemy in the east. In his aforesaid self-interpretation Kallay goes on to boast, "I do not wish to appear immodest, but I wonder where else among the suffering nations a premier answered a German ultimatum by such a declaration, made under the most public circumstances, at that moment when the German troops were on the Caucusus." As already noted, Kallay explained his pro-German utterances by claiming that he was forced to act in that way so as not to stir up German doubts as to the nature of his true outlook. This approach was common after the war. In his book *A Year without End*, Moshe Zandberg describes his vulgar treatment of the history teacher, who had tormented him after the German invasion of Hungary. About a year after the end of the war, the teacher came to him to apologize, claiming "that he was aware that he had insulted me badly two years ago, but I must believe him that he had no alternative, for the fascists were following him around, thinking he was against them, and so he was forced to behave in such a way in order to deceive them." Moshe Zandberg, *A Year without End*, 10 (in Hebrew). It should be noted that Kallay was not the only Hungarian leader whose opinions were changed by the vicissitudes of war. On June 22 Bishop Ravasz spoke in the Calvin Square church in Budapest, and his talk was even broadcast on the state radio. In his speech he said, "This morning, when the radio announced the outbreak of war between Germany and Russia, many Hungarians breathed a sigh of relief: the problem, which was open and demanded a solution, was finally going to be solved. The Russian threat enveloped Europe like a nightmare. We are finally going to be rid of it!" When the Hungarian Second Army was poised to leave for the Russian front in May 1942, Ravasz addressed the soldiers "fighting for the justice of God's land, for the Kingdom of Jesus, and thus for survival on earth" in an open letter. Yet in November 1943 Ravasz wrote, "The decisive factor which has always guided Hungarian public opinion is a true desire for peace, for the survival and the welfare of Europe.... The moment occasionally comes, when one has to jump from the flaming aircraft, for that is the only way to survive." Szenes, *Befejezetlen Mult*, 44.

178. Katzburg, *Hungary and the Jews*, 198. For the Jewish Estate Expropriation law, see ibid., 191–200.
179. *Nemzeti Ujsag*, March 20, 1942, 1–4.
180. Ibid., 4.
181. Ibid., March 21, 1942, 5, 6.
182. The report appeared in a paper distributed nationally, *Reggeli Magyarorszag*, March 31, 1942, 5.

183. *Nemzeti Ujsag,* April 21, 1942, 1–3. In his book, mentioned above in n. 177, Kallay devoted a single short sentence to explain his public announcement of the deportation of eight hundred thousand Jews: "It also meant that the 800,000 Jews would be there [remain in Hungary] until after the war and that until then they would not be harmed." Kallay, *Hungarian Premier,* 99. There is, however, no doubt at all that Kallay's audience, which included simple people as well as members of Parliament, did not understand this literal interpretation of his announcement. This can be understood from the comments made by those referring to this section of his speech, which are adduced below. The German foreign office also understood Kallay's announcement as it was worded. In a memorandum presented to the German foreign minister, Ribbentrop, by the deputy-secretary of the foreign ministry, regarding his meeting with the Hungarian ambassador in Berlin on October 2, 1942, the deputy-secretary wrote, "I reminded Mr. Sztojay of the statements regarding the Jewish question made by Prime Minister Kallay in his first speech before the Parliament. These statements had proved that Prime Minister Kallay showed a special understanding of the solution of the Jewish question in our sense, and apparently was willing to solve this problem for Hungary as soon as possible." Mendelsohn, *Selected Documents,* vol. 8, 203–4.
184. *Nemzeti Ujsag,* May 30, 1942, 3.
185. Ibid., June 6, 1942, 7. The idea of deporting the Jews appears again and again from the early 1920s, having been raised both by various intellectuals and by politicians. See Cohen, *Illuminations,* 333 (in Hebrew).
186. Miklos Gardos, *Nemzetvesztok a Nepbirosag Elott* (The Destroyers of the Nation before a People's Court; hereafter Gardos, *Nemzetvesztok*), Budapest, 1971, 135.
187. *Nemzeti Ujsag,* June 6, 1942, 7.
188. Ibid., June 11, 1942, 3.
189. Ibid.
190. Ibid., June 10, 1942, 5. In the issue that carried the newspaper report of the speech delivered by the minister of agriculture, there also appeared Kallay's announcement as given to the parliamentary correspondents: "I am satisfied with the debate in Parliament, for I am convinced that even those who criticized this bill are aware of its importance."
191. Ibid., May 30, 1942, 3.
192. Ibid.
193. Ibid., June 11, 1942, 3.
194. Ibid.
195. Ibid., June 16, 1942, 2.
196. Ibid.
197. Katzburg, *Hungary and the Jews,* 200.
198. In 1935 the churches owned over a million *hold* of land. Nearly 90 percent of this was owned by the Catholic church. Gergely, *PPK,* 373. It should

be noted that the Reformed church—which at the time was in possession of some one hundred thousand *hold* of land—took a different approach to the so-called agrarian reform. In the summer of 1939 the Association of Spiritual Shepherds of the Reformed church held a national convention in the town of Cegled. The convention considered the importance of a just distribution of agricultural land. The main speaker at the convention was Bishop Ravasz: "We are well aware that if we want to guarantee a fairer income to those who suffer deprivation, we must take it from those who have too much." The newspaper reporting on the convention explains, "Laszlo Ravasz undoubtedly expressed not only the view of the Reformed church, but also the feelings and views of the vast majority of Hungarian public opinion.... His deeply rooted Hungarian audience well understands that which the Bishop merely hinted at." *Magyar Nemzet,* August 29, 1939, 8. If we take into account the fact that Ravasz's speech was delivered one short week after the promulgation of the second anti-Jewish law, we, too, shall succeed in understanding just what the speaker was getting at, and we will realize to whom the bishop was referring when he spoke of "those who have too much."

199. Ibid., 104. The session was held on May 16, 1923.
200. See ibid., 229, 232, 239, 243, 304.
201. Ibid., 251. The session was held on October 4, 1938.
202. Ibid., 260. The protocol is dated January 13, 1939.
203. Ibid., 275. The protocol is dated October 16, 1940.
204. *Reggeli Magyarorszag,* October 5, 1943, 5.
205. *Nemzeti Ujsag,* March 20, 1942, 3, 4.
206. Ibid., 4.
207. Ibid., June 10, 1942, 5.
208. Ibid., March 14, 1942, 3.
209. Ibid., May 5, 1942, 3.
210. Ibid.
211. Ibid., March 20, 1942, 1.
212. Venetianer, *Zsidosag,* 20–21. The existence should be noted of common ground shared by the leaders of the Catholic and Evangelical churches based on the antisemitism shown by the early Christian king.
213. Ibid., 21–22.
214. *Reggeli Magyarorszag,* May 7, 1942, 5. Another resolution taken at the convention: "Jewish students studying at the high schools of the Reformed church will henceforth be released from their obligations in writing, drawing, and handcrafts on Sabbaths and Jewish festive days."
215. Ibid., June 8, 1943, 7.
216. Ibid., October 6, 1942.
217. Ibid., March 25, 1943, 5. For the sake of comparison, note an extract from one of Hitler's speeches in the Reichstag: "The Jews have maneuvered the British Empire into a most hazardous crisis. The Jews have been the carriers

of the bacteria of the Bolshevik plague which threatens Europe with oblivion." *Nemzeti Ujsag,* April 28, 1942, 5. See also Laszlo Endre's views in *Ujnemzedek,* June 26, 1944. At the session of the Synod of Catholic Bishops held on January 13, 1939, the anti-Jewish legislation was discussed. Shvoy said, "The Synod of Bishops agrees fully with the intention to put an end to Jewish destructiveness.... Its comments are intended to serve in defense of Christian justice." Gergely, *PPK,* 259.

218. *Nemzeti Ujsag,* March 20, 1942, 2. The present writer clearly recalls that in the summer of 1942, in the region in which he lived (Jaras), the regional authorities ruled against the sidelocks and beards of Jewish males. The official regional medical officer expressed his professional opinion before the regional authorities that the beards and sidelocks were liable to serve as breeding grounds for lice, which, in their turn, might facilitate the spread of typhus (anyone familiar with the subject of lice knows that typhus is spread by a louse completely different from the kind that infests hair). In light of this medical opinion, the regional authorities ordered all the men and boys in about half a dozen towns and villages under regional jurisdiction to cut off their sidelocks and their beards. In the village in which the present writer lived, the village authorities added a further regulation. The local gendarmes hunted down Jewish girls with long hair, arrested them in the street, and brought them to the village council buildings, where the village barber cut off all their hair—to the applause of the village mob that had gathered to observe the event. The case described above was not exceptional, and local initiatives that exaggerated in carrying out steps against the Jews were a common occurrence in those days. The Synod of Roman Catholic Bishops appointed a committee to deal with problems involving Catholics of Jewish origin because of the implementation of the anti-Jewish legislation. The committee chairman, the bishop of Kalocsa, reported to the Synod of Bishops the numerous complaints received by his office—fifteen or twenty per week—most of which referred to various groups that did more than the law required, dismissing workers whose dismissal was not required by the law. Gergely, *PPK,* 271. The date of the protocol is March 3, 1940.

219. *Uj Elet—Katolikus Szocialis es Vilagnezeti Szemle,* the first issue of 1943, 50–51. The semiofficial organ of the Catholic church reported the cancellation of the permits held by Jewish tradesmen and craftsmen in the region of Sub-Carpathia, about a year before the appearance of the list quoted herein. In cases, too, where the permits of Jews were not canceled "Jews were not permitted to practice their businesses in the main streets of the large towns.... Those Jews whose continued activity might endanger that of Christian businessmen were not permitted to continue with their businesses as before." *Nemzeti Ujsag,* January 9, 1942.

220. *Reggeli Magyarorszag,* July 17, 1942, 3. Even the Organization of Christian

Merchants, "Baross," encouraged its members to exhibit a crucifix in their shops.

221. Ibid., October 20, 1942, 5.

222. Ibid., October 23, 1942, 5. Kallay went even further in his book in the way he treated the last section of his speech quoted below. He adjusted the excerpt to the theory he had developed concerning his positive approach to the Jews: "I tried to win over to my side the better elements of the Hungarian nation and tried to offer some comfort to the Jews." We, of course, have already read Kallay's words of "comfort" in the relevant newspaper report. However, in an excerpt from his book, Kallay made a slight change in the text of his speech. He omitted the word "Jews" when he spoke of "disseminators of poison" and replaced it by "certain individuals." Here is the corrected excerpt: "I wish to establish one point here: on the Jewish question, I am prepared to take all steps which will support, satisfy, and promote the political, economic, and ethical aims of the nation. But I am not willing to promote the base, private interests of certain individuals; nor to allow the [Jewish] question, in these, its last phases, to poison and corrupt the atmosphere more than it did in its heyday." Kallay goes on to explain that he was referring to those elements "who can see no other problem in this country except the Jewish problem." Kallay, *Hungarian Premier*, 123. Reading Kallay's book leads one to believe that not only did he offer the Jews comfort, but he even defended them by attacking the "certain individuals" who were hostile to the Jews. We are thus faced by two versions of the passage: one an innocent newspaper report, published the day after the speech was delivered, and the other Kallay's version as composed after the war in an attempt to describe in a positive fashion his period as prime minister. From the generally hostile context of the speech and its antisemitic tones, it is most likely that the early version is the correct one. One must not wonder at Kallay for not expecting anyone to compare the two versions at any time in the future. Yet, unfortunately, even respected historians make use of Kallay's book as a source for their research, and not only quote excerpts from it but even accept his interpretation of his own statements and deeds.

223. *Reggeli Magyarorszag*, October 23, 1942.

224. Ibid., May 13, 1943.

225. Ibid., August 27, 1943. Mihalovics served in several high-ranking positions in the Catholic church. From time to time the Synod of Bishops entrusted him with special assignments. Among other things, he served as national director of Actio Catholica. See Gergely, *PPK*, 24, 179, 252, 277, 280, 294.

226. *Reggeli Magyarorszag*, August 27, 1943.

227. Ibid., October 5, 1943, 5. Bishop Ravasz spoke up in a similar vein: "In the western democracies people are being unrestrainedly incited against the

states which enacted laws against the Jews, including Hungary.... Local
Jewry must vehemently reject such allegations, for they are an integral part
of the war campaign of incitement." *Budapesti Hirlap,* April 18, 1939, 5.
The Protestants and Methodists in Nazi Germany spoke similarly. See
Gutterridge, *Open Thy Mouth,* 75, 78–79.

228. When Kallay reported the event to Parliament, he spoke of 2,550 Serbian
casualties. He made no mention of Jewish casualties. *Nemzeti Ujsag,* June
16, 1942, 2.

229. At a murder trial where the accused were members of the Arrow-Cross
party, held in Budapest in 1956, one of the accused described the sounds
of Christmas Eve in 1944: "It was the eve of Holy Christmas and we had
arranged a magnificent dinner.... After dinner the girls of our families were
sent home, while we continued drinking, and when everyone's mood was
already high, Szelepcsenyi [one of the officers in the group] said: 'The front
is drawing very near and we must destroy our enemies, and we must clean
out the basement.' " Afterwards there is a description of the terrible torments inflicted upon the basement dwellers, Jews and Jewesses who had
been collected up by Arrow-Cross men in the city streets, a gang rape of
the Jewish girls, and finally the brutal murder of all the unfortunates—
representatives of "the enemy whose battle front was approaching the center
of Budapest." Jozsef Solyom, *Szabo Laszlo, A Zugloi Nyilas Per* (The Trial
of the Zuglo Arrow-Cross Men), Budapest, 1967, 134. The present writer
had been drafted into the forced labor battalion that was annexed by the
civil defense forces in the city of Szeged. The job of the battalion was to
deal with the damage caused by the bombing of the Allied air forces. On
June 2, 1944, a heavy bombing took place on the Szeged train station, and
all railway lines were destroyed. To repair a few lines, partially but immediately, we worked nonstop for over twenty-four hours. In addition to
our team of guards, an anti-Communist Russian engineer who had left
Russia at the time of the Bolshevik Revolution supervised our labors. This
person did not stop urging us on incessantly, while commenting on our
being Communists, Bolsheviks, G.P.U. agents, and saying that "all Jews
are accursed Communists."

230. *Reggeli Magyarorszag,* February 24, 1944.

231. Ibid., February 27, 1944.

3. 1944

1. Jozsef Darvas, *Varos az ingovanyon* (City on a Dung Heap), Budapest,
1945, 92–93.

2. Quoted in Ilona Beneschofsky and Elek Karsai, *Vadirat a nacizmus ellen:
Dokumentumok a Magyarorszagi Zsidouldozeshez* (An Indictment against
Nazism: Documents of the Persecution of the Jews in Hungary; hereafter
Karsai, *Vadirat*), vol. 1, Budapest, 1958, 38.

3. Moshe Zandberg, *Year without End,* Jerusalem, 1966, 9 (in Hebrew). See also *The Diary of Eva Heiman,* Jerusalem, 1964, 84 (in Hebrew).

4. Levai, *Black Book,* 99.

5. I. Bibo, *Harmadik ut* (The Third Way), 237. Quoted by Asher Cohen, "Illustrations to the Background of the Holocaust of Hungarian Jewry," in Milleth, *Open University Studies in Jewish History and Culture* (hereafter Cohen, "Illustrations"), Tel-Aviv, 1983, 327 (in Hebrew).

6. Karsai, *Vadirat,* vol. 1, 88–89.

7. Cohen, "Illustrations," 326.

8. Karsai, *Vadirat,* vol. 1, 50–51. In his memoirs Horthy blames his policy of nonintervention in Jewish matters on German pressure. "On April 2nd Dr. Veesenmayer had been instructed by the German Foreign Office that I should be excluded from all political activity." Nicholas Horthy, *Memoirs* (hereafter Horthy, *Memoirs*), London, 1956, 218. It should be noted that the premier's announcement preceded by a number of days the date Horthy mentioned as that of his meeting with Veesenmayer, and so one may reasonably doubt the exactness of his memoirs.

9. Levai, *Black Book,* 102–5.

10. The formal ruling forbidding traveling appeared only on April 7, 1944. See Karsai, *Vadirat,* vol. 1, 127–28. Nevertheless, on the day after the German invasion the authorities arrested many Jews who had arrived at Budapest railway stations without prior knowledge of the German invasion, of the prohibition against traveling, or of the siege of the railway stations.

11. Levai, *Black Book,* 228–31. See also *Uj Magyarsag,* April 23, 1944, 5.

12. *Uj Nemzedek,* May 2, 1944, 5. For the sake of comparison, note that at the Fourth Lateran Council, which gathered under the leadership of Pope Innocent III in 1215, the following was stated: "Thus it sometimes happens that by mistake Christians have intercourse with Jewish or Saracen women. ... Therefore, lest these people, under cover of an error, find an excuse for the grave sin of such intercourse, we decree that these people (Jews and Saracens) of either sex ... shall easily be distinguishable from the rest of the populations by the quality of their clothes; especially since such legislation is imposed upon them also by Moses." Freeman, *Intolerance,* 23.

13. Karsai, *Vadirat,* vol. 1, 50–51.

14. Ibid., vol. 1, 92–93.

15. Ibid., vol. 1, 94–95.

16. Ibid., vol. 1, 124–27.

17. Ibid., vol. 2, 44. One of the witnesses at the Eichmann trial, Dr. Martin Paldi, who was a member of the Judenrat of one of the ghettos, described in his testimony the intolerable living conditions in the ghetto before they were sent to Auschwitz. He related that a German officer said to him, "Here you live like pigs; you will be transferred to Germany, where you will live normal lives with your families. There you will work." *The Attorney-General against Adolf Eichmann, Testimony* (hereafter *Attorney-General*), vol. 2, Jerusalem,

1963, 795. Considerable cynicism was thus necessary to describe the appearance of the ghetto after its inhabitants had left as was done by a local Catholic newspaper in a Hungarian town on June 21, 1944. The newspaper was called *Veszpremi Hirlap*, with a prominent sub-heading: "A Political Christian Newspaper." The owner and publisher of the paper was the Provincial Church Press. It wrote as follows: "They removed the Jews and took them to concentration camps. All Monday they were accompanied in groups to the train station, so that all, from all over the country, would be gathered together in a single place. After the evacuation of the ghetto we went to see the condition in which they left the place." The reporter describes what he saw in the empty ghetto: a large number of eggs, much flour and jam; women's purses with delicate, fragrant perfumes; vast piles of clothing and suitcases and plenty of the fat of the land scattered everywhere. The reporter concludes, "As long as the Jews were in the ghetto, they had no reason to complain about their livelihoods, for various kitchens took care of their needs. There was a kosher kitchen, a dietetic kitchen, and even a nonkosher kitchen there." Kis, *Megjelolve*, 230–31.

18. Levai, *Black Book*, 139.
19. Ibid., 146. The writer relies on testimony given after the war by Marton Zoldi, who was a liaison officer in the gendarmerie between the Hungarian and German executors of the deportations. Obstinate rumors claimed that the Hungarian government paid the government of the German Reich a considerable sum in return for the evacuation of the Jewish residents of Hungary. From Endre's statements after the war it would seem that two and a half billion *reichsmarken* was the sum paid. Ibid., 147.
20. Levai, Jeno, *Endre Laszlo: A Magyar Haborus Bunosok Listavezetoje* (Laszlo Endre: At the Head of the List of Hungarian War Criminals; hereafter Levai, *Endre Laszlo*), Budapest, 1945, 70.
21. Karsai, *Vadirat*, vol. 3, 38–39. For purposes of comparison, note that on July 6, 1944, Angelo Rotta, the apostolic representative in Budapest, visited Sztojay. Summarizing the meeting, Sztojay wrote, "The nuncio admitted the fact that there exists a certain Jewish danger and that it is necessary to eliminate that danger, but he stressed that this must be carried out while taking into consideration Christian morality." Ibid., vol. 3, 96.
22. Levai, *Black Book*, 235–40.
23. *Uj Magyarsag*, May 14, 1944, 6.
24. *Pesti Hirlap*, June 7, 1944, 3.
25. For the sake of comparison, note that during the debate on the second anti-Jewish law in the Upper House, Cardinal Seredi said, "It is not sufficient to make use of the law to block those Jews who should be blocked. It is also important to eliminate the phenomena which they have introduced into our public life in economics and society and to eliminate that Jewish spirit because of which the government has deemed it fitting to table this bill." *Nemzeti Ujsag*, April 1, 1939, 1.

26. *Uj Nemzedek,* May 18, 1944, 5.
27. *Uj Nemzetor,* April 7, 1944; quoted by Karsai, *Itel A Nep* (The People Judge), Budapest, 1967, 114.
28. *Uj Magyarsag,* May 12, 1944, 5.
29. Karsai, *Vadirat,* vol. 1, 95.
30. *Uj Nemzedek,* June 26, 1944, 5. In comparison, Bishop Ravasz stated during the debate about the second anti-Jewish law in the Upper House on April 17, "We may not alter the fact that Judaism differs from Hungarianism, as a race, as a religion, in its fate, and in its historical situation. The foreign quality of the Jewish spirit is the consequence of all these. Christian culture and national life must take this fact into account." *Pesti Hirlap,* April 18, 1939, 5.
31. Levai, *Black Book,* 151.
32. Ibid., 139.
33. Ibid., 139–40.
34. Ibid., 140.
35. Ibid., 238.
36. Karsai, *Vadirat,* vol. 2, 27. See also ibid., vol. 1, 123. Karsai relies on a memorandum prepared on May 27, 1944, by Dr. Halasz, an advisor to the interior ministry. In this memorandum he sums up succinctly the content of discussions held with Endre and Baky in the small meeting room of the ministry on April 7, 1944. This date also appears on the Baky document.
37. Ranki Gyorgy, *1944 Marcius 19,* Budapest, 1968, 159–60, 255 256. Quoted by Cohen, "Illustrations," 326.
38. Cohen, "Illustrations," 326–27.
39. Mendelsohn, *The Holocaust,* vol. 8, 221.
40. Ibid.
41. Himler, *Igy Neztek Ki,* 116.
42. For the cessation of the deportations, see this part, n. 109.
43. Munkacsi Erno, *Hogyan Tortent?: Adatok es Okmanyok a Magyar Zsidosag Tragediajahoz* (How Did It Happen?: Details and Documents of the Tragedy of Hungarian Jewry; hereafter Munkacsi, *Hogyan Tortent?),* Budapest, 1947, 213–14. According to another source, Veesenmayer added, "This was so vast a police action that its execution was made possible within three months only because of the complete cooperation and enthusiasm showed by the Hungarian authorities and their executive branches." Gardos, *Nemzetvesztok,* 133.
44. Munkacsi, *Hogyan Tortent?,* 213.
45. Livia Rotkirchen, "Hungarian Jewry in the Holocaust Period: A General Survey." *Symposium on the Hungarian Jewish Leadership under the Test of the Holocaust,* pamphlet published by Yad Va-Shem, Jerusalem, 1976, 51.
46. Gerald Reitlinger, *The Final Solution* (hereafter Reitlinger, *Final Solution*), New York, 1953, 431.

47. R. Major, *The Churches and the Jews in Hungary,* Chicago, 1966, 378–79.
48. Father Jozsef Elias made this statement in an interview held in the mid-1980s. The interview is included in Szenes, *Befejezetlen Mult,* 73. See also ibid., 56, 69.
49. Karsai, *Vadirat,* vol. 2, 75–76.
50. Reported in *Pesti Hirlap,* January 14, 1939.
51. Reported in *Nemzeti Ujsag,* April 1, 1939, 1.
52. Reported in *Budapesti Hirlap,* April 16, 1939, 3. Bishop Glattfelder expressed a similar opinion in the debate on the same subject. See *Nemzeti Ujsag,* April 1, 1939, 2.
53. *Harc,* August 12, 1944, 5.
54. Cohen, "Illustrations," 340.
55. Szenes, *Befejezetlen Mult,* 55–56.
56. Ibid., 140.
57. Rudolf Vrba and Alan Bestic, *Factory of Death* (hereafter Vrba, *Factory of Death*), London, 1964, 213 ff., 226–28.
58. Szenes, *Befejezetlen Mult,* 54, 60–61, 95–96, 111–14, 138–39. For the date of the arrival of the Vrba Report in Budapest and its distribution, see also the testimony of Pinhas Freudiger, then chairman of the orthodox community and member of the Jewish Central Committee in 1944, at the Eichmann trial. *Attorney-General, Testimony,* vol. 2, 756. See also Braham, *Politics of Genocide,* vol. 2, 710–11.
59. Levai, *Black Book,* 91.
60. Ibid., 92.
61. Karsai, *Vadirat,* vol. 1, 108–9.
62. Levai, *Black Book,* 92.
63. Ibid., 118.
64. Seredi based his standpoint upon the church's ancient approach, believing in the superiority of Christianity to other religions, especially Judaism. Thus, it is not fitting for the Jews to enjoy any superiority relative to Catholic believers. Here are a number of examples: Pope Gregory VII wrote in 1081 to Alfonso IV of Castille, "We admonish Your Highness that you must cease to suffer the Jews to rule over Christians and exercise authority over them. For to allow Christians to be subordinate to Jews, and to be subject to their judgment, is the same as to oppress God's church and to exalt the synagogue of Satan." Malcolm Hay, *Thy Brother's Blood,* 35. The Third Lateran Council, which convened under the leadership of Pope Alexander III in 1179, strengthened the earlier church prohibition of the employment of Christians by Jews. Freeman, *Intolerance,* 23. At the Fourth Lateran Council in 1215, under the leadership of Pope Innocent III, the employment of Christians by Jews and the employment of Jews in public office were prohibited, "since it is quite absurd that any who blaspheme against Christ

should have power over Christians.... We forbid that Jews be given preferment in public office since this offers them the pretext to vent their wrath against Christians." Ibid. St. Thomas Aquinas, a thirteenth-century Christian theologian, ruled, "It would be unreasonable to permit the Jews, in a Christian state, to exercise the functions of government, thereby subjecting Catholics to their authority." Ibid., 4. Pope Eugene IV ruled in 1442, "Christians shall not allow Jews to hold civil honor over Christians." Ibid., 27. Cardinal Seredi was also able to rely on the doctrine postulated by a known extreme antisemite of his own generation, Karoly Wolf, the leader of the antisemitic Christian party, who had declared, "We must guarantee the economic supremacy of Hungarian Christians.... We do not desire to see our Christian colleagues in an inferior position." *Magyarsag*, July 2, 1933, 4. The Evangelical church took a stand identical with that of the Catholic church. In a circular the church distributed among its pastors on July 10, 1944, it reported its appeal to the government with regard to the converts. One of its demands was "to remove Jewish converts from the influence of the Jewish Council.... As long as they are under the influence of the Jewish Council, they are liable to be persecuted, mocked, ridiculed, and oppressed." Karsai, *Vadirat*, vol. 3, 130–31.

65. Ibid., vol. 1, 78.
66. Levai, *Black Book*, 119–20.
67. Ibid., 120–21.
68. Ibid., 120.
69. Ibid., 121–22.
70. Karsai, *Vadirat*, vol. 2, 59–60.
71. Ibid., vol. 2, 53.
72. Ibid., vol. 3, 310–12. See also Levai, *Black Book*, 92. Similarly, see Albert Bereczky, *Hungarian Protestantism and the Persecution of the Jews* (hereafter Bereczky, *Protestantism*), Budapest, 1945, 14.
73. Levai, *Black Book*, 93.
74. Karsai, *Vadirat*, vol. 3, 311.
75. Ibid.
76. Levai, *Black Book*, 218.
77. Ibid., 217. It was undoubtedly the ancient tradition of the church that the Protestant bishops, and even the cardinal, faced: "Practically all papal letters commanding princes and prelates to refrain from maltreating Jews described the latter as 'perfidious,' 'ungrateful,' or 'insolent' people. The recipients of these recommendations might well be excused for not heeding instructions to protect 'the Synagogue of Satan' or 'Jewish reprobates' or 'arrogant unbelievers.' Lapide, *The Three Last Popes*, 70. See also Karsai, *Vadirat*, vol. 3, 7.
78. Levai, *Black Book*, 197. The nuncio stressed that the struggle against the

Jews not be waged "beyond the borders dictated by the laws of nature," i.e., that as long as the struggle is waged within "the laws of nature," it is not to be condemned. The nuncio could have relied upon the ancient church approach expressed in the words of Pope Innocent III, who ruled in 1199: "Although the Jewish perfidy is in every way worthy of condemnation, nevertheless, because through them the truth of our own faith is proved, they are not to be severely oppressed by the faithful." Freeman, *Intolerance*, 21. "Christian tradition . . . asserts that the Jews may live among the Christians as a degraded and inferior class so that the faithful Christian may observe the fate of those who are guilty of deicide and who stubbornly refuse to accept the true religion." Y. Katz, *From Prejudice to Destruction* (hereafter Katz, *Prejudice*), Cambridge, Mass., 1980, 20. A similar approach is revealed by a comment made by Bishop Ravasz. After his speeches in the Upper House favoring the adoption of the second anti-Jewish law, he added an appeal to the government "to show delicacy and goodwill, together with the strong arm it applies in executing the law." *Pesti Hirlap*, April 18, 1939, 3.

79. Levai, *Black Book*, 197–98.

80. Ibid., 199–200.

81. Ibid., 200–201. Krumey, then one of the heads of the German mission to Hungary, told a member of the Jewish Council, "It is a German system, to send people together with their families, for then they work better and do not long for their families." *Attorney-General, Testimony*, vol. 2, 755.

82. Karsai, *Vadirat*, vol. 3, 93.

83. Ibid., vol. 3, 93–99.

84. Ibid., vol. 3, 170–71. The idea of showing mercy to the converts in order to facilitate the deportation of the Jews seems to have been accepted in government circles. In its session of August 22, 1944, the government discussed practical ways of deporting a quarter of a million Budapest Jews and sought a way to do so without making unnecessary noise. The interior minister said, "The number of converts in the Budapest area is about 20,000. The idea is that by refraining from deporting the converts, the deportation of the other Jews will be made possible." Ibid., vol. 3, 329.

85. Ibid., vol. 3, 19–22.

86. Ibid., vol. 3, 206–7.

87. Ibid., vol. 3, 104–5. Karsai, the editor of the book, comments on Winckelman's statement: "As scholars know today, Seredi did not intervene with Horthy against the brutal approach to the Jews."

88. Himler, *Igy Neztek Ki*, 117. See also Y. Z. Moor, *The Catholic Church and the Extermination of the Jews in Hungary* (hereafter Moor, *Catholic Church*), Quadrant, Sydney, Australia, May-June 1966, 69.

89. The writer's conversation with Rabbi Professor Meir Weiss in his home in

Jerusalem on April 23, 1985. The bishops quoted expressed an opinion acceptable in Christian theology, and here are a number of examples: "The statement by Dietrich Bonhoeffer [a German theologian, anti-Nazi fighter, and victim of the Nazi regime] proves how deep the roots of anti-Jewish prejudice are, even among the best Christian theologians. The following excerpt is taken from a lecture he delivered in April 1933: 'The steps taken by the state against the Jews—on April 1st a boycott was declared against Jewry—are linked with the church in a special way. In the church of Jesus the concept never faded of "the chosen people" who crucified the Savior of the world, having to bear the curse resulting from its actions by means of a long history of suffering.' " Charlotte Klein, *Anti-Judaism in Christian Theology* (hereafter Klein, *Anti-Judaism*), Philadelphia, 1957, 118. The German Archbishop Groeber distributed a Shepherds' Epistle in March of 1941. In his letter he made use of numerous antisemitic expressions, accused the Jews of crucifying Jesus, and added, "the self-imposed curse of the Jews, 'His blood be upon us and upon our children,' has come true terribly until the present time." Gunter Lewy, *The Catholic Church and Nazi Germany* (hereafter Lewy, *Church and Germany*), New York, 1964, 294. See also Gutterridge, *Open Thy Mouth*, 71.

90. Szenes, *Befejezetlen Mult*, 139.
91. Ibid., 145, and see also Levai, *Black Book*, 207.
92. Szenes, *Befejezetlen Mult*, 176–78.
93. Levai, *Black Book*, 192–93.
94. Ibid., 207–10. See above, n. 77.
95. *Budapesti Hirlap*, April 16, 1939. See also above, part 2, n. 79. Of the many expressions voiced in Hungary over the long years in the spirit of Seredi's statement, we will note here only one. An antisemitic member of Parliament proposed in 1939, "If negative economic features appear, it will be desirable to declare the collective responsibility of the Jews." *Magyarsag*, February 4, 1939, 6.
96. A Hungarian historian, Istvan Bibo, wrote in the fall of 1948, "Even during the period between March 19 and October 15 the churches saw no reason to change their stand relative to the government and government officials whom they knew well . . . they included the Hungarian government together with those who stood behind them, the mad, idolatrous, criminal Hitlerite regime." Bibo's study appeared in the October-November 1948 issue of the Hungarian periodical *Valasz* (Response) under the heading "The Jewish Question in Hungary after 1944." Quoted in Szenes, *Befejezetlen Mult*, 86.
97. Ibid., 67. See also ibid., 26, 148–49, 154. With regard to Raffay's appeal to Seredi, see Karsai, *Vadirat*, vol. 3, 9–10. Raffay's appeal is dated June 27, 1944. For Seredi's negative reply, see ibid., 111–12. In his reply rejecting the proposal of cooperation, Seredi writes that even without this intrachurch cooperation, "we are succeeding in achieving our aim."

98. Levai, *Black Book,* 221–22.

99. The rules of censorship did not apply to church publications, and the churches did not have to request advance authorization for their publications. In contrast, printing houses were obligated to present the authorities with one copy of whatever they printed. And so, the manager of the printing house presented a copy of the letter to the attorney-general's office in Esztergom, where the cardinal had his residence. The attorney-general passed the letter along to his superiors. Ibid., 211. There is another version that claims that the manager of the local post office, out of curiosity, examined the contents of one of the envelopes given him by the cardinal's office for posting. When he discovered the nature of the contents of the envelope he reported this to his superiors. The minister of trade and transport awarded the diligent post office manager a monetary prize of a thousand *pengo.* Szenes, *Befejezetlen Mult,* 154.

100. Ibid., 155 ff. See also Levai, *Black Book,* 211–13.

101. See Karsai, *Vadirat,* vol. 3, 93–99.

102. Levai, *Black Book,* 214.

103. Ibid.

104. Ibid., 222–23. Karsai, *Vadirat,* vol. 3, 154–55.

105. Moor, *Catholic Church,* 72. The writer relies on documents 5435/1944 and 5882/1944 in the cardinal's archives in Esztergom.

106. Kis, *Megjelolve,* 234.

107. Braham, *Destruction of Hungarian Jewry,* vol. 2, 625. The bishop—named Mindszenty—who became cardinal after the death of Seredi, wrote a book called *My Memoirs* after the war. In his book he claims that neither he nor the Franciscan friar was aware of the aim of the prayer session organized by the Arrow-Cross party. It is difficult to imagine that the leader of the Arrow-Cross party neglected to inform the Franciscan friar of the aim of the thanksgiving service, and he clearly had no reason to hide it from him, especially since they announced both the service and its aim in fliers distributed in advance throughout the town of Veszprem. Moreover, the organization of public prayer sessions in cathedrals was not an everyday affair, nor was it the job of the leaders of the Arrow-Cross party. It is not reasonable that the priest in charge made no inquiries of the organizers of the service as to just what they wanted to give thanks for. The bishop also claims that in the end the thanksgiving prayer was not held at all. This claim is disproved both by Veesenmayer's report and by the testimony of Veszprem residents who remember the holding of the thanksgiving prayer session clearly. Kis, *Megjelolve,* 234–36.

108. Karsai, *Vadirat,* vol. 3, 63.

109. In his telegram to Berlin of July 6, Veesenmayer himself raises the possibility that the deterioration of the military situation was one of the reasons why the Hungarian government decided to put an end to the deportations. Ibid., vol. 3, 81–82.

110. Ibid., vol. 3, 4–5.

111. Ibid., vol. 3, 81–82. It is a reasonable assumption that the decoded telegrams were present in the background of Imredi's speech, delivered a few days after he had heard of them. In his speech he attempted to evade both the responsibility of the Hungarians in general and his own personal responsibility in particular for the treatment the Hungarians gave the Jews. "Contrary to the pernicious rumors being spread outside our borders, it may be stated certainly that not a drop of Jewish blood has been spilt—neither by the authorities nor by any Hungarian individual." *Nemzetor,* July 14, 1944, 2.

112. Karsai, *Vadirat,* vol. 3, 80. With regard to the reasons for the cessation of the deportations many theories have been raised since the war. The accepted assumption is that they were stopped as a result of the intervention of neutral countries maintaining diplomatic relations with Hungary. In this context the activities of the Holy See and its emissaries have particularly been stressed. In light of the material in this book, it is more likely that the Hungarian leaders were alarmed—simply alarmed—by the contents of the decoded telegrams. Support for this assumption can be found in the fact that the Hungarian leaders completely ignored all the warnings and appeals made to them from the time of the German invasion until these telegrams arrived and indicated that they were in the future to be tried for their deeds.

113. Levai, *Black Book,* 161, 182–84. Later on the authorities put off the target date until June 24. See also Karsai, *Vadirat,* vol. 2, 113–18, 162–66, 187–94, 203–22, 279–83, 290–308, 344–48. The Hungarian authorities treated the BBC threats seriously. In a document prepared by the Commission for Housing Affairs in the Capital, which deals with the location of the ghetto, there appear the considerations regarding the concentration of the Jewish residences. "It is not desirable for broad residential areas to be cleared of Jews, for in case of a terrorist attack from the air the Christian residents of these areas will be subjected to bombing from the air, whereas the residents of the ghetto will be spared them." Ibid., vol. 1, 302. Another consideration in determining "the Jewish buildings" appears in a newspaper article proposing "that it be taken into consideration that modern, favorably located, low-rental buildings be included in the list of Christian buildings. 'Jewish buildings' should be those which are located on side streets, old, neglected buildings or, on the other hand, modern residential buildings where rents are highest." Ibid., vol. 2, 191.

114. Ibid., vol. 2, 238. The homes of Jews now evacuated were placed at the disposal of those Christians who were compelled to evacuate their apartments as a result of their being designated Jewish buildings, or at the disposal of those Christian families whose apartments had been destroyed in Allied bombings from the air. The Jewish evacuees were to prepare inventories of the contents of their apartments, and were permitted to take with them only a minimal amount of vital clothing. Ibid., vol. 2, 164.

115. Ibid., vol. 2, 316–17.
116. Ibid., vol. 3, 114.
117. Ibid., vol. 3, 329. Separating the converts from the Jews takes on fateful significance in light of Jaross's statement quoted here. He would seem to have been inspired by the approach adopted by the priesthood, which consistently demanded that in every case the Jews and the converts were to be separated. The following episode, which might be considered comic were it not for the tragic element it contains, can serve to illustrate the rigid stance taken by the priests with regard to the separation of converts from Jews. Representatives of the organization of converts were brought urgently to the interior ministry on July 31 at 4 P.M. A prominent official of the ministry and a gendarmerie officer in charge of dealing with the Jews told them that all the converts were to move to special buildings intended for converts only, thus carrying out to the full their separation from the Jews. While the homes of the converts were also to be marked by a yellow Star of David, a distinction was to be made between them and those of the other Jews by means of a cross to be affixed over the yellow Star of David. The transfer of the thousands of converts—who had just crowded into their new apartments—was to be carried out in six days, by 8 P.M. on August 6. When the representatives of the converts tried to protest, pointing out the physical difficulty in carrying out this decree, the government representatives expressed their astonishment at the converts' representatives' reservation, claiming that the very separation of their residential quarters resulted from the request made by the priests and the pressure they brought to bear on the authorities to carry out that separation. The representatives of the converts were to be satisfied and grateful for the government's acquiescing with the request of the priesthood and agreeing to carry out this separation. Ibid., vol. 3, 305–8.
118. Ibid., vol. 3, 76.
119. Ibid., vol. 3, 152–53. A study of the protocol of that meeting shows that the number of Jews included in paragraph b was between fifty and sixty thousand as well. This means that the Hungarian government offered between 100,000 and 120,000 Jews in return for the removal of the Gestapo from Hungary. Ibid., vol. 3, 374–75, 379.
120. Katzburg, *Antisemitism*, 177.
121. Macartney, *October Fifteenth*, vol. 2, 283, n. 1. Horthy's consistency should be noted. In a letter to Prime Minister Teleki he wrote on October 14, 1940, "As regards the Jewish problem, I have been an anti-Semite throughout all my life, I have never had contact with Jews." Miklos Szinai and Laszlo Szucs, *The Confidential Papers of Admiral Horthy* (hereafter Szinai, *Confidential Papers*), Budapest, 1965, 150. To Hitler he wrote on May 7, 1943, "I hope that I may without any conceit refer to the fact that in my time I was the first to raise my voice against the destructive attitude

of the Jews and since then appropriate measures were taken by me to force back their influence." Ibid., 249. In a talk with Veesenmayer on July 4, 1944, Horthy said, "Back after the World War my name was involved in the struggle against Judaism and against Bolshevism. Such an image was created, and now we have not done more than to realize that image created a long time ago." Karsai, *Vadirat*, vol. 3, 77.

122. Nagy-Talavera, *Green Shirts*, 212.

123. Nicholas Horthy, *Memoirs*, 161.

124. Szenes, *Befejezetlen Mult*, 198, 212–15. In the memoirs he published in 1953 Horthy claims that only in August 1944 did he learn of the fate of those deported. This claim of Horthy's is denied by Dr. Sandor Torok, the converted journalist who was appointed deputy chairman of the Council of Converts in the summer of 1944, and who was directly responsible for handing over the report to Horthy. We also learn that Horthy received the report at the same time from another source as well. See ibid. Horthy's claim can be understood on the basis of the efforts made after the war by many involved directly or indirectly in the mass murder of Jews to clear themselves of these heavy allegations, or at least to limit their part in the crimes.

125. Karsai, *Vadirat*, vol. 3, 23.

126. When the message was being written, there were no longer any Jews in Hungary outside of Budapest. The aim of this sentence is clearly to deceive.

127. Levai, *Black Book*, 306–7.

128. Karsai, *Vadirat*, vol. 3, 276, 280–81.

129. Ibid., vol. 3, 390–91.

130. Levai, *Black Book*, 319.

131. Ibid., 321, 328, 330. See also Karsai, *Vadirat*, vol. 3, 29–30, n. 57.

132. Ibid., vol. 1, 202. Hungarian law required the would-be convert to inform the offices of his community/church of his desire to leave his previous religion and adopt a new one. Only after receipt of certification of doing so was he permitted to turn to the community/church he desired to join in order to arrange for the conversion procedure.

133. Ibid. The interview with the rabbi appeared in the Jewish community newspaper *A Magyar Zsidok Lapja* (Newspaper of Hungarian Jewry), in its issue of April 20, 1944, a month after the German invasion. A few years after the war Dr. Sandor Torok said, "the government promised the churches to separate the Jews from the converts, and even if the Jews were deported from Budapest, the converts would not be deported. This was, understandably, never made public, but the rumor spread, causing a vast wave of baptism applications." Szenes, *Befejezetlen Mult*, 203.

134. Karsai, *Vadirat*, vol. 3, 156–58.

135. Braham, *Politics of Genocide*, vol. 2, 1029. Braham does not make this claim explicitly, but the text paints just such a picture. According to Dr.

Sandor Torok's testimony, Ravasz, too, referred to what was happening
to the Jews, saying, "I didn't want it to be this way." Szenes, *Befejezetlen
Mult,* 199.

136. Kis, *Megjelolve,* 93.

137. Levai, *Black Book,* 292–93. Seredi was consistent, remaining faithful to
his principles and to the opinion he had expressed a few years earlier on
this subject. See *Pesti Hirlap,* December 22, 1938. Seredi expressed a similar
opinion at the session of the Synod of Bishops on January 13, 1939. See
Gergely, *PPK,* 257.

138. Karsai, *Vadirat,* vol. 3, 215–18.

139. Ibid., vol. 3, 132.

140. Ibid., vol. 3, 195–96. An activist of one of the Protestant churches wrote
a book just before the end of the war in which he attempts to present in
a positive light the Protestant churches and their attitude to the Jews during
the war and even before. He wrote that the church leaders had to ignore
the rules of their own churches on many occasions on behalf of people
whose lives were in danger. They ignored the preparatory period needed
to prepare the would-be converts for their baptism, and baptized many and
provided them with conversion certificates. With the help of these certificates, it was possible to deceive the authorities. Bereczky, *Protestantism,*
27–28. In light of the documents contradicting Bereczky quoted in this
book, and in light of the fact that Bereczky provides no documentation
whatever in support of his claims, these may be considered creative hind-
sight after the war, intended to disguise the behavior of his church during
the persecution of the Jews. For the one-sidedness of Bereczky's book, see
also Szenes, *Befejezetlen Mult,* 85–87.

141. Karsai, *Vadirat,* vol. 3, 212. The letter is dated July 17, 1944.

142. Ibid., vol. 3, 213–14. The writer is certainly referring to Seredi's instruction
concerning conversion procedures promulgated on July 24, and adduced
below.

143. *Harc,* August 12, 1944.

144. Karsai, *Vadirat,* vol. 3, 257–58.

145. Ibid., vol. 3, 593–97.

146. Ibid., vol. 3, 383–84. The use of the term "laborers being sent to work in
the Reich" served as a code that meant being sent to the death camps. In
the messages dispatched in the summer of 1944 by the director of the local
jail in the town of Sarvar to the Budapest police, the following wording
appears regularly: "I hereby inform you that the detainee...has been
handed over to the German Army so that he may be provided with work
in Germany." In the letters there appear various personal details of the
person being deported, including his date of birth. From these details we
learn that among those detainees who "were sent to work" there was a
74-year-old woman and a two-year-old toddler. Ibid., vol. 3, 179 ff.

147. *Uj Magyarsag,* May 12, 1944, 5. A newspaper interview with Laszlo Endre

after he flew to visit thirty-four towns to supervise the deportations personally.

148. *Magyarorszag,* June 16, 1944, 5. Some two months before the beginning of the operation in which Jewish books were destroyed, a newspaper interview was held with Kolozsvary-Borcsa, whom the newspaper describes as "a fearless fighter for Christian ideals... who will work tirelessly for the Hungarian spirit and for the true Christian spirit." *Pesti Hirlap,* April 16, 1944. In a speech he delivered at the ceremony inaugurating the operation of destroying Jewish books, Kolozsvary-Borcsa recalled the inspiring memory of the late Bishop Prohaszka, who was "one of the pioneers of the concept of the struggle against Jewish literature." See above, part 2, nn. 31, 88.

149. Karsai, *Vadirat,* vol. 1, 313–14. See also above, part 2, n. 100.

150. Ibid., vol. 1, 299–300. Quoted from the newspaper *Pesti Hirlap,* May 6, 1944.

151. Ibid., vol. 3, 137.

152. Ibid., vol. 2, 185–86.

153. Szenes, *Befejezetlen Mult,* 234. Quoted from the Catholic periodical *Egyedul Vagyunk.*

154. *Pesti Hirlap,* April 23, 1944, 2.

155. Ibid., April 16, 1944. See above, n. 107.

156. Ibid.

157. *Uj Nemzedek,* May 9, 1944, 8.

158. *Uj Magyarsag,* June 27, 1944, 6.

159. *Harc,* July 8, 1944, 4.

160. *Uj Nemzedek,* May 18, 1944, 5. The minister of economics, Imredi, spoke in a similar tone. See *Nemzetor,* July 14, 1944, 2.

161. Karsai, *Vadirat,* vol. 3, 507–8. The bishop's reply was given on September 6, 1944.

162. Ibid., vol. 3, 395.

163. Ibid., vol., 1, 262–64.

164. *Uj Nemzedek,* June 21, 1944, 7.

165. Karsai, *Vadirat,* vol. 1, 236.

166. Ibid., vol. 3, 226.

167. Ibid., vol. 3, 353–55.

168. Ibid., vol. 1, 66–69. As already noted, the Catholic chief inspector quotes government directive ME 1210/1944, dated March 29, 1944, promulgated in the official newspaper on March 31, 1944, under that number. The document composed by the Catholic chief inspector mentions two additional government directives: paragraphs 9 and 16 of Law XV of 1941, as well as directive number 1730/1944. These two directives deal with the definition of who the relevant anti-Jewish laws apply to. See also ibid., vol. 2, 355.

169. Ibid., vol. 3, 381–89.

170. Ibid., vol. 3, 447.

171. Ibid., vol. 3, 501. The instructions of the Catholic education inspectors and the pressures applied by the priests for the total separation of Jewish and convert residences reflected the common attitude demanding absolute separation from the Jews. It is not impossible that the atmosphere generated by this approach is the explanation for the demand made by Catholic prostitutes to be separated from their Jewish counterparts. Macartney, *October Fifteenth*, vol. 2, 276; Nagy-Talavera, *Green Shirts*, 204.

172. Kis, *Megjelolve*, 74.

173. From a letter by the bishop of Gyor to Cardinal Seredi, dated June 17, 1944. Szenes, *Befejezetlen Mult*, 234.

174. In the winter of 1944 he attempted to save a nun from a Russian soldier who was about to rape her. The soldier shot and killed him.

175. Personal testimony in the Yad Va-Shem Archives, given in October 1983 by L.G., who lives in Hungary and desires to preserve his anonymity. He added pictures to his testimony, and they were marked with the number 1359. A set of four pictures describing the final stages of the deportation from the town of Soltvadkert also appears in the final pages of Szenes, *Befejezetlen Mult*. In one of these pictures, a white patch may be discerned alongside one of the coaches. L.G.'s explanation: after the coach was padded with lime, it was decided to use it to transport the gendarmes who accompanied the deportees. For this purpose the coach was swept out and cleaned. The white patch next to the coach was created out of the lime dust swept out of it. In the pictures one can clearly see the accompanying gendarmes.

176. According to the men of office 06, after they completed the Eichmann file for the prosecution in preparation for his trial in Jerusalem in 1961–1962, and after they had made a study of the Holocaust over a long period of time—in their conversation with the newspaperman Dezso Schon, *A Jeruzsalemi Per* (The Jerusalem Trial), Tel-Aviv, 1962, 272.

177. Ibid., 377.

178. R. Major, *Churches*, 379.

179. Szenes, *Befejezetlen Mult*, 230.

180. Gergely, *PPK*, 24, 157.

181. *Magyarsag*, January 25, 1939, 9.

182. Szenes, *Befejezetlen Mult*, 87.

183. Nagy-Talavera, *Green Shirts*, 230. This event took place after October 15, 1944.

Index

Academic professionals, 164
Accepted religions, 17–18, 143, 144–45
Actio Catholica, 58, 61–65, 243, 262n. 78, 273n. 226
Adamovics, Jozsef, 9, 10–12
Ady, Endre, 263n. 82
Agrarian reform, 24, 125, 156, 157, 265n. 115
Agricultural workers, 22, 155–56, 157–58, 161
Allies, 207, 215, 229
Ammon, Kurt, 140
Anchor-cross, 70
Antal, Istvan, 119–20, 161–62, 198, 211, 213
Anti-Christianity: and internationalism, 55
Anti-Communist Committee, 49
Anti-Jewish legislation, 4, 48, 61, 65, 77, 79–169, 176, 191, 201, 205, 242; Catholic church and, 97–99; demand for additional, 128–33; effects of, on Jews, 94–100, 117–19, 145; first, 82–90, 91, 93, 94–100, 251n. 121; implementation of, 130–31, 163, 272n. 218; justification of, 96; opposition to, 110–11, 112–13; Protestant churches and, 95–97; second, 64, 100–06, 110–11, 112–13, 119–28, 133, 145, 190, 209, 248n. 71; Teleki and, 34; third, 133–40

Anti-Jewish triangle (regime/church/people), 82, 169, 176, 236–38
Antisemitic activity, organized, 8
Antisemitic argument, 38
Antisemitic coalition, 43
Antisemitic decrees, 132. *See also* Decrees imposed on Jews
Antisemitic movements, 22, 29–30, 65–75
Antisemitic organizations, 56–57
Antisemitic party, 8, 11, 19–20
Antisemitism, 4, 8, 36, 43–44, 76–77, 174–75, 242–44; of Arrow-Cross party, 75; Catholic church and, 29–30, 64–65, 70; of Catholic People's party, 20, 22–23; Christian (1930s), 48–55; clerical, 235; and Judaism, 132; legitimacy of, 82, 132; in Parliament and Upper House, 81–82; popular (1930s), 56–65; priesthood and, 8, 33–34, 76; and readiness of Hungarians to expel the Jews, 188–89; reasons for, 95–96; as self-defense, 8, 179; in Union of Awakening Hungarians, 30–33
Apor, Vilmos, 240
Apponyi, Gyorgy, 154
Arad (town), 26
Arkangyal, Boris, 30
Arrow-Cross party, 65–75, 92, 102, 122, 140, 144, 221; and anti-Jewish legislation, 126, 128–30; and explusion

DATE DUE

1/01

DEMCO